# The Nuclear Freeze Campaign

# The Nuclear Freeze Campaign

## Rhetoric and Foreign Policy in the Telepolitical Age

J. Michael Hogan

Michigan State University Press
East Lansing
1994

All Michigan State University Press books are produced on paper which meets the requirements of American National Standard of Information Sciences—Permanence of paper for printed materials ANSI Z23.48-1984.

Printed in the United States of America

Michigan State University Press
East Lansing, Michigan 48823-5202

02 01 00 99 98 97 96 95 94 1 2 3 4 5 6 7 8 9 10

Library of Congress Cataloging-in-Publication Data

Hogan, J. Michael, 1953-
The nuclear freeze campaign : rhetoric and foreign policy in the telepolitical age / J. Michael Hogan.
p. cm. — (Rhetoric and public affairs series)
Includes bibliographical references and index.
ISBN 0-87013-367-5
1. Nuclear disarmament—United States—History. 2. Antinuclear movement—United States—History. 3. Peace movements—United States—History. 4. United States—Politics and government—1981-1989. I. Title. II. Series.
JX1974.H59 1994
327.1'74—dc20 94-26660
CIP

Cover photograph: Ellen Shub/THE PICTURE CUBE

# Contents


| | |
|---|---|
| Acknowledgments | vii |
| Introduction | 1 |

**Part I**
**The Nuclear Freeze Campaign**

| | | |
|---|---|---|
| Chapter 1. | The Radical Ethos in Reagan's America | 13 |
| Chapter 2. | The Rhetoric of Doom | 37 |
| Chapter 3. | The Rhetoric of Political Medicine | 61 |
| Chapter 4. | The Rhetoric of Nuclear Education | 81 |

**Part II**
**The Freeze Campaign and Institutional Politics**

| | | |
|---|---|---|
| Chapter 5. | Managing Dissent in the Catholic Church | 99 |
| Chapter 6. | Popular Sovereignty and the House Freeze Debate | 119 |

**Part III**
**Portraits of the Public**

| | | |
|---|---|---|
| Chapter 7. | The Rhetoric of a Telepolitical "Movement" | 141 |
| Chapter 8. | The Rhetoric of Polling | 169 |

| | |
|---|---|
| Conclusion | 185 |
| Appendix: Polling on the Freeze | 209 |
| Bibliography | 239 |
| Index | 259 |

# Acknowledgments

I never participated in the nuclear freeze campaign, so I have a different perspective than Pam Solo, Douglas Waller, David Meyers, and others who have written on the subject. I do owe a debt to those writers, however, as well as to a number of other former freeze activists who provided insights and artifacts. This book may be critical of the strategies and tactics of the freeze campaign, but it does not question the good intentions of those who participated.

The Freeze campaign merely symptomized a larger illness in the American body politic, an illness that infects people of all ideological stripes and has only grown worse since the early 1980s. That illness, a sort of political malnourishment that Kathleen Hall Jamieson, James Davison Hunter, and others also have written about in recent books, has resulted from gradual, almost imperceptible changes in how Americans discuss and debate public issues. Increasingly over the past several decades, the American public has been asked to perform the hard labors of democratic governance on a steady diet of political junk food.

In *Eloquence in an Electronic Age*, Jamieson presents Ronald Reagan as the consummation of these trends. The "Great Communicator's" success, Jamieson argues, rested upon a mode of speaking that traditionally would have been condemned as "effeminate": a conversational style built upon dramatizing, storytelling, and self-revelation. According to Jamieson, Reagan's rhetoric, while exploiting television's power to convey images and emotions, also "defied traditional logic and our usual tests of evidence." As such, it not only immunized Reagan from political attack, but also in Jamieson's view, subverted public discussion of his polices and ideas.

In *Culture Wars*, Hunter makes note of seemingly unrelated trends in American public discourse. Focusing not upon the gentle, even "effeminate" persuasion of Ronald Reagan but the strident, uncompromising "grammar of hostility" in contemporary moral debates, Hunter worries that "voices of quiet, reflective passion"—indeed, the voices of the majority of Americans—have been drowned out in today's cultural climate by rhetorical extremists.

In the final analysis, however, Jamieson and Hunter are describing two sides of the same coin. Both Reagan and the cultural warriors practice the politics of the televisual age—the politics of images and "sound bites," of anecdotes and feelings. Advocates of all ideological persuasions, both in and outside of the political mainstream, routinely substitute storytelling for argument, images and emotions for information and ideas. And the inevitable result is a democratic polity starved of the knowledge it needs to sustain itself, a public driven toward apathy and cynicism by the sense that they have no say in the political process.

Students of American politics continue to debate who or what is to blame for the impoverishment of public discourse in America. Do the new communicative technologies, not only television but direct mail and other new media, dictate the superficiality and polarization of contemporary public debate? Or do the people behind those technologies—the media barons, the journalists, the political commentators, and the talk-show hosts—deserve most of the blame? Still others, of course, blame the politicians and political activists, and virtually all place some measure of blame on the public itself. This book, while embracing all of these explanations in part, ultimately resists the last explanation: the tendency to blame the public. I believe that what V. O. Key argued three decades ago remains true today: that while the American people sometimes act in odd ways indeed, they generally behave as responsibly and rationally as one can expect, *given* the clarity of the alternatives put before them and the quality of the information upon which they must base their decisions.

I am indebted to Martin J. Medhurst, the senior editor of the Michigan State University Press series on Rhetoric and Public Affairs, for pointing out some of my own rhetorical excesses in the original manuscript for this book. I will continue to insist that the book was much better before he exorcised my sarcastic demon, but I say this only to irritate Marty. I also thank Jay Mechling of the University of California—Davis for steering me toward a better understanding of the apocalyptic tradition and for making countless other suggestions that improved this book. Finally, I owe major debts of gratitude to three people who contributed very directly to particular chapters. David Olsen, now at California State University—Los Angeles, contributed significantly to chapter 4, first by writing a term paper on "nuclear education" while a student at the University of Virginia, then by conducting much of the research and collaborating with me on a previously published version of the chapter. Leroy Dorsey, now at Texas A&M University, contributed similarly while a doctoral student at Indiana University. As my collaborator on an earlier version of chapter 6, Dorsey diligently researched the twisting paths of various freeze resolutions as they made their way through Congress. And Ted J. Smith III, my former colleague at Virginia and my frequent collaborator on polling and all things statistical, deserves much of the credit for chapter 8 and the Appendix. Smith collected the polling data reported in this book, tracked down fugitive polls, and helped me unravel the mysteries of the data as the co-author of a report published in *Public Opinion Quarterly*. He deserves full credit for the comprehensiveness of the opinion data in this book but none of the blame for any errors or tediousness of interpretation.

Less obvious contributions to this book have been made by countless other people. Jim Andrews, my department chair at Indiana as I competed the manuscript, understood better than I my need for time off, a minimum of distractions, and research assistance. Shawn Parry-Giles provided much of that research assistance while a doctoral student at Indiana, but made much more significant contributions over the years as a friend and adviser. Glen Williams, now at Texas A&M, likewise spent many hours listening to me ramble while a doctoral student at Indiana, all the while pretending that I made perfect sense. And Jim Aune and Michael Osborn, while contributing little directly to this book, have contributed immeasurably over the years to my personal and scholarly growth. Both have been the best of friends and inspirational role models. They taught me that there is more to life than career advancement, and that success does not have to come at the expense of humor and humanity.

I trust that nobody who knows me well, including my mother, will be offended that I choose not to dedicate this book to any of them. Instead, I dedicate it to the memory of a remarkable white German Shepherd, known around these parts as Cosmo-the-Wonderdog. My constant companion and, yes, my best friend for the past decade-and-a-half, Cosmo has been gone now for more than a year, but he returns as a bittersweet memory with each passing thunderstorm. The great poets have reflected little upon the mystical therapy of canine companionship, so the understated, low-brow eloquence of Neil Young will just have to do: "He was the best old hound dog I ever did know."

J.M.H.

# Introduction

> The nuclear freeze movement is a rarity in twentieth-century America in two respects: its pure spontaneity and its power as a public phenomenon. As such, it is comparable in American history to our movement for independence in the eighteenth century that gave birth to the nation; to the movement to abolish slavery in the nineteenth century that saved the nation; and to the movements in recent years for civil rights, the equal rights of women, and an end to the Vietnam war.[1]
>
> Edward M. Kennedy and Mark O. Hatfield, *Freeze!*

In March 1980, a young arms control activist named Randall Forsberg first proposed a bilateral freeze on the testing, production and deployment of new nuclear weapons.[2] Conceived as a mechanism for reuniting and reinvigorating the peace movement,[3] the freeze quickly attracted support from a broad array of mainstream political groups as well. By the spring of 1982, the freeze had been endorsed by hundreds of politicians and political groups,[4] and Congress began a two-year debate over various freeze resolutions.[5] Meanwhile, freeze activists lobbied hard for state and local freeze resolutions and circulated petitions to put freeze referenda on local ballots. By January of 1982, more than two dozen city councils, 300 towns, and 6 New England state legislatures had passed freeze resolutions.[6] By November the list of freeze resolutions had grown to include 275 city governments, 12 state legislatures, and 446 New England town meetings, and in the fall elections freeze referenda won in 8 states, the District of Columbia, and over two dozen cities.[7]

The freeze campaign drew its political momentum, in large measure, from depictions of public support for the initiative. Describing support for the freeze as broad-based and rapidly growing, news commentators spoke mystically about public opinion rising up "with a singular message, as if a great revelation had come to the common imagination."[8] In 1982, *Newsweek* reported that "a cross section" of Americans, including "homemakers and businessmen, clerks and doctors, clergymen, teachers, scientists and even military men," had "suddenly enlisted" in this "loosely linked, burgeoning campaign to end the nuclear arms race." Their numbers were "mushrooming," the newsmagazine reported, growing faster than "even their own leaders ever expected."[9] Similarly, *Time* reported that the freeze attracted "broad-based support" from "across the socioeconomic spectrum."[10] In March 1982, the newsmagazine declared the freeze movement "far more broadly based" than the antiwar movement of the 1960s and began a cover story on the phenomenon under the Victor Hugo quotation, "No army can stop an idea whose time has come":

> An idea whose moment may have arrived is sweeping the U.S.—for better or for worse. From the halls of Congress to Vermont hamlets to the posh living rooms of Beverly Hills, Americans are not only thinking about the unthinkable, they are opening a national dialogue on ways to control and reduce the awesome and frightening arsenals of the superpowers.[11]

The polling industry provided the empirical foundation for such stories. Between 1980 and 1984, the pollsters asked hundreds of questions about nuclear weapons and strategic arms policy, and they marvelled at the strong, often overwhelming support for the freeze initiative. Some polls showed upwards of 90 percent of the public supporting the freeze,[12] creating the curious spectacle of a protest movement that almost everybody supported. For years, the pollsters had reported that Americans did not pay much attention to the nuclear threat. But now, according to pollster Louis Harris, the public was not only "genuinely frightened" but "frightened in an activated as opposed to a passive way."[13]

All this was not lost on the politicians. In Congress, supporters of a freeze resolution echoed the journalists and the pollsters, warning their colleagues that they could ignore the freeze movement "only at political peril for themselves and for their political parties."[14] Convinced that millions of Americans had sent them a powerful message,[15] the House of Representatives twice debated the issue, finally passing a freeze resolution in the spring of 1983 by nearly a two-to-one margin.[16]

On the campaign trail, the freeze assumed even greater prominence. In February 1984, the *CBS Evening News* reported that Democratic presidential hopefuls had begun "falling all over each other, trying to court the freeze movement," because the polls had identified nuclear war as "the number one concern on the minds of the voters."[17] And as early as July of 1984, CBS News reported that "questions about the President's sincerity on arms control" had become a political problem for the Republicans.[18] Right up through the fall the news media continued to insist that nuclear war was "high on the list" of voter concerns, with the polls showing that most Americans wanted more action on arms control than they had seen from Ronald Reagan.[19] With the freeze campaign threatening to "organize millions upon millions of freeze voters" in 1984,[20] even seasoned political observers predicted that the freeze just might "do to Ronald Reagan what Vietnam did to Lyndon Johnson."[21]

Reagan's landslide reelection, of course, put an end to such talk. In 1984, the movement that promised to revolutionize American politics "not only failed to defeat the President," it failed even to make "the peace issue a major campaign topic." For the freeze campaign, the 1984 elections proved a "demoralizing flop."[22] Nor did the nuclear freeze campaign leave a legacy of new strategic arms policies. Even supporters admitted that the House freeze resolution was more symbolic than substantive, and in any case the Senate refused to go along. Shortly after the resolution passed, it was back to business as usual, with the House voting to fund the MX missile just 20 days after the freeze vote.[23] As Helen Caldicott conceded in retrospect: "In terms of pragmatic results, we haven't gotten rid of one weapon. . . . We haven't had any impact on Congress."[24]

The nuclear freeze campaign thus remains a political paradox. How does one account for such a powerful, grass-roots movement having so little impact? How could it disappear so suddenly without a trace? And why did it have so little impact upon electoral politics and strategic arms policy? One answer might lie in the rhetoric of the freeze activists themselves. The very "telepolitical" strategies that won abundant and sympathetic news coverage for the freeze campaign may have doomed it to failure in institutional political contexts and generated only superficial and transitory public support. By pandering to journalistic conventions, the freeze campaign attracted headlines and created the appearance of a powerful grass-roots movement. But that movement proved a political mirage, as fleeting as the images and sound bites of contemporary TV news.

## The Nuclear Debate and Telepolitical Journalism

Questions of nuclear weapons and strategic policy historically have posed significant obstacles to public involvement in the political process. Citizens attending to the nuclear debate must grapple with extremely complex issues, made all the more incomprehensible by technical jargon and a "jungle of mysterious acronyms."[25] Talk of telemetry encryption, circular error probable, and throw weight hardly invites public deliberation. Even the best-informed citizen may retreat from discussions of ICBMs, IRBMs, SLBMs, MIRVs and MARVs. No wonder that polls have shown that most Americans consider nuclear issues too complicated for the public to decide.[26]

Rhetorical scholars have long sensed an Orwellian conspiracy behind the nuclear debate. Treating nuclear jargon as some sort of anti-democratic plot to obfuscate the issue, Edward Schiappa, among others, has argued that the "rhetoric of nukespeak" allows politicians "to avoid and to constrain" public deliberation over nuclear defense strategy.[27] Similarly, Walter R. Fisher, in elaborating his theory of the "narrative paradigm," has suggested that people in privileged positions deliberately discredit popular discourse about nuclear issues with a "subversive pattern of ideological, bureaucratic, and technical arguments." In the nuclear debate, Fisher suggests, public argument is typically "overwhelmed by privileged argument," reducing the public to spectators rather than participants in the democratic process.[28]

The nuclear freeze movement supposedly changed all that. Echoing the freeze campaign itself, many of these same writers have celebrated the freeze campaign as a "democratization" of the nuclear debate—a sort of revolution against the rhetorical tyranny of the politicians and the experts. Fisher, for example, developed his narrative paradigm for the express purpose of circumventing the "inevitable subversion" of the freeze movement's "bible"—Jonathan Schell's *The Fate of the Earth*—by the technical standards of the prevailing "rational paradigm." According to Fisher, Schell's book was "exemplary of contemporary moral argument intended to persuade a general audience, the 'public,'" for it displayed, not specialized knowledge, but a narrative rationality accessible to all.[29] Similarly, rhetorical critic Rebecca S. Bjork has claimed that the freeze movement transformed "an apathetic public willing to cede control to the experts" into an activist public "crying No to the authority of the existing hierarchy." Bjork identified two characteristics of the freeze campaign's rhetoric that supposedly accounted for its broad grassroots support: its emphasis on moral concerns and its simplicity. According to Bjork, the moral simplicity of the freeze campaign appealed to millions of "concerned citizens confused by the paradoxes and intricacies of the arms race."[30]

The nuclear freeze campaign may well have democratized the nuclear debate, but it did so only in the sense that television has democratized American culture generally: by appealing to the lowest common denominator, by titillating rather than educating, by dramatizing, sensationalizing, and oversimplifying complex issues. Indeed, the nuclear freeze campaign did not merely reflect television culture, it aggressively exploited the new style of journalism spawned by this culture.[31] Appealing to changing conceptions of news, the freeze campaign was to the American public dialogue what dramatizations, "info-tainment," and "docudramas" are to journalism: rhetorical mutations of an honorable tradition. Blurring distinctions between fact and fiction, and wallowing in emotionalism, the freeze campaign designed its rhetorical strategies not to enlighten the public but to attract media attention.

As Kathleen Hall Jamieson has argued, electronic journalism has spawned a whole new conception of political eloquence. In place of the rational, instrumental, and impersonal style that historically has characterized American public discourse, the "electronic age" has encouraged a more emotional and intimate style that Jamieson labels effeminate. In place of policy analysis and deliberative argument, the electronic age invites "visual assertions" and "synecdochic phrases"—"mere shards" of political argument that can be "telegraphed to the national audience by the news media." According to Jamieson, Ronald Reagan epitomized this degraded sense of eloquence, substituting storytelling for argument, personality for a "reasoned invitation to judgment."[32] Yet Jamieson might just as well have been talking about the nuclear freeze campaign, for this too put on quite a telepolitical "act."

Concocted by peace activists hoping to broaden their political base, the very concept of a freeze arose out of a concern not so much with policy as with public relations. Considered simple enough to be understood by a public weaned on television, the freeze masked the peace movement's larger political agenda behind a simple metaphor with broad appeal: the image of a spiraling arms race frozen in place. In the rhetoric of the Nuclear Weapons Freeze Campaign, the freeze represented a cluster of emotionally provocative images, not a specific arms control initiative or a new kind of treaty. Skirting the technical and political controversies of the nuclear debate, the freeze campaign rested instead upon apocalyptic scenarios and celebrity appeals. Its strategy was not to democratize the nuclear debate but to sidestep that debate altogether.

For a time, at least, the strategy worked. By the middle of 1982, the freeze dominated the news and Americans were said to be flocking to the cause by the millions. Yet that very success came back to haunt the peace activists who founded the campaign. Increasingly coopted by mainstream politicians and the news media itself, the freeze campaign's telepolitical rhetoric took on a life of its own. No longer did it call attention to the peace movement's broader political agenda or even to the freeze initiative itself. Leaving the peace activists who founded it in the wake of its sudden success, the nuclear freeze became something of a cultural fad.

To offer such a reading is not to take sides in the freeze debate. Jamieson is right to lament that Ronald Reagan has come to define eloquence, and those who have complained about nukespeak likewise have a point. Yet neither should we allow our longings for peace to blind us to the freeze campaign's rhetorical transgressions. Both sides in the freeze debate oversimplified the issues. Both sides fudged the facts and substituted fear appeals for evidence and sound reasoning. We already have a whole genre of critical literature condemning Ronald Reagan's rhetoric as "unrealistic, simplistic, and misinformed."[33] This book applies the same rhetorical standards to the nuclear freeze campaign.

## Rhetoric and Democracy in the Telepolitical Age

A decade has passed since the nuclear freeze campaign dominated the discourse of our national political life. Yet our memories of the freeze remain shrouded in political myths—myths that obscure both the history of the campaign and its larger political lessons. This, of course, is not the first book about the freeze, and it may not be the last. It is, however, the first *not* grounded in two related myths: that the campaign was, at least in some senses, a great success, not only winning a number of important political victories, but also "reforming" Ronald Reagan, and that the campaign, at least for a time, enjoyed widespread public support, spawning a grass-roots movement that cut across socio-economic classes and eventually attracted a large majority of the American people.

Since former freeze activists have written most of the campaign's postmortems, it hardly comes as a surprise that they claim some measure of success.

Some even claim that they won the debate. Insisting that "the movement vanished" only "when it was no longer necessary," David S. Meyer, a freeze organizer and researcher at the Institute for Defense and Disarmament Studies, points to a legacy of institutionalized movement organizations and nuclear education programs. As a result of the campaign, Meyers argues, "expression of nuclear concern" no longer requires "extra-institutional social mobilization." Furthermore, Meyers boasts that the campaign, in effect, reformed Ronald Reagan, forcing the "extremely popular president to return to long-established bipartisan policies he had consistently eschewed and had vigorously criticized." As Meyers writes:

> The Ronald Reagan who talked of limited nuclear war and joked of beginning to bomb the Soviet Union in five minutes was replaced by a president committed to world peace, a Ronald Reagan who saw his landslide victory as a mandate for arms control, one who looked forward to the day when "all nations can begin to reduce nuclear weapons and ultimately banish them from the face of the earth."

From this perspective, then, the freeze campaign can be seen "as a political triumph," according to Meyer—"a demonstration of a responsive democratic polity and of the limits on executive policy."[34]

Such a claim, of course, rests upon the second, even more prevalent myth about the freeze campaign: that it inspired a strong grass-roots movement and attracted overwhelming public support, at least for a time. For former freeze activists, the question is not *whether* the campaign ever had "the people" behind it, but rather what happened to that support. Why was such a powerful grass-roots movement unable to translate this support into votes for pro-freeze candidates or into passage of the freeze initiative itself? How could it be that "one of the largest grass-roots social change movements in the history of the country" could fade so rapidly, failing to translate its "massive public support into real political power?" For Pam Solo, one of the founders of the campaign and the former chair of the Nuclear Weapons Freeze Committee's Strategy Committee, this is the ultimate question to arise out of the freeze debate, a question that in turn raises larger questions about the integrity of the democratic process itself: "Can the Freeze, or any citizens' movement, gain the power to move from protest to policy? Is national security decisionmaking susceptible to public opinion?"[35]

Most former freeze activists retain at least some faith in the democratic process. According to Solo, the freeze campaign at least *began* a long process of "educating" the public, and for a time it successfully transformed "the issues and the language used by politicians" to facilitate discussion of nuclear issues, breaking from "the dominant discourse of arms control and the cold war." But just as this "war of ideas" was beginning to bear fruit, according to Solo, "the movement narrowed its agenda, which in turn constrained its educational program and confined its politics." Concerned with answering its right-wing critics and remaining "respectable" among "political and arms control elites," freeze advocates began defending the initiative on "technical grounds," thereby straying from their "original goal of breaking out of arms control 'negotiations as usual' and challenging the new militarism." For Solo, the lesson is clear: that in order "to develop a mass base" with "potential to develop political power without being co-opted," peace activists must "promote political literacy with a dynamic education strategy that recognizes the peculiarities of our culture and language and does not overlook the continuing impact of television on our political life as a nation."[36]

This book draws very different conclusions about the nuclear freeze campaign. I argue that the freeze campaign never set out to educate the public. Rather, it was designed from the outset to circumvent deliberations over policy, to attract media attention with telepolitical appeals. Instead of a "war of ideas," the freeze campaign waged a war of images, slogans, and bandwagon appeals. Substituting passion for argument and celebrity for expertise, the freeze campaign disguised the political agenda of its founders behind an innocuous, almost apolitical rhetoric designed to make the news. When the freeze campaign changed strategy, deciding to focus upon electoral politics and congressional lobbying, mainstream political forces indeed coopted that rhetoric. But lacking political substance from the outset, the campaign never stood much of a chance of prevailing in institutional contexts or of building a strong foundation of public support.

As Fox Butterfield wrote in 1982, the nuclear freeze campaign can provide "special insights into the American political process and the state of the public mind and character."[37] For some, these insights inspire optimism: the freeze campaign "democratized" the nuclear debate and pointed the way for effective public involvement in the political process. For others, they inspire pessimism: the freeze campaign, despite its broad grass-roots support, never really changed things; "the will of the people," in the final analysis, did not really count.

In a sense, I dispute both these views, suggesting that the public never had a *chance* to make a difference. As V. O. Key argued in the mid-1960s, the American people are quite capable of asking "central and relevant questions of public policy, of governmental performance, and of executive personality."[38] Yet such questions cannot be answered by a colloquial idiom of public debate that values "feelings over information, personality over character."[39] As Jamieson argues, if citizens are to "deliberate fully and judge justly," then "public discourse must be enriched by *logos* as well as *ethos* and *pathos*, statement as well as proof."[40] By pandering to journalistic values, neither side in the freeze debate met this prerequisite of democratic deliberation. Like too many of today's journalists, both sides rejected Key's classic democratic dictum: "voters are not fools."[41]

## NOTES

1. Edward M. Kennedy and Mark O. Hatfield, *Freeze! How You Can Help Prevent Nuclear War* (New York: Bantam Books, 1982), 160-61.
2. Randall Forsberg, *Call to Halt the Nuclear Arms Race* (St. Louis: Nuclear Weapons Freeze Campaign, 1980).
3. Randall Forsberg, "The Shared Origins of the Directory and the Nuclear Freeze Movement," in *American Peace Directory, 1984*, edited by Melinda Fine and Peter M. Stevens (Cambridge: Ballinger, 1984), vii-viii.
4. Adam M. Garfinkle, *The Politics of the Nuclear Freeze* (Philadelphia: Foreign Policy Research Institute, 1984), 77-121.
5. Douglas C. Waller, *Congress and the Nuclear Freeze: An Inside Look at the Politics of a Mass Movement* (Amherst: University of Massachusetts Press, 1987).
6. Garfinkle, *The Politics of the Nuclear Freeze*, 84.
7. John Herbers, "Widespread Vote Urges Nuclear Freeze," *New York Times*, 4 November 1982, A22.
8. CBS News, *CBS Evening News*, 22 March 1982, microfiche transcript, 8-9.
9. David M. Alpern, et al. "A Matter of Life and Death," *Newsweek*, 26 April 1982, 20.
10. "Freeze March," *Time*, 14 June 1982, 24.
11. James Kelly, "Thinking About the Unthinkable," *Time*, 29 March 1982, 10.
12. See "Americans Assess the Nuclear Option," *Public Opinion* 5 (August/September 1982): 39.
13. Jamie Kalven, "A Talk with Louis Harris," *Bulletin of the Atomic Scientists* 38 (August/September 1982): 3-4.
14. U.S. Congress, House, "Providing for Consideration of House Joint Resolution 138, Calling for a Mutual and Verifiable Freeze on and Reductions in Nuclear Weapons," 98th Cong., 1st sess., *Congressional Record*, daily ed., vol. 129, no. 33 (16 March 1983), H1218.
15. Ibid., H1274.
16. See "House OKs, Senate Rejects Nuclear Freeze," in *1983 Congressional Quarterly Almanac*, ed. Mary Cohn (Washington, D.C.: Congressional Quarterly, 1983), 205-11.
17. CBS News, *CBS Evening News*, 13 February 1984, microfiche transcript, 10.
18. CBS News, *CBS Evening News*, 2 July 1984, microfiche transcript, 1.
19. CBS News, *CBS Evening News*, 28 September 1984, microfiche transcript, 3.
20. CBS News, *CBS Evening News*, 3 December 1983, microfiche transcript, 5.
21. Midge Costanza quoted in Alpern, et al. "A Matter of Life and Death," 21.
22. Steve L. Hawkins and John W. Mashek, "Antinuclear Campaign Reawakens," *U.S. News and World Report*, 27 January 1986, 22.
23. Waller, *Congress and the Nuclear Freeze*, 290.
24. Quoted in "Disarmament Groups Seek Rallying Point After Faltering on Atom Freeze," *New York Times*, 18 August 1985, 22.
25. Albert Carnesale, et al., *Living With Nuclear Weapons* (New York: Bantam, 1983), 11.
26. See question 81 in the Appendix.
27. Edward Schiappa, "The Rhetoric of Nukespeak," *Communication Monographs* 56 (September 1989): 254. See also Steven Hilgartner, Richard C. Bell, and Rory O'Connor, *Nukespeak: Nuclear Language, Visions, and Mindset* (San Francisco: Sierra Club Books, 1982); Sam Totten, "Orwellian Language in the Nuclear Age," *Curriculum Review* 23 (April 1984): 43-46.

28. Walter R. Fisher, "Narration as a Human Communication Paradigm: The Case of Public Moral Argument," *Communication Monographs* 51 (March 1984): 11-12.
29. Fisher, "Narration as a Human Communication Paradigm," 11-15. Elaborating upon the notion that storytelling is somehow more "democratic" than rational argument, Fisher claims that his "narrative paradigm" provides "a radical democratic ground for social-political critique," for "narrative rationality" is presumably "inimical to elitist politics," condemning "the sort of hierarchy . . . marked by the will to power, the kind of system in which elites struggle to dominate . . . or that makes the people blind subjects of technology" (9).
30. Rebecca S. Bjork, "Reagan and the Nuclear Freeze: 'Star Wars' as a Rhetorical Strategy," *Journal of the American Forensic Association* 24 (Winter 1987): 183-85, 192.
31. See John Fiske, *Television Culture* (London: Methuen, 1987), esp. 281-308. Fiske's argument, of course, is that television has encouraged a sort of journalistic discourse that, in terms of narrative conventions, cannot be distinguished from fictional texts.
32. Kathleen Hall Jamieson, *Eloquence in an Electronic Age: The Transformation of Political Speechmaking* (New York: Oxford University Press, 1988), 67-117.
33. William F. Lewis, "Telling America's Story: Narrative Form and the Reagan Presidency," *Quarterly Journal of Speech* 73 (August 1987): 280. For criticisms specifically of Reagan's nuclear discourse, see G. Thomas Goodnight, "Ronald Reagan's Reformulation of the Rhetoric of War: Analysis of the 'Zero Option,' 'Evil Empire,' and 'Star Wars' Addresses," *Quarterly Journal of Speech* 72 (November 1986): 390-414 and Janice Hocker Rushing, "Ronald Reagan's 'Star Wars' Address: Mythic Containment of Technical Reasoning," *Quarterly Journal of Speech* 72 (November 1986): 415-33.
34. David S. Meyer, *A Winter of Discontent: The Nuclear Freeze and American Politics* (New York: Praeger, 1990), 269, 272.
35. Pam Solo, *From Protest to Policy: Beyond the Freeze to Common Security* (Cambridge: Ballinger, 1988), xiv.
36. Solo, *From Protest to Policy*, 23, 51, 52.
37. Fox Butterfield, "Anatomy of the Nuclear Protest," *New York Times Magazine*, 11 July 1982, 14.
38. V. O. Key Jr., *The Responsible Electorate: Rationality in Presidential Voting, 1936-1960* (New York: Vintage, 1966), 7-8.
39. Kenneth Cmiel, *Democratic Eloquence: The Fight Over Popular Speech in Nineteenth-Century America* (Berkeley: University of California Press, 1990), 259. Cmiel argues that the rise of the "colloquial style" in public advocacy is "*not* simply the result of electronic media," tracing it back to such sources as Henry Ward Beecher's "theology of feeling" and Dale Carnegie's teachings in the early twentieth century. This book does not dispute that, but it does suggest that the trend toward a more "colloquial" style of public discourse has been accelerated greatly by television journalism.
40. Jamieson, *Eloquence in an Electronic Age*, 241.
41. Key, *The Responsible Electorate*, 7.

# Part I

# The Nuclear Freeze Campaign

Chet Seymour/THE PICTURE CUBE

## Chapter One

# The Radical Ethos in Reagan's America

> I will regard with benevolence a revival of freeze pressure upon an administration subsequent to Reagan, but I do feel the United States peace movement should be raising its sights to more radical and more ambitious goals, such as the roots of the Cold War itself, since I think that paradoxically, by taking the easy route of the lowest common denominator, the necessary criticism of the United States militarism has been blunted.[1]
>
> E. P. Thompson

Politics often defy logic—moreso than ever in the telepolitical age. In the early 1980s, we witnessed the curious spectacle of Ronald Reagan proposing "truly substantial reductions" in the superpower arsenals and seemingly utopian schemes to render nuclear weapons "impotent and obsolete."[2] Meanwhile, his critics in the peace movement rallied around a far more modest initiative: a proposal to "freeze" nuclear arsenals at existing levels.

Yet literal, policy-oriented readings fundamentally miss the point of the nuclear freeze debate. Just as Reagan's "Star Wars" initiative may be interpreted as a rhetorical strategy to disarm his critics,[3] the freeze initiative is best understood, not as an arms control initiative, but as a domestic political campaign. For a peace movement scattered and isolated since the Vietnam era, the freeze provided an effective, albeit short-lived rallying point. Dispirited by the Reagan landslide in 1980, the peace movement discovered in the freeze a powerful metaphor that rejuvenated their organizations, enhanced their fund-raising efforts, and generated abundant and sympathetic news coverage.

The campaign for a nuclear freeze originated with veteran peace activists. Yet determined to broaden their political base, they stifled their usual ideological agenda and instead spoke metaphorically of an arms race "frozen" in place. Substituting slogans, images, and bandwagon appeals for policy analysis, the official rhetoric of the Nuclear Weapons Freeze Campaign cultivated a mainstream image and skirted most of the substantive controversies of the nuclear debate. For a time, the strategy worked. Yet the freeze campaign soon resurrected the classic dilemma of radical politics in America: the conflict between political pragmatism and ideological purity. The more freeze activists reached out to the

American public, the more they bickered among themselves over ideological and strategic issues. And the more attention the freeze attracted, the more mainstream political forces coopted the crusade.

## The Origins of the Freeze

As Adam Garfinkle has written, the nuclear freeze campaign was "first born and subsequently organized" by a handful of special interest groups—organizations of the "professional left"—including the American Friends Service Committee (AFSC), the Fellowship of Reconciliation (FOR), and the Women's International League for Peace and Freedom (WILPF). To be sure, many of these activists sincerely worried about the arms race. But as Garfinkle has argued, "politicizing the nuclear issue" also became a means for enhancing their political relevance and clout. "It was, put colloquially, a power trip—a way to make these tiny, fringe organizations more important to other public advocacy groups that were closer to the center of the political spectrum."[4]

A young arms control analyst named Randall Forsberg first formally articulated the freeze proposal itself. An English major at Barnard College in New York, Forsberg taught at a private school before marrying a Swedish student and moving to Stockholm in 1967. Hired as a typist by the government-sponsored Stockholm International Peace Research Institute, she soon became interested in arms control, and in 1974 she returned to the United States to pursue graduate studies in international relations at MIT. A few years later she founded her own research institute, The Institute for Defense and Disarmament Studies (IDDS) in Brookline, Massachusetts. As head of this "think tank," she wrote the brief, nontechnical manifesto of the nuclear freeze campaign: *Call to Halt the Nuclear Arms Race.*[5]

Nobody was more candid about the domestic political motivations behind the freeze proposal than Forsberg herself. In her introduction to *The American Peace Directory*, a guide to anti-nuclear and disarmament groups published by the IDDS in 1984, Forsberg reminisced about her role in launching "the national movement for a US-Soviet nuclear-weapons freeze." While compiling the *Directory*, Forsberg recalled, she realized that "the peace movement was at a nadir, experiencing a post-Vietnam backlash that had decreased the number of activists to a few thousand." What the movement lacked, she reasoned, was a "shared, short-term goal." If all the groups could work together "on a common short-term goal—instead of being splintered by advocacy of competing medium- and long-term goals"—she believed that their chances of achieving *any* goal would be "greatly increased." Thus she searched for an issue that would "command the support of most peace groups" as well as appeal to "the majority of the U.S. public." Initially, she "proposed twin-goals to be undertaken simultaneously, one concerning nuclear weapons, the other concerning conventional (non-nuclear) armed forces." But she quickly "decided that even though nuclear freeze and nonintervention policies would complement and strengthen one another in many ways, it would be too complicated for activist groups to promote two seemingly unrelated goals at the same time." Concluding that one of the issues would have to be "tackled first, leaving the other to a later campaign," Forsberg settled upon the freeze "as the best focus for a common campaign intended to last several years."[6]

In fleshing out her idea, Forsberg joined forces with the American Friends Service Committee (AFSC), the Quaker pacifist organization founded in 1917. Revising a call for a three-year, unilateral nuclear moratorium issued by the AFSC in 1979,[7] Forsberg arrived at her proposal for a bilateral, verifiable nuclear freeze. Substantively, of course, Forsberg's revision differed radically from the original AFSC proposal, transforming a call for *unilateral disarmament* into a relatively modest plan for *bilateral arms control.* Nevertheless, the AFSC distributed Forsberg's *Call* as the centerpiece of a campaign dubbed "The New Manhattan Project," and the results proved startling. Sales of AFSC disarmament literature quadrupled during just one year of the campaign, with one AFSC pamphlet selling over 5,000 copies in but a single month.[8]

Other peace groups quickly jumped on the bandwagon. Some, like the Fellowship of Reconciliation (FOR) and Pax Christi, had religious roots like the AFSC. Others, such as the WILPF, came out of secular, neo-Marxist traditions. Yet whatever their histories, all opposed American "imperialism" and "interventionism" abroad. All sympathized with the "developing world" and urged unilateral disarmament by the United States. All drew linkages between America's foreign policy and its domestic social ills. None of these groups abandoned their historic principles to campaign for the freeze. Yet neither did they reveal these principles to the American people. Cultivating a moderate, mainstream political image, their broader political platforms comprised the hidden agenda of the nuclear freeze campaign.

## The Hidden Agenda

Randall Forsberg's efforts to rally support for the freeze initiative began with a speech to 600 peace activists at the annual convention of Mobilization for Survival (MOBE) in December of 1979. Founded in the spring of 1977, MOBE consisted of some 280 peace and environmental groups, including the AFSC, Clergy and Laity Concerned (CLC), the War Resisters' League (WRL), and the WILPF.[9] As a national coalition of veteran activists, MOBE seemed the logical organizational home for the freeze campaign. Yet as David Meyer has noted, Forsberg's *Call* initially received mixed responses from MOBE. Not only had the group developed its own proposal for a nuclear moratorium, but it generally advocated a "wide range of political activity linking many issues."[10]

Nevertheless, the peace groups continued to discuss the freeze in less formal strategy meetings in early 1980, and at least some became convinced of the potential of the freeze as an organizing vehicle. In February, several of the groups, including the AFSC, CALC, FOR, and Forsberg's IDDS, decided to print and distribute the *Call to Halt the Nuclear Arms Race*, and in April they distributed 5,000 copies. By the summer of 1980, the AFSC, CALC, and FOR had formally endorsed the freeze proposal, and a number of other groups, including IDDS, WILPF, Sojourners, the Riverside Church, World Peacemakers, Pax Christi, and the Coalition for a New Foreign and Military Policy (CNFMP) had declared the freeze an "organizing priority." In March of 1981, the First National Nuclear Weapons Freeze Conference brought 300 activists from around the country together at Georgetown University to consider a unified national campaign strategy. Mapping out a three-to-five year strategy for achieving a bilateral freeze, the conference decided upon four major goals: demonstrating the potential of the freeze; building broad and visible public support; focusing that support on policy makers and creating a major national debate; and winning the debate and making the freeze a national policy objective.[11]

For a group such as the AFSC, the freeze campaign marked a striking change in mission. Since organizing around efforts to counsel conscientious objectors to World War I, the AFSC had always been known as a Quaker peace group. Yet the AFSC historically remained on the fringes of American politics, promoting utopian images of a world without violence and calling for America to lay down its arms. Throughout its long history, the AFSC seemed almost deliberately to cultivate the image of a lonely voice in the political wilderness.

Early in its history, the AFSC remained closely associated with the Quaker religion. Following World War II, however, the AFSC's Quaker connections gradually gave way to a "radical pacifism" based upon social scientific rather than religious justifications for collective nonviolence and passive resistance.[12] In 1962, for example, the AFSC published Mulford Sibley's *Unilateral Initiatives and Disarmament*—a call for unilateral disarmament by the United States and "nonviolent resistance" to any Soviet invasion. Proposing an elaborate scheme for educating the American people "in the techniques and theory of non-cooperation, civil disobedience and the peaceful strike," Sibley wrote of how the "soldiers of the occupation would be respected as persons," while their policies "would be undercut by techniques of non-cooperation."[13] In 1969, the AFSC marked another milestone in its political evolution with the publication of *Anatomy of Anti-Communism*. Authored by a "working party" of the AFSC's Peace Education Division, *Anatomy of Anti-Communism* set out to destroy the "myths about the Communist" that served "as a camouflage for conservative and, on occasion, reactionary policy" in the United States. Arguing that the Communist had as good "a case against the Western world as the Western world has a case against him," the study equated the "political servitude" imposed by communist regimes with "parliamentary capitalism's perpetuation of economic misery."[14]

As the AFSC entered the 1980s, it continued to invoke its religious roots, describing itself as "a contemporary expression of Quaker beliefs" and celebrating "a denial that violence can ever be right."[15] But as the *New Republic's* Stephen Chapman has observed, the group preached an increasingly selective pacifism, criticizing human rights violations only in countries allied with the U.S. while endorsing "any number of explicitly violent movements" opposed to U.S. policy.[16] Proclaiming solidarity with the PLO and other liberation movements,[17] the AFSC emphasized the linkages between the "the violence of war" and "the violence of human misery and exploitation." As one brochure summarized the group's philosophy, the AFSC sought "nothing less than the abolition of war," and that meant recognizing "that oppression, sexism, and a denial of human and economic rights" were at "the roots of violence and war."[18]

The AFSC typified the religious groups that dominated the early freeze coalition.[19] Although they affiliated with a variety of denominations, all subscribed to what James Davison Hunter has called the "progressivist vision,"[20] preaching a theology of peace and justice that went well beyond just freezing the arms race. Like the AFSC, the Fellowship of Reconciliation, an interdenominational peace group also dating back to World War I, historically published calls for the United States to "lay down its arms, scrap its warplanes, missiles, and submarines, disband its troops, and leave itself only the organization and weapons needed for local police and for normal patrols of its borders."[21] Pax Christi, the leading Catholic freeze group, likewise preached unilateral disarmament and developed elaborate plans for "nonviolent resistance to invasion" and "conversion of the economy to peace-based work."[22]

None of these religious groups seemed troubled by allegations that they politicized religion.[23] Invoking "liberation" or "political" theology, all celebrated what they called a "deprivitized" religion concerned with more than just personal salvation. Treating "Christian social action" as a "constitutive part" of their "personal faith commitment," they believed that "transformation of the world and transformation of the individual go hand in hand," and they viewed "the spread of thermonuclear weapons" as threatening to "the liberation of everyone."[24] All of these groups recognized, as the Fellowship of Reconciliation emphasized in its literature, that the freeze "would not in itself involve disarming nuclear weapons that now exist." They supported it only "as a first step toward worldwide disarmament," while they continued to emphasize "initiatives for unilateral disarmament."[25]

The same might be said about the secular groups initially involved in the freeze coalition. None of them supported the freeze as an end in itself. All came out of ideological traditions that, like liberation theology, treated nuclear weapons as but one symptom of a larger corruption. As Garfinkle has noted, virtually all of the religious and secular freeze groups were "knit together" by an "interlocking directorate," and all shared pretty much the same world view.[26] Although the religious groups may have couched their advocacy in the language of religious morality, their interpretations of world affairs differed little from those of the secular, neo-Marxist groups.

The Women's International League for Peace and Freedom, the peace group founded in 1915 with Jane Addams as its first president, perhaps best represents the various ideological strains of the secular freeze groups. Since its Third International Congress in 1921, the WILPF has been dedicated to transforming the American "economic system in the direction of social justice." Campaigning tirelessly for a new, "non-exploitative society"—a society based upon socialist principles—the WILPF identified the free enterprise system as the root of all evil in the modern world. As the group's pamphlet, *Principles and Policies*, explained: "Production for private profit rather than for human needs fosters war, racism, violence, and social and economic injustice. Fundamental economic change is needed to achieve more equitable distribution of resources through public ownership of the sources of wealth and the participation of workers in the control of industry." The WILPF was never only a socialist group, however, nor was it only a peace group. In the same pamphlet, the WILPF's list of concerns ranged from global ecology, to civil rights and the rights of women, to "the militarism, racism, and demands for sexual, social and political conformity which undermine our entire educational system."[27] Like the religious freeze groups, the WILPF drew linkages among a host of domestic and foreign policy issues, calling itself "a multi-issue, multi-racial organization emphasizing the connections between war and poverty, racism and economic exploitation and sexism and violence." And like the religious freeze groups, the WILPF viewed its foreign and domestic agendas as "inseparable, two sides of the same coin."[28]

At first glance, the WILPF might seem a strange political bedfellow of Quakers and Catholics. With its explicitly neo-Marxist political orientation, the WILPF seemed indifferent, if not hostile, toward religion. Yet as James Dougherty has observed, "the affinity of liberation theology with the Marxist view of human existence" should be "obvious,"[29] particularly in the realm of foreign affairs. Sympathetic to Third World "liberation" movements, the religious and secular freeze groups shared opposition to U.S. imperialism. All traced the evils of American foreign policy to capitalistic acquisitiveness, and all perceived linkages between American interventionism abroad and the oppression of minorities, women, and poor people at home. As Richard McBrien has written, "The God of liberation theology . . . is a God whose primary, if not sole, passion is the freeing of the oppressed from the bondage of economic, racist or sexist exploitation."[30] The WILPF and most other secular freeze groups worshipped very much the same "God"—and the same "holy trinity" of race, class, and gender.

Even as they organized around the freeze, most of these veteran peace activists criticized the initiative as too "timid about the larger, more crucial issue of disarmament." Even Mark Neidergang of Forsberg's IDDS conceded that the freeze was "not very good" as "political analysis." But articulating the rationale animating Forsberg and the rest of the early freeze advocates, Neidergang observed that the freeze had "amazing" power as "a tool for getting people involved in these issues and for bringing them to a more critical analysis" of American foreign policy. "It gets tens of millions of people thinking about nuclear war. It opens up people's minds." In the past, Neidergang argued, "the left has not been able to do that." But in the freeze campaign the Left had found an issue with appeal to "a lot of new people from religious and professional backgrounds," and "even some conservatives" had begun to see the light.[31]

Yet the rhetoric of the freeze campaign actually did little to promote this more critical analysis of American foreign policy. Eschewing the wide-ranging critiques of American politics and culture historically characteristic of peace movement rhetoric, the new campaign focused narrowly upon the idea of a freeze and exhibited none of the language of "radicalism"—that ideological jargon and stridency of tone that has long relegated peace activists to the political fringes. Couching their advocacy in more moderate tones, Forsberg and her allies focused upon the horrors of nuclear war and spoke in politically innocuous metaphors. Skirting the major controversies of the nuclear debate, they refused to debate technical issues, and they refrained from attacking Ronald Reagan or any other specific "enemy." In short, they spoke an essentially apolitical language, and for a time, at least, the strategy paid off.

## The Rhetoric of the Freeze Clearinghouse

In February 1982, the Second National Freeze Conference convened in Denver, Colorado. Attended by freeze organizers from around the country, the conference reflected upon the success of the plan developed at the Georgetown conference. Phase I, they decided, had already succeeded; they had demonstrated the "potential of the Freeze idea." Now they could focus on Phase II of the plan: "Building broad and visible public support for the freeze." Specifically, the strategy for 1982 called for: gathering one-and-a-half million signatures on Freeze petitions by mid-October; getting the endorsements of at least "ten nationally-prominent individuals and organizations per major constituency"; putting Freeze referenda on the ballot "in as many locales as possible"; expanding the campaign to include all fifty states; and, by the end of 1982, "gaining the support of 150 Members of the U.S. House of Representatives and 35 Members of the U.S. Senate."[32]

At the time, these goals seemed ambitious, even unrealistic, but they soon proved quite modest. By the end of 1982, the petition drive had netted nearly two-and-a-half million signatures,[33] and in the November elections more than eleven-and-a-half million voters supported the freeze in 48 state and local freeze referenda.[34] By February 1983, 348 city and 64 county councils had passed freeze resolutions, along with 446 New England Town Meetings and nearly a dozen state legislatures.[35] On 5 August 1982, the House of Representatives narrowly defeated a freeze resolution, but in the spring of 1983 a freeze resolution passed the House by nearly a two-to-one margin.[36]

How did they do it? How did peace groups long relegated to the fringes of American politics suddenly become major players? For answers, we must take a closer look at the official voice of the Nuclear Weapons Freeze Campaign: the National Clearinghouse established in St. Louis in January of 1982.

Headed by a Vietnam-era draft resister, Randall Kehler,[37] the National Freeze Clearinghouse reflected important changes in the strategic thinking of the American peace movement. With a professional staff of twelve, including a "national media coordinator,"[38] it brought a new coherence and sophistication to peace movement advocacy. In all of its materials, the Clearinghouse carefully cultivated a mainstream political image, emphasizing institutionalized political activities and setting a moderate tone for the campaign. Serving as a "gatekeeper" of sorts, it jealously guarded the image of the campaign against the rhetorical excesses of its more radical supporters. As Kehler explained, even the site selected for the new Clearinghouse cultivated a mainstream image: "St. Louis presented us with the image we wanted, one of a movement anchored in Middle America."[39]

As a national Clearinghouse, the St. Louis office devoted most of its energies to coordinating the activities of state and local freeze groups. In a list of "resources" published by the Clearinghouse, most of the "information material" was geared to committed activists: a quarterly *Freeze Newsletter* and monthly *Freeze Updates* to help supporters "keep track of developments in the fast-growing Nuclear Weapons Freeze Campaign"; a Freeze Campaign Information Packet, including reprints of articles and a sample newsletter; a Leaflet Sampler, containing five of "the best Freeze leaflets produced by local organizations around the country"; and a State of the Campaign Report, to help activists put their "local efforts in the context of the National Campaign." Similarly, the "organizing tools" distributed by the Clearinghouse were all designed to aid and coordinate local campaigns: an "ad kit" containing fourteen camera-ready advertisements and "complete instructions" for placing the ads; a Congressional District Petitioning Packet, containing "everything you need to know to start a petitioning campaign in your Congressional district"; a Fundraising Packet, with "helpful hints for local fundraising"; and a Freeze Media Kit, described as a "step-by-step manual for local freeze groups who want to make better use of their local print and broadcast media." With all of these materials, the Clearinghouse promoted a mainstream political strategy. Instead of "confronting the warmakers," the Clearinghouse advocated "Depolarizing Disarmament Work"—as it titled one article containing advice on "how to make personal interactions more productive."[40]

In addition to coordinating local efforts, the Clearinghouse served as the official public voice of the freeze campaign on the national level. Producing slick "national brochures" and direct-mail literature, the Clearinghouse boasted of using "the best of contemporary advertising techniques to convince the American public that the Freeze is essential to our common future." It also distributed a series of seven *Fact Sheets* designed for public consumption, as well as promotional paraphernalia typical of an election campaign: campaign buttons, bumper stickers, and freeze window stickers "designed to be placed on your front door or window."[41] With these materials, the Clearinghouse set the slogans, the strategic priorities, and the official positions of the freeze campaign at the national level. Touching only perfunctorily upon the technical controversies of the nuclear debate, the Clearinghouse targeted its appeals to Middle America. While materials aimed at committed activists often attacked the Reagan administration, the public face of the Clearinghouse remained non-partisan—even apolitical. Instead of controversies, the Clearinghouse spoke of consensus, projecting the image of a non-partisan "people's campaign" rooted in "common sense."

The controlling imagery of the Clearinghouse campaign is perhaps best illustrated by one of its two national brochures: a shiny, eight-page mailer featuring the slogan, "Freeze: Because Nobody Wants a Nuclear War." Juxtaposed above and below the slogan on the cover of the pamphlet were images reminiscent of Lyndon Johnson's infamous "Daisy Ad" in the 1964 presidential campaign: a huge mushroom cloud billowing up behind a crowd of children, some apparently singing, others looking worried. Turning the cover, the reader confronted the "reality" of nuclear war: a wide-angle photograph, spread out across the bottom of two pages, dramatically depicting the devastation of Hiroshima. Elaborating upon the images, the text explained that, at minimum, 140,000,000 Americans would die in an all-out nuclear war. If even a fraction of the existing nuclear arsenals were ever exploded, "our nation and much of the rest of the world would be transformed into a vast, burning graveyard and civilization as we know it could no longer exist."[42]

Logically, of course, the slogan accompanying these images denied their political relevance. "Nobody wants a nuclear war," the Clearinghouse conceded in all of its literature. And as if to confirm the point, freeze pamphlets quoted from a broad spectrum of "establishment" figures—Russian and American leaders, liberals and conservatives, military men, scientists, and religious leaders—all testifying to the horrors of nuclear war. In just this one brochure, former U.S. Ambassador to the U.S.S.R., George Kennan, former Defense Secretary Harold Brown, Soviet leader Leonid Brezhnev, retired Rear Admiral Gene LaRocque, Pope John Paul II, and even Ronald Reagan all testified in bold-faced inserts to the fact that, in Reagan's words, "a nuclear war cannot be won and must never be fought."[43]

At the same time, however, the whole freeze campaign implicitly tapped anti-elitist and populist sentiments, vaguely condemning *all* politicians and experts and portraying the freeze as a common sense alternative born of the people. "For the past 35 years," read one Clearinghouse mailer, "world leaders have not ended this common nightmare. It is clearly up to us."[44] Other Clearinghouse materials vaguely criticized "military and civilian planners" who spoke "openly of fighting and winning nuclear wars," government officials who "no longer think much" about ending the arms race, and people who "think arms control is too complicated for ordinary citizens to understand."[45] One *Fact Sheet* devoted entirely to citizen involvement in the campaign explained that the Freeze Campaign was "helping the American people to take back from the experts the one issue that threatens to kill us all." The *Fact Sheet* concluded, "Through the freeze campaign, the *common sense of the American people is being heard. . . .* Until now, we have generally left the issue to the experts. But with the Freeze Campaign . . . 'The nuclear issue is being taken away from the priesthood.'"[46]

The "nuclear priesthood"—a darkly mysterious cabal of pro-war politicians and experts—served as the primary enemy of the freeze campaign. Criticizing an abstraction with no political voice, the campaign avoided the appearance of partisanship.[47] In the rhetoric of the Clearinghouse, the enemy also included all who favored traditional approaches to arms control; indeed, tradition itself functioned as something of a "devil term." And the Clearinghouse opposed the usual product of traditional negotiations: the arms control treaty. Metaphorically, at least, the freeze represented something altogether different from a "traditional treaty." According to the Clearinghouse, it represented an entirely new approach to arms control.

Throughout the literature of the National Freeze Clearinghouse, the metaphor of a freeze largely remained just that—a metaphor rather than a detailed arms control proposal. Criticizing traditional arms control treaties as too complicated,[48] the Clearinghouse touted the very simplicity of the freeze as its greatest virtue. As the first freeze *Fact Sheet* explained: "It says simply: *enough is enough*: there are too many nuclear weapons around for our own good, so let's stop making them."[49] Evoking still more metaphorical images, the fifth in the series of Clearinghouse *Fact Sheets* offered a sporting explanation of "why the freeze will work": "If you want to stop a football game, you don't set up new rules for how to play it. You just blow the whistle. That's what the Freeze would do to the nuclear arms race."[50] Even the failure of conventional arms control treaties was explained, not with historical argument or expert testimony, but with an obliquely pertinent simile: "Arms control treaties fail because they try to solve a problem while weapons makers add to it. It's like asking someone on a diet to cut down on bread, but eat a lot of potatoes."[51]

The freeze thus became—at least metaphorically—something altogether different from an arms control treaty. Treaties, by definition, were "too complicated": "They don't say, simply: stop."[52] Of course, the very comprehensiveness of the freeze idea—its embrace of "delivery systems" as well as "weapons," and its coverage of "testing" and "production" as well as "deployment"—would have necessitated wide-ranging and difficult negotiations—and, of course, a negotiated *treaty*.[53] In its public literature, however, the Clearinghouse insisted that a freeze could be negotiated "quickly," for it would not require "complicated comparisons of different weapons systems." According to the Clearinghouse, the freeze would be easy to negotiate precisely because it called for a halt in "the testing, production and deployment of ALL nuclear weapons and their delivery systems for both sides."[54]

The notion that the freeze could be negotiated "quickly," without complicated comparisons, rested upon a crucial assumption: that the superpowers already had roughly equivalent arsenals. The Reagan administration disputed the point, of course, but the Clearinghouse rarely debated the President. Occasionally citing expert opinion, the Clearinghouse did mention a 1982 Defense Department report that concluded that the United States and the Soviet Union were "roughly equal in strategic nuclear power."[55] And a freeze *Fact Sheet* on the issue quoted from a number of "experts," including MIT Professor William Kaufman, Desmond Ball of the "respected" International Institute for Strategic Studies, Nobel physicist Hans Bethe, and former Defense Secretary Robert McNamara—all denying that the Soviets held a nuclear advantage.[56] More commonly, however, the Clearinghouse noted the difficulty of comparing the two arsenals—distinguishing between warheads and missiles, for example, or between the size and the effectiveness of weapons—and simply dismissed the whole matter. Rising above "all the confusion" about the nuclear balance, the Clearinghouse declared that both sides already had "more than enough nuclear weapons to deter attack" and concluded: "The important question is not who's ahead, but how do we stop the contest." Declining to debate such a "complicated matter," the Clearinghouse again substituted metaphors for political argument: "It is not like a foot race in which one side or the other is 'ahead,' depending on the number of weapons it has. . . . The two sides have built so many extremely powerful weapons that they are like two children in a room with gasoline all over the floor. It doesn't really matter if one has six matches and the other seven. What matters is that neither one light even one match."[57]

The Clearinghouse also gave short shrift to the second major technical issue raised by critics of the freeze: the question of verification. In materials prepared for committed activists, the Clearinghouse matched experts with the administration, citing "former government officials" and other "experts" who agreed that "a freeze would be much easier to verify than a series of complex arms reduction agreements."[58] But in its public literature, the Clearinghouse appealed, somewhat ironically, to faith in technology, assuring readers that scientific verification was an important part of the freeze proposal and that existing technologies would make verification easy. According to one Clearinghouse brochure, "already proven reconnaissance satellites, radar and seismic tests" would "help prevent cheating" by either country.[59] And virtually all the Clearinghouse literature presented some version of the "Russian-license-plate" theme: "Satellite photographs are so accurate that they can read license plates on Russian cars."[60]

In the final analysis, the whole case for the freeze rested upon the answer to one key question: "But What About the Soviets?" With polls identifying distrust of the Soviet Union as the chief obstacle to support for the freeze,[61] the

Clearinghouse devoted considerable energy to proving that the Soviets could be counted upon to live up to such an agreement—based on their record. Over the years, the United States and the Soviet Union had signed many nuclear arms control agreements, one Clearinghouse *Fact Sheet* argued, and even the Defense Department acknowledged that Soviet compliance with those agreements had been good. Yet the Clearinghouse stopped far short of the revisionist portrait of the Soviet Union found in most peace movement literature. Recognizing that most Americans simply did not trust the Russians, the Clearinghouse tried to empathize: "The Russians will go on supporting people we oppose and running their country in ways we don't like. The Freeze will not end our political differences. But it will lessen the chance that we'll blow ourselves up over those differences." Adopting a pragmatic tone, the Clearinghouse ultimately insisted that we did not *need* to trust the Russians, for the Russians did not "want to get blown up any more than we do":

> We don't have to trust the Russians in order to freeze the nuclear arms race. As Averell Harriman, veteran US negotiator with the Russians, has said, "You can trust the Russians—to act in the Russian interest." *Mutual self-interest is the key to the Freeze, not trust.* . . . In fact the Russians have their own reasons for stopping the nuclear arms race—the same reasons we have. *The Freeze will improve the national security of both countries by reducing the military threat they pose to each other,* and by enabling their economies to better serve the needs of their people.[62]

In 1982, the Second National Freeze Conference identified only one strategy for selling the freeze on positive grounds: "Visibly link the Freeze to key economic issues uppermost in people's minds."[63] Targeting its economic appeals to Middle America, the Clearinghouse eschewed the usual peace movement pathos about "robbing the poor." Instead, it emphasized the impact of the arms race on inflation, jobs, interest rates, and government services. "Most of us believe that military spending is good for the economy," observed one Clearinghouse brochure. "In fact it is inflationary. . . . Military spending also provides us with over a million fewer jobs than would be created if the same amount were spent in the civilian sector."[64] Elaborating the point, another brochure cited a recent Pentagon commissioned study that concluded that "military spending increases will boost inflation measurably, drive up interest rates, and increase bottlenecks in critical labor and materials markets." According to the brochure, the freeze would save approximately half of the budget devoted to nuclear weapon-related programs—a savings of $22,000,000,000—which then could be used "to aid our seriously ailing economy, assist the over 10 million Americans who are now out of work, and restore vital human services that are being eliminated."[65]

All of these issues—the nuclear balance, verification, Russian trustworthiness, and economic benefits—received fuller treatment in the Clearinghouse materials designed for committed freeze activists. In a series of ten position papers prepared by Connecticut freeze activists, for example, such issues as parity, verification, and Soviet treaty compliance were treated in detail. The Clearinghouse also distributed reprints of an article by Randall Forsberg published in *Scientific American*, an article by Senator Mark Hatfield for the American Enterprise Institute's Foreign Policy and Defense Review, and an excerpt on verification from an article by Mark Niedergang of the Institute for Defense and Disarmament Studies—all fairly technical materials designed for committed freeze activists. In addition, the Clearinghouse advertised the publications of affiliated peace groups, including SANE, the Coalition for a New Foreign and Military Policy, Clergy and Laity Concerned, the AFSC, the Traprock Peace Center, and Women's Action for Nuclear Disarmament. All these materials contained more vigorous, partisan attacks on the Reagan administration as well as more detailed treatments of the major issues of the freeze debate. All were designed, in the Clearinghouse's words, "to help deepen understanding of Freeze-related issues among Freeze workers."[66]

In the Clearinghouse's view, however, the American people had no interest in a deeper understanding. As Forsberg herself put it in the original *Call*, the pros and cons of arms control treaties were simply "too technical for the patience of the average citizen."[67] The Clearinghouse thus skirted most of the technical and political questions surrounding the freeze, at least in materials designed for public consumption. Indeed, the dominant appeal in all of the Clearinghouse's literature—materials aimed at both activists and the public at large—had nothing at all to do with arms control or the merits of the freeze. Determined to demonstrate the respectability of the freeze among political elites, the Clearinghouse relied heavily upon bandwagon appeals, urging support for the freeze on the grounds that so many others supported it.

## The Freeze Bandwagon

From its earliest days as a peace movement initiative, the freeze campaign prominently featured lists of endorsers, usually on the back page of brochures and direct-mailings. An edition of Forsberg's *Call* distributed in 1981 carried a list of twenty-seven endorsers and urged supporters to allow their own name to be used "in printing and publicizing the Freeze."[68] The literature of the AFSC's "New Manhattan Project" likewise emphasized that the group was but "one of a number of social, religious and civic organizations" promoting the freeze, and it claimed that the initiative already had broad, public support. "Across the country," one AFSC freeze brochure boasted, "people are joining to call a halt to the arms race: mothers and fathers, electricians and executives, teachers, scientists, farmers, carpenters—Republicans and Democrats, 'liberals' and 'conservatives'—citizens of this country who want to live free from the threat of nuclear war."[69]

For a time, such claims were clearly exaggerated. Reflecting the origins of the campaign in the traditional peace movement, the FOR's list was dominated by such pacifist religious groups as Pax Christi and the Riverside Church Disarmament Program, along with secular peace groups including MOBE and the WILPF. The individuals on the FOR's edition of the *Call* were all peace movement activists: Forsberg herself, Richard Barnet of the Institute for Policy Studies, and Victor Sidel of Physicians for Social Responsibility, to name just a few.[70] The AFSC's list of "supporters" contained a smattering of nationally prominent liberals, including John Kenneth Galbraith and Shirley Chisholm, along with a handful of state legislative bodies and elected officials.[71] But neither list supported claims of broad, non-partisan support. While a few mainstream liberals appeared, the lists remained for the most part a "who's who" of the peace movement. Some of the coalitions listed, such as MOBE and the Coalition for a New Foreign and Military Policy, consisted of such stridently left-wing groups as the War Resisters' League and Women Strike for Peace.[72]

The National Clearinghouse of the Nuclear Weapons Freeze Campaign set out to mute this radical image. Determined to broaden the base of support for the freeze, it declared "getting the endorsements of at least ten nationally-prominent individuals and organizations per major constituency" a major goal of its 1982 strategy.[73] As Forsberg herself reportedly explained, the freeze could not hope to succeed if its support reflected only the "pacifist-vegetarian anti-corporate value system" of the peace groups, nor could it succeed by their preferred strategies of direct action and civil disobedience.[74] For the cause to succeed, it needed support from the political center and from groups and institutions *inside* the "establishment."

Editions of Forsberg's *Call* distributed in 1982—now under the National Clearinghouse banner—reflected this strategic thinking. Not only did they bear lists of "endorsers" nearly three times longer than those on earlier editions, but also more prominent, more moderate names replaced most of the peace activists on the earlier lists. On the Clearinghouse's list, the American Friends Service Committee, the Fellowship of Reconciliation, and the Women's International League for Peace and Freedom were nowhere to be found. Also disappearing from the list were Richard Barnet of the Institute for Policy Studies, Clergy and Laity Concerned, and the Coalition for a New Foreign and Military Policy. In place of religious radicals, one found names that at least sounded more mainstream: Theodore Hesburgh of Notre Dame, the "14th World Methodist Council," and the United Presbyterian Church, USA. Pax Christi had been transformed into "131 Catholic Bishops." Among secular endorsers, peace activists had given way to mainstream politicians, labor leaders, civil rights leaders, and academics—including several Nobel Laureates. Even the YWCA had jumped on the freeze bandwagon, along with singers Paul Simon, Joan Baez, and Bonnie Raitt.[75]

In February 1983, the Clearinghouse issued a new eight-page "Prominent Endorsers List." Providing only "a sampling that illustrates the range of support for the Freeze proposal," the single-spaced, double-columned document listed 473 individuals and groups endorsing the freeze, divided into eighteen categories ranging from the arts to the military, from business to religion, and from labor unions to Hollywood's "rich and famous." Balanced by more mainstream supporters, many of the radical founders of the campaign now returned to the list, often making for strange political bedfellows. Along with the radically anti-military War Resisters League, the list included a number of retired military personnel and government war strategists. Richard Barnet and Marcus Raskin, co-founders of the Institute for Policy Studies, now joined forces with major corporate executives. Daniel Ellsberg and William Sloane Coffin appeared alongside the Reverend Billy Graham, while a group called Prolifers for Survival joined hands with Eleanor Smeal of the National Organization for Women. From the Gray Panthers to the American Pediatric Association, from Young Democrats to a group of Republican party officials, the "Prominent Endorsers List" spanned a broad spectrum of occupational, associational, and political interests. Architects, lawyers, economists, and farmers all had their own freeze groups, as did college fraternities, minorities, environmentalists, health workers, and labor groups. Even the U.S. Ski Team appeared on the list, as did a California company specializing in "Natural Nectar Products."[76]

Celebrity name-dropping may have seemed a curious rhetorical strategy for a self-styled "people's campaign." While the Clearinghouse railed against the politicians and the experts, its "Prominent Endorsers List" had plenty of both. Yet the Clearinghouse's bandwagon appeal reached beyond the prominent to include that most important yet elusive of endorsers: the American public. Emphasizing not only the breadth but the diversity of public support for the freeze, one *Newsletter* described pro-freeze opinion as broad-based and non-partisan: "It includes both conservatives and liberals, young and old, whites and non-whites."[77] Similarly, a Clearinghouse *Fact Sheet* devoted entirely to the issue of support for the initiative asserted that the freeze had "very *broad support.*" The *Fact Sheet* explained: "Both Republicans and Democrats vote for it. It wins support from business people and labor, from religious leaders and lay people, from people of all races, all economic classes, and from all parts of the country. . . . Seven major national public opinion polls all show the American people favoring the Freeze by a large majority." The *Fact Sheet* quoted pollster Louis Harris calling support for the freeze "an incredible phenomenon" and insisting that the support for the freeze "cuts right across the spectrum of social and political divisions in this country."[78]

Yet even some of the top leaders of the campaign seemed to doubt the knowledge and motivation of those who expressed support for the freeze. In the *Freeze Newsletter* of January 1983, for example, National Coordinator Randall Kehler warned his fellow freeze advocates that policy makers in Washington continued to ask skeptical questions: "Can the momentum be sustained? Can Freeze organizers keep the movement from becoming fragmented?" And even Kehler seemed to suspect that support for the freeze was only skin deep: "How many of our supporters are capable of answering the Administration's basic arguments against the Freeze—that it would leave the U.S. in an inferior position, that it isn't verifiable, and that it would undermine efforts to negotiate real reductions in Geneva?[79]

The Clearinghouse's bandwagon appeals functioned rhetorically to establish the respectability of the freeze among political elites and to portray the campaign as the "voice of the people." Yet many of the ideologues initially behind the initiative never felt comfortable with a bandwagon strategy. Fearful of cooptation by elites, and skeptical about their own claims of public support, many feared that such an approach would only dull the critical edge of the initiative and allow politicians to defuse it with token concessions. Such thinking was at the root of internal dissension that soon sabotaged the freeze campaign—dissension that first manifested itself during planning for the freeze rally in New York in June of 1982.

## Coming Apart in New York City

In its "national brochure," *Freeze: Because Nobody Wants a Nuclear War*, the freeze Clearinghouse boasted about the movement's greatest achievement: the gathering of "close to 1,000,000 people" in New York City on 12 June 1982—"the largest political demonstration in American history." According to the Clearinghouse brochure, the huge throng that gathered in Central Park called "for the U.S. and the Soviet Union to freeze and reverse the arms race and redirect military funds to human needs."[80] As it turned out, that was indeed the official slogan for the rally. Yet the slogan itself hinted at the splintering of the freeze coalition that began during planning for the New York demonstration, as some hoped to focus narrowly upon the freeze while others preferred to emphasize disarmament and domestic social issues. As the product of negotiation and compromise between these factions, the New York rally did not really "call" for any particular political initiatives, and it arguably signaled the beginning of the end for the freeze as a peace movement issue.

The New York rally testified to the classic dilemma of radical politics in America. On one side of the dispute that broke out during planning for the rally was the June 12 Rally Committee, which included the AFSC, FOR, Pax Christi, Greenpeace, SANE, and the Riverside Church Disarmament Program, along with most of the other older, established peace groups. This coalition, which listed some 80 national organizations as endorsers, hoped to focus the rally upon the call for a bilateral freeze, attracting "as broad a cross-section of the American public as possible." On the other side was a smaller coalition, the Third World and Progressive People's Coalition (TWPPC), led by the Reverend Herbert Daughtry of the Black United Front (BUF). This faction demanded a much more radical agenda, emphasizing unilateral disarmament, racism, economic injustice, and a host of other issues. It preferred ideological purity to political pragmatism. The result, as Dave Lindorff observed in the *Village Voice*, was three months of "vicious infighting," with organizers of the rally "so busy battling each other" that they "barely had time to print fliers."[81]

In the end, Mobilization for Survival helped engineer something of a compromise. MOBE's leaders generally sympathized with the TWPPC's "third world" agenda and they became publicly upset with efforts to exclude black and "revolutionary" groups from the rally. But as part of the original rally committee, they also hoped to attract the largest crowd possible to the New York demonstration. After repeated negotiations, the factions finally agreed upon a steering committee of thirteen organizations and a long list of speakers. The list of speakers included a number of "establishment" liberals, including Representatives Edward Markey of Massachusetts, Mickey Leland of Texas, and Toby Moffett of Connecticut. But so too did it include a number of radicals, including Daughtry, David Dellinger, Seymour Melman, Winona La Duke of the American Indian Movement, and Norma Becker of the War Resister's League. Putting the best face on the whole dispute, David Meyer has called this final compromise a "triumph of diversity."[82] But it might also be called a triumph of confusion, for it resulted in a rally that virtually defied interpretation.

For some of the speakers at the June 12 rally, the gathering remained a demonstration of support for the freeze—and nothing else. "We have done it," Randall Forsberg boasted to the crowd. "The nuclear freeze campaign has mobilized the biggest peacetime peace movement in United States history."[83] For Forsberg and most of the other founders of the campaign, the rally also signaled an important turning point in the campaign. Viewing the rally as the culmination of a grass-roots protest, Forsberg urged the assembled masses to channel their political energy into the electoral arena. "We will remember in November," Forsberg repeatedly intoned during her address to the crowd.[84]

For other speakers, however, the New York rally had little to do with the freeze. The Reverend Daughtry railed against cuts in programs for the poor; a representative of the African National Congress alleged that South Africa had plans to develop nuclear weapons for use against that country's blacks; Rubin Zemora of the Revolutionary Democratic Front of El Salvador criticized American arms shipments to that country; and Bella Abzug emphasized the paucity of women among America's elected officials.[85] One speaker even insisted that "there can be no disarmament without the independence of Puerto Rico."[86] Furthermore, many viewed the turnout, not as a sign that the time had come for mainstreaming the movement, but as the start of a new era of massive demonstrations, civil disobedience, and "direct action" against the "warmakers." Just two days after the peaceful New York rally, for example, some 1,600 demonstrators were arrested trying to "Blockade the Bombmakers" outside the New York missions of the five nuclear powers.[87]

Confused by the mixed messages of the June 12 rally, some observers cynically concluded that the rally had nothing at all to do with politics. "It's a scene," observed Michael Levin in the *New York Times.* "How many of the hundreds of thousands who attended did so because they wanted to see what hundreds of thousands of people look like?" Besides, they got "first-rate entertainment at the right price": "Bruce Springsteen and Jackson Browne do not provide free concerts at the drop of the hat, and seldom appear on the same bill."[88] Even some of the top freeze organizers left the New York rally uncertain about what it all meant for the future of the campaign, and by the end of the year that uncertainty had evolved into a kind of mid-life crisis. "Everybody gets tired," observed NWFC director Randall Kehler in December as the campaign's leadership gathered in San Francisco to ponder how to keep the momentum going. "We need short-term goals to get people involved again."[89]

When the Third National Freeze Conference convened in St. Louis in February of 1983, the leadership of the campaign reached a fateful decision. Inspired by the narrow defeat of the House freeze resolution in August 1982, and by the success of freeze resolutions in the November elections, they decided that their best hope for the future lay in further "mainstreaming" of the movement. Further narrowing the agenda of the campaign and focusing upon institutional politics, the conference decided upon two major goals for the next two years: bringing "overwhelming citizen pressure to bear on the U.S. Congress" to reject specific new weapons proposed by the Reagan administration, and "laying the groundwork for making the Freeze a decisive factor in the 1984 Presidential and Congressional elections."[90] As *U.S. News* reported, freeze leaders admitted that such a strategy risked undermining the "universal emotional appeal" of the freeze and alienating supporters who shunned "overly partisan politics." Yet so too did they recognize that "the simple appeal to freeze nuclear arsenals" had begun "running out of steam."[91] While the polls still showed broad public support for the idea, they admitted that the "softness" of that support remained a "clear liability," making the campaign vulnerable to "right-wing opposition" and threatening its momentum. Further, they realized that the campaign had failed to have any significant impact on the arms control process. As the 1983 strategy document put it, "it is important to remember that despite [the] impressive list of Freeze successes in 1982, the Administration succeeded in getting Congress to pass the largest military budget in U.S. history, a budget which included billions of dollars for new and destabilizing first-strike nuclear weapons."[92]

The change in strategy embraced by the Third National Freeze Conference clearly had some positive effects. As its leaders had hoped, the shift to a more moderate, institutional focus helped to insulate the campaign against Ronald Reagan's charge that "some who want the weakening of America" were "manipulating" the freeze movement.[93] Indeed, the charges only provided another opportunity for freeze supporters to tout the "immense size" of the movement and the "unassailable political, professional and religious credentials" of its leaders.

Instead of discrediting the campaign, the charges only allowed freeze supporters to rage in righteous indignation against Reagan's fearmongering and "McCarthyite Red-baiting."[94] Furthermore, the new strategy directly led to the most important political victory claimed by the campaign: the House freeze resolution passed in May of 1983. As it became more and more respectable to support the freeze, even some who had voted against the freeze in 1982 voted for it in 1983, and the resolution finally passed by nearly a two-to-one margin.

Yet victory in the House came at the cost of many of the peace activists who had formed the core of the freeze coalition. Convinced that the cause had been coopted, many on the left complained that the campaign had lost its "independent clout" and had become little more than "a junior partner in Democratic Party struggles."[95] Furthermore, as freeze activist David Meyer has suggested, the House resolution meant something very different from what the peace groups had in mind when they originally rallied around the freeze idea:

> The nuclear freeze came to obscure the activities of the groups that gave rise to it. The national campaign defined itself and its goals more narrowly, until winning passage of a Congressional freeze resolution overwhelmed all other goals. Divorced from its roots, the freeze was domesticated by mainstream politicians whose analysis of the arms race and arms control bore little relation to that of the freeze initiators.[96]

Above all, the change in strategy transformed the 1984 elections into a life-or-death test of the freeze campaign. Convinced that high levels of support in the polls could be transformed into votes, the campaign diverted almost all of its energy toward defeating Ronald Reagan in 1984. As a result, Reagan's landslide reelection wrote the campaign's political obituary. Not only did the news media declare the movement "dead," but freeze activists by the thousands were left completely demoralized. Reflecting back on the results, even such dedicated activists as Randall Forsberg seemed to give up the fight. "The grass-roots people who poured in thousands of hours over the last few years through their work on the freeze are tremendously disappointed and frustrated," Forsberg told the *New York Times* in August of 1985. "We felt that the degree of commitment and devotion had to make a difference, and the shock of what happened in the 1984 elections left us reeling."[97]

For some peace activists, the lesson of the freeze campaign's "demoralizing flop" in the 1984 elections was that they needed still more "Madison Avenue techniques."[98] For others, the lesson was quite the opposite: that it had been a mistake for peace activists to abandon their comprehensive critiques of American "militarism" in favor of narrow, mainstream political objectives. According to Pam Solo, an early freeze organizer, "the pressure to narrow the agenda, limit the arguments, and remain 'respectable' seemed compelling" at the time, but as a result the campaign lost its ability "to define the problem and set the terms of the debate." It became just "an arms control movement—not a peace and disarmament movement—and its attention became riveted on technical debates that damaged its popular base."[99]

Yet the lessons to be learned from the fate of the freeze campaign may be far more complicated than either of these viewpoints. Solo is right to focus our attention on questions of discourse. Yet the freeze campaign never comprehensively critiqued American "militarism," nor did it ever become a real "arms control movement." At bottom, the campaign was a grand, mass-mediated fear appeal. From the start, it rested in large measure upon a disturbing yet politically irrelevant "rhetoric of doom."

## Notes

1. E. P. Thompson, letter to Pam Solo, January 1986, quoted in Solo, *From Protest to Policy*, 3.
2. Ronald Reagan, "United States Foreign Affairs Policy: Arms Reduction," *Vital Speeches of the Day*, 1 December 1981, 100; Ronald Reagan, "Address to the Nation on Defense and National Security, March 23, 1983," in U.S. President, *Public Papers of the Presidents of the United States* (Washington: Office of the *Federal Register*, National Archives and Records Service, 1953-), Ronald Reagan, 1983, 443.
3. See Bjork, "Reagan and the Nuclear Freeze," 181-92.
4. Garfinkle, *The Politics of the Nuclear Freeze*, 5-8.
5. See Butterfield, "Anatomy of the Nuclear Protest," 32.
6. Randall Forsberg, "The Shared Origins of the Directory and the Nuclear Freeze Movement," in *American Peace Directory, 1984*, edited by Fine and Steven, vii-viii.
7. Peter Pringle, "Putting World War III on Ice," *Inquiry*, July 1982, 15.
8. See American Friends Service Committee, *The Choice is Life Itself: AFSC Programs for Disarmament*, brochure distributed by the AFSC, Philadelphia, 1982, 1984.
9. Solo, *From Protest to Policy*, 31.
10. Meyer, *A Winter of Discontent*, 147-48, 162.
11. Solo, *From Protest to Policy*, 46-48, 57-58.
12. See Elizabeth Walker Mechling and Jay Mechling, "Hot Pacifism and Cold War: The American Friends Service Committee's Witness For Peace in 1950s America," *Quarterly Journal of Speech* 78 (May 1992): 176-85.
13. Mulford Sibley, *Unilateral Initiatives and Disarmament* (Philadelphia: American Friends Service Committee, 1962), 34-36.
14. American Friends Service Committee, *Anatomy of Anti-Communism: A Report Prepared for the Peace Education Division of the American Friends Service Committee* (New York: Hill and Wang, 1969), vi, xv. The "working party" included James E. Bristol, Holland Hunter, James H. Laird, Sidney Lens, Milton Mayer, Robert E. Reuman, Athan Theoharis, and Bryant Wedge. Much of the historical material of the book is drawn from Sidney Lens' *The Futile Crusade: Anti-Communism as American Credo* (Chicago: Quadrangle Books, 1964.)
15. American Friends Service Committee, *An Introduction to Working with AFSC*, brochure distributed by the AFSC, Philadelphia, 1984; American Friends Service Committee, *Introduction to the American Friends Service Committee*, brochure distributed by the AFSC, Philadelphia, 1985.

16. Stephen Chapman, "Shot From Guns," *New Republic*, 9 June 1979, 15.
17. See American Friends Service Committee, *A Compassionate Peace: A Future for the Middle East* (New York: Hill and Wang, 1982). See also Leon Wieseltier's critical review, "Partisan Compassion," *The New Republic*, 16 June 1982, 37-39.
18. American Friends Service Committee, *The Choice is Life Itself.*
19. Well over half of the twenty-seven endorsers listed on an edition of Forsberg's *Call to Halt the Nuclear Arms Race* distributed by the Fellowship of Reconciliation in 1981 had religious affiliations. These included: Church Women United, Clergy and Laity Concerned, the Mennonite Central Committee, the Sisters of Loretto, Sojourners, and the National Council of Churches.
20. James Davison Hunter, *Culture Wars: The Struggle to Define America* (New York: Basic Books, 1991), 113-16.
21. W. H. Ferry, *Farewell to Arms: A Case for Unilateral Disarmament* (Nyack, New York: Fellowship Publications, 1978), 4.
22. Mary Lou Kownacki, ed., *A Race to Nowhere: An Arms Race Primer for Catholics* (Chicago: Pax Christi USA, n.d.), 72, 78.
23. See, for example, CBS News, "The Gospel According to Whom?" *60 Minutes*, 23 January 1983, network transcript, 1-12; William Safire, "Bullies in the Pulpit," *New York Times*, 14 March 1983, A15.
24. Mary I. Buckley, "Freedom as Personal and Public Liberation," in *Liberation, Revolution, and Freedom: Theological Perspectives*, edited by Thomas M. McFadden (New York: Seabury Press, 1975), 30-31.
25. Randall Forsberg, *Call to Halt the Nuclear Arms Race*, FOR edition (Nyack, New York: Fellowship Reconciliation, 1981).
26. Garfinkle, *The Politics of the Nuclear Freeze*, 1-2.
27. Women's International League for Peace and Freedom, *Principles and Policies*, brochure distributed by the Women's International League for Peace and Freedom, Philadelphia, 1985.
28. Women's International League for Peace and Freedom, *What WILPF Stands For . . .*, brochure distributed by the Women's International League for Peace and Freedom, Philadelphia, n.d.
29. James E. Dougherty, *The Bishops and Nuclear Weapons: The Catholic Pastoral Letter on War and Peace* (Hamden, Connecticut: Archon Books, 1984), 106.
30. Richard P. McBrien, *Catholicism* (Minneapolis: Winston Press, 1981), 317-18.
31. Jay Walljasper, "Who's Who in the Nuclear Freeze Campaign," *In These Times*, 21-27 April 1982, 12.
32. Nuclear Weapons Freeze Campaign, "From Popular Mandate to Public Policy: 1983 Strategy Proposal," presented to the Third National Freeze Conference, St. Louis, February 1983, 1-2.
33. Nuclear Weapons Freeze Campaign, "The Freeze Campaign: What You Can Do," *Fact Sheet 2*, distributed by the NWFC National Clearinghouse, St. Louis, January 1983, 2.
34. Barbara Roche, "Citizens Lobby for a U.S./Soviet Nuclear Weapons Freeze," *Freeze Newsletter*, January 1983, 4.
35. Nuclear Weapons Freeze Campaign, "State of the Campaign: Proposal for a Mutual U.S.-Soviet Nuclear Weapons Freeze," distributed by the NWFC National Clearinghouse, St. Louis, 17 February 1983, 1-2.
36. For the most complete account of the congressional debate, see Waller, *Congress and the Nuclear Freeze.*
37. Pringle, "Putting World War III on Ice."

38. Nathaniel Sheppard Jr., "Center for Nuclear Freeze Set Up in St. Louis," *New York Times*, 23 March 1982, A19.
39. Ibid.
40. Nuclear Weapons Freeze Campaign, *Resources*, brochure distributed by the NWFC National Clearinghouse, St. Louis, n.d., 1-2.
41. Ibid., 2.
42. Nuclear Weapons Freeze Campaign, *Freeze: Because Nobody Wants a Nuclear War*, brochure distributed by the NWFC National Clearinghouse, St. Louis, n.d.
43. Ibid.
44. Nuclear Weapons Freeze Campaign, *Now*, brochure distributed by the NWFC National Clearinghouse, St. Louis, n.d.
45. Nuclear Weapons Freeze Campaign, *Freeze*, 2; Nuclear Weapons Freeze Campaign, "The Freeze Campaign," 2.
46. Nuclear Weapons Freeze Campaign, "The Freeze Campaign," 1-2.
47. One of the few times that Reagan is mentioned by name in a brochure, for example, the Clearinghouse calls his START initiative a "welcome shift" that might be "coupled with a proposal to freeze the existing arsenals as a first step" and suggests that it proves that "our leaders are beginning to listen" to the freeze movement (See Nuclear Weapons Freeze Campaign, *Freeze*).
48. Nuclear Weapons Freeze Campaign, "The Freeze and Arms Control," *Fact Sheet 5*, distributed by the NWFC National Clearinghouse, St. Louis, February 1983, 2.
49. Nuclear Weapons Freeze Campaign, "The Freeze: Why Now?" *Fact Sheet 1*, distributed by the NWFC National Clearinghouse, St. Louis, January 1983, 1.
50. Nuclear Weapons Freeze Campaign, "The Freeze and Arms Control," 3.
51. Ibid., 4.
52. Ibid., 1.
53. As freeze critic Colin S. Gray observed, the notion of an immediate freeze "never stood a chance of being translated into U.S. policy, let along of being negotiable with the Soviet Union," for "reasons of technical difficulty alone." Furthermore, "by the time a formal freeze agreement had been designed that could accommodate the major objections of domestic critics *and* the concerns of the Soviet military establishment, nothing of much merit (to freeze proponents) would remain" (Colin S. Gray, "Making Sense of the Nuclear Freeze Debate," in *The Nuclear Freeze Controversy*, edited by Keith B. Payne and Colin S. Gray [New York: University Press of America, 1984], 156).
54. Nuclear Weapons Freeze Campaign, "The Freeze and Arms Control," 1-2.
55. Nuclear Weapons Freeze Campaign, "The Freeze: Why Now?" 1; Nuclear Weapons Freeze Campaign, *Freeze*.
56. Nuclear Weapons Freeze Campaign, "The Freeze and the Military Balance," *Fact Sheet 4*, distributed by the NWFC National Clearinghouse, St. Louis, February 1983, 1-2.
57. Ibid., 4.
58. David Keppel, "Verification," Connecticut Freeze Campaign Position Paper, distributed by the NWFC National Clearinghouse, St. Louis, n.d., 1.
59. Nuclear Weapons Freeze Campaign, *Now*.
60. Nuclear Weapons Freeze Campaign, "The Freeze: Why Now?" 1.
61. See, for example, questions 37 and 38 in the Appendix.
62. Nuclear Weapons Freeze Campaign, "The Freeze and the Soviet Union," *Fact Sheet 3*, distributed by the NWFC National Clearinghouse, St. Louis, January 1983, 1.
63. Nuclear Weapons Freeze Campaign, "From Popular Mandate to Public Policy," 2.
64. Nuclear Weapons Freeze Campaign, *Now*.

65. Nuclear Weapons Freeze Campaign, *Freeze.*
66. Nuclear Weapons Freeze Campaign, *Resources*, 1.
67. Forsberg, *Call to Halt the Nuclear Arms Race*, FOR edition, 3.
68. Ibid., 4.
69. American Friends Service Committee, *The Future is in Our Hands: Freeze the Arms Race, U.S.-U.S.S.R*," brochure distributed by the AFSC New Manhattan Project, New York, n.d.
70. Forsberg, *Call to Halt the Nuclear Arms Race*, FOR edition, 4.
71. American Friends Service Committee, *The Future is in Our Hands.*
72. See the list of groups supporting the Coalition for a New Foreign and Military Policy in *Coalition Close-Up*, "Join the Coalition Network," Spring/Summer 1982, 20.
73. Nuclear Weapons Freeze Campaign, "From Popular Mandate to Public Policy," 2.
74. Meyer, *A Winter of Discontent*, 163.
75. Randall Forsberg, *Call to Halt the Nuclear Arms Race*, NWFC rev. ed. (St. Louis: NWFC National Clearinghouse, 1982), 4.
76. Nuclear Weapons Freeze Campaign, "Prominent Endorsers List," distributed by the NWFC National Clearinghouse, St. Louis, February 1983.
77. Nuclear Weapons Freeze Campaign, "The Nuclear Weapons Freeze Campaign," *Freeze Newsletter*, January 1983, 2.
78. Nuclear Weapons Freeze Campaign, "The Freeze Campaign," 1.
79. Randall Kehler, "Message from the National Coordinator," *Freeze Newsletter*, January 1983, 3.
80. Nuclear Weapons Freeze Campaign, *Freeze*, 4.
81. Dave Lindorff, "War in Peace: The Fight for Position in New York's June 12 Disarmament Rally," *Village Voice*, 20 April 1982, 12.
82. Meyer, *A Winter of Discontent*, 187.
83. Robin Herman, "Rally Speakers Decry Cost of Nuclear Arms Race," *New York Times*, 13 June 1982, 43.
84. Meyer, *A Winter of Discontent*, 187.
85. Herman, "Rally Speakers Decry Cost of Nuclear Arms Race," 43.
86. Ronald Radosh, "The 'Peace Council' and Peace," *New Republic*, 31 January 1983, 17-18.
87. Meyer, *A Winter of Discontent*, 188.
88. Michael Levin, "The Springsteening of Disarmament," *New York Times*, 19 June 1982, 25.
89. Judith Miller, "Advocates of Arms Control Ponder Some New Moves," *New York Times*, 5 December 1982, E5.
90. Nuclear Weapons Freeze Campaign, "From Popular Mandate to Public Policy," 4.
91. James Wallace, "Nuclear Freeze Crusade: Gaining or Waning?" *U.S. News and World Report*, 25 April 1983, 18-19, 21.
92. Nuclear Weapons Freeze Campaign, "From Popular Mandate to Public Policy," 3.
93. Reagan made the charge in a speech to veterans' groups in Columbus, Ohio, on 4 October 1982. He toned down but basically reiterated the charges in two subsequent news conferences, in November and December. In November, Reagan claimed that "foreign agents" had been "sent to help instigate" such demonstrations as the June 12 rally in New York, and on December 10 he mentioned several "well-documented articles" that proved the Soviets' "participation" in the peace movement. The White House backed up Reagan's charges with several State Department reports focusing upon the World Peace Council and several articles from the *Reader's Digest*,

*Commentary*, and the *American Spectator*. The House Select Committee on Intelligence released a report in December that concluded that the Soviets had attempted to influence the American peace movement, but the report concluded that "Soviet agents have had no significant influence on the nuclear freeze movement." Similarly, the FBI released a partially declassified report in March 1983, that concluded that "Soviet-controlled" organizations had participated "at the highest levels" in planning for the June 12 demonstration and that the Soviets sought to "capitalize" on the American peace movement. But the FBI concluded that the Soviets did not "directly control or manipulate" the movement. See "President Says Foes of U.S. Have Duped Arms Freeze Group," *New York Times*, 5 October 1982, A22; Leslie Maitland, "Sources Are Cited for Charge of Soviet Tie to Arms Freeze," *New York Times*, 13 November 1982, 7; Judith Miller, "President Says Freeze Proponents May Unwittingly Aid the Russians," *New York Times*, 11 December 1982, 9; Judith Miller, "Soviet Role in Freeze Movement Found Minor," *New York Times*, 10 December 1982, A15; and Leslie Maitland, "F.B.I. Rules Out Russian Control of Freeze Drive," *New York Times*, 26 March 1983, 1, 7.

94. Frank Donner, "But Will They Come? The Campaign to Smear the Nuclear Freeze Movement," *The Nation*, 6 November 1982, 457.
95. Alexander Cockburn and James Ridgeway, "Has the Freeze Failed?" *Village Voice*, 7 June 1983, 22.
96. Meyer, *A Winter of Discontent*, xvii.
97. "Disarmament Groups Seek Rallying Point After Faltering on Atom Freeze," 22.
98. See Hawkins and Mashek, "Antinuclear Campaign Reawakens," 22.
99. Solo, *From Protest to Policy*, 23-25.

# Chapter Two

# The Rhetoric of Doom

> Let us consider . . . some of the possible ways in which a person in a targeted country might die. He might be incinerated by the fireball or the thermal pulse. He might be lethally irradiated by the initial nuclear radiation. He might be crushed to death or hurled to his death by the blast wave or its debris. He might be lethally irradiated by the local fallout. He might be burned to death in a firestorm. He might be injured by one or another of these effects and then die of his wounds before he was able to make his way out of the devastated zone in which he found himself. He might die of starvation, because the economy had collapsed and no food was being grown or delivered, or because existing local crops had been killed by radiation, or because the local ecosystem had been ruined, or because the ecosphere of the earth as a whole was collapsing. He might die of cold, for lack of heat and clothing, or of exposure, for lack of shelter. He might be killed by people seeking food or shelter that he had obtained. He might die of an illness spread in an epidemic. He might be killed by exposure to the sun if he stayed outside too long following serious ozone depletion. Or he might be killed by any combination of these perils.[1]
>
> Jonathan Schell

Jonathan Schell redefined "overkill." A person dies just once, but Schell killed us again and again as he imagined a nuclear holocaust in *The Fate of the Earth.* Widely hailed as the "bible" of the nuclear freeze movement,[2] *The Fate of the Earth* became the archetype of a genre of nuclear horror stories, partly historical but mostly speculative, designed to simplify the issues of the arms race and to bring about an emotional realization of the nuclear threat. Virtually every artifact of the nuclear freeze campaign, regardless of its ultimate point or purpose, included some variation upon Schell's apocalyptic theme. More than any other artifact, *The Fate of the Earth* defined the telepolitical strategy of the nuclear freeze campaign.

Of course, Jonathan Schell did not invent apocalyptic rhetoric. Apocalyptic visions have been common in American religious discourse, and end-of-world prophecies have been a staple of the American political and literary traditions. The dawning of the "nuclear age" brought about a revival of the apocalyptic tradition, and peace activists shaped another apocalyptic revival with a wave of doomsday films and videotapes in the late 1970s. Yet it remained for Jonathan Schell to bring such discourse to the mainstream of the nuclear debate. Not only depicting the impending holocaust but exploring its philosophical and political implications, Schell became the intellectual prophet of the freeze campaign and *The Fate of the Earth* its secular "bible."

In an earlier era, *The Fate of the Earth* might have been dismissed as fantasy. In the 1980s, however, it became a celebrated model of "public moral argument," hailed for cutting through the "nukespeak" of the political "establishment" and "democratizing" the nuclear debate. In fact, Schell never wrote *The Fate of the Earth* for the "ordinary citizen." But he did inspire the arbiters of popular culture to echo his warnings in everything from TV movies—most notably, of course, ABC's *The Day After*—to Sunday newspaper supplements and mass-market paperbacks. *The Fate of the Earth* made it fashionable to commiserate over our doom.

The prominence of apocalyptic discourse in the freeze debate reflected a strange illogic, even a sort of parochialism, among many freeze activists. With the exception, perhaps, of a few religious cranks,[3] nobody is in *favor* of nuclear war. Yet freeze activists seemed to assume that all who failed to join their cause must be longing for the holocaust. And, by the same token, they assumed that all who came to fear nuclear war inevitably would join their cause. Yet fear of nuclear war does not dictate a particular political solution, and freeze activists did little to channel fear into support for the freeze. By saying so little about the freeze proposal itself, they failed to heed an important lesson of the apocalyptic tradition: that the rhetoric of doom, if it is to persuade and motivate, must mitigate fear with a measure of hope.

## The American Apocalyptic Tradition

As Joseph Dewey has observed, "every culture, every age in the Hebraic-Christian tradition has formulated a considerable canon of apocalyptic literature."[4] For whatever reason, however, apocalyptic rhetoric has been especially prominent in the American religious tradition. Indeed, as Douglas Robinson has pointed out, "the very idea of America in history *is* apocalyptic, arising as it did out of the historicizing of apocalyptic hopes in the Protestant Reformation."[5] The New England Puritans, with their apocalyptic jeremiads, created a mode of public expression that "persisted through the eighteenth century, and helped sustain a national dream through two hundred years of turbulence and change."[6] That dream—the "national dream of an American Age," the dream of "a great paradisal future to be ushered in by America"—remained strong even into the early twentieth century.[7] Apocalyptic preaching may have cooled a bit since Jonathan Edwards' "flamethrowing rhetoric of imminent judgment."[8] But in our own generation, echoes of Puritan apocalyptic have been heard from such "hard-core" apocalyptists as Billy Graham, Hal Lindsey, Jerry Falwell, and Oral Roberts.[9]

The form or structure of religious apocalyptic also has been evident in "a great deal of *secular* discourse" throughout American history. In fictional literature, images of the end of the world have been so "commonplace," so "fundamental to American writing as to be virtually ubiquitous,"[10] and apocalyptic thought has undergirded the "central secular ideas" of the American political tradition, including "progress, manifest destiny, economic growth, and scientific advance."[11] Apocalyptic interpretations also have been offered for many of America's great political crises, from the Revolution itself to World War I.[12] As Barry Brummett has observed, secular apocalyptics generally have focused upon narrower and more varied subjects than religious apocalyptics—specific economic, ecological, civil, or military concerns. But they employ a "structure of argument that parallels . . . religious apocalyptic exactly," creating a "system of order" that makes sense out of chaos.[13]

Given the prominence of end-of-world prophecies in American cultural history, it hardly comes as a surprise that the atomic bomb would inspire an apocalyptic revival. Giving religious prophecies of a fiery end to the world a chilling new resonance, the bomb inspired even President Truman to biblical allusion: "It may be the fire of destruction prophesied in the Euphrates Valley era, after Noah and his fabulous ark."[14] Other politicians, military leaders, journalists, and even the atomic scientists themselves likewise found "sufficient language" to describe "the bomb" only "in the radical vocabulary of religion." As Dewey has written, a variety of commentators "marked the similarities between the blasts that decimated Hiroshima and Nagasaki and the images associated with the traditional Christian apocalypse: the suddenness, the all-engulfing fire, the disturbing completeness of obliteration."[15] And in doing so, they found comfort; God had *planned* for America to have "the bomb." As Senator Edwin C. Johnson of Colorado put it: "God Almighty in His infinite wisdom [has] dropped the atomic bomb in our lap."[16]

Less hopeful visions of the atomic future came from secular writers in the late 1940s, particularly authors of speculative fantasy and science fiction. As Paul Boyer has noted, the fictional portraits of nuclear apocalypse were "almost invariably bleak and pessimistic."[17] In the 1960s, however, a variety of other writers began to offer more hopeful visions. As Dewey has argued, contemporary apocalyptic literature may be set in "a most treacherous post-Hiroshima landscape." Yet, for the most part, American writers have adapted a timeless and ultimately optimistic theme to the nuclear age: "the will to live and to love in a fragile world."[18]

In all its various manifestations—religious and secular, historical and futuristic, factual and fantastic—the American apocalyptic tradition has been more than a tradition of nihilistic doomsaying. Assigning purpose to seemingly random historical events, doomsayers acknowledge uncertainty and pain, as

Brummett has suggested, but they also must, if they hope to inspire action, provide the "assurance of deliverance." Indeed, predictions of "an end, a new world, the Second Coming, or a disaster" are but "secondary to, and derivative from," the ways in which apocalyptic rhetoric "comforts and empowers an audience that finds itself in a context of anomie and chaos."[19] In short, the rhetoric of doom generally is but preliminary to religious or political prescription. During the freeze campaign, however, it often seemed an end in itself.

## The Rhetoric of the Peace Documentary

For the American peace movement, the nuclear freeze campaign marked a "coming of age"—a coming of the media age, to be more precise. "Americans spend as much time watching television as they spend doing almost anything else," observed a publication of the Media Network, an organization promoting "alternative media" for "grassroots organizing." Media were no longer to be considered "extras or luxuries"; they had become "an integral part of organizing for disarmament":

> Many people who might not read a piece of literature or go somewhere to hear a speech can be attracted to see a film. Films are considered entertainment and so are not as intimidating to newcomers as a formal meeting might be. Because of their visual power, films make information accessible in ways that literature or speeches cannot. They have the ability to involve people emotionally, making issues that might otherwise be seen as abstract, concrete and real.[20]

For the peace movement, involving people "emotionally" meant confronting them with "the bomb." Building an industry of significant proportions, peace activists produced hundreds of films, slide shows, and other audiovisual materials in the early 1980s, most sounding a rhetoric of apocalyptic doom. Distributed through an extensive network of peace organizations, commercial outlets, and educational "media centers," these materials served not only as tools of recruitment but as a major source of revenue for many of the peace groups. A *National Directory of Audiovisual Resources on Nuclear War and the Arms Race*, published by the University of Michigan Media Resources Center in 1984, provides some sense of the scope of the "peace film" industry: 313 organizations distributing audiovisual resources on nuclear war were listed, along with a total of 399 films, videotapes, and slide shows. Like many who distributed such materials, the editors of the *National Directory* considered themselves "educators," but they also confessed to strong political motives in rating the entries: "We have tried to be intellectually honest in assigning ratings; but, the reader should be aware of our own biases that the arms race is insane and that nuclear war would be an unparalleled catastrophe."[21]

As a concession to the other side, the *National Directory* listed two films by the American Security Council defending the Reagan administration's policies: *Countdown for America* and *The SALT Syndrome.* As it turns out, however, these two films alone endorsed a strong nuclear deterrent, and both rated a lowly 1 on the Center's 10-point scale for overall quality and a 10 on its scale of political bias.[22] By contrast, the Center for Defense Information's *War Without Winners*, a film featuring Russian and American citizens "expressing their fears, thoughts, and hopes about the future in an age of nuclear weapons that can incinerate civilization in minutes," rated a 7 on quality and a comparatively low 5 on political bias.[23] Even the National Film Board of Canada's *If You Love This Planet*, a film that the U.S. Department of Justice labeled foreign "propaganda," rated a comparatively moderate 7 on political bias.[24]

Most telling, however, were the ratings affixed to the dozens of films emphasizing the "human" effects of nuclear weapons or apocalyptic themes. Most of these films focused upon the bombings of Hiroshima and Nagasaki, and they invariably rated very high in quality and low in political "bias." The Media Resources Center described one film, entitled *Hiroshima: A Document of the Atomic Bombing*, as a "sensitive treatment of the holocaust's victims," concentrating on "the survivor's constant need for medical attention, their deep psychological wounds, and their inability to fit into everyday life." Yet according to the Center, the concept of bias was "not applicable" to this film; it had *no* political bias.[25] Similarly, a short, animated film entitled *Booom* presented "various scenarios for planetary self-destruction, both planned and accidental," and ultimately posed the question: "Is this the end?" Again, the Media Resources Center declared that the concept of bias was "not applicable" to the film; it contained no "political" message.[26] Even a film entitled *Doomsayers* earned the Center's "no bias" rating. According to the Center, the concept of political bias was "not applicable" to this film featuring Dr. Helen Caldicott and other well-known "prophets of doom."[27]

Offering "films for all ages," the editors of the *National Directory* declared many of their offerings appropriate for "schools of all types and levels."[28] *Bombs Will Make the Rainbow Break*," for example, featured children testifying to "the impact of growing up in a world on the brink of nuclear holocaust." The *Directory* explained, "Their art portrays nuclear devastation, their words express their confusion and fear."[29] Another film, entitled *In the Nuclear Shadow*, also featured young people (from seven to seventeen years of age) expressing "fear that they will never grow up, a sense of helplessness, and anger at adults whom they feel have betrayed them by threatening their future with nuclear weapons."[30] For $100, one could purchase a videotape of perhaps the youngest anti-nuclear activists in America reflecting upon their doom: *Third Graders Discuss Nuclear Issues.*[31]

For a time, the rhetoric of doom remained largely confined to peace movement circles. All that changed when Jonathan Schell published *The Fate of the*

*Earth*. Not only depicting the holocaust but contemplating its philosophical and moral implications, Schell made it "respectable"—indeed, quite fashionable—to "think about the unthinkable." Seemingly overnight, the news media began to take notice, and the possibility of nuclear war suddenly became news. Like the peace documentaries that preceded him, Schell did not offer much hope of escaping the nuclear dilemma. Nevertheless, his vision had great appeal among the political commentators and journalists who set the public agenda.

## Jonathan Schell and the Rhetoric of Extinction

Jonathan Schell, a staff writer for *The New Yorker* and author of three previous books, published *The Fate of the Earth* in 1982. First serialized in *The New Yorker* and later discounted for the Book-of-the-Month Club's 1.2 million members from $11.95 to just $2.25,[32] *The Fate of the Earth* quickly became the "publishing sensation" of the 1980s. Even before the first printing hit the shelves, Alfred A. Knopf ordered a large second printing, and "feverish bidding" erupted over the paperback rights.[33] It may never be "looked back upon as a crucial event in the history of human thought," as its dust jacket boasted, but it did prove by far the most successful of the dozens of anti-nuclear books flooding the market in the early 1980s.[34]

Many of the new anti-nuclear books imitated the distinctive character of *The Fate of the Earth*: its effort to describe nuclear war in "human" rather than "statistical" terms.[35] In Schell's view, nuclear war could best be understood, not by talk of megatonage or throw weight, but by dwelling in specific, colorful, and gory detail upon the physical and emotional effects of nuclear war on people. Schell claimed to base his projections largely on government reports on the effects of nuclear weapons.[36] But he did not borrow their language. In place of the technical and "sanitized" apocalyptic of "official" nuclear war scenarios, Schell created images that shocked and dismayed.

In the first part of the book, Schell moved inexorably from the known effects of the single, relatively small bomb dropped on Hiroshima through several speculative scenarios, each presuming detonation of more and bigger bombs. Eventually he arrived at the ultimate obscenity of all-out nuclear war between the superpowers. At no point, however, did Schell lose sight of individual suffering. Ironically, he even contemplated the extinction of the species from a distinctively human point-of-view.

Like virtually all prophets of nuclear doom, Schell began his story with a return to Hiroshima. In recalling the scene, he told of the darkness and of the erie silence broken only by the cries of the injured. A "housewife" recalled seeing "a mother, driven half-mad while looking for her child," only to find him with his "eyes . . . half-closed . . . his mouth . . . white, pursed, and swollen." His head "looked like a boiled octopus." Another survivor recalled "a stark naked man standing in the rain with his eyeball in his palm." Several spoke of the "processions of the injured"—processions "of a kind that had never been seen before in history." With blackened skin hanging loosely from their faces and bodies, most were "like walking ghosts," while those "still capable of action often acted in an absurd or an insane way.[37]

Given that "what happened at Hiroshima was less than a millionth part of a holocaust at present levels of world armament," Schell conceded that the effects of nuclear war today would be "scarcely imaginable." But imagine them he did, in concrete detail that belied his caveat about "the difficulty of making reliable predictions about an event that has no precedent." Describing the effects of both a single one-megaton bomb and a twenty-megaton bomb dropped on New York—with the specific city and the vivid, concrete descriptions obscuring the speculative character of the scenarios—he described how people would be "burned, battered, crushed, and irradiated in every conceivable way." If New York were the target of a one-megaton bomb, "the city and its people would be mingled in a smoldering heap." Following detonation of a twenty-megaton bomb, "New York and its suburbs would be transformed into a lifeless, flat, scorched desert in a few seconds."[38]

Escalating the emotional assault on the reader, Schell's final scenario depicted an all-out attack on the United States, which he predicted would involve ten thousand separate one-megaton bombs. Dashing any hope that some portions of the nation might survive, Schell wrote: "In the first moments of a ten-thousand megaton attack on the United States . . . flashes of white light would suddenly illumine large areas of the country as thousands of suns, each one brighter than the sun itself, blossomed over cities, suburbs, and towns. In those same moments, when the first wave of missiles arrived, the vast majority of the people in the regions first targeted would be irradiated, crushed, or burned to death." The "thermal pulse" would then "subject . . . one-sixth of the total land mass of the nation" to "a level of heat that chars human beings. . . . Tens of millions of people would go up in smoke." And as the attack proceeded

> as much as three-quarters of the country could be subjected to incendiary levels of heat, and so, wherever there was inflammable material, could be set ablaze. In the ten seconds or so after each bomb hit, as blast waves swept outward from thousands of ground zeros, the physical plant of the United States would be swept away like leaves in a gust of wind. The six hundred thousand square miles already scorched . . . would now be hit by blast waves . . . and virtually all the habitations, places of work, and other man-made things there—substantially the whole human construct in the United States—would be vaporized, blasted, or otherwise pulverized out of existence.[39]

In Jonathan Schell's imagination, all of these effects, along with the "gross ecological consequences" that also would result from nuclear war, would result in "the extinction of mankind." Then treating all-out war as inevitable if the superpowers continued to maintain nuclear arsenals of any sort, the second part of the book explored the philosophical implications of extinction. Contemplating the meaning of life in page after page of quotations from Edmund Burke, Hannah Arendt, Kant, Pericles, Lucretius, and Freud, among others, Schell philosophically dissected the concept of extinction and reflected upon its moral implications. Finally, following consideration of Socrates' trial and biblical teachings, he arrived at his grand philosophical revelation: "there can be no justification for extinguishing mankind."[40]

In the third and final part of *The Fate of the Earth*, Schell offered his "solution" to the problem of nuclear weapons. If the human race were to be spared total extinction, he declared, there would have to be a "complete rearrangement of world politics." The only hope rested upon abolishing the existing system of sovereign nation-states and replacing it with a "new common world" based on "respect for human beings, . . . respect for the earth," and "respect for God or nature, or whatever one chooses to call the universal dust that made, or became, us." National sovereignty was "at the very core of the political issues" involved in the nuclear debate, he argued, and "those who favor complete nuclear and conventional disarmament, as I do . . . admit that their recommendation is inconsistent with national sovereignty." Schell concluded by polarizing the issue into two, presumably mutually exclusive choices: "On the one side stand human life and the terrestrial creation. On the other side stands a particular organization of human life—the system of independent, sovereign nation-states." For Jonathan Schell the choice was clear: "Our present system and the institutions that make it up are the debris of history. They have become inimical to life, and must be swept away."[41]

Not so long ago, Jonathan Schell might have been relegated to the ranks of misfits and cranks—another self-anointed prophet proclaiming the imminence of our doom.[42] In the early 1980s, however, Schell became a folk hero, the mushroom cloud a cultural icon of sorts, as critics and political commentators gushed over *The Fate of the Earth*. As Theodore Draper has observed, *The Fate of the Earth* not only sold well, it received "a rapturously favorable reception." Even partially critical reviews were "unduly respectful," reminding Draper of the reaction to "that classic of puerility, *The Greening of America*, also first published in *The New Yorker*."[43] Calling the book both "eloquent" and "timely," Bill Moyers considered *The Fate of the Earth* "destined to be one of that small number of books which occasionally play a great part in opening the public mind to dimly perceived truths." Comparing the book to Rachel Carson's *Silent Spring* and Solzhenitzyn's *Gulag Archipelago*, Moyers dreamed of Ronald Reagan and Leonid Brezhnev, sitting alone with their interpreters, "reading aloud and slowly from *The Fate of the Earth*."[44]

To be sure, Jonathan Schell had his critics. A handful of intellectuals on the left wondered how Schell's "interminable vaporings" could possibly command such "vast audiences,"[45] while the right could only respond with ridicule and satire. "Nuclear nonthink," William F. Buckley, Jr. headlined his commentary on *The Fate of the Earth* in the *National Review*,[46] while Vic Gold of the *American Spectator* sensed a "ghostwriter" behind the scenes: "You've heard the joke, now read the book. . . . Woody Allen, come out from behind that curtain. I see your hand, you irreverent rascal."[47] Still others complained about contradictions in Schell's reasoning or accused him of "tinkering with evidence to make it serve his purpose." According to Theodore Draper, for example, Schell's "strange illogic" constituted a "travesty of thinking about nuclear war."[48]

Yet for many commentators, the "illogic" of *The Fate of the Earth* was, in a sense, its greatest virtue. Precisely *because* it subverted "rational" debate over nuclear weapons and strategic policy, the book presumably helped democratize the nuclear debate, spearheading a revolution of sorts against the rhetorical tyranny of the politicians and the experts. According to Walter R. Fisher, for example, *The Fate of the Earth* was "exemplary of contemporary moral argument intended to persuade a general audience, the 'public.'" As such, it was not to be judged by the "ideological, bureaucratic, and technical arguments" of privileged elites, but by standards of "narrative rationality" common to all. Indeed, Fisher developed his "narrative paradigm"—one of the most influential rhetorical theories of the 1980s—for the express purpose of circumventing the "inevitable subversion of *The Fate of the Earth*" by conventional standards of logic and rationality. According to Fisher, *The Fate of the Earth* represented a mode of discourse "inimical to elitist politics," for it eschewed the "privileged argument" of the "experts" and appealed to a "public" of "untrained thinkers."[49]

Upon closer examination, however, *The Fate of the Earth* seems a remarkably curious model of "public moral argument." Clearly, the book was never intended for an audience of "ordinary citizens." Ordinary citizens do not read *The New Yorker.* Ordinary citizens do not ponder the teachings of Plutarch, Kafka, Kant, Camus, Socrates, and Lucretius. As Schell contemplated our "terrestrial biological inheritance" or the "claustrophobic isolation" of our "doomed present,"[50] it is hard to imagine an audience of enraptured ordinary citizens. If *The Fate of the Earth* was a model of discourse for ordinary citizens, then "ordinary citizen" has lost all meaning.

Even if ordinary citizens *were* to have read *The Fate of the Earth*, it is difficult to imagine them struck by its "narrative rationality"—that logic of "good reasons" determined by their "inherent awareness of *narrative probability*"—the sense of "what constitutes a coherent story"—and their "constant habit of testing *narrative fidelity*," or "whether the stories they experience ring true with the stories they know to be true in their lives."[51] Would ordinary citizens sense "narrative probablity"—coherence or consistency—in a book that criticizes the "fear-filled, thought-stopping epithets" of the pro-nuclear "establishment" after vaporizing, crushing, burning, and irradiating its readers for more than 100 pages?[52] Would they sense "narrative fidelity"—that quality of "ringing true" in the context of everyday experience—in a hypothetical scenario of nuclear armageddon? One can scarcely imagine stories more remote from the everyday experiences of ordinary citizens than Schell's tale of all-out nuclear war, his portrait of a planet devoid of all life, or his vision of "reinventing" the world and establishing a benevolent "one-world" government.

Above all, it is hard to imagine ordinary citizens satisfied by Schell's solution to the nuclear threat. Although freeze activists claimed *The Fate of the Earth* as an endorsement, a strict reading of the book actually casts the freeze advocates who lionized Schell into the enemy camp. In Schell's polarized world, proponents of the freeze aligned with all those other "timid" and "crippled" thinkers who sought political solutions within the framework of the existing international order.[53] By Schell's logic, they too, in effect, practically favored nuclear annihilation. As the Harvard Nuclear Study Group has suggested, the challenge of the nuclear age lies not in escaping "to a fictional utopia" but in discovering "how to live with nuclear weapons in ways that are successively safer."[54] *The Fate of the Earth* contributed nothing to meeting that challenge. It enticed readers into an unthinking world of fear and pessimism, and it failed to show them any way out.

According to Barry Brummett, "real" apocalyptic must be historically deterministic, and for that reason he excludes *The Fate of the Earth* because of "Schell's clear belief that human action can avert nuclear disaster."[55] But did Schell really believe that "human action" could bring about the "solution" he proposed in *The Fate of the Earth*? The answer seemed to come in 1984, when Schell published a follow-up to *The Fate of the Earth* titled *The Abolition*. Suddenly more realistic about solutions to the arms race, Schell now offered qualified praise of the freeze initiative, arguing that it answered "the urgent need to head off the next advance in the arms race, which promises to be a particularly perilous one." At the same time, however, he observed that "the freeze proposal was adopted by the movement perhaps as much for its political 'salability' as for its merits," and he criticized freeze advocates for failing to articulate goals beyond this "first step." Hence the need for a second book: this time advocating "an agreement abolishing nuclear arms." Under Schell's new scheme, the nations of the world would agree to establish "not world government, in which all nations are fused into one nation, but its exact opposite—a multiplicity of inviolate nations pledged to leave each other alone." In 1982, Jonathan Schell wanted to reinvent the world. By 1984, he favored incremental change and the preservation of national sovereignty: "In political affairs, it's a great advantage to be able to start with what is in place and improve on it, rather than have to start over. An agreement freezing the world's boundaries in place and abolishing nuclear arms while keeping deterrence in force by retaining the ability to rebuild them offers this advantage."[56]

To debate Schell's consistency or the feasibility of his solution is, however, to miss the point. *The Fate of the Earth's* impact did not stem from its philosophical arguments, nor from its appeal to ordinary citizens, nor from its promise of a solution. Instead, the influence of *The Fate of the Earth* stemmed from its scenario of the holocaust, which apparently struck an emotional chord in many readers and translated effectively into the grammar of television. Not surprisingly, Schell-like scenarios quickly became common on television news, as well as on a host of documentaries and even entertainment programs. The best-known of these productions, of course, was a made-for-television movie: ABC's docudrama of nuclear war, *The Day After.*

## The Docudrama of Doom

Of all the evidence for the deleterious effects of television on contemporary public discourse, perhaps none is more convincing than the controversy over ABC's *The Day After.* A docudrama of the "undocudramable," as Paul Attanasio called it,[57] *The Day After* neither documented much of anything nor did it aspire to particularly high artistic standards, even for a television movie. Yet, eagerly anticipated by freeze activists for months before its airing, *The Day After* became the watershed event of the entire freeze debate. Confident that the film would send Americans by the millions flocking to their cause, freeze activists published "viewing guides," launched direct-mail and petition campaigns, and screened pirated videocassettes of the film at freeze gatherings across the nation.[58] Some even established toll-free numbers to channel the "fall-out" from the movie into support for the freeze.[59]

"Watch 'The Day After,'" advised one viewing guide in advance of the movie, "But Don't Watch It Alone." Right after the movie, the guide advised, "encourage people to get up, walk around, or talk with others before the discussion begins. You may want to serve refreshments as a transition into the discussion."[60] In New York, 1,000 people crowded into the Riverside Church to watch the movie on big-screen television, while activists in San Francisco provided a television and a translator for Spanish-speaking citizens.[61] ABC refused to sell pro-freeze advertising during the movie itself, but that did not stop freeze activists from buying spots on local affiliates. "It doesn't have to be the end," Paul Newman declared in one of the ads. "We don't have to stand idly by while the politicians and bureaucrats make seemingly rational plans and policies, which, if ever carried out, will deny our children a future." In another ad, Meryl Streep urged women to "join millions of moms in sharing information about the prevention of nuclear war."[62]

In the midst of all this, ABC executives maintained their political innocence. As they were quick to point out, the movie took no stand on the freeze, nor did it explicitly criticize the policies of the Reagan administration. Appearing on *60 Minutes*, Brandon Stoddard, president of ABC Motion Pictures, insisted "again and again and again" that *The Day After* was never intended as a political movie. "We don't discuss whether deterrence is good or bad," he insisted, and it had "nothing to do" with a nuclear freeze. According to Stoddard, *The Day After* was merely a "what if" movie, and he just could not understand why critics of the freeze were so "irritated" by the movie and supporters so "overjoyed."[63]

Media critics have supported the network's claims to political innocence. Arguing that ABC actually sought to depoliticize the film, Rubin and Cummings have pointed out that the movie "carefully avoided describing what prompted the nuclear exchange,"[64] while Foss and Littlejohn have argued that the movie merely tapped into existing "fantasy themes" about nuclear war.[65] In the context of the freeze debate, however, such readings not only ignore the reactions of political activists on both sides of that debate, but also the visual and verbal "text" of the movie itself. A close reading of that text—an examination of the political and moral lessons taught by the film—in fact reveals an aggressively political movie. While it is true that the movie never explicitly attacked the Reagan administration or endorsed the freeze initiative, it did echo virtually every major theme of the freeze campaign: the inevitable failure of deterrence, the futility of Civil Defense, and the corruption of all political authority, from the President on down.

Set in the areas around Kansas City and Lawrence, Kansas, the plot of *The Day After* is well-known: "typical" midwesterners go about the business of everyday life as newscasts in the background tell of a growing crisis in Europe. Gradually, the newscasts assume more prominence; they begin to interrupt the discourse of wedding plans, farming life, and the ubiquitous small-town barber shop. Finally, they take center stage on a small television in the kitchen of Dr. Oates (Jason Robards) and his wife, interrupting their flirtatious banter. As the "Special Report" details the escalating crisis, Dr. Oates asks: "You want to go in the living room and watch? "No," responds his wife, "I just want to go upstairs and get into bed . . . with you!"[66]

Soon the panic begins, with motorists jamming the highways and hoarders fighting over the last few morsels at the grocery store. As the panicking crowd moves through the check-out lines (where, curiously, the checkers and baggers remain calmly at their posts), an excited citizen relays the latest news from his transistor radio: "They just hit one of our ships in the Persian Gulf. . . . We hit 'em back, one of their ships, ya' know?" Shortly thereafter, the ground begins to shake, people look toward the skies, and the most memorable scene of the movie unfolds: missiles rising out of the Kansas wheatfields. At the college football game, the realization sets in. One woman asks: "What's going on?" Perhaps it is a test, she speculates, or some kind of warning. But other fans know that Minuteman missiles are headed for Russia. "They take about thirty minutes to reach their targets," one man explains. Another responds ominously: "So do theirs, right?"

After several minutes of mass chaos in the streets, the Russian missiles arrive, delivering their proper sequence of technical events: the blinding flash, the electromagnetic pulse, the fireballs, and the great mushroom clouds. In a red-tinted sequence of nuclear test footage and special effects, buildings are shredded, forests set ablaze, and flesh-and-blood human beings dissolve into x-ray skeletons. Finally, there is nothing left but smoldering ruins, but all of our major characters miraculously have survived. Unfortunately, that only leaves us to watch them die slowly over the last half of the movie. The make-up artists are now called upon to depict the insidious effects of radiation, while the scriptwriters begin preaching their political and moral "lessons."

Both do their jobs heavy-handedly. Blood is spattered everywhere; all the characters are smeared with black soot; most characters bear Frankenstein-like scars about the face and head. As the visual images of misery and death accumulate, the dialogue becomes progressively more preachy. All things official are predictably skewered. The government's emergency supplies run out, and soldiers open fire on those still clamoring for food. An official of the National Emergency Reconstruction Administration addresses a group of farmers, instructing them to scrape off the top four or five inches of their top soil before planting new crops. One farmer responds sarcastically: "And do what with it? . . . Where'd you get all this . . . good advice? Out of some government pamphlet?" Yet another scene testifies to the complete breakdown of law-and-order, as a victim relays rumors of firing squads summarily executing looters and other alleged criminals. Clinging to his now irrelevant sense of justice, a doctor responds incredulously: "Without a trial?" Finally, the President addresses what is left of the nation, absurdly claiming a victory of sorts: "During this hour of sorrow, I wish to assure you that America has survived this terrible tribulation. There has been no surrender, no retreat from the principles of liberty and democracy for which the free world looks to us for leadership."

The lessons implicit in the plot of the movie were obvious, of course: question authority, and if that does not work, ignore, ridicule, sabotage, or rebel against the government. Yet *The Day After* went well beyond knee-jerk anti-authoritarianism, confirming a variety of more specific peace movement claims. Most obviously, of course, the film demonstrated how all planning for a nuclear war is folly. As we witness the exchange of a handful of tactical nuclear weapons escalate rapidly into a full-scale holocaust, we learn the absurdity of planning for battlefield or limited uses of nuclear weapons.[67] Similarly, Civil Defense and evacuation plans are depicted as exercises in futility, as stampeding crowds never quite make it to the shelters and cars pile helter-skelter on the roadways. The film also goes to great lengths to confirm claims by Physicians for Social Responsibility that all planning for an emergency medical response to nuclear war is fruitless. With much of the program set in the small university hospital in Lawrence—apparently the only medical facility left standing—we witness first-hand how hospitals would be overrun by mobs of injured survivors, and how pain-relieving drugs and other medical supplies would soon be depleted. With doctors the featured victims, the film strongly endorsed claims by Physicians for Social Responsibility that there could be no medical response to nuclear war.[68]

*The Day After* criticized U.S. strategic policies with a bit more subtlety. Yet in the sequence of events, one could find visual confirmation of some of the peace movement's most troubling claims. As the missiles rise out of their silos *before* the Russian bombs arrive, for example, the film confirms peace movement allegations that the government has routinely lied to us; we do, it turns out, have a doctrine of launch-upon-warning. Indeed, by depicting confirmation of the Soviet attack *after* the launchings, the film confirmed the suspicions of some peace activists that government strategists may be planning a preemptive strike. Most obviously, of course, *The Day After* confirmed a basic premise of all peace movement rhetoric: that security based upon deterrence is fragile at best. Watching *The Day After*, we never learned for sure who first "pushed the button." Somebody may have pushed it by mistake; perhaps it was an accident. Whatever the scenario, it did not matter. Deterrence failed; everybody died.

Above all, *The Day After* taught a purely secular moral lesson: there are no truths worth dying for; there is only death itself. That lesson was most poignantly conveyed by the final scene of the movie. As Dr. Oates heeded some perverse calling to return to his home, he took the viewer on a guided tour of a desolate landscape where the only reality was death: soldiers loading the body bags and firing squads at work. Stumbling through the rubble and stepping over bodies, he finally located the remains of his home. There he discovered a family of squatters huddled around what was once his own doorstep. At first, he angrily demanded that they vacate his property. Then, dramatically, he fell to his knees, apparently realizing the absurdity of his property rights. As one of the squatters comforted Dr. Oakes in an awkward embrace, the camera slowly withdrew, providing a broad vista of death and destruction. Finally, the scene faded into a printed trailer that only compounded the horror and offered only the faintest glimmer of hope: "The catastrophic events you have just witnessed are, in all likelihood, less severe than the destruction that would actually occur in the event of a full nuclear strike against the United States. It is hoped that the images of this film will inspire the nations of this earth, their peoples and leaders, to find the means to avert the fateful day."

Viewers who sat through the entire list of credits received a somewhat different message. There, at the end of the trailer, came the classic disclaimer: "The persons and events depicted in this film are fictitious. Any similarity to actual persons, living or dead, or to actual entities or events, is purely coincidental." Furthermore, the 45-minute *Viewpoint* special aired immediately following the movie, at least according to some observers, further divorced the film from reality and neutralized "any possible political message."[69] Opening the program with yet another disclaimer, Ted Koppel again reminded viewers that *The Day After* was, after all, "only a movie": "There is—and you probably need it about now—there is some good news. If you can, take a quick look out the window. It's all still there. Your neighborhood is still there; so is Kansas City and

Lawrence. . . . What we have all just seen . . . is sort of a nuclear version of Charles Dickens' *Christmas Carol.*"[70]

Yet Dickens' *Christmas Carol* rarely inspires follow-up news specials. If ABC executives really hoped to neutralize *The Day After* politically, it seems curious that they would invite such political luminaries as Secretary of State George Schultz, Henry Kissinger, William F. Buckley, Carl Sagan, and Elie Wiesel to comment on the film.[71] Furthermore, ABC covered *The Day After* as a major news event on its regular news programs. On *World News Tonight*, Peter Jennings emphasized that the Entertainment Division, not the News Division, had produced the film, and Jack Smith reminded viewers that the network had refused to sell advertising to anti-nuclear groups.[72] Yet the bottom line remains that ABC News, and even competing network news programs, covered a fictionalized account of nuclear war as the major news event of the entire freeze debate.[73]

All this is not to say that ABC deliberately set out to endorse the nuclear freeze campaign. While scriptwriter Ed Hume confessed his "long sympathy" for the disarmament movement,[74] ABC programming executives arguably had different motives. For a network in the throes of a dramatic ratings decline and threatened by corporate raiders, *The Day After* proved a blessing.[75] Attracting an estimated 106 million viewers in 38.5 million American homes, it became, at the time, the most watched made-for-TV movie in the history of television.[76] ABC executives made much of the fact that they lost money on the movie, pointing to high production costs and the reluctance of advertisers to sponsor the film.[77] Yet aired during the November "sweeps" (when advertising rates are determined), *The Day After* proved the one bright spot in an otherwise disastrous year for ABC.[78]

Ironically, *The Day After* proved less of a blessing for the nuclear freeze campaign. When all was said and done, the movie's political impact was barely noticeable. Phone banks set up to counsel frightened viewers received virtually no calls,[79] and surveys of audience reactions showed that the movie produced only minimal to moderate levels of fear among both children and adults.[80] Moreover, polls taken following the movie suggested that it had little, if any, effect on support for the freeze. One poll taken after the broadcast showed Reagan's job-approval rating "still rising bullishly,"[81] while another actually showed a slight increase, from 37 percent to 41 percent, in those who felt the United States was doing all it could to avoid nuclear war. That same poll, which questioned viewers both before and after the movie, also showed approval of Reagan's defense policies increasing from 54 percent to 58 percent, and Reagan actually did better against Walter Mondale after the movie (53 percent to 37 percent) than before it was shown (49 percent to 38 percent).[82]

Perhaps, as Paul Attanasio has argued, the reaction to *The Day After* confirmed that "once television decides to tackle an issue dramatically, it reliably signals that no one is really interested anymore."[83] Yet there may be another, more far-reaching explanation: that the American people recognized that the film did not "tackle an issue" at all. Freeze activists assumed that *The Day After* would panic people into support for the freeze, but the film made no argument for the freeze or any other specific arms control policy. *The Day After* may have scared some people, but it lacked a key element of the apocalyptic tradition: the promise that we might be delivered from fear by faith or political commitment.

## The Science of Fear

In the fall of 1983, a group of scientists led by Carl Sagan introduced a new strain of apocalyptic discourse into the freeze debate: the rhetoric of nuclear winter. Simply stated, the theory of nuclear winter held that even a small exchange of nuclear weapons—on the order, perhaps, of 500 of the world's 18,000 nuclear weapons—would throw so much dirt, soot, and smoke into the atmosphere that the earth would be plunged into darkness and subfreezing temperatures, a "winter" lasting long enough to create "a real possibility of the extinction of the human species."[84]

Unlike the doomsday scenarios that preceded it, the theory of nuclear winter was based upon "extensive scientific studies," and it had been "endorsed by a large number of scientists."[85] For a combination of reasons, however, nuclear winter remained tangential to the freeze debate. Not only did it come too late to make much difference,[86] but it became mired in scientific controversy.[87] In addition, the rhetoric of nuclear winter lacked journalistic appeal. Not only had the devastation of nuclear war become old news, but the "winter" scenario itself—a scenario of long-term climatic change—could not be visually depicted or dramatized as powerfully as the usual attack scenario.

In the final analysis, however, the rhetoric of nuclear winter failed for the same reason that *The Fate of the Earth* and *The Day After* failed: it remained curiously unconnected to the freeze initiative itself. Sagan himself said more than most doomsayers about the policy implications of his scenario.[88] Yet those implications had nothing at all to do with the freeze; indeed, they only made the freeze once again seem dangerously timid. In arguing that the world's arsenals had to be cut below the threshold at which nuclear winter might be triggered, Sagan spoke vaguely of "a more than 90-percent reduction" and of cuts to "well below" 1,000 total warheads.[89] Like Jonathan Schell, Sagan wanted, not a freeze at existing levels,[90] but a "very steep decline in the total number of warheads in the world."[91] More than that, he wanted, like Schell, to reinvent politics:

> Given the magnitude of the potential loss, no policy declarations and no mechanical safeguards can adequately guarantee the safety of the human species. No national rivalry or ideological confrontation justifies putting the species at risk. . . . The problem cries out for an ecumenical perspective that rises above cant, doctrine

> and mutual recrimination, however apparently justified, and that at least partly transcends parochial fealties in time and space.[92]

Sagan's lukewarm endorsement of the freeze echoed virtually all of the prominent doomsayers of the early 1980s. For most, the freeze simply did not go far enough. Indeed, some of the best-known doomsayers, such as Ground Zero's Roger Molander, actually opposed the freeze initiative on the grounds that it might stall efforts to cut nuclear arsenals.[93] Still others turned apocalyptic warnings into arguments for the Reagan administration's policies. The Department of Defense, for example, invoked the threat of nuclear winter in arguments for modernization of America's strategic forces, for limited nuclear war doctrines, and for more vigorous development of the Strategic Defense Initiative.[94]

It comes as no surprise that the rhetoric of doom sometimes backfired on the freeze campaign. At the dawn of the nuclear age, a similar campaign met a similar fate: the so-called "scientists' movement" of the late 1940s. Dismayed that their invention had been used to destroy two cities, a number of the scientists originally involved in the Manhattan project organized in 1945 to shape future atomic energy policies. Opposed to efforts to place atomic research and development under military control, the scientists pressed for peaceful development of atomic energy under international authority and the banning of all nuclear weapons. Their campaign won widespread support from political leaders, civic groups, and editorial writers. While polls showed support for the general idea of international control, however, they also showed more than 70 percent of Americans opposed to giving up "the secret of making atomic bombs."[95]

Disturbed by such findings, the scientists launched a five-year campaign to change public opinion, a campaign of "shameless propaganda" based "almost wholly on fear." Taking their crusade to "the village square," they tried, in the words of one of the scientists, to "scare the pants off" the public. As one scientist explained their strategic thinking: "Only one tactic is dependable—the preaching of doom." Scheduled to address a group of radio executives, one scientist was advised to "scare the living hell out of them," while another received the following advice about his speech to the same group: "It would probably be most useful to our cause to make this a blood and thunder speech about no defense and the horrible consequences of another world war."[96]

From the start, critics expressed doubts about the scientists' strategy. Reinhold Niebuhr complained that the whole campaign misread human nature, while others predicted that it would only numb public awareness and promote political withdrawal. Some even feared that such a campaign might lead to a national orgy of hedonism and self-indulgence. But whatever the concern, all correctly predicted that the strategy would fail. By 1951, even Eugene Rabinowitch, a key figure in the movement, conceded that the effort had been worse than a failure; it had only encouraged more hawkish attitudes. "While trying to frighten men into rationality," Rabinowitch lamented, they had only frightened many "into abject fear or blind hatred."[97]

The lesson of the scientists' movement may be seen as the lesson of apocalyptic movements throughout American history: that fear alone is not enough. Apocalyptic discourse, if it is to persuade and motivate, must not only frighten but promise salvation. It seems a curious theory of public psychology indeed that holds that fear, administered in massive doses, should inspire political action.[98] Yet that is precisely the theory of public psychology behind much of the freeze campaign's rhetoric, and it went hand-in-hand with a larger historical and cultural perspective that limited the appeal of the freeze campaign to a disaffected "New Class."

## Notes

1. Jonathan Schell, *The Fate of the Earth* (New York: Alfred A. Knopf, 1982), 24.
2. "Who's Who in the Movement," *Newsweek*, 26 April 1982: 22.
3. Helen Caldicott, among others, has insisted that "millions of fundamentalist Christians, led by Jerry Falwell and others," believe "that the world will be consumed by fire, as in nuclear war, and that one third of men with the mark of God on their foreheads will go straight up to heaven." According to Caldicott, they believed that nuclear war would bring about "the rapture," and they were "actually praying for it to happen." In reality, of course, Falwell preached no such thing. He advocated "peace-through-strength" as the best means for *avoiding* nuclear war; he never expressed any desire *for* nuclear war. See Helen Caldicott, *Missile Envy: The Arms Race and Nuclear War* (New York: Bantam, 1985), 331-32 and Jerry Falwell, *Nuclear War and the Second Coming of Jesus Christ* (Lynchburg, Virginia: Old Time Gospel Hour, n.d.), audiocassettes.
4. Joseph Dewey, *In a Dark Time: The Apocalyptic Temper in the American Novel of the Nuclear Age* (West Lafayette: Purdue University Press, 1990), 11.
5. Douglas Robinson, *American Apocalypses: The Image of the End of the World in American Literature* (Baltimore: Johns Hopkins University Press, 1985), xi.
6. Sacvan Bercovitch, *The American Jeremiad* (Madison: University of Wisconsin Press, 1978), xi.
7. Robinson, *American Apocalypses,* xi.
8. Dewey, *In a Dark Time,* 21.
9. See Barry Brummett, *Contemporary Apocalyptic Rhetoric* (New York: Praeger, 1991), 3, 41-43.
10. Robinson, *American Apocalypses,* xi.
11. Brummett, *Contemporary Apocalyptic Rhetoric,* 6.
12. See Dewey, *In a Dark Time,* 15-16.
13. Brummett, *Contemporary Apocalyptic Rhetoric,* 5-6, 31.
14. Quoted in Dewey, *In a Dark Time,* 3.
15. Dewey, *In a Dark Time,* 5-6.
16. Quoted in John Lewis Gaddis, *The United States and the Origins of the Cold War, 1941-1947* (New York: Columbia University Press, 1972), 245.

17. Paul Boyer, *By the Bomb's Early Light: American Thought and Culture at the Dawn of the Atomic Age* (New York: Pantheon, 1985), 258.
18. Dewey, *In a Dark Time,* 43.
19. Brummett, *Contemporary Apocalyptic Rhetoric,* 31, 38.
20. Barbara Solow, *Mobilizing Media: A National Report on How the Peace Movement Has Used Films and Other Media in Grassroots Organizing and Education* (New York: Media Network, 1983), 2, 5.
21. Karen Sayer and John Dowling, eds., *1984 National Directory of Audiovisual Resources on Nuclear War and the Arms Race* (Ann Arbor: University of Michigan Media Resources Center, 1984), 2.
22. Ibid., 16, 38.
23. Ibid., 43.
24. Ibid., 25. On the controversy surrounding the film see Robert D. McFadden, "3 Canadian Films Called 'Propaganda' by U.S.," *New York Times,* 25 February 1983, C4; Richard Grenier, "The Politicized Oscar," *Commentary,* June 1983, 70; and J. Justin Gustainis, "Propaganda and the Law: The Case of Three Canadian Films," in *Propaganda: A Pluralistic Perspective,* edited by Ted J. Smith III (New York: Praeger, 1989), 115-26.
25. Sayer and Dowling, *1984 National Directory of Audiovisual Resources on Nuclear War and the Arms Race,* 23.
26. Ibid., 13.
27. Ibid., 26.
28. Ibid., 2.
29. Ibid., 13.
30. Ibid., 26.
31. Ibid., 40.
32. Strobe Talbott, "A Grim Manifesto on Nuclear War," *Time,* 19 April 1982, 20.
33. Avon Books secured the paperback rights for $375,000, and at least ten foreign publishers also secured rights to the book. See Talbott, "A Grim Manifesto on Nuclear War," 20.
34. Of the 130 books on a *Publisher Weekly* checklist of nuclear subjects in March of 1982, as Edwin McDowell reported, more than 80 percent had been published since 1980. While not all of these books sold well in bookstores, many sold well "outside normal trade-book distribution channels—for example, through the efforts of antinuclear organizations and church groups." Edwin McDowell, "Nuclear Books Proliferating, but Few Sell Well," *New York Times,* 4 November 1982, C25.
35. Schell, *The Fate of the Earth,* 36.
36. Ibid., 4-5.
37. Ibid., 38-43.
38. Ibid., 6, 45-46, 50, 53.
39. Ibid., 55-57.
40. Ibid., 130.
41. Ibid., 177-78, 218-19, 221.
42. In literature, as Robinson has noted, critics have treated apocalyptic writings as "inhabiting some fanatical fringe worthy only of the critical attention needed to dismiss it." Apocalypses generally have been considered "freaks or sports, the eccentric imaginative spawn of dangerous cranks from whom readers cannot be overly protected" (Robinson, *American Apocalypses,* 3).

43. Theodore Draper, "How Not to Think About Nuclear War," *New York Review of Books*, 15 July 1982, 36.
44. CBS News, *CBS Evening News*, 22 March 1982, microfiche transcript, 8-9.
45. Alexander Cockburn and James Ridgeway, "Will the Freeze Movement Be More Than a Fad?" *Village Voice*, 13 April 1982, 6.
46. William F. Buckley Jr., "Nuclear Nonthink," *National Review*, 4 February 1983, 140.
47. Vic Gold, Review of *The Fate of the Earth*, by Jonathan Schell, *American Spectator*, July 1982, 36-37.
48. Draper, "How Not to Think About Nuclear War," 36-38.
49. Fisher, "Narration as a Human Communication Paradigm," 9, 11-12, 15.
50. Schell, *The Fate of the Earth*, 172-73.
51. Fisher, "Narration as a Human Communication Paradigm," 8.
52. Schell, *The Fate of the Earth*, 162.
53. Ibid., 161-62.
54. Carnesale, et al. *Living With Nuclear Weapons*, 19.
55. Brummett, *Contemporary Apocalyptic Rhetoric*, 35.
56. Jonathan Schell, *The Abolition* (New York: Avon Books, 1984), 92-93, 146-47, 191.
57. Paul Attanasio, "Big Bang, Little Box," *New Republic*, 5 December 1983, 13.
58. On a segment of *60 Minutes* about the controversy surrounding the movie, Ed Bradley observed: "We don't know how key members of the nuclear freeze movement obtained advance copies of the film, but they did, and they are using it in a nationwide campaign to win converts to their cause" (CBS News, "The Week Before *The Day After*," *60 Minutes*, 13 November 1983, microfiche transcript, 7).
59. As *Time* reported, several dozen freeze groups, including the Campaign Against Nuclear War and Physicians for Social Responsibility, sponsored TV commercials urging viewers to call 1-800-NUCLEAR, "before it's too late." By "week's end," the newsmagazine reported, "some 50,000 people" had called "for more information" (James Kelly, "Fallout From a TV Attack," *Time*, 5 December 1983, 38).
60. Robert Karl Manoff, "The Week After," *Nation*, 10 December 1983, 589.
61. Kelly, "Fallout From a TV Attack," 38.
62. CBS News, "The Week Before *The Day After*," 8.
63. Ibid., 9-10.
64. David M. Rubin and Constance Cummings, "Nuclear War and Its Consequences on Television News," *Journal of Communication* 39 (Winter 1989): 43.
65. Karen A. Foss and Stephen W. Littlejohn, "*The Day After*: Rhetorical Vision in an Ironic Frame," *Critical Studies in Mass Communication* 3 (September 1986): 317-36.
66. ABC Motion Pictures, *The Day After*, Embassy Home Video, 1983, videocassette. All quotations from the film are transcribed from the videotape.
67. Alton Frye of the Council on Foreign Relations told *Time* magazine that he considered the scenario of escalation in *The Day After* "unrealistic" (Kelly, "Fallout From a TV Attack," 40).
68. Timothy J. Hayes, a medical doctor, served as a "research advisor" on the film's crew.
69. Rubin and Cummings, "Nuclear War and Its Consequences on Television News," 52.
70. ABC News, "'The Day After'—Nuclear Dilemma," *Viewpoint*, 20 November 1983, microfiche transcript, 2.
71. Schultz assured viewers that nuclear war was "not acceptable" in the view of the Reagan administration, while Henry Kissinger dismissed the film as "simple minded." On the other side, Carl Sagan warned that a nuclear war would be far worse than depicted in the film and criticized Reagan's arms build-up, while Elie

Wiesel just said he was "scared." See ABC News, "'The Day After'—Nuclear Dilemma," 2, 4, 5, 7, 9.

72. Rubin and Cummings, "Nuclear War and Its Consequences on Television News," 52.
73. On the *CBS Evening News*, for example, *The Day After* received more coverage than any other event of the entire freeze debate. See Meyer, *A Winter of Discontent*, 124.
74. CBS News, "The Week Before *The Day After*," 10.
75. As Huntington Williams has pointed out in an "insider's" account of the decline of ABC, the network that had fourteen of the Nielson top twenty shows (including eight of the top ten and all five of the top five shows) during the 1978-79 season had, by the fall of 1984, plunged into third-place in the ratings and soon thereafter was taken over by Capital Cities Communications. At the start of the 1983-84 season, as Williams puts it, "ABC was skimming along at high speed without traction, like a car on ice—an accident waiting to happen," and the "rave reviews and high ratings" garnered by *The Day After* provided one of the few bright spots during the network's dramatic decline (Huntington Williams, *Beyond Control: ABC and the Fate of the Networks* [New York: Atheneum, 1989], esp. 119, 185, 187, 211).
76. Initial estimates that *The Day After* reached 46 million American homes (62 percent of the night's total audience) were later revised downward to 38.5 million. Whatever the exact figures, it was at the time the highest-rated made-for-television movie in history. ABC's own polling revealed that 53 percent of the sample had viewed the film and an additional 40 percent knew about it. In addition, ABC's poll revealed that 82 percent of the viewers subsequently discussed the film with others, making *The Day After* "more talked about" than *The Winds of War* or *Roots*. See Kelly, "Fallout From a TV Attack," 38; Rubin and Cummings, "Nuclear War and Its Consequences on Television News," 43; Foss and Littlejohn, "*The Day After*," 317, 319; and Stanley Feldman and Lee Sigelman, "The Political Impact of Prime-Time Television: 'The Day After,'" *Journal of Politics* 47 (May 1985): 556.
77. *The Day After* cost approximately $7 million, about three-times as much as the typical television movie, yet ABC was forced to sell spots for only $100,000 apiece—$35,000 below its original asking price. On *60 Minutes*, Stoddard declared that ABC would have aired the film even if no spots had been sold. Attanasio, "Big Bang, Little Box," 13; Jeff Gottlieb, "Prime-Time Patriotism: ABC Atones for *The Day After*," *Mother Jones*, January 1987, 42; CBS News, "The Week Before *The Day After*," 11.
78. Stoddard tried to repeat that success during the February 1987 sweeps with another politically controversial project: the twelve-hour miniseries *Amerika*. Teaching a much different political lesson, *Amerika* was in the works even as *The Day After* aired, but it was widely seen as an attempt by ABC to appease right-wing critics of *The Day After*. In any case, it seemed to confirm that Stoddard had no particular political agenda in choosing story lines for his projects. He simply seemed convinced that controversy attracted big ratings. Unfortunately, *Amerika* proved even more costly than *The Day After* (more than $50 million, by one projection), and it did not attract nearly as much attention. As a result, the network lost an estimated $20 million on the miniseries. See Gottlieb, "Prime-Time Patriotism," 26-29, 42-44; and Williams, *Beyond Control*, 254.
79. The Federal Emergency Management Agency (FEMA), for example, assigned extra staff to answer an anticipated flood of calls from frightened viewers. Yet the agency received just three calls on the Monday following the film's airing and only four more on Tuesday. See Tom Morganthau, "After 'The Day After,'" *Newsweek*, 5 December 1983, 62.

80. See Joanne Cantor, Barbara J. Wilson, and Cynthia Hoffner, "Emotional Responses to a Televised Nuclear Holocaust Film," *Communication Research* 13 (April 1986): 272.
81. Morganthau, "After 'The Day After,'" 62.
82. Kelly, "Fallout From a TV Attack," 39. Other studies confirmed that the movie had little effect on political attitudes, although one pair of researchers argued that it did have some impact on the salience of the nuclear issue. See Feldman and Sigelman, "The Political Impact of Prime-Time Television,'" 556-77.
83. Attanasio, "Big Bang, Little Box," 13.
84. Carl Sagan, "The Nuclear Winter," *Parade*, 30 October 1983, 7.
85. Carl Sagan, "Nuclear War and Climatic Catastrophe: Some Policy Implications," *Foreign Affairs* 62 (Winter 1983/84): 259.
86. The findings of Sagan and his colleagues were first presented at a scientific conference in Cambridge, Massachusetts in April of 1983. They did not go public until the end of October, when they presented their findings to a conference on the "World After Nuclear War" in Washington, D.C. On October 30, Sagan warned of "nuclear winter" in the Sunday newspaper supplement, *Parade*, and on November 20 he appeared on the ABC *Viewpoint* special to warn that the reality of nuclear war would be much worse than depicted on *The Day After*. The actual results of the research, however, did not appear for yet another month, in the December 23 issue of *Science*. Thus, by the time the nuclear winter campaign began in earnest, the freeze already had disappeared from the news. As a result, nuclear winter became an academic issue in the literal sense: it generated considerable discussion among academics and scientists, but it had little impact on public debate. By the time Sagan and Turco published their book on the subject, not only the freeze debate but the Cold War had ended. See Sagan, "Nuclear War and Climatic Catastrophe," 259; Sagan, "The Nuclear Winter," 4-7; ABC News, "'The Day After'—Nuclear Dilemma," 4; R. P. Turco, et al., "Nuclear Winter: Global Consequences of Multiple Nuclear Explosions," *Science* 222 (23 December 1983): 1283-92; John Maddox, "What Happened to Nuclear Winter," *Nature* 333 (19 May 1988): 203; and Carl Sagan and Richard Turco, *A Path Where No Man Thought: Nuclear Winter and the End of the Arms Race* (New York: Random House, 1990).
87. Almost as soon as Sagan and his colleagues announced their theory, other scientists criticized their one-dimensional model of atmospheric processes. As atmospheric scientists Starley L. Thompson and Stephen H. Schneider pointed out, the climatic model employed by Sagan and his colleagues "did not take into account north-south and east-west directions, but instead treated the earth as a homogeneous all-land sphere having a temperature that depended only on the up-down direction (atmospheric altitude). Thus, the model had no geography, no winds, no seasons, instantaneous spread of smoke to the hemispheric scale, and no feedback of atmospheric circulation changes on the rate of smoke washout by rainfall." More sophisticated models predicted some cooling of temperatures in the wake of a nuclear exchange, but Thompson and Schneider pointed out that "the oceans, with their vast storage of heat, would reduce the magnitude of average continental cooling by a factor of two in the summer, compared to the cooling calculated by assuming a land-covered planet." Thus, they concluded, the changes would more closely resemble a nuclear "fall" than a nuclear "winter." See Starley L. Thompson and Stephen H. Schneider, "Nuclear Winter Reappraised," *Foreign Affairs* 64 (Summer 1986): 985, 987.
88. See especially Sagan, "Nuclear War and Climatic Catastrophe," 275-83.
89. Sagan, "Nuclear War and Climatic Catastrophe," 284; ABC News, "'The Day After'—Nuclear Dilemma," 9.

90. Sagan generally talked about the freeze only when asked, and he endorsed it only as "an excellent first step." See ABC News, "'The Day After'—Nuclear Dilemma," 12.
91. ABC News, "'The Day After'—Nuclear Dilemma," 16.
92. Sagan, "Nuclear War and Climatic Catastrophe," 292.
93. On Molander's opposition to the freeze, see Garfinkle, *The Politics of the Nuclear Freeze*, 82.
94. See Thompson and Schneider, "Nuclear Winter Reappraised," 983.
95. Boyer, *By the Bomb's Early Light*, 49-58.
96. Ibid., 59-75.
97. Ibid., 72-73, 93.
98. Not only does such a theory of public psychology seem disconfirmed by historical experience, but also by most experimental studies in the psychology of fear. For a review of that literature, see Alice H. Eagly and Shelly Chaiken, *The Psychology of Attitudes* (Fort Worth: Harcourt Brace Jovanovich, 1993), esp. 432-47.

Ellen Shub/THE PICTURE CUBE

## CHAPTER THREE

# THE RHETORIC OF POLITICAL MEDICINE

> . . . there aren't communist babies and capitalist babies—a baby is a baby is a baby.[1]
>
> Helen Caldicott

If Jonathan Schell was the theologian of the nuclear freeze movement, Helen Caldicott was its tent-revivalist. Preaching with fire-and-brimstone fury to millions of Americans on television, in books and popular magazines, and at huge public rallies, Caldicott simply dominated media coverage of the freeze debate. She was one of two movement personalities most frequently quoted in national news coverage of the freeze.[2] She appeared regularly, not only on the evening news programs, but also on morning news shows, television newsmagazines, talk shows, new specials, and documentaries.[3] She was profiled by *People*, *Life*, *Family Circle*, and a host of other magazines. Her traveling symposium on the "Medical Consequences of Nuclear War" generated "thousands of newspaper stories and TV spots in local and national outlets."[4] Her two books, *Nuclear Madness* and *Missile Envy*, were best-selling Bantam paperbacks.[5] She appeared in a number of anti-nuclear films and even "starred" in the controversial Academy Award-winning documentary, *If You Love This Planet.*[6] By virtue of her media visibility alone, Caldicott earned her popular title: "Mother of the Nuclear Freeze Movement."

As a pediatrician, of course, Caldicott was no more an expert on nuclear weapons than Robert Oppenheimer was an expert on prepubescent maladies. But constantly reminding audiences of her medical credentials, she practiced what she called political medicine,[7] speaking metaphorically of "the final epidemic" and gravely warning that "the prognosis is guarded."[8] Her second book, *Missile Envy*, was billed on the cover as "an expert's account of the frightening facts behind our blind rush toward atomic disaster." More an account of her personal journey from pediatrician to anti-nuclear activist, the book is perhaps best described as a political autobiography. Elaborating her views on everything from Vietnam to video games, it revealed far more about Helen Caldicott than about the nuclear threat.

Few would dispute Caldicott's claim that she provided a catalyst for the freeze movement, and she may not have exaggerated when she claimed to have recruited the majority of all people who responded to the appeals of peace organizations in the early 1980s.[9] Many of her recruits themselves became influential activists, mimicking both Caldicott's persona and her rhetorical style. With Caldicott's blessing, freeze activists by the hundreds copied her rhetorical trademark, dubbed the "bombing run" speech by campaign insiders.[10] Meanwhile, her books served as briefing papers for scores of additional activists, providing argumentative themes, facts and figures, testimony, and anecdotes. Videotapes featuring Caldicott provided the drawing card and focal point for many a freeze gathering.

Caldicott was in many ways the archetypal, even stereotypical, freeze activist: well-educated, professionally successful, and economically secure. She epitomized the sort of New Class activist that led Robert Coles to dub the freeze movement "the crusade of the leisure class."[11] More significantly, she symbolized the notion that New Class professionals—not only physicians but lawyers, teachers, musicians, and others—should play a special role in the nuclear debate. Her personal crusade most directly inspired the resurrection of Physicians for Social Responsibility (PSR)—an organization of activist medical professions dormant since the early 1960s—and its sister group, the International Physicians for the Prevention of Nuclear War (IPPNW).[12] But PSR in turn inspired dozens of copy-cat groups, such as Educators for Social Responsibility and even Architects, Designers, and Planners for Social Responsibility.[13]

In the brief period that the freeze movement flourished, Caldicott's rhetoric—and her style of rhetoric—received much of the credit. When the movement faltered in 1983-1984, it was only natural that she would attract at least part of the blame. Like Jonathan Schell, Caldicott wallowed in gruesome scenes of atomic death and destruction, and like Schell she did little to channel fear into support for the freeze. By the middle 1980s even many anti-nuclear activists had begun to sense that shock therapy may not be the best therapy, concluding that Caldicott only promoted "psychic numbing" and encouraged political "paralysis."[14] Furthermore, they began to realize that fear did not necessarily translate into support for the freeze. As Paul Boyer concluded from his historical review of anti-nuclear fear appeals: "Once fear is unleashed, the direction of its political expression is wholly unpredictable. Certainly the early activists learned to their regret that it is easier to terrify the public than it is to channel that terror into sustained and constructive political action."[15]

Yet the roots of Caldicott's failure reached deeper than this. Like Schell, Caldicott's apocalyptic was grounded, not in religious faith, but in a secular, progressivist world view embraced by but a small minority of the American people.[16] Grounding all ethical judgment in humanistic principles, she scoffed at the cultural myth of America as God's chosen people. In its place, she embraced a neo-Marxist, revisionist interpretation of history that cast America as the evil villain of world affairs. Like the New Left historians from whom she borrowed, Caldicott blamed virtually all the violence and suffering in the world upon the greed of America's ruling class, while she completely absolved the Soviet Union and other adversaries of the United States of blame. To many within the peace movement, Caldicott preached a fundamental historical faith. But the vast majority of Americans in the 1980s not only rejected Caldicott's secular progressivism, but continued to view the Soviet Union as an untrustworthy adversary necessitating a strong nuclear defense.[17]

Caldicott constantly betrayed her disdain for the very people she set out to persuade. She did not consider the American people merely numb or ignorant about the nuclear threat. She considered them mentally disturbed and morally corrupt. Invoking comparisons to Nazi Germany, Caldicott railed against virtually every aspect of American politics and culture, and she held the American people morally culpable for the crimes of their leaders. By the journalistic standards of the televisual era, Caldicott's rhetoric may have been eloquent. But in the context of mainstream cultural values and political mythology, her rhetoric was radical, irrational, alien, and condescending.

## Psychic Numbing and the Rhetoric of the Bombing Run

Although many viewed Jonathan Schell as the intellectual founder of the freeze campaign, Schell was neither the first nor the most accomplished apocalyptic prophet of the freeze campaign. Schell learned his art from a number of physicians and scientists who specialized in this "modern-day branch of eschatology,"[18] and PSR, along with the IPPNW, targeted a broader, more genuinely public audience than did Schell. Moreover, Caldicott and her colleagues went well beyond Schell, offering not only more detailed and gruesome scenarios of nuclear mayhem, but also a psychological rationale for the rhetoric of doom. Following Robert Jay Lifton, the activist doctors declared that the American people suffered from psychic numbing: a condition similar to the psychological defense of denial and the behavioral state of apathy.[19] And by the curious logic of political medicine, apocalyptic rhetoric provided the only possible cure.

Dr. Caldicott thus called it therapeutic to induce feelings of severe discomfort in people so that they would act to prevent "the final epidemic."[20] Similarly, psychologist John E. Mack wrote of the need for an emotional realization of nuclear warfare while introducing the IPPNW's volume, *Last Aid*: "Only by understanding the agonizing suffering and slow death of countless others through burning, crushing, and radiation sickness can we wrest the control of human destiny from the destructive instruments we have so heedlessly spawned."[21]

In "treating" the public's numbness, the political doctors typically began, like Schell, with gruesome accounts from the victims of Hiroshima. Dr. Caldicott presented what she called clinical descriptions of the survivors of Hiroshima in her popular Bantam paperback, *Missile Envy*: "There were about thirty men . . . all in exactly the same nightmarish state: Their faces were wholly burned; their eye sockets were hollow; the fluid from their melted eyes had run down their cheeks. . . . Their mouths were mere swollen, pus-covered wounds which they could not bear to stretch enough to admit the spout of a teapot."[22] The IPPNW's Dr. Michito Ichimaru offered even more wrenching recollections of his childhood in Nagasaki in the IPPNW volume *Last Aid.* Meanwhile, his credentials as a leukemia specialist sustained an aura of medical expertise:

> When I went outside . . . I met many people coming back from Urakami. Their clothes were in rags and shreds of skin hung from their bodies. They looked like ghosts with vacant stares. I cannot get rid of the sounds of crying women in the destroyed fields. . . . There were dead bodies everywhere. . . . In [a small tub] . . . was the body of a desperate man who had sought cool water. There was foam coming from his mouth, but he was not alive.
>
> As I got nearer to school, there were black charred bodies, with the white edges of bones showing in the arms and legs. A dead horse with a bloated belly lay by the side of the road.[23]

Like Schell, the political physicians used accounts from Japanese survivors as springboards for predicting the results of nuclear war today. Verbally dropping a 15- or 20-megaton bomb on the hometown of her audience, Caldicott piled image upon image, building to an emotional crescendo of mind-numbing horror. Starting at Ground Zero, she would begin with the image of a "hole three quarters of a mile wide and 800 feet deep." Progressively moving outward, she paused to create additional images at various distances from the epicenter of the blast. At six miles, for example, every building would be flattened and every person killed. At twenty miles away, those who happened to glance at the blast could have their eyes melted. At twenty-six miles, people would spontaneously ignite and become "walking, flaming torches." At forty miles, people would be instantly blinded by burns to the eyes—and so on and on.[24]

Like a modern-day Jonathan Edwards, Caldicott created the very picture of hell: "huge fires," fueled by winds of "1,000 miles per hour," consuming "1,500 to 3,000 square miles."[25] Yet unlike religious prophets of doom, the secularist doctors promised no life ever-after. Instead, they simply wallowed in images of intense human suffering, albeit sanitizing those images a bit with medical jargon. As Caldicott concluded her scenario: "All the people within the bombed areas will die alone, from a combination of trauma, burns, radiation illness, and starvation . . . with no relatives and no help from doctors or health workers even to give them pain-relieving drugs."[26] Similarly, Bernard Lown, the American cardiologist who helped found IPPNW, sprinkled his otherwise even more gruesome scenario of all-out nuclear war with medical lingo: "More than 200 million men, women, and children would be killed outright. . . . Crushing injuries, fractures, perforated viscera, contusions of internal organs, charred extremities, and uncertain radiation exposures, as well as psychiatric derangements, would be commonplace."[27]

Medical metaphors dominated the rhetoric of the crusading physicians, sustaining at all times the aura of expertise. "As individual physicians," the IPPNW wrote in an open letter to Reagan and Chernenko in 1984, "we must at times tell families that the condition of a patient is 'critical.' After careful study . . . we must collectively issue the warning that it is now not a single human life but all human life that is in critical condition."[28] In introducing the PSR book *The Final Epidemic*, Caldicott wrote that "the world is moving rapidly toward the final medical epidemic, thermonuclear war." She concluded by sprinkling the analogy liberally with medical jargon: "This planet can be compared to a terminally ill patient infected with lethal 'macrobes' which are metastasizing rapidly. . . . Time is short. The prognosis is guarded. But the analogy of the terminally ill patient in the intensive care unit who occasionally survives because of dedicated medical, scientific and nursing efforts seems appropriate."[29]

Whether appropriate or not, such analogies served to depoliticize the doctors' crusade. In *Missile Envy*, Caldicott rarely addressed the concerns of a doctor (much less of a pediatrician), yet the book was one long medical metaphor, from the Freudian interpretation of the arms race suggested by the title itself, to chapters entitled "Prognosis," "Case History," "Physical Examination," "Pathogenesis," and "Etiology." In the same book, Caldicott even disguised a bizarre *ad hominem* attack on Ronald Reagan as a medical diagnosis, recounting a seventy-five minute interview she had with Reagan on 6 December 1982. According to Caldicott, Reagan called the Russians "evil, Godless communists" while admitting that he had never met a Russian. Reagan just could not understand the "facts" that Caldicott presented: the fact that the nuclear balance was equal, for instance, and the fact that the American navy was superior to that of the Soviets. Even Reagan's own daughter Patti supposedly took Caldicott's side during the discussion, producing a Pentagon document supporting Caldicott's view. Yet apparently in the grips of some paranoid disorder, Reagan dismissed the document as a forgery. Caldicott concluded her account with a snap diagnosis of Reagan's mental disorder:

> I was shocked by this interview. He is not a man of great intelligence, and he lacked both empathy and a deep understanding of the complex subject of nuclear weapons. . . . Further, he is an old man, and old men are prone to obstruction of cerebral vessels by atheromatous plaques causing small strokes which, without producing obvious damage, may affect the thinking process.[30]

As Richard Grenier observed, Caldicott tried to assure us as a doctor that it was "medically contra-indicated to do anything that might alarm those poor, fearful, old men in the Kremlin."[31] Yet she rarely offered a specific prescription. Occasionally, she paid lip service to the freeze, but only as a first step in "rapid bilateral nuclear disarmament."[32] More commonly, she soared toward utopia, advocating immediate and unilateral disarmament by the United States and a wholesale reconstitution of the human spirit. If the United States were simply to dismantle its nuclear arsenal tomorrow, Caldicott assured readers of *Nuclear*

*Madness*, the Russian people "would heave a momentous sigh of relief" and somehow compel "their own leaders to follow America's moral initiative toward nuclear disarmament."[33] Eventually such an initiative would lead to a Schell-like utopia, free of national distinctions and based on fundamental changes in "the whole psychology of the human race." "Humankind" must "understand that they can't fight anymore," Caldicott declared in articulating her solution to the nuclear arms race.[34]

As Taylor Branch observed in the *New York Times Book Review*, Caldicott fluctuated between such utopian and desperate cries "for a wholesale transformation of human nature" and "a politician's call for the nation to elect women and Democrats in 1984."[35] Yet while she occasionally spoke to the practicalities of electoral politics, there remained in her corpus of discourse virtually no defense of the freeze proposal itself. The oddity of the one public advocate perhaps most identified with the freeze saying virtually nothing about it invites a deeper level of analysis. It takes us back to the roots of the freeze campaign in a set of New Left historical premises that not only warranted Caldicott's calls for unilateral disarmament but defined the narrow boundaries of her public appeal.

## Medicinal History

As Hayden White has written, "there is no such thing as politically innocent historiography."[36] A work of history, as Megill and McCloskey have pointed out, "does not derive chiefly from solitary illumination in the archives." Rather, it is an attempt at persuasion; in other words, "the writing of history is rhetorical." Historians may "resist the notion that their writing is 'rhetorical'"[37]; indeed, as White has suggested, some might consider the notion shocking or even offensive.[38] But that may be because most historians equate the term rhetoric with mere ornamentation or bombast.[39] Recognizing that historiography is always shaped by problems in the present,[40] most historians undoubtedly would agree with Edwin Black: "History is a long, long time. Its raw material is an awesome garbage heap of facts, and even the man who aspires to be nothing more than a simple chronicler still must make decisions about perspective."[41]

Still, some histories are more rhetorical than others, and none have been more rhetorical than the New Left histories of the Vietnam era. Rejecting the ideal of objectivity, New Left historians unabashedly placed their craft in the service of "the Movement." Searching for a useable past and debunking any and all traditional accounts, they claimed a license—indeed, a moral duty—to promote alternative interpretations. As the introduction to David Horowitz's history of the Cold War revealed, the New Left revisionists hardly would have been shocked to hear that historiography might be rhetorical:

> *The Free World Colossus* was written in the winter of 1962-3 . . . . At that time the cold war was still regarded as America's holy crusade to save the world from Communist totalitarianism, and it was not easy to find a publisher in the United States ready to print such a book. The intellectual atmosphere was frigid, both on and off campus, and remained so until the birth of a mass anti-war movement created a new climate in which dissenting theory and analysis could begin to develop with some self-confidence. To the extent that *The Free World Colossus* . . . assisted the growth of this movement by advancing a new understanding of cold war history, I am satisfied that the effort put into research and writing was not wholly in vain.[42]

For many New Left historians, the most important lessons of history involved American foreign policy, and particularly the origins and character of the Cold War. The need to understand Vietnam—its causes and consequences—especially focused attention upon a prolific group of historians associated with William Appleman Williams and the University of Wisconsin—the so-called Wisconsin School of diplomatic history. Often writing in an argumentative rather than a narrative style, the Wisconsin revisionists fundamentally rewrote the entire history of the Cold War era, beginning with the event that started it all: the atomic bombing of Hiroshima and Nagasaki.

Dismissing the official U.S. explanation, Gar Alperovitz issued the most troubling moral indictment of the entire revisionist project: the notion that the United States dropped the atomic bombs on Japan, not to end the war, but to intimidate the Russians. As Alperovitz explained his thesis: "The common belief is that the question is closed, and that President Truman's explanation is correct: 'The dropping of the bombs stopped the war, saved millions of lives.' My own view is that presently available evidence shows the atomic bomb was not needed to end the war or to save lives—and that this was understood by American leaders at the time."[43] Even some fellow revisionists voiced disagreement with Alperovitz's conclusion, insisting that the evidence remained inconclusive.[44] But all the revisionists helped Alperovitz paint a new portrait of the Soviets: the Soviets as victims of U.S. aggression.

Assaulting the prevailing historical consensus, the revisionists wrote of the Soviets' defensive, even conservative policy in the Cold War era, contrasting it with American hysteria over an imaginary Russian plot. They blamed virtually all tension and violence in the post-war world, quite simply, on America's "militant intervention into the affairs of literally every area of the world."[45] America's moralistic rhetoric, they argued, only masked the true motive force behind American foreign policy: the acquisitiveness and greed of the ruling class. "The rhetoric of opposition to [communist] aggression," as Horowitz put it, was a "mere cover for containing internal change" that might threaten America's economic interests in foreign nations.[46]

At the heart of much New Left revisionism was the "Open Door thesis" of William Appleman Williams—the notion that the driving force behind

American foreign policy historically had been the "firm conviction, even dogmatic belief" that "America's *domestic* well-being" depended upon "sustained, ever-increasing overseas economic expansion."[47] This thesis, of course, shaped the economic determinism definitive of the revisionist perspective. As revealed in Gabriel Kolko's *The Roots of American Foreign Policy*, the revisionists could be relentless in their elaboration of the Open Door theme:

> The dominant interest of the United States is in world economic stability, and anything that undermines that condition presents a danger to its present hegemony. . . . In today's context, we should regard United States political and strategic intervention as a rational overhead charge for its present and future freedom to act and expand. One must also point out that however high that cost may appear today, in the history of the United States diplomacy specific American economic interests . . . have often defined the national interest on the assumption that the nation can identify its welfare with the profits of some of its citizens. . . . The costs to the state as a whole are less consequential than the desires and profits of specific class strata and their need to operate everywhere in a manner that, collectively, brings vast prosperity to the United States and its rulers.[48]

Although the revisionist interpretation of the Cold War came under sharp attack within the academy and eventually was subsumed in a "post-revisionist" synthesis,[49] it provided—and continues to provide—a body of unquestioned premises in the rhetoric of the peace movement. It undergirds today's rhetoric of nuclear disarmament no less than it informed the critique of the Vietnam war. If anything, it had become even more firmly entrenched—and even less subject to critical examination—by the early 1980s. And nowhere was that more evident than in the rhetoric of Helen Caldicott.

As a foreigner, Caldicott confessed, she knew little about American history when she first came to this country. But convinced that the past held the key to understanding how we got ourselves "embroiled in this potential nuclear disaster," she "decided to review the history of the United States since its inception."[50] The chief product of that review, a chapter of *Missile Envy* entitled "Case History," did not merely reveal Caldicott's debt to the revisionists. Remarkable for its superficiality, it demonstrated how the Open Door thesis could function in public discourse to simplify and condemn all of America's past.

Beginning with the Declaration of Independence, Caldicott reflected upon the framing of the Constitution, ripped through the entire nineteenth century, and arrived at the birth of the military-industrial complex at the turn of the century—all in just over five pages. For Caldicott, the first hundred years of American history required no more elaborate discussion because one revisionist theme explained all: "the acquisitive, possessive individualism of the capitalist ethic."[51]

Pausing to discuss at greater length the birth of the military-industrial complex, Caldicott recited still more catch phrases of New Left revisionism.

America's rise to military power in the late nineteenth century, she insisted, was driven by the profit motives of steel-company executives, and at this time "the characteristics of the modern military-industrial relationship—political deals, kickbacks, cost overruns, favoritism—began to emerge." In contrast to the proud, spiritually motivated, and increasingly mighty nation one reads about in conventional histories, Caldicott's America "hobbled into the twentieth century with its working class increasingly prey to severe depressions, which are characteristic of totally unfettered capitalism."[52] Dismissing Theodore Roosevelt's rhetoric, she suggested that the Panama Canal was built solely for the purposes of U.S. trade access,[53] and she discerned essentially the same motivations behind Wilson's suppression of rebellions in China, Haiti, and Mexico. Concluding her history of America from its inception to World War II, she explicitly invoked the Open Door thesis, suggesting how economic interests had perverted the Founders' vision:

> The economic and political self-interest of the predominant leaders in the United States succeeded in preventing the kinds of revolutionary changes that had been enshrined as part and parcel of American ideology in the Declaration of Independence!
>
> It seems clear that in its relations with other countries, the United States has pursued an aggressive, often antidemocratic, policy, more intent on *opening the doors* for resource and labor exploitation than on implementing democratic norms and political practices.[54]

Caldicott played fast and loose with the historical details. On occasions, she dismissed contrary evidence outright, as when she deflected the entire thrust of American foreign policy rhetoric in the first half of the twentieth century as a "false rubric of responsibility and goodwill." On other occasions, she simply concluded the opposite of what her own evidence showed. At one point, she recalled how President Wilson proclaimed it "a very perilous thing to determine the foreign policy of a nation in terms of material interest," yet "regardless of these sentiments," Wilson suppressed "popular attempts at revolution" to protect American business interests.[55]

When Caldicott finally reached World War II, she simply ignored Hitler's aggressions and the expansionist designs of the Japanese. Indeed, she ignored the war altogether, save one major event: the day the Americans, for no good reason, dropped the first atomic bomb on the people of Hiroshima. Carefully avoiding any mention of events leading up to the bombing, Caldicott revealed the foundations of her bombing run speech. In clinical detail, she described the aftermath of the bombings:

> People exposed to heat equal to that of the sun . . . were vaporized and left only their shadows on the pavement behind them. Children were seen running along

> the streets with their skin falling off their bodies like veils. A woman lay in the gutter with her back totally burned, and as she died, her baby suckled at her breast. A man stood acutely shocked, holding his eyeball in the palm of his hand. Bodies lay in all areas. Tongues were swollen and protruded from the mouths; eyes were eviscerated by the blast and hung on the cheeks.[56]

Caldicott returned again and again to such "clinical" descriptions, and in *Missile Envy* she even presented photographs of a badly charred Japanese baby and of a "child growing up minus a hand, and very scarred."[57] But Caldicott's goal was never merely to shock or to sicken the reader. Rather, she seemed to suggest, following Alperovitz, that it had all been totally unnecessary. Presenting the "truth" about Truman's motivations, Caldicott dismissed the official explanation as obviously fallacious, for "the Japanese had already opened peace negotiations through the Soviet Union." Furthermore, she transformed a statement by Truman on the eve of the first atomic test—a statement that most took as a reference to the Japanese—into a threat against the Russians: "If it explodes as I think it will, I'll certainly have a hammer on those boys."[58] From this evidence, Caldicott could draw only one conclusion:

> Why were those bombs used? It is said that they saved 500,000 American lives that would otherwise have been lost during the invasion of Japan—obviously a fallacious argument because of the ignored peace proposal. At the same time, Russia, a professed ally which had shouldered an enormous burden during World War II, was being branded as an enemy by the American President. Was [the bomb dropped] because of the incipient hostility toward the Soviet Union held by a few hard-line anti-Communists close to the seat of power and by other influential individuals?[59]

As Caldicott reached the post-war era in her "case history," she outdid even *Pravda* in creatively rewriting history to render Soviet actions legitimate and defensive. Yes, she admitted, the Soviets invaded Afghanistan, but that was a "defensive action in response to an unacceptable challenge to strategic Soviet interests in an area of vital concern." Yes, she admitted, there had been some bloodshed during the Solidarity uprising, but if there had been "less belligerency" on the part of the United States, the Soviet Union would have felt "freer to moderate its tough posture within Poland." Yes, she admitted, the Soviets had made a puppet of Cuba, but Cuba was "literally pushed into the hands of the Soviet Union" by U.S. economic sanctions. In any case, events in Cuba all worked out for the better, for Castro and his communist planners had "performed miracles with their people."[60]

In contrast to the ever-benevolent Soviet Union, Caldicott's post-war America was the "big global bully."[61] Relying heavily upon "madness" metaphors, Caldicott blamed the arms race entirely on America's "passionate hatred and paranoia" toward communism and portrayed the Soviet Union "essentially as the victim of America's craziness."[62] During Truman's presidency, according to Caldicott, Stalin proved to be "a reasonable man, interested in cooperation," but "a faction of old hard-liners in the State Department, who were notoriously pompous, anti-Semitic, tolerant of Hitler, and ultrareactionary, persuaded Truman to adopt a hard-line posture toward the Soviet Union." Subsequently, the "right wing" in American politics became virtually omnipotent, dictating the foreign policy of even the most liberal of presidents. Concluding her historical review with a sympathetic portrait of Jimmy Carter, Caldicott wrote: "He was a good man, but misguided and misled, and not strong enough to avoid being outmaneuvered by the hawks—a handful of hostile men who had gained enormous power in a political vacuum created by the lack of knowledge and widespread apathy of the vast American electorate."[63]

There is little mistaking where Caldicott learned her American history. Not surprisingly, the very first source cited in her historical chapter was William Appleman Williams' *America Confronts a Revolutionary World*.[64] Even more telling were the assumptions and the conclusions of Caldicott's history—all unmistakably the product of New Left revisionism. Caldicott bought wholesale the assumption of economic determinism: that "all men, or at least all capitalists, are motivated primarily by greed and acquisitiveness, and that we can disregard whatever other explanations they may have given for their actions."[65] The plot in her discussion of the Cold War was but a rerun of the revisionists' melodramatic portrayal of the superpower competition—a struggle between the American bullies and the benevolent, defensive Soviet Union. Echoing the revisionists, she proclaimed: "The history is well-chronicled. It is clear that the Soviet-Cuban Communist expansionism is only an excuse for the preordained economic expansionism of the United States of America."[66] Her version of America's use of the atomic bomb was, of course, Gar Alperovitz's controversial thesis presented as obvious truth. And, ultimately, her conclusions about the subsequent nuclear arms race embraced the revisionist view that the United States was entirely to blame.

Taylor Branch has been virtually alone among critics and political commentators in calling attention to Caldicott's "dreadfully simplistic, error-ridden synopsis of American history."[67] Yet perhaps more than anything else, that history shaped Caldicott's solution to the arms race—immediate, complete, and total disarmament by the United States. Suggesting that the peace-loving Russians would gladly disarm if we just asked them nicely, Caldicott metaphorically reduced the arms race to a marital spat, calling upon the United States to "capitulate," render itself "vulnerable," and make "the first move" to "give love."[68] Such was Caldicott's "simple, obvious, and easy" solution,[69] and it was a solution licensed by the revisionist version of Cold War history.

Most Americans, however, learned a different history, and polling data suggest that most continued to embrace those conventional views well into the

1980s. In 1945, the vast majority of Americans supported the atomic bombing of Japan, and in 1982 a large majority (63 percent) still considered the bombing "necessary and proper."[70] Furthermore, Americans continued to reject the revisionists' portrait of a defensive and benevolent Soviet Union. As Everett Carll Ladd has concluded from a review of survey data: "At no time since World War II have Americans shown any confidence that the Soviet Union could be trusted to uphold the spirit and letter of a nuclear arms limitation agreement." In the early 1980s, large majorities of Americans continued to believe in the necessity of a strong nuclear deterrent. Indeed, "large majorities" of Americans "have asserted consistently" since the arms race began that they would be "willing to risk the destruction of the United States rather than be dominated by the Russians."[71]

In a sense, the theory of psychic numbing conceded the marginal status of the revisionist view. Much as New Left revisionists dismissed public attitudes as the product of false consciousness, the rhetoric of political medicine explained away the public's disagreement with a theory of psychological denial. Yet for Caldicott, the problem went much deeper. She considered the American people not merely ignorant or numb about the nuclear threat but fundamentally corrupt. She despised virtually everything about the American people and their culture, and she blamed all Americans for the crimes of their leaders. In short, Caldicott disdained the very people she aspired to persuade, and that fact defined the limits of her appeal.

## "Political Medicine" and the Public

The notion that an ignorant and apathetic public counts for nothing in American politics has long been a staple of New Left revisionism. Challenging both our political mythology and a major premise of most traditional diplomatic histories,[72] the revisionists painted a portrait of a public duped into quiescence by ruling class appeals to "a broader social welfare and erstwhile consensus."[73] In *The Roots of American Foreign Policy*, Gabriel Kolko again articulated the revisionist perspective with startling conviction. The "close and serious student of American foreign relations," Kolko wrote, could "rarely, if ever, find an instance of an important decision made with any reference to the alleged general public desires or opinions." According to Kolko, "the fact that a ruling class makes its policies operate, even when the mass of society ceases to endorse them" was "a central reality most analysts perpetually exclude from a descriptive explanation of American society."[74]

The theory of psychic numbing, of course, rested upon a similar view of the public mind. "Diagnosing" the public's support for America's nuclear deterrent as the product of psychological denial, Caldicott and her imitators not only rationalized the rhetoric of doom but also insulated themselves against ordinary standards of reasoning and evidence. Caldicott's bombing run speech rested upon a host of technical assumptions, yet even her supporters acknowledged that she was "a little casual with the facts." As Harvard physicist Richard Wilson commented: "The people that I trust think she's exaggerating [the effects of nuclear war] by about a factor of five or ten. . . . She's completely stopped a lot of technical people from being able to support her."[75]

Caldicott, however, worried little about the "facts" or "technical people." Calling technical questions trivial and irrelevant,[76] she explained: "I'm a teacher, and you can't give the public a lecture in physics . . . because they'd go to sleep."[77] Even more commonly, she invoked the medical metaphor, comparing her approach to how a doctor might explain disease to a patient—as if doctors routinely lied to their patients about the severity of their illnesses.[78] Attributing all resistance to her views to a mass psychiatric disorder, she considered the American people not merely ignorant or apathetic but "in the grips of a pervasive mental illness."[79] Their "passionate hatred and paranoia" toward communism was a "pathological condition,"[80] and their attitudes toward nuclear war constituted "passive suicide." "When a suicidal patient is seen by a physician," Caldicott concluded in a telling analogy, "that patient is hospitalized because he or she is mentally sick and needs help."[81]

Yet Caldicott had little sympathy for her suicidal patients. Criticizing virtually every aspect of American life, she expressed an all-encompassing disdain for the American people and held them morally responsible for their "illness." One constant theme was how only "lack of knowledge and widespread apathy" could explain why Americans voted the way they did.[82] In *Missile Envy*, she recalled how she was "so perplexed and alarmed" by the "self-righteous, paranoid, warlike sentiments" in response to the Iranian hostage crisis that she just wanted "to run away."[83] Delving still further into the public's "illness," she railed against "hot tubs, Jacuzzis, fancy cars, gourmet foods, fur coats, and fashionable clothes" as evidence of a "hedonistic" and "manic denial" of the nuclear reality. Drawing her favorite historical analogy, she declared America the moral equivalent of Hitler's Germany, where "self-oriented, egocentric, pleasure-seeking activities"—an "atmosphere of manic hedonism"—allowed people to deny the reality of Der Fuehrer's atrocities.[84] In *Nuclear Madness*, she even suggested that Americans might develop a higher moral consciousness by emulating Russians: "Still, most Americans remain strangely silent [about the arms race], as if mesmerized into a feeling of safety and security. I find this self-delusion difficult to understand. . . . I know several people . . . who have recently lived in Russia for a number of years. They report that almost every Russian with whom they have made contact spoke spontaneously of a fear of the imminence of atomic war."[85]

It is difficult to imagine people responding positively to a rhetoric that questioned their intelligence, their mental health, and ultimately their morality. And there is at least anecdotal evidence that listeners occasionally did react to Caldicott, not with the indifference of the numb, but with resentment, even hostility. After witnessing Caldicott speak at his son's graduation at Salem State College, for example, one working-class Bostonian interviewed by Robert Coles released this telling "torrent of outrage" against Caldicott's whole crusade:

> We come there to see our son get a college degree—the first person in our family to get one—and she's there telling us the world is sick, sick. She said it's "terminal," I remember. And she said we're sticking our heads in the sand—she didn't say that, she said something that meant that, that we're all numbed out, I remember. Everyone but her and her friends! How does she know? What gives her the right to think every single person in the hall isn't as worried as she is about a nuclear war? She talks down to you! She's telling us we should be like her in our ideas and what we do, or she'll call us "sick," and the whole earth dying. Then she talked about these kids who think the world is coming to an end soon, because of a nuclear war, and how that's mighty good and smart of them, and if we aren't thinking the same way, we're a bunch of saps! And if we had the god-damned gall to want some other kind of message on the day our kid was getting his diploma, and getting ready to have the first office job of anyone in this family, I'll tell you, then tough luck for us—and aren't we the dopes and the blind fools to expect that, when any day now the nukes will go off and that'll be the end, and here we are, whistling Dixie! . . . Will you tell me who in hell is in favor of those goddamned bombs?[86]

As Coles observed, "this man's rage was not that of someone whose complacency had been abruptly undermined." This was a man who "knew quite well what was happening in the world. He prided himself always on the careful attention he gave to the daily newspaper and to the *CBS Evening News*." He resented being called sick because he blocked the nuclear threat out of his mind and tried to lead a normal life. He suspected that Caldicott and her friends—those obsessed with the remote possibility of nuclear annihilation—were the ones who really were sick. He obviously sensed Caldicott's disdain for ordinary Americans, and Caldicott's scenario of a benevolent Russia following America's "moral initiative" toward disarmament simply did not ring true. As the man explained: "I remember when the Russian tanks went into Hungary. Look at Poland and Afghanistan." He wondered whether Caldicott herself was numb to the suffering of Russians murdered or exiled by their own government.[87]

Helen Caldicott had little to say to this sort of American. Ordinary Americans may not always have noticed when she fudged the facts. But Caldicott's hostility toward American culture could hardly have escaped notice, nor could one have missed her attitude of self-righteous superiority. Helen Caldicott did not address a public whose "consent is requested," providing "knowledge sufficient for informed decisions by those urged to act or suffer the consequences of choices."[88] Rather, she lectured the American people as if they were children, denying their capacity for "knowledgeable choice and active participation."[89]

The rhetoric of political medicine was not a public but an anti-public rhetoric. It was the rhetoric of a privileged elite with serious doubts about the ordinary citizen's capacity for reasoned judgment. Assaulting the emotions, Caldicott and her imitators tried to bully Americans into political deference, and when that did not work they dismissed the public as ignorant, deluded, or even immoral. Americans may not have understood all the technical issues involved in the freeze debate, and they may not have paid close attention. But most probably did recognize the difference between an argument and an insult.

## Notes

1. Helen Caldicott, "A Commitment to Life," *The Humanist*, September/October 1982, 11.
2. Meyer, *A Winter of Discontent*, 128.
3. CBS News, for example, not only repeatedly presented excerpted versions of Caldicott's "bombing run" on the *Evening News*, but also featured Caldicott in a segment of *60 Minutes*. In the *60 Minutes* feature, entitled "The Bomb," CBS recorded Caldicott speaking to an audience in San Francisco. See CBS News, "The Bomb," *60 Minutes*, 9 May 1982, microfiche transcript, 2-8.
4. Tom Ricks, "Dr. Caldicott Goes to War," *Washington Journalism Review* (October 1982): 36.
5. Helen Caldicott, *Nuclear Madness: What You Can Do!* (New York: Bantam, 1980); Caldicott, *Missile Envy*.
6. *If You Love This Planet* (National Film Board of Canada, 1982) was among the three films distributed by the National Film Board of Canada labeled "political propaganda" by the U.S. Department of Justice in February 1983. See McFadden, "3 Canadian Films Called 'Propaganda' by U.S.," C4. For critical commentary on the film, see Grenier, "The Politicized Oscar," 70. Other films featuring Caldicott included *Eight Minutes to Midnight*, Mary Benjamin, 1981; *The Freeze*, Barbara Zheutlin, 1983; *The Last Epidemic*, Impact Productions, 1981; *Dr. Helen Caldicott: Caring for an Endangered Planet*, Original Face Video, 1982; *One Million Hiroshimas*, Michael Anderson Films, 1982; *What About the Russians*, Impact Productions, 1983; and *Women and Power in the Nuclear Age*, High Hopes Media, 1980.
7. Caldicott, *Nuclear Madness*, 73.
8. Helen Caldicott, Introduction, in *The Final Epidemic: Physicians and Scientists on Nuclear War*, edited by Ruth Adams and Susan Cullen (Chicago: Educational Foundation for Nuclear Science, 1981), 1, 3.
9. "Helen Caldicott on Tactics," *Bulletin of the Atomic Scientists* 42 (May 1986): 45.
10. Peter M. Sandman and JoAnn M. Valenti, "Scared Stiff—Or Scared Into Action," *Bulletin of the Atomic Scientists* 42 (January 1986): 12.
11. Robert Coles, "The Freeze: Crusade of the Leisure Class," *Harper's*, March 1985, 21-23. For analyses of other New Class peace campaigns, see Mechling and Mechling, "Hot Pacifism and Cold War," esp. 187-91 and Elizabeth Walker Mechling and Gale Auletta, "Beyond War: A Socio-Rhetorical Analysis of a New Class Revitalization Movement," *Western Journal of Speech Communication* 50 (Fall 1986): 388-404.
12. IPPNW, founded by American cardiologist Bernard Lown and Soviet cardiologist Dr. Evgueni Chazov, won the Nobel Peace Prize in 1985. Not surprisingly, Chazov's official

positions as Kremlin cardiologist and Soviet Minister of Health clouded the award in controversy. Critics called it ironic that a Soviet official who once helped discredit Nobel Prize winner Andrei Sakharov should himself receive the Peace Prize some twelve years later. See Anthony Lewis, "The Neglected Question," *New York Times*, 30 July 1981, A19.

13. See Nuclear Weapons Freeze Campaign, "Prominent Endorsers List."
14. Sandman and Valenti, "Scared Stiff—or Scared Into Action," 12-13.
15. Paul Boyer, "A Historical View of Scare Tactics," *Bulletin of the Atomic Scientists* 42 (January 1986): 19.
16. As James Davison Hunter has observed, the secularist community in America has grown rather dramatically since the 1950s and 1960s, but by 1990 it still constituted only about 11 percent of the population. And not all of that 11 percent share the "progressivist" views of people like Helen Caldicott. While most secularists are drawn to the "progressivist impulse" in American culture, a few (neo-conservative intellectuals, for example) are drawn toward the "orthodox" impulse. See Hunter, *Culture Wars*, 45-46, 75-76.
17. Everett Carll Ladd, "The Freeze Framework," *Public Opinion* 5 (August/September 1982): 20, 41.
18. Talbott, "A Grim Manifesto on Nuclear War," 20.
19. Robert Jay Lifton, "Psychological Effects of the Atomic Bombings," in *Last Aid: The Medical Dimensions of Nuclear War*, edited by Eric Chivian, et al. (San Francisco: W. H. Freeman, 1982), 67. See also Robert Jay Lifton, *Death in Life: Survivors of Hiroshima* (New York: Random House, 1968) and Robert Jay Lifton and Richard Falk, *Indefensible Weapons: The Political and Psychological Case Against Nuclearism* (New York: Basic Books, 1982).
20. Caldicott, *Missile Envy*, 291.
21. John E. Mack, Introduction, in *Last Aid: The Medical Dimensions of Nuclear War*, edited by Eric Chivian, et al. (San Francisco: W. H. Freeman, 1982), 2.
22. Caldicott, *Missile Envy*, 284.
23. Michito Ichimaru, "Nagasaki, August 9, 1945: A Personal Account," in *Last Aid: The Medical Dimensions of Nuclear War*, edited by Eric Chivian, et al. (San Francisco: W. H. Freeman, 1982), 43-44.
24. Caldicott, *Missile Envy*, 283-91.
25. Ibid., 285, 288.
26. Ibid., 290.
27. Bernard Lown, "Physicians and Nuclear War," in *Last Aid: The Medical Dimensions of Nuclear War*, edited by Eric Chivian, et al. (San Francisco: W. H. Freeman, 1982), 9.
28. Peter Kerr, "Physicians Urge End to Arms Race," *New York Times*, 10 June 1984, 17.
29. Caldicott, Introduction, in *The Final Epidemic*, edited by Adams and Cullen, 1, 3.
30. Caldicott, *Missile Envy*, 15-22.
31. Grenier, "The Politicized Oscar," 70.
32. Caldicott, *Missile Envy*, 358.
33. Caldicott, *Nuclear Madness*, 78.
34. Caldicott, "A Commitment to Life," 7.
35. Taylor Branch, Review of *Missile Envy*, by Helen Caldicott, *New York Times Book Review*, 29 July 1984, 13.
36. Hayden White, "Rhetoric and History," in *Theories of History: Papers Read at a Clark Library Seminar, March 6, 1976*, by Hayden White and Frank E. Manuel (Los Angeles: William Andrews Clark Memorial Library, 1978), 24.

37. Allan Megill and Donald N. McCloskey, "The Rhetoric of History," in *The Rhetoric of the Human Sciences: Language and Argument in Scholarship and Public Affairs*, edited by John S. Nelson, Allan Megill, and Donald N. McCloskey (Madison: University of Wisconsin Press, 1987), 221-22.
38. White, "Rhetoric and History," in *Theories of History*, by White and Manuel, 3-4.
39. In his Bancroft Prize-winning history of the Cold War, for example, John Gaddis analyzes Henry Wallace's speech at Madison Square Garden when "stripped of its rhetoric" and concludes that "the rhetoric in Wallace's speech attracted more attention than its substance" (Gaddis, *The United States and the Origins of the Cold War*, 339).
40. Megill and McCloskey, "The Rhetoric of History," in *The Rhetoric of the Human Sciences*, edited by Nelson, Megill, and McCloskey, 221, 223.
41. Edwin Black, "The Second Persona," *Quarterly Journal of Speech* 56 (April 1970): 109-19.
42. David Horowitz, *The Free World Colossus: A Critique of American Foreign Policy in the Cold War*, 2nd ed. (New York: Hill and Wang, 1971), 3, 7.
43. Gar Alperovitz, *Atomic Diplomacy: Hiroshima and Potsdam* (New York: Vintage, 1965), 14.
44. See Gabriel Kolko, *The Politics of War: The World and United States Foreign Policy, 1942-1945* (New York: Random House, 1968), 421-22, 538-43.
45. Kolko, *The Politics of War*, 622.
46. Horowitz, *The Free World Colossus*, 403.
47. William Appleman Williams, *The Tragedy of American Diplomacy*, rev. ed. (New York: Delta Books, 1962), 11.
48. Gabriel Kolko, *The Roots of American Foreign Policy: An Analysis of Power and Purpose* (Boston: Beacon Press, 1969), 55, 84-85.
49. Some critics of the Wisconsin School, such as John Gaddis, insisted that American policy makers "did not accord the Open Door the importance revisionist historians have given it" and argued that the revisionists had "fallen prey to an old methodological fallacy: the single-cause interpretation of history." Others, such as Arthur Schlesinger Jr., went further, proclaiming it time "to blow the whistle" on the revisionists' attempts to blame the United States "for everything that has gone wrong in the world in the last twenty years." Robert Maddox even alleged that the revisionists had doctored the evidence, claiming that all the major books of the Wisconsin School were "based upon pervasive misusages of the source materials." According to Maddox, the "most striking characteristic of revisionist historiography" was "the extent to which New Left authors have revised the evidence itself." Nevertheless, the revisionist interpretation helped shape a new generation of post-revisionist Cold War histories in the 1970s—histories that, as Martin McCauley has observed, avoided "the polarities of blame-it-all-on-the-Soviets or blame-it-all-on-the-Americans." According to McCauley, post-revisionist historians recognized that the Cold War was "so infinitely complex that no generalizations about who was to blame" would suffice, and they tried "to stand back from the battle, avoid blatant partisanship and . . . to pass a cold, critical eye over the 'sins' of all participants." See John L. Gaddis, "A Revisionist Monolith: American Foreign Policy and the Origins of the Cold War," in *Recent American Foreign Policy: Conflicting Interpretations*, 2nd ed., edited by Lawrence S. Kaplan (Homewood, Illinois: Dorsey Press, 1972), 360-61; Arthur M. Schlesinger Jr., Letter to the Editor, *New York Review of Books*, 20 October 1966, 37; Robert J. Maddox, *The New Left and the Origins of the Cold War* (Princeton: Princeton

University Press, 1973), 10-11; Martin McCauley, *The Origins of the Cold War* (New York: Longman, 1983), 14.

50. Caldicott, *Missile Envy*, 44-45.
51. Ibid., 45-50.
52. Ibid., 50-51.
53. Ibid., 52. Roosevelt, of course, disavowed economic motives for building the canal, instead championing the project on strategic and even spiritual grounds—as a project that might inspire the "martial spirit" in the American people. See J. Michael Hogan, *The Panama Canal in American Politics: Domestic Advocacy and the Evolution of Policy* (Carbondale: Southern Illinois University Press, 1986), 19-56.
54. Caldicott, *Missile Envy*, 52 (emphasis added).
55. Ibid., 50, 52-53.
56. Ibid., 57.
57. Ibid., 286-87.
58. As Jonathan Daniels has suggested in his 1950 study of Truman, this statement obviously referred to "the still unconquered Japs," but it could be interpreted as sending at least an implicit warning to the Russians, "with whom he was having difficulty in shaping a collaboration for lasting peace" (Jonathan Daniels, *The Man of Independence* [Philadelphia: J.B. Lippincott Co., 1950], 266).
59. Caldicott, *Missile Envy*, 58.
60. Ibid., 88, 101-3.
61. Ibid., 331.
62. Robert L. Ivie, "Metaphor and the Rhetorical Invention of Cold War 'Idealists,'" *Communication Monographs* 54 (June 1987): 176-78.
63. Caldicott, *Missile Envy*, 64, 83.
64. William Appleman Williams, *America Confronts a Revolutionary World, 1776 to 1976* (New York: William Morrow and Co., 1976).
65. Gaddis, "A Revisionist Monolith," in *Recent American Foreign Policy*, edited by Kaplan, 361.
66. Caldicott, *Missile Envy*, 97.
67. Branch, Review of *Missile Envy*, 13.
68. Caldicott, *Missile Envy*, 314.
69. Caldicott, *Nuclear Madness*, 78.
70. "Americans Assess the Nuclear Option," 33.
71. Ladd, "The Freeze Framework," 41.
72. In 1940, for example, Thomas Bailey treated public opinion as the motive force in American foreign policy, concluding that "the American people, exercising their democratic privilege and enjoying freedom of speech and press, have shaped their own foreign policies." Traditionally, even critics of foreign policies shaped by public opinion, such as Hans Morgenthau and George Kennan, agreed that American policies did in fact reflect public opinion. They argued, as Ernest May observed in 1964, that "this should not be so—that policy should come to a larger extent from calculation by experts." See Thomas A. Bailey, *A Diplomatic History of the American People* (New York: F.S. Crofts, 1940), 756; and Ernest R. May, "An American Tradition: The Role of Public Opinion," in *Theory and Practice in American Politics*, edited by William H. Nelson (Chicago: Phoenix Books, 1967), 102.
73. Joyce Kolko and Gabriel Kolko, *The Limits of Power: The World and United States Foreign Policy, 1945-1954* (New York: Harper and Row, 1972), 333-34.
74. Kolko, *The Roots of American Foreign Policy*, xii-xiii, 13.

75. Ricks, "Dr. Caldicott Goes to War," 38.
76. "Helen Caldicott on Tactics," 45.
77. Ricks, "Dr. Caldicott Goes to War," 38.
78. Ibid., 38.
79. Caldicott, *Missile Envy*, 332.
80. Ibid., 44-45.
81. Ibid., 332.
82. Ibid., 83.
83. Ibid., 45.
84. Ibid., 331.
85. Caldicott, *Nuclear Madness*, 77.
86. Coles, "The Freeze," 21-22.
87. Ibid., 21-22.
88. G. Thomas Goodnight, "Public Discourse," *Critical Studies in Mass Communication* 4 (December 1987): 431.
89. G. Thomas Goodnight, "The Personal, Technical, and Public Spheres of Argument: A Speculative Inquiry in the Art of Public Deliberation," *Journal of the American Forensic Association* 18 (Spring 1982): 215.

## Chapter Four

# The Rhetoric of Nuclear Education

> Radiation sickness is caused by: (a) nuclear fallout, (b) electricity, (c) sitting too close to a radiator, (d) TV.[1]
>
> *Choices: A Unit on Conflict and Nuclear War*

The National Education Association (NEA), with some 1.7 million members, is among "the largest, best organized, and most energetic interest groups in the United States."[2] Through its Congressional Contact Team, its political action committee (NEA-PAC), and various other tools of lobbying and electioneering, the NEA has long been a powerful force on Capitol Hill, and political candidates at all levels covet the group's endorsement.[3] It was of no small significance, then, when the NEA formally endorsed the nuclear freeze campaign in 1982,[4] proclaiming that children had a "right" not "to grow up in the terrifying shadow of a possible nuclear holocaust."[5]

In speeches and essays throughout the early 1980s, the leadership of the NEA insisted that teachers had not only a moral but a professional obligation to become freeze activists. Speaking before the Second Special Session of the U.N. Disarmament Conference in June of 1982, for example, NEA president Willard H. McGuire complained that, in the past, political leaders had "misused the instrument of organized education to shape policies that have led tragically and inexorably to international ill-will, aggression and war." McGuire called it imperative that teachers "not permit the precious instrument of education ever again to become the tool of irrational leaders who would pervert the world's youth into believing that there is nobility in militarism."[6] Meanwhile, the NEA's Executive Director, Terry Herndon, founded Citizens Against Nuclear War (CANW), and provided headquarters for the coalition of some 26 anti-nuclear groups in the NEA offices in Washington.[7] Railing against "redundant weapons" paid for "with dollars stripped from the millions of children served by Head Start or from the millions served by Title I," Herndon echoed McGuire's suggestion that teachers had a professional obligation to protest: "There is something antithetical about choosing to teach and tolerating the perpetual threat of social destruction. . . . Teachers are—they must be—enemies of war."[8]

Labor and professional groups have always been involved in political activities, of course, yet the NEA's role in the nuclear debate went well beyond providing organizational and financial support for the freeze. Ostensibly in its professional capacity, the NEA also spearheaded efforts to bring "nuclear education" to America's classrooms. Not only did the NEA lobby local school boards and even state legislatures to mandate nuclear education,[9] but also it developed, tested, and marketed the most popular curriculum guide for such programs: *Choices: A Unit on Conflict and Nuclear War.*[10] Designed for junior-high-school classes, *Choices* provoked a storm of controversy, not only among educators, but on the national political scene. In obvious reference to the NEA and *Choices*, even President Reagan lashed out at "those who have promoted curriculum guides that seem to be more aimed at frightening and brainwashing American schoolchildren than . . . stimulating balanced, intelligent debate."[11]

Given that more rank-and-file teachers voted for Ronald Reagan than Jimmy Carter in 1980,[12] the NEA's support for the freeze raised an important issue within the educational community: who speaks for America's teachers? Beyond that, it raised broader questions about the politics of American education and about the ethics of public advocacy. Why bring "the bomb" into America's classrooms? And what defines genuinely educational materials and distinguishes such materials from political propaganda? Finally, what are the implications of the schools and the children themselves becoming involved in partisan political debates? Answers to these questions may be found by examining the rationale for nuclear education, the rhetoric of *Choices*, and the role of nuclear education in the larger freeze debate.

## The Rationale for Nuclear Education

At the dawn of the nuclear age, the U.S. government called upon all citizens to enlist in the "army of civil defense" and portrayed knowledge about how to survive as a source of power.[13] Not surprisingly, this thinking extended into the nation's classrooms. Concerned that fears of "the bomb" could jeopardize the emotional health of an entire generation of American young people, educators across the country developed programs designed to provide children with "a sense of security" in an "age of anxiety." Teachers eagerly cooperated with the government in developing such programs, hoping to attract federal dollars and to silence critics who suspected "progressive" educators of "poisoning young minds with communistic ideology."[14]

Proclaiming that children required "a different kind of education for the nuclear age,"[15] professional educators in the 1980s voiced similar concerns. Suggesting that an epidemic of nuclear fears among children had broken out with the election of Ronald Reagan, proponents of "nuclear education" warned that those fears threatened to create a new generation of aimless pessimists. Helen Caldicott, a strong advocate of nuclear education, presented some of the testimony typically offered as proof of this "growing problem" in *Missile Envy:*

> Piper Herman, at Swampscott Junior High School, age twelve, said, her voice trembling, "I just get so scared thinking that tomorrow I might not wake up, and that would just be the end." . . . Catherine Rich, age twelve, from Swampscott, said, "I had nightmares of the bombs slowly floating towards me. I could feel my blood spurting all over the place." . . . Susan Sweeney, age seventeen, said, "As for a career, it seems like it is a waste to go to college and to build up a career and then get blown up someday."[16]

Proponents of nuclear education buttressed such anecdotal evidence with survey data. Educators for Social Responsibility (ESR), a group in the forefront of the freeze campaign, conducted a survey of 2000 students and found that 90 percent believed there would be a nuclear war, and 87 percent did not think they would survive it.[17] Similarly, a survey of 1000 young people in the Boston area (sponsored by the American Psychiatric Association) found, in Caldicott's words, that almost all believed they would "never grow up, never get jobs, never get married or have children of their own" because they would "be killed in a nuclear war."[18]

According to nuclear educators, a sense of powerlessness among children compounded the problem. Lacking sufficient understanding of both nuclear issues and the political system, students did not realize that they would be called upon someday to help decide America's nuclear policies. Thus a second rationale for nuclear education emerged: education for citizenship. Paul Fleisher, a Richmond, Virginia teacher who participated in the testing of *Choices*, acknowledged that the subject of nuclear war could sometimes be "uncomfortable and frightening." But, Fleisher concluded: "Our republic works best when an informed public considers the important issues of the day from all perspectives. . . . Citizens must examine our nation's policies on these issues and make informed choices. As educators, our task is to give students the skills and knowledge that they need to become effective citizens."[19]

Critics doubted from the start that such concerns motivated the nuclear educators. Observing that virtually all of the nuclear curricula had been developed by groups involved in the campaign for a nuclear freeze, many considered such programs, quite simply, political propaganda. Some of the nuclear educators, such as the Jobs with Peace Education Task Force, made very little effort to disguise their political motives. As a political group created specifically to protest against the Reagan administration, Jobs with Peace had no business, save political business, developing educational curricula, and its leftist, anti-Reagan stance emerged forcefully throughout its materials.[20] The NEA, on the other hand, had at least some credibility as a professional group, and it not only claimed curriculum development as a professional function but also insisted that its materials on nuclear war were not politically biased. *Choices*, the NEA argued, was an educational resource, not political propaganda.

The distinction between education and propaganda is very slippery, of course. But the nuclear educators themselves often drew the distinction, contrasting "truly educational" with "pseudo-educational, propagandistic" information on war and peace.[21] The editors of a special edition of *Social Education* devoted to nuclear education elaborated on some of the key differences:

> Indoctrination is the antithesis of education, and, as such, it should be anathema to every teacher. Education has at its heart a free and open exchange of ideas. It avoids the preaching of dogma, and the suppression of conflicting opinions. . . . We need to teach the factual truth about the nuclear world and the consequences of nuclear war.[22]

As one examines the NEA's *Choices*, the rationales and purposes articulated by the nuclear educators themselves provide a framework for raising some essential questions. Was *Choices* really designed to assuage the "numbing paralysis of fear" and the "sense of powerlessness" among children?[23] Was the curriculum balanced and factual, offering not the preaching of dogma but a free and open exchange of ideas and conflicting opinions? In short, did *Choices* aim to educate rather than propagandize? A close reading of the document raises a number of very serious doubts; indeed, it suggests a conscious and deliberate attempt to exploit American schoolchildren for political purposes.

## *Choices:* The Rhetoric of Doom and Political Misinformation

In the 1950s, teaching about nuclear war "domesticated" nuclear capabilities. Saying little about the actual effects of nuclear weapons, the programs treated "the bomb" as just an ordinary (albeit more powerful) weapon. In animated films and comic books distributed to millions of schoolchildren, Bert the Turtle compared surviving a nuclear attack to learning how "to cross streets safely" or "what to do in case of fire." "DUCK to avoid the things flying through the air," Bert cheerily advised, "and COVER to keep from getting cut or even badly burned." "Duck and Cover" epitomized the politics of that era's nuclear education: civil defense was just another precaution—and atomic holocaust just another hazard—of everyday life.[24]

Proponents of nuclear education in the 1980s also professed a desire to lessen children's fears. Yet the NEA's *Choices*, the best-known of the curriculum guides, was a far cry from Bert the Turtle. Indeed, it seemed almost deliberately designed, not to soothe, but to increase fear and pessimism among children. Grounded in the rhetoric of doom, *Choices* seemed to embrace Jonathan Schell's view that nuclear war should be discussed in "human" rather than "statistical" terms. Somehow the NEA concluded that an alleged epidemic of fear among children could best be cured by bombarding children with gruesome scenes of people being vaporized, burned, crushed, melted, irradiated, or otherwise pulverized out of existence by a virtually inevitable nuclear holocaust.

*Choices* opened with Harvard Professor and PSR activist John E. Mack expounding upon this curious logic in a message to teachers. Insisting that "young, and even very young, children" had become increasingly "afraid of dying in a nuclear war," Mack insisted that "the experience of living with the threat of imminent annihilation" had produced "a significantly adverse impact on the emotional lives of young people." Youngsters were therefore grateful for information on these subjects that was "presented in a meaningful and objective manner." Acknowledging that "much of what is contained in this unit is difficult and often unpleasant to contemplate," Mack argued that such materials nonetheless helped "young minds visualize and experience the nuclear reality in a way that is not threatening."[25]

*Choices*' idea of "not threatening" became evident immediately, as Lesson One exposed children, "perhaps for the first time," to "the destructive power of the atomic bomb." Acknowledging in teacher notes that "the unit does not pursue the reasons for targeting populated cities," it emphasized instead the "unbelievable ruin" wrought by the U.S. bombing of Japanese cities, as portrayed in two personal accounts by survivors of the attack. The first described how people near ground zero "literally evaporated and only their shadows remained," and how "others were turned to charred corpses." It detailed how those who survived were badly burned and doomed by the "large black drops" of a radioactive, "deadly rain." It described the "endless line of injured people" marching through the black rain and the burning flames toward the outskirts of the city. The burns made their "skin hang down"; their hands looked like "those of ghosts."[26]

The second narrative detailed the experiences of a 14-year-old Japanese youngster, bringing the horrors closer to home for the junior-high-school classes. Recounting his first impressions upon regaining consciousness, the 14-year-old recalled his frantic effort to find his mother and his 5-year-old sister in the darkness: "Terribly frightened, I thought I was alone in a world of death and groped for any light. My fear was so great I did not think anyone would truly understand. When I came to my senses I found my clothes in shreds. . . . It was quiet, very quiet, an eerie moment. I discovered my mother in a water tank. She had fainted. Crying out, 'Mamma, Mamma,' I shook her to bring her back to her senses. After coming to, my mother began to shout madly for my sister, 'Eiko, Eiko!" Thus the story ended, with no word on the fate of the five-year-old.[27]

The emotional assault peaked in Lesson Four, with a discussion of the much greater destructive power of modern nuclear weapons. The first worksheet of the lesson compared the power of the Hiroshima bomb with modern nuclear weaponry. Today's total nuclear arsenal, it pointed out, had 1,000,000 times more power than the bomb dropped on Hiroshima. ("One million times larger is a lot—it's hard to understand! Can you figure out how many miles long a line will be that is a million times longer than one inch?") It then compared an eight-inch representation of the MX missile with a one-quarter inch version of the Hiroshima bomb. Commenting on the difference the worksheet stated: "One warhead in the new MX missile is about 25 times stronger than the Hiroshima bomb. Each MX missile alone carries ten warheads! . . . Plans now call for 100 MX missiles; how many Hiroshima bombs would that be?" Students then moved on to another worksheet detailing "the long-term effects on those who are not immediately killed by the explosion" in a nuclear attack. The worksheet emphasized how radiation would cause even people living far away from an explosion to "lose their appetite and hair," to become "constantly nauseated," and to "eventually die." They concluded the lesson by contemplating the effects of a one-megaton bomb dropped on their own home town. Students used a compass to draw concentric circles on a map of their city, detailing the proportions of family and friends that would be dead, burned, or blinded at familiar locations.[28]

*Choices* supplemented its grotesque consideration of nuclear effects with a discussion of the "issues" surrounding the decision to drop the bomb. From a "factual account," the children learned that President Truman also had "choices": one group of advisors had argued that a mere demonstration of the weapon, perhaps on an uninhabited island, would induce surrender. But for reasons that remained a mystery to the children, Truman chose to disregard the more humane alternative, preferring instead to use atomic weapons on people for the first time in history.[29]

*Choices'* apocalyptic rhetoric and its interpretation of Truman's decision clearly raised questions of balance, if not of factual accuracy. One wonders, for example, why the unit explicitly sidestepped the reasons for targeting the two cities, why Japan's surprise attack on Pearl Harbor was not even mentioned, or why there were no equally gruesome descriptions of, say, the Bataan Death March. One also might question *Choices'* interpretation of Truman's decision to drop the bomb, with its obvious grounding in the New Left revisionism of Gar Alperovitz and others.[30] It is true, of course, that the United States first used atomic weapons, and *Choices'* interpretation of Truman's decision had at least some intellectual credibility as the product of a popular, albeit controversial, school of academic historiography. But clearly *Choices* failed to provide a balanced treatment of history; it emphasized only the suffering of the Japanese, while it simply ignored the American government's explanation for the bombing.

Other lessons in *Choices* were likewise politically slanted, as they further developed the theme that the United States was the major villain in the nuclear arms race. In one lesson, *Choices* treated the arms race as essentially a technological rather than a political phenomenon, and it graphically illustrated how the United States had been responsible for nine of twelve technological "firsts." This lesson not only laid historical blame for the arms race almost entirely upon the United States, but also it implied the utter futility of any new weapons development and suggested that the arms race would end if the United States simply stopped developing new weapons. Still another lesson emphasized that the Soviet Union, but not the United States, was bordered by "unfriendly countries," and that Russia had lost about 31 million people in war compared to only 1 million for the United States. The suggestion, of course, was that Russia was more understandably militarized; its policies were more defensive in nature and justified by its history.[31]

Critics of nuclear education pointed out that *Choices* made "no reference to the ideology of Marxism-Leninism, to the brutal Soviet regime, or to the Soviet Union's imperial expansion since 1945."[32] Barry Goldwater complained that the unit failed even to "mention the numerous acts of Soviet aggression on its own people and neighboring countries."[33] While emphasizing America's technological superiority, *Choices* also neglected to point out that the United States "neither struck nor threatened to strike" even when it enjoyed a nuclear monopoly.[34] None of these criticisms challenged the truth of *Choices'* historical claims (the Soviets indeed lost more men in war, and the United States did in fact pioneer most nuclear technology). But again, the critics were right to question the balance of *Choices.* Even the orthodoxy of the liberal establishment assigns at least some blame to the Soviets for escalating the arms race.

*Choices'* lesson on American budget priorities raised more serious questions, as the factual errors were so grievous as to suggest deliberate misinformation. Developing the argument that money for defense deprived Americans of domestic services, *Choices* contained a game on budget priorities in which the students first divided 20 tokens by priorities such as health care, parks, schools, roads, police, and the military. They then contemplated the fact that the actual budget of the United States distributed, in effect, nine of the twenty tokens to the military, leaving only one for social needs (education, food, jobs, and social services), two for health (medical research and programs for the elderly, handicapped, and poor), one for science and politics, and so on.[35] The outcome was predictable, of course, with students undoubtedly shocked at how many tokens piled up for the military.

Simple arithmetic reveals that *Choices'* budget game attributed 45 percent of the budget—nine of twenty tokens—to the military. This, of course, was simply not true. Defense spending during the 1980s consistently ran between 26 and 29 percent of the federal budget. One might add that *Choices* said nothing about Soviet military spending. The fact that the Soviets spent about 14 percent of their GNP on the military, compared to less than 7 percent for the United States, certainly would have put the matter in a much different light.[36] Also, *Choices* presented national defense as a monolithic category, while categories of domestic spending were divided into more specific sub-categories (social needs, for instance, was divided into education, food and nutrition, job training, and social services). This masked two important facts: that a large portion of the national defense category was comprised, not of weapons procurement, but of personnel costs and retirement pay, and that strategic nuclear forces typically accounted for less than 20 percent of the defense budget.[37] Finally, *Choices* encouraged students to think that federal military spending was at the expense of such vital domestic needs as public schools, police, and firefighters. The truth, of course, is that funding for police and firefighters comes almost entirely from local sources, and public schools receive more than 90 percent of their funding from state and local revenues.[38]

*Choices'* lesson on the balance of nuclear forces also was blatantly misleading and constituted, in effect, an endorsement of the nuclear freeze. Totally ignoring the controversy over the matter at the heart of the freeze debate, *Choices* presented the "fact" that the United States was far ahead of the Soviets in total nuclear forces: the U.S. had 9,500 warheads, a worksheet in Lesson Seven noted, while the Soviets had but 7,500. The worksheet also included maps of the two countries showing missile-submarine bases, major airfields, missile-launching sites, and missile-testing centers. In completing the worksheet, students were asked to compare the two countries in terms of major airfields and missile-launching sites. In doing so they discovered again that the United States had a significant advantage: U.S. airfields outnumbered Soviet airfields 44 to 21, while U.S. missile-launching sites outnumbered those of the Soviets by 10 to 5.[39]

The lesson comparing maps of the two countries displayed the most obvious bias in *Choices'* materials on the nuclear balance. Aside from the fact that the number of bases or launching sites really says nothing about nuclear capabilities, students were asked to compare only airfields and missile-launching sites—areas in which the United States had an advantage—while nothing was said about missile-submarine bases or missile-testing centers. The maps showed the Soviets enjoying a 3-2 advantage in the former and a 4-2 advantage in the latter.

A more subtle but much more significant problem was that *Choices* employed only the number of warheads as the measure of total nuclear capabilities. Yet as the Harvard Study Group on Nuclear Weapons has pointed out, it is totally meaningless to compare the numbers of nuclear weapons without considering their characteristics: their accuracy, their vulnerability, their destructive power, and the like.[40] The Soviets, for instance, packed more than twice as much destructive force (7,868 to 3,505 megatons) in their numerically smaller arsenal.[41]

Measuring "who's ahead" in the arms race is an extremely complicated business, of course, and a junior-high-school curriculum could not have been expected to resolve all the controversies. But if *Choices* had been truly designed to educate, one would have expected to find at least some acknowledgment that the matter was controversial. The President, the Secretary of Defense, and a host of defense experts obviously did not consider it a fact that the United States was far ahead of the Soviets in the early 1980s. No wonder that Barry Goldwater was "outraged to read that the highly debatable question on nuclear superiority" had been "resolved" by *Choices.*[42] Even the *Washington Post,* while supporting the freeze editorially, chastised the NEA for its blatantly biased treatment of the nuclear balance: "The materials show us far ahead of the Russians. The matter is surely debatable, but arguments to the contrary are buried in a reprinted article in the appendix."[43]

By misinforming students about the issues in the nuclear debate, the NEA raised serious doubts that it aimed to educate children for responsible citizenship. Those doubts grew when one considered *Choices'* civic lessons, or its message about politicians and the political system. In Lesson Eight, children were taught how to recognize propaganda—"opinion in the form of fact"—in the nuclear debate. As the first exercise in a worksheet for the lesson, the students critiqued a newspaper report of President Reagan's televised "dense pack" speech in November 1982. Another exercise attributed a fictitious statement on law-and-order, first to President Kennedy, then to Adolf Hitler. The intent of the lesson was unmistakable: to teach children that even the President of the United States might make propagandistic statements and that they should "evaluate the meaning of something apart from who said it."[44]

*Choices*' final two lessons followed logically from these lessons. Celebrating dreams of political utopia and anti-establishment political activism, they incited kids to reject and rebel against the corrupt political world of their parents. "The wild dream is the first step to reality," Lesson Nine proclaimed, before recommending songs that might "encourage creativity." *Choices* first recommended John Lennon's "Imagine"—a controversial attack on religion and patriotism as the chief causes of war. *Choices* also recommended Pete Seeger's "Ain't Gonna Study War No More"—a pacifist anthem calling for the total abolition of the military. Moving from utopian visions to political activism, Lesson Ten suggested such activities as investigating the role the military plays in the community: "Are weapons produced at a local plant? Is research and development in progress at a local university? Are weapons stored at a nearby base?"[45] *Choices* stopped short of stirring the children to storm the fences of the local weapons depot. But at schools with nuclear education, as Ronald Alsop reported, students formed "nuclear-awareness clubs" and staged "rallies reminiscent of Vietnam era activism."[46]

Deputy Undersecretary of Education, Gary L. Bauer, called *Choices* "leftist indoctrination aimed at turning today's elementary students into tomorrow's campus radicals."[47] Yet even this view seemed a bit naive, for the NEA was not content to wait for the next generation to embrace its political agenda. The NEA had a much more immediate goal: to enlist the emotional and moral force of children in the campaign for a nuclear freeze. *Choices* did not prepare children for political activism. It suggested that children protest now by organizing rallies in their community, exploiting local media, raising money for "an organization . . . that the class wants to support," or gathering signatures to place a freeze referendum on the local ballot. A story invoked at the outset and again at the conclusion of the unit, "The Hundredth Monkey," communicated the essence of this message. In the story, the elder monkeys ignored a "social improvement" (washing potatoes before eating them) discovered by their children until the hundredth youngster achieved the "new awareness." The lesson? When "only a limited number of people know of a new way, it may remain in the minds of only these people. But there is a point at which if only one more person tunes in to a new awareness, the idea is strengthened so that it reaches almost everyone!" The story concluded: "Your awareness is needed in preventing nuclear war. You may be the 'Hundredth Monkey.'"[48]

*Choices* encouraged teachers to consult outside readings, but it recommended only those readings, audiovisual materials, and political organizations that echoed its message. Almost all of the dozens of resources cited for further study were "intricately bound up with the peace movement."[49] Of fifteen audiovisual resources, only two (both films by the American Security Council) could be called pro-defense. The literature of the peace movement also dominated the list of thirty books and articles in *Choices*, with only three "hawkish" works listed. Of the thirty-three organizations listed in *Choices*, twenty-five could be found in the national directory of the peace movement, the *American Peace Directory*,[50] and five or so others probably should have been included. It is little wonder that teachers who used *Choices* often displayed an almost unbelievable ignorance of the issues and varying perspectives of the nuclear debate. One teacher who tested the unit reportedly contended that the materials were "justifiably biased in favor of a nuclear freeze" because "nuclear war is wrong."[51]

Perhaps more disconcerting than the content of *Choices* itself was the NEA's response to criticism of the curriculum. Calling *Choices* a "conservative document" and a "piece of Americana," the NEA's Sharon Robinson insisted that it was "ideologically neutral." "To those who suggest that *Choices* is propagandistic," Robinson responded, "we would ask only that they read the document"[52]—as if none of the critics had bothered. Other NEA officials responded in propagandistic fashion themselves, deflecting substantive criticism with arguments *ad hominem*, reverse red-baiting, scapegoating, and allegations of conspiracy. When American Federation of Teachers President Albert Shanker criticized the NEA's involvement in the nuclear freeze movement, the NEA's Gary Watts responded that "Shanker is well-known as one of the country's most hawkish union leaders" and accused him of "right-wing, McCarthy-like tactics."[53] The NEA's Bob McClure found *Human Events* a useful scapegoat, accusing the "reactionary right wing newspaper" of instigating a "concerted effort of the far right to get *Choices*." Proclaiming it the policy of the NEA to "react with fact," McClure proved otherwise by dismissing all the critics as proponents of propaganda to "indoctrinate young people."[54]

It was troubling enough that the nation's largest organization of professional educators sensed some logic in trying to calm the fears of young people by assaulting their senses with grotesque scenes of atomic death and destruction. It was even more troubling that they misinformed children about the issues, and that they taught them to reject the politics of their parents and to celebrate utopian and anti-establishment political views. But perhaps most troubling of all is the possibility that the NEA's leaders really could not understand all the furor.

Contrary to the NEA's conspiracy theory, the "far right" was not alone in condemning *Choices*. Some of the harshest criticism came from the *Washington Post*, which editorially concluded: "This is not teaching in any normally accepted—or, for that matter, acceptable—sense. It is political indoctrination."[55] It is true that Barry Goldwater and other conservatives were in the forefront of opposition to nuclear education. But one did not need to be conservative to agree with Goldwater that if *Choices* were "truly an educational tool, it would present both sides of the case giving equal weight to each viewpoint."[56]

## Nuclear Education and the Freeze Debate

Not all mental health experts and educators agreed with those experts who "gravely" reported that kids had suddenly become terrified of nuclear war and that this fear was "ruining their lives."[57] In 1985, Harvard child psychiatrist Robert Coles wrote that "in years of work with children and youth all over this country . . . I have not met the children Dr. Caldicott and others described."[58] Joseph Adelson and Chester E. Finn Jr. also considered the problem exaggerated, calling the research on children's nuclear fears "amateurish." Most of the evidence consisted of "anecdotes rather than data," they argued, and the surveys were "essentially worthless."[59]

Even assuming that some kids had become troubled by visions of the holocaust, there remained the question of who was to blame. Advocates of nuclear education, of course, were quick to blame Reagan's arms build-up for traumatizing the children. Helen Caldicott argued that kids just had "to listen to President Reagan make a speech renaming the MX missile 'the Peacekeeper' to realize they [were] living in an insane world."[60] A much more believable hypothesis, however, is that children picked up such fears from their parents and teachers. "Again and again," Coles argued, "I find that the children who have taken this issue to heart are from well-off families whose parents are themselves involved in the nuclear freeze movement."[61] And both the children's testimony and the survey research cited by the nuclear educators pointed to their own programs as the most likely source of such fears.

As the kids spoke of Hiroshima and the "human effects" of the bomb, or when they claimed to "feel sorry for the Russians,"[62] it seemed clear that they learned more from nuclear education than from Ronald Reagan. Similarly, survey research showed that kids had little confidence in what the President, military leaders, or even the clergy told them on this subject. The data showed kids to be more likely than their parents to be sympathetic toward the Soviets, to favor more radical measures like unilateral disarmament, and to reject the argument that America's deterrent must be strengthened.[63] Again, these hardly seem like attitudes developed spontaneously while watching the President on television.

Advocates of the freeze had strong political motives for frightening children. Talk of traumatized children proved a useful tool for recruiting concerned parents. Listening to the "experts" of the freeze campaign, parents learned that their kids could be "tremendously reassured" by their political activism. Freeze advocates were fond of telling the story of a teacher who discovered only one child in her class unafraid of nuclear war. When asked why he was not scared, the little boy replied: "Because my daddy is out every night trying to prevent it."[64]

Most significantly, freeze advocates convinced many parents that involving the children themselves in protest could be effective therapy. As a result, the freeze campaign gained a potent political weapon: the media spectacle of innocent children crying out against the Reagan arms build-up. Focusing upon the prominent role of children in demonstrations staged by the nuclear freeze campaign, reporters provided positive, even celebratory coverage. In reports from the freeze rally in New York on 12 June 1982, even the staid *New York Times* gushed about the children. "If there was one single symbol of [the freeze rally]," Anna Quindlen reported, "it was a small child. There were hundreds, perhaps thousands of them . . . a testimonial to the oft-stated belief that marching for an end to the nuclear arms race meant marching for a future for future generations."[65] Never mind that children, as a rule, do not attend political demonstrations of their own accord. In the *Times*' coverage we witnessed children leading the march and serving up quotable profundities. "This is very important," nine-year-old Gregory Barger reportedly said of his first demonstration. "If there is a nuclear war, a lot of us children will die, and some of us could be very important to the future of America."[66]

Other parents encouraged their children to join such groups as the Children's Campaign for Nuclear Disarmament (CCND). Inspired by Helen Caldicott, the CCND was best known for organizing a letter-writing campaign, traveling to Washington, and reading thousands of anti-Reagan letters in front of the White House. One typically angry child asked the President: "Who will cry for me when I am dead from your pro-war actions?" Another echoed *Choices*' lesson on budget priorities: "How can you say you're for peace when most of our economy is going towards the military."[67] At one point, schoolchildren were sending more than 100 such letters a day to the White House.[68]

Some children were even dragged before congressional committees to testify about their nuclear neuroses and the need for a freeze. "I think about the bomb just about every day now," a sixteen-year-old girl told the House Select Committee on Children, Youth, and Families at hearings in September 1983. "It's hard to live with the possibility that we might not ever get a chance to grow up." At the same hearings, twelve-year-old Gerald Orjuela lectured the committee about Hiroshima: "Parts of people literally melted under the blast. A bone was sticking out from the socket where there once was an arm. The shadows of people left imprinted on the floors and walls when the heat flash vaporized them. Pitiful piles of entrails that were once known as human beings." The presumably unrehearsed youngster mocked the President's rhetoric ("Is it right to call a nuclear missile 'peace keeper'?") before concluding that America was "criminalizing Newton, Dalton, Einstein, Lucretius, and Democritus, great pioneers in the Atom." That left it for eleven-year-old Jessica Fiedler to instruct the committee on the policy needed to save the children: "I think we should put a freeze on nuclear weapons."[69]

Perhaps some children indeed became frightened by the prospects of nuclear war in the early 1980s. Perhaps nuclear education of some sort might have proven beneficial. But how were children reassured by contemplating how people melted at Hiroshima, by memorizing half-truths and falsehoods about the issues of the nuclear debate, or by learning that their political system held no hope of a solution? How were children soothed by the sort of shock treatment Alsop witnessed in a "nuclear classroom" in New Jersey? "A six foot bomb was assembled from papier mache and chicken wire, air raid sirens were sounded and students screamed and writhed on the ground as they pretended to be blinded or killed by the fiery blast."[70]

The NEA's *Choices* clearly failed to serve the rationale offered for nuclear education, and by the nuclear educators' own definitions, it could be considered propagandistic. The teachers who promoted such curricula were either well aware that they were politicizing American education, or (perhaps worse) they were incapable of understanding why people might object to such programs.[71] Whatever the explanation, the whole controversy over nuclear education gave new meaning to "a nation at risk." Considering nuclear education, as Adam Garfinkle suggested, a parent could not be faulted for wondering whether a public school was "still a safe place to send a child."[72]

## Notes

1. Union of Concerned Scientists, Massachusetts Teachers Association, and the National Education Association, *Choices: A Unit on Conflict and Nuclear War* (Washington: National Education Association, 1983), 52. Hereafter cited as *Choices*.
2. Chester E. Finn Jr., "Teacher Politics," *Commentary*, February 1983, 29.
3. The NEA describes its Congressional Contact Team as a grassroots network that "maintains continuous liaison with individual Senators and Representatives" while lobbying for a Legislative Program established by the NEA's annual Representative Assembly. The Legislative Program also forms the basis of a NEA-PAC candidate questionnaire, which helps to determine the candidates NEA-PAC will support. In the 1982-83 Annual of *Today's Education*, Willard McGuire, president of NEA, reflected upon the NEA's "immersion in the tooth-and-claw realities of partisan politics" and declared the efforts successful. Of 1,413 candidates supported by NEA-PAC since 1972, McGuire observed, 78 percent had won, and McGuire deemed NEA lobbying pivotal in such legislation as the 1976 extension of the Voting Rights Act and the 1979 act creating the Department of Education. In presidential politics, as Theodore White has observed, teachers also became a major force in the 1970s—"far and away" the

most organized of the special interest groups within the Democratic Party. At the 1980 Democratic National Convention, the NEA sent 464 pro-Carter delegates—up from 265 in 1976. The Carter delegation, quipped Senator Daniel Patrick Moynihan, had become "a wholly-owned subsidiary of the NEA." See the National Education Association, *The NEA Legislative Program for the 99th Congress* (Washington, D.C.: NEA Government Relations, 1985), 2-4; Willard McGuire, "Why We Fight," *Today's Education* (1982-83 Annual): 119-20; and Theodore White, *America in Search of Itself: The Making of the President, 1956-1980* (New York: Warner Books, 1982), 333-34.

4. See *Today's Education* (1982-83 Annual): 182, 186.
5. National Education Association, *To Speak of Peace*, brochure distributed by the NEA, Washington, D.C., n.d.
6. Quoted in National Education Association, *To Speak of Peace*.
7. "26 Groups Join in Campaign for Arms Freeze," *New York Times*, 17 October 1982, 44.
8. Terry Herndon, "A Teacher Speaks of Peace," *Phi Delta Kappan* 64 (April 1983): 529, 531-32.
9. Larry Dieringer, "The Challenge of Legislation and School Board Resolutions," [Educators for Social Responsibility] *Forum*, Fall 1985, 1-2, 4; Ronald Alsop, "'A' is for Atom: Nuclear War Becomes Hot Topic in Schools, Stirs Up Controversy," *Wall Street Journal*, 24 May 1983, 1, 22.
10. *Choices* was field-tested by 47 teachers in 34 states, and it was first published in March 1983. By June of the following year, it already had gone into its fifth printing. See *Choices*, 2, 5.
11. Eloise Salholz, with Mary Lord and Dianne H. McDonald, "Teaching About Nuclear War," *Newsweek*, 18 July 1983, 78.
12. Finn, "Teacher Politics," 29.
13. See Elizabeth Walker Mechling and Jay Mechling, "The Campaign for Civil Defense and the Struggle to Naturalize the Bomb," *Western Journal of Speech Communication* 55 (Spring 1991): esp. 112-13.
14. See JoAnne Brown, "'A Is For Atom, B Is for Bomb': Civil Defense in American Public Education, 1948-1963," *Journal of American History* 75 (June 1988): 68-90.
15. Tony Wagner, "Educating for Responsibility in a Nuclear Age," *Media and Methods*, 20 (November 1983): 24.
16. Caldicott, *Missile Envy*, 334-35.
17. Mary McCory, "Administration Fires Back With Its Own Schoolbook on A-War," *Washington Post*, 9 June 1983, A3.
18. Helen Caldicott, "Growing Up Afraid: The 37th Summer of the Bomb," *Family Weekly*, 8 August 1982, 4.
19. Paul Fleisher, "Teaching Children About Nuclear War," *Phi Delta Kappan* 67 (November 1985): 216.
20. Jobs With Peace Education Task Force, *Crossroads: Quality of Life in a Nuclear Age* (Boston: Jobs with Peace Education Task Force, 1982).
21. Douglas Sloan, "Preface: Toward an Education for a Living World," in *Education for Peace and Disarmament: Toward a Living World*, edited by Douglas Sloan (New York: Teachers College Press, 1983), 9.
22. Betty Reardon, John Anthony Scott, and Sam Totten, "Nuclear Weapons: Concepts, Issues, and Controversies," *Social Education* 47 (November/December 1983): 473.
23. Ibid., 474.
24. Brown, "'A Is For Atom, B Is for Bomb,'" 80-87.

25. *Choices*, 4.
26. Ibid., 11, 14-16.
27. Ibid., 16.
28. Ibid., 34, 37-39.
29. Ibid., 15.
30. See J. Michael Hogan, "The Rhetoric of Historiography: New Left Revisionism in the Vietnam Era," in *Argument and Social Practice: Proceedings of the Fourth SCA/AFA Conference on Argumentation*," edited by J. Robert Cox, Malcom O. Sillars, and Gregg B. Walker (Annandale, Virginia: Speech Communication Association, 1985), 345.
31. *Choices*, 15, 44, 47, 64-65.
32. Ernest W. Lefever, "Teaching History and Politics in the Age of Nuclear Arms," *Phi Delta Kappan* 67 (November 1985): 217.
33. Barry Goldwater, "NEA's Nuclear 'Choices,'" *Washington Post*, 18 June 1983, A20.
34. Ernest W. Lefever and E. Stephen Hunt, "Education, Propaganda, and Nuclear Arms," *Phi Delta Kappan* 64 (June 1983): 728.
35. *Choices*, 58-59.
36. U.S. Department of Commerce, *Statistical Abstract of the United States, 1986* (Washington: Department of Commerce, 1985), 331, 336.
37. Garfinkle, *The Politics of the Nuclear Freeze*, 106.
38. Gene I. Maeroff, "Curriculum Addresses Fear of Atom War," *New York Times*, 29 March 1983, C4.
39. *Choices*, 64-66.
40. Carnesale, et al., *Living With Nuclear Weapons*, 115-26.
41. Strobe Talbott, "Living with Mega-Death," *Time*, 29 March 1982, 19, 22.
42. Goldwater, "NEA's Nuclear 'Choices,'" A20.
43. "Political Teaching," *Washington Post*, 5 April 1983, A14.
44. *Choices*, 72-73, 76.
45. Ibid., 79-80, 84.
46. Alsop, "'A' is for Atom," 1.
47. David Hoffman, "NEA Criticized for Curriculum on Nuclear War," *Washington Post*, 8 June 1983, A10.
48. *Choices*, 20, 82-84.
49. Maeroff, "Curriculum Addresses Fear of Atom War," C4.
50. *American Peace Directory, 1984*, edited by Fine and Steven, 10-42.
51. "Political Teaching," A14.
52. Sharon Robinson, "Of History, Peace, and Choices," *Social Education* 47 (November/December 1983): 487-88.
53. Harry Bernstein, "Teacher Unions Swing Right and Left in Battle," *Los Angeles Times*, 11 July 1983, section 4, page 1.
54. Bob McClure, Telephone interview with David Olsen, 24 April 1986.
55. "Political Teaching," A14.
56. Goldwater, "NEA's Nuclear 'Choices,'" A20.
57. Charles Krauthammer, "Kid's Stuff," *New Republic*, 13 February 1984, 10-11.
58. Coles, "The Freeze," 22.
59. Joseph Adelson and Chester E. Finn, "Terrorizing Children," *Commentary*, April 1985, 29-30.
60. Caldicott, *Missile Envy*, 334.
61. Robert Coles, "Children and the Bomb," *New York Times Magazine*, 8 December 1985, 61.

62. Caldicott, *Missile Envy*, 334-35.
63. Barry Sussman, "Young People in Area Fear a Nuclear War," *Washington Post*, 19 February 1984, A1, A16-A17.
64. Marcia Yudkin, "When Kids Think the Unthinkable," *Psychology Today*, April 1984, 25.
65. Anna Quindlen, "About New York," *New York Times*, 13 June 1982, 43.
66. Robert D. McFadden, "A Spectrum of Humanity Represented in the Rally," *New York Times*, 13 June 1982, 42.
67. Marcia Yudkin, "Young Activists," *Psychology Today*, April 1984, 24-25.
68. Nicholas Hentoff, "Student Letters to Reagan on War Stir Their Own Tempest in Senate," *Wall Street Journal*, 14 September 1983, 30.
69. U.S. Congress, House, Select Committee on Children, Youth, and Families, *Children's Fears of Nuclear War*, 98th Cong., 1st sess., 20 September 1984, 21-26.
70. Alsop, "'A' is for Atom," 24.
71. Supporters of nuclear education typically portray attempts to establish such programs as courageous crusades against spineless administrators and ignorant parents who "do not wish nuclear issues to be raised in any form, and view discussion as the stuff of rebellion, subversion, even treason" (Paul Rogat Loeb, *Hope in Hard Times: America's Peace Movement in the Reagan Era* [Lexington, Massachusetts: Lexington Books, 1987], 131).
72. Garfinkle, *The Politics of the Nuclear Freeze*, 32.

# Part II

# The Freeze Campaign and Institutional Politics

MacDonald Photography/THE PICTURE CUBE

## CHAPTER FIVE

# MANAGING DISSENT IN THE CATHOLIC CHURCH

> We are called to be peacemakers, not by some movement of the moment, but by our Lord Jesus.[1]
>
> *The Challenge of Peace*

The American Catholic bishops, speaking in their corporate voice as the National Conference of Catholic Bishops (NCCB), would seem the quintessential "establishment"—the voice of an ancient and conservative religious institution. In the early 1980s, however, they suddenly found themselves in the middle of the freeze debate, designated by some observers as leaders of the new anti-nuclear movement. Steve Goldzwig and George Cheney have even used the word revolutionary to describe the *Pastoral Letter on War and Peace* approved by the bishops in 1983. According to Goldzwig and Cheney, the *Pastoral Letter on War and Peace* "implicitly linked Catholic moral teaching to the arguments of the international peace movement, a process involving sharp criticism of the Reagan Administration's arms policies."[2]

Clearly, it is problematic to treat the American Catholic bishops—members of a notoriously conservative institutional hierarchy—as leaders of a revolutionary social movement. The *Pastoral Letter on War and Peace* did echo some of the language of the freeze campaign, repeating its call for a halt to the testing, production, and deployment of new nuclear weapons. Indeed, it employed the exact same language as the freeze campaign's clarion call: Randall Forsberg's *Call to Halt the Nuclear Arms Race*.[3] At the same time, however, the pastoral letter also dissociated the bishops' efforts from secular peace movements, and it said little with which conservative Catholics or even the Reagan administration could not agree. The American Catholic bishops never intended, nor did they write, a manifesto of the nuclear freeze campaign.

The *Pastoral Letter on War and Peace* represented a genuinely collective statement by the Catholic bishops, forged by committee over a two year period in three successive drafts, and ultimately amended further by the entire conference of bishops in May of 1983. It was the product both of negotiations and compromise within the drafting committee and of an ongoing dialogue with various audiences inside and outside the Church. As Goldzwig and Cheney have suggested, such a process may have been unusual within a church accustomed to doctrinal pronouncement. But that hardly made it revolutionary. To the contrary, it was typical of how institutions manage internal political dissent, and it virtually guaranteed a politically moderate pastoral letter.

The text of the *Pastoral Letter on War and Peace* already has been scrutinized in thousands of pages of published commentary, and stripped of its institutional context it may be read as a radical statement. However, a full understanding of the letter dictates analysis, not just of the final text, but also of the debate that gave rise to the letter and shaped its evolution. From such a perspective, the *Pastoral Letter on War and Peace* is best seen as an attempt not to promote but to diffuse a radical Catholic challenge to American defense policy. Growing out of an atmosphere of escalating anti-nuclear activism by the Catholic New Left, the letter reclaimed for the bishops the right to define Church teachings on war and peace, and it reflected the wide diversity of views within the Catholic community on the moral, political, and technical issues of the nuclear debate. The letter may have been claimed by anti-nuclear activists within the Church, and many journalists may have been persuaded by that claim. But both the pastoral letter and the process by which it was constructed actually served to correct the Catholic New Left and to announce that the Catholic Church remained squarely in the mainstream of American political thought. The *Pastoral Letter on War and Peace* functioned rhetorically not to foster but to manage dissent.

## The Catholic New Left and Nuclear Weapons

As leaders of a immigrant Church, American Catholic bishops historically have "plunged headfirst into symbolic and emotional bursts of American patriotism."[4] The Catholic Church, perhaps more than any other, has been supportive, "almost jingoistic in [its] endorsements of U.S. foreign policy."[5] During World War II, Eric Goldman has observed, "a good part of the American [Catholic] hierarchy was sharply anti-Soviet," and "aspirations for unchallengeable Americanism" led some Catholics to play major roles in the communist witch hunts of the 1950s.[6] In the 1960s, the American Catholic Church was among the last to question America's role in Vietnam. As late as November 1966 the Catholic bishops went on record proclaiming the American presence in Vietnam justified,[7] and not until 1971 did the bishops embrace the view that the costs of the war had come to outweigh its benefits.[8]

Not all Catholics agreed with their official leadership about the Vietnam War. While the established Church remained notably conservative, a Catholic resistance movement, led by the Berrigan brothers and others, challenged not only American foreign policy but also the right of the established Church to define the Catholic conscience.[9] After the war, the Catholic New Left increasingly embraced the broader agenda of political and liberation theology. Envisioning a Church with a primarily political mission, Catholic New Leftists entered the 1980s celebrating a deprivatized theology, emphasizing not personal salvation but the social and political agenda of secular liberation movements.[10]

By the early 1980s, the growing influence of New Left politics could be seen in Catholic educational institutions and in the Catholic media. A Roper survey of religious educators in 1982 revealed that nearly half (46 percent) of the professors in Catholic seminaries and schools of religion agreed or strongly agreed that "the U.S. would be better off if it moved toward socialism," and 54 percent even went so far as to profess that a "good Catholic" could not endorse laissez-faire capitalism. On foreign and military affairs, 82 percent of the Catholic teachers favored reductions in military spending, and 57 percent deemed "repressive regimes aligned with the United States" a "greater problem in the world today" than "Communist expansion."[11]

Meanwhile, such widely read publications as the *National Catholic Reporter* began editorializing in tones once reserved for *The Catholic Worker*, calling for unilateral disarmament and romanticizing the Berrigans and others for their defiant protests.[12] Even the comparatively moderate *Commonweal*, while concerned that Catholic support for unilateral disarmament might have deleterious effects both "on the church's place in American society and on the peacemaking process," praised the "compelling moral arguments" behind the idea and called it worthy of "serious and prayerful discussion."[13] Like the *National Catholic Reporter*, *Commonweal* routinely praised demonstrators who defied the law, comparing them to the "early abolitionists" who also were considered "crazy by more realistic citizens."[14]

Even within the ranks of American bishops, it became acceptable—indeed, quite fashionable—to preach a New Left gospel of unilateral disarmament and civil disobedience. In 1981, Archbishop Raymond Hunthausen of Seattle called the Trident submarine "the Auschwitz of Puget Sound" and proclaimed support for unilateral disarmament "a moral imperative for followers of Christ." In the same speech, Hunthausen urged people to withhold half of their federal taxes "in non-violent resistance to nuclear murder and suicide."[15] Meanwhile, Bishop Walter Sullivan toured his heavily defense-oriented Richmond diocese declaring it immoral to produce or be associated with nuclear weapons.[16] And in Amarillo, Texas, home of the Pantex plant that serves as the final assembly point for U.S. nuclear weapons, bishop Leroy T. Matthiesen urged Catholics "involved in the production and stockpiling of nuclear bombs to consider what they are doing, to resign from such activities and to seek employment in peaceful pursuits."[17]

In the context of growing media coverage of the freeze campaign, the anti-nuclear bishops gained public recognition far beyond their own dioceses. Matthiesen and Hunthausen were featured in dozens of sympathetic interviews and stories, both in the Catholic press and in major national news media.[18] The previously little-known Matthiesen appeared on *60 Minutes* and *The Phil Donahue Show*, and became a featured attraction at college convocations sponsored by the Union of Concerned Scientists, a leading pro-freeze organization.[19] Other bishops were quick to jump on the media bandwagon, establishing common cause with the new stars of the Catholic hierarchy through their own dramatic gestures. In October 1981, twenty-eight other bishops joined with Matthiesen in a statement proclaiming even the possession of nuclear weapons immoral, and a flood of similar statements by individual bishops followed, creating "a stunning picture of a hierarchy up in arms over the arms race."[20]

Phyllis Zagano has observed that "the preponderance of those bishops who gained the public eye" during the freeze debate were part of a "minority cadre" of pacifist bishops. Yet "through the magnification of a cathode-ray tube," their personal opinions seemed to take on "added moral authority."[21] More importantly, their visibility promoted the growth of Pax Christi, USA, the American branch of the international Catholic pacifist organization founded in the 1950s. By 1983, Pax Christi counted nearly sixty of America's 295 bishops among its members (including many from America's largest urban dioceses), with some twenty-five of those members joining in a single year between 1980 and 1981.[22] Pax Christi remained a small minority within the Catholic hierarchy, but its rapid growth and its visibility in the media often led observers to conclude that it had "overturned the balance of political power within the American Catholic hierarchy."[23]

Pax Christi may not have taken over the Church, but it did become a significant voice. Dominating the moral debate over nuclear weapons within the Church, the group offered many Catholics something the institutional Church did not: a comprehensive Catholic response to the hottest political issue of the early 1980s. Pax Christi's distinctive anti-nuclear message—a message addressing not only moral but political and technical issues as well—began to appear in sermons and in the Catholic media as commonly as official Church pronouncements. Only by understanding the implications of that message both for individual believers and for the Church as a social institution can we fully understand the origins and significance of the debate over the *Pastoral Letter on War and Peace.*

## Pax Christi and the New Catholic Pacifism

Pax Christi, USA., like virtually all political advocacy groups, proclaims educational work its top priority. Bishop Thomas Gumbleton, president of the group at the time of the freeze debate, spoke of helping Catholics to "clarify their own attitudes and positions" on nuclear weapons, and he introduced a Pax Christi anti-nuclear manifesto, *A Race to Nowhere,* as an educational resource. Pax Christi, he wrote, hoped only to help Catholics tap the "resources in the Gospel" and in the established "social teachings of the Church." At the same time, however, Gumbleton acknowledged that *A Race to Nowhere* aimed "to bring the teaching of the Church to bear on the shaping of public opinion," to enlist support for "the growing peace movement," and to persuade readers to "join us in Pax Christi."[24] These goals, of course, suggested not an educational exercise but political persuasion. Indeed, these goals necessitated a radical revision of Church teachings and a repudiation of its essentially conservative political and social tradition.

Pax Christi's very existence rested upon a revisionist theological premise—the notion that there were two traditions of Catholic teaching on the morality of war. Although Pax Christi acknowledged that the "just war theory" had "formed the basis for Church teaching on war" from "the 5th century on," the group suggested two reasons for proclaiming pacifism the more legitimate Christian philosophy. First, pacifism represented the older of the two traditions, dating back to the very first Christian community. Second, it was the tradition most true to the Gospels, according to Pax Christi, for nonviolence was "at the heart" of Jesus's message:

> It can be argued that the just war doctrine is based, not on the life and teachings of Jesus, but upon pagan philosophies and the religiously neutral natural law: a universal morality, binding on all peoples. And sometimes the ethic of natural law and the ethic of the Gospels clash.[25]

Pax Christi acknowledged that the "just war theory" remained the official doctrine of the Catholic Church, but they insisted that pacifism had been "gaining respect and recognition by Church authorities and in Church documents."[26] The threat of nuclear weapons apparently was not responsible for this development, for Pax Christi taught that nuclear warfare was "condemned equally by our pacifist and just-war convictions." The Church already "judged that nuclear war, involving weapons of mass destruction, cannot be squared with the just war theory," Pax Christi argued, and the group declared that even the possession of nuclear weapons for deterrent purposes had been "condemned by the Church" on just war grounds.[27]

The Church's growing "respect and recognition" of pacifism, then, supposedly grew not out of the nuclear threat but out of a "recent Biblical renewal."[28] And its implications for American defense policy likewise went far beyond questions about nuclear weapons. Pax Christi did not stand just for nuclear disarmament. With official Church teachings supposedly mandating nuclear disarmament already, Pax Christi advocated complete and unilateral disarmament, both nuclear and conventional. In Pax Christi's vision, an unarmed America could meet military invasions with passive, nonviolent resistance. The populace would simply "paralyze an invader by refusing to give logistic support and by instigating insubordination among the invading troops." The invaders could be expected to take "bloody reprisals," but Pax Christi insisted that this would result in "*far fewer* casualties" than any sort of armed defense. Pax Christi expressed confidence that if the American people would just study the rationale for such a policy, they would "accept the changes required through democratic consent." Then could begin "the conversion of the economy to peace-based work," the "training of literally millions of citizens in nonviolent resistance to invasion," and the elimination of all military forces. The "ex-military" could "play a key training and organizing role" in this process, while international agencies ("probably the U.N.") could "take over the responsibility for securing international waterways and mediating international disputes."[29]

Pax Christi's vision rested upon political as well as theological revisionism. Most obviously, it rested upon a portrait of the Soviet Union that obviated any need for deterrence or defense. "Much of the early revolutionary zeal on which the USSR was founded is now gone," Pax Christi argued, and the Soviets' harsh treatment of satellite states was defensive and perfectly understandable in light of the "American threat"—something "rarely discussed in the United States."[30] Countering the "dehumanization" common to war-making rhetoric, Pax Christi urged readers to think of the Soviets "simply as *people*." And as people, of course, they were no different than Americans: "When you say the Soviets are your enemies, you are not just talking about an atheist official in the Kremlin; you are also speaking about the Jewish milkman from a small farm town, a Christian mother of five living in a Moscow apartment house, priests, rabbis, and religious—all who live in the Soviet Union and love their country as you do yours."[31]

Even if the Soviets were to invade and occupy an unarmed America, Pax Christi apparently foresaw the sort of benign occupation portrayed in the ABC mini-series *Amerika*, in which "few Americans were executed," nobody was "arbitrarily sent to forced-labor camps," and dissidents were exiled, "not to an arctic waste but to a comparatively balmy Nebraska."[32] Even from a religious point of view, Pax Christi suggested that living under a Soviet regime would be no worse than living in contemporary Western society. One still could have faith in a communist country, and Pax Christi insisted that religious persecution in the Soviet Union was no worse than in "fanatically anti-communist" countries. Under every government, Pax Christi concluded, "real Christianity is a struggle. The seduction of 'godless materialism' in the West can be as destructive as the repressions under 'godless communism.'"[33]

Indeed, Pax Christi's America was so corrupt, so greedy, and so militaristic that a Soviet invasion almost seemed like a blessing. In contrast to its benevolent Soviet Union, Pax Christi's America supported "corrupt and unpopular governments around the world." Its foreign aid programs were designed, not "to help poor people in developing countries," but "to 'pay back' many times its cost into the pockets of U.S. corporations." Its reckless military spending caused unemployment, inflation, and a failure to address human needs at home. In America, Pax Christi proclaimed, the government spent "one tax dollar in two" on the military, while only "one in six" dollars was spent on the military in the rest of the world.[34] The government's budget documents, by contrast, showed only about one in four American tax dollars going to the military in the early 1980s.[35]

Pax Christi may not have gotten the numbers right, but it did tell a good story. Employing modern-day parables, it suggested that American Catholics were morally obligated to oppose their country's foreign and military policies. One narrative in *A Race to Nowhere* told the story of Franz Jaegerstatter, a deeply religious Austrian who was beheaded for refusing to cooperate with Hitler. Pax Christi apparently considered Hitler's Germany perfectly analogous to the United States. Another featured narrative, entitled "Requiem for an Arms Peddler," likewise taught that Catholics could not, in good conscience, be "loyal subjects of our nation's military-industrial complex." Focusing upon a Defense Department employee who was "catapulted from an ordinary government worker into the world's most select group of weapons peddlers," the story told how visions of death one night led the worker to a deep certainty that he must quit his job. Sitting before his fireplace, he envisioned M-60 machine guns he sold being used against "friends of mine—people I had dealt with"—by a revolutionary firing squad. As the wall blossomed bright red, "the older men, some cut in half, slumped to the ground," and good educations became "red-gray brain fragments plastered to the wall." The moral of the story? It went well beyond the evils of the arms trade, as the man realized the immorality of any role in defense industries or the military:

> I saw American mothers and fathers working in a Pennsylvania factory assembling fuses for cluster bombs. Just ordinary people doing their jobs. We peddlers sold them to a Mideastern country. Just doing our jobs. A few years later good mothers, fathers, and children in southern Lebanon are shredded into fragments by the same bombs dropped by pilots. Just doing their jobs.[36]

Pax Christi was determined to enlist not only individual Catholics but the institutional Church in its crusade for disarmament. The group argued that disarmament deserved the same effort from the Church as abortion, and it advocated "concrete actions" and "a massive education program" in all Catholic institutions: schools, parishes, seminaries, newspapers, and magazines. Catholic schools must be turned into peace schools, Pax Christi declared, and "an ROTC unit on a Catholic campus should be as rare as an abortion clinic; a military recruiter as suspect as a speaker from Planned Parenthood." In addition, Pax Christi proposed support groups similar to those in the pro-life campaign to provide material as well as moral support for "conscientious objectors and those employed by the military or in arms production who want to switch jobs." Pax Christi even suggested that the Church sponsor "a Peace Tax Fund where those who don't want to contribute tax money to the military can channel it to humanitarian concerns."[37]

Pax Christi acknowledged that Church support for such measures could be costly, for "it is safe to assume that the state is more tolerant of an anti-abortion Church than it will be with one that confronts the war economy." The group even predicted that Catholic institutions might lose their tax-exempt status. But Pax Christi actually seemed to relish such prospects, evoking biblical images of unwarranted persecution and glorious redemption. Establishing common cause with liberation theologists in Latin America, Pax Christi spoke of the monolithic, conspiratorial enemy: "To challenge the war economy here is to antagonize the same deadly forces that are waging battle against the Church in Latin America. We can expect organized persecution. If liberation theology is the Exodus theme of Latin American Christians, a peace theology is what will push United States Christians toward an unknown 'Promised Land.'"[38]

The *Pastoral Letter on War and Peace* takes on a very different meaning when viewed in the context of Pax Christi's campaign to transform the Catholic Church into a peace Church. It may be tempting to view the letter as a response to the secular freeze debate or to reckless talk about nuclear warfare emanating from the Reagan administration.[39] Yet Pax Christi's anti-nuclear crusade preceded the secular freeze campaign, and it peaked just as the Reagan administration settled into office. From an evolutionary perspective, the letter's relevance to secular politics was a later concern; it had been vigorously debated within the Catholic community and it had evolved through two drafts before it attracted widespread attention outside of the Church. The letter was designed, first and foremost, to answer religious and political challenges posed by Pax Christi. And, understood in that context, it answered the peace activists with a thundering rebuke.

## Managing Dissent in the Pastoral Letter

Secular media reported that the *Pastoral Letter on War and Peace* reflected radical change in Catholic teachings on war and peace, allied the Church with the secular peace movement, and condemned the Reagan administration's nuclear arms policies. A front-page story in the *New York Times* reported that many Catholics considered the letter's "forceful and historic position" the "boldest and most decisive step on social issues in the history of the American hierarchy." It marked for the bishops a new "leadership role in the effort for disarmament," the *Times* reported, and its "tone of distrust of nuclear strategy and its implied criticism of the Reagan Administration's military policies" made it "the most challenging statement by any national or regional conference of bishops thus far."[40] In the *Washington Post*, we even read that this "about face" on issues of war and peace signaled "the most significant revolution within the American Catholic Church since its start in 1634."[41]

Yet considering the *Pastoral Letter on War and Peace* in the context of Pax Christi's challenge, one is hard-pressed to discover anything revolutionary about it. Indeed, the final document is better described as counterrevolutionary, for it clearly reaffirmed traditional Church doctrine and rejected Pax Christi's political conclusions in favor of a decidedly mainstream stance. Even the process by which the committee prepared the letter served to diffuse rather than promote a revolutionary challenge to traditional Church teachings and to American defense policy. Holding hearings of a sort, subjecting each draft of the letter to public scrutiny and comment, and ultimately fogging the most divisive issues in thick clouds of calculated ambiguity, the bishops provided an object lesson in parliamentary-style compromise and the management of dissent.

Consider, first, the process employed in preparing the pastoral letter. Goldzwig and Cheney may be correct, at least hyperbolically, that the committee's interactive procedure—the fact that they consulted extensively both within and outside of the Church and invited open discussion—was revolutionary within a Church accustomed to doctrinal pronouncement.[42] But symbolically that very process also legitimized disagreement—even celebrated diversity—within the Church, and it functioned to balance the views of Pax Christi against those of more conservative elements. The committee's procedures were those not of revolution but of representative democracy and parliamentary deliberation, and they virtually guaranteed a pastoral letter inimical to Pax Christi's crusade.

At the outset, Pax Christi seemed poised to secure from the National Conference of Bishops something akin to *A Race to Nowhere.* Not only did Pax Christi's initiative lead to the appointment of the ad hoc Committee on War and Peace in the first place,[43] but the group lobbied hard for an initial agenda of twelve issues they deemed "particularly urgent and in need of moral clarification."[44] Church leaders tried to balance the five-man committee between pacifist and just-war advocates. But the committee included Pax Christi president Thomas Gumbleton, two other bishops who quickly emerged as Pax Christi supporters, and a very influential staff with a history of anti-war activism.[45]

From the very beginning, however, the leadership of committee chair Archbishop Joseph Bernardin of Cincinnati steered the committee toward a middle ground. Known as a mediator and a builder of consensus, Bernardin presided over a series of hearings—fourteen sessions between July 1981 and July 1982—at which the committee and its staff heard from a diverse array of experts in nuclear strategy, moral theology, and other relevant fields.[46] As the committee worked on the letter, Bernardin involved each member as well as the staff in the writing process, and the committee as a whole debated and amended virtually every sentence until they reached consensus. Perhaps most importantly, the committee remained open to outside criticism throughout the entire process, with committee members diligently plowing through thick piles of correspondence following release of each draft and continuing to meet with interested parties.[47]

Pax Christi and its supporters dominated the first wave of criticism, both in the seven hundred pages of commentary sent directly to the committee and in the Catholic news media.[48] The committee assuaged some of the pacifists' concerns in the second draft with, among other changes, a more detailed discussion of the nonviolent tradition. Still, the pacifists did not get the clear, unambiguous condemnation of nuclear weapons they demanded.[49] Nevertheless, the second draft moved too far to the left for many conservative Catholics,[50] and Vatican officials, the Reagan administration, and a group of Catholic Members of Congress added their voices to a second wave of criticism dominated by calls for a more realistic document.[51] The third and final draft took account of many of these criticisms, and the result was a significantly more conservative statement.[52] Even the Reagan administration praised the third draft as "substantially improved over the previous versions" and as "an important and serious contribution."[53]

Pax Christi had one last opportunity to save its letter at the special meeting of the entire Conference of Bishops on 2-3 May 1983. But again, procedural constraints conspired against the pacifists, forcing them to compromise their most basic principles in order to secure even relatively minor changes in the document. Limited to proposing amendments to specific passages, the pacifists won a few symbolic victories, but the Conference's "desire to remain clearly within the present limits of universal church teaching" also led to the defeat of numerous pacifist amendments.[54] In the end, the pacifists tallied more victories than defeats,[55] but most of the changes were barely noticeable. Overall, as the final text of the document reveals, the *Pastoral Letter on War and Peace* remained a remarkably conservative document.

The bishops' conservatism was perhaps most evident in their final resolution of the most fundamental theological question at issue in the Catholic debate over war and peace. In the spirit of compromise, the bishops granted pacifist teachings some legitimacy, recognizing non-violence as one of "two distinct moral responses" to war and peace in Church history.[56] Yet at the insistence of the Vatican,[57] the letter forcefully rejected pacifism as a Church or Gospel mandate for public policy, calling it only one of two "options open to individuals." Governments, the letter argued, had not only a "right to legitimate defense" but a "duty to protect the welfare of the people entrusted to their care." The letter continued: "The council and the popes have stated clearly that governments threatened by armed, unjust aggression must defend their people. This includes defense by armed force if necessary as a last resort." Later, the bishops even cautioned against pacifism as a personal philosophy, observing that the Church recognizes the right of a government to "require military service of its citizens." The letter warned that "a citizen may not casually disregard his country's conscientious decision to call its citizens to acts of 'legitimate defense.'"[58]

On the more specific issues of the nuclear debate, the pastoral letter again paid lip service to the pacifists while fundamentally rejecting the substance of their teachings. The bishops appeared to begin the section on "war and peace in the modern world" with the clear-cut "no" to nuclear weapons the pacifists had been demanding. But they employed the just war theory as the sole source of moral criteria in judging actual policies, and ultimately they retreated into a maze of qualifications and ambiguity. It is clear that "we must reject nuclear war," they began, "but it is much less clear how we translate a 'no' to nuclear war into the personal and public choices which can move us in a new direction." The bishops did make two things clear: they rejected not only unilateral disarmament but also the advice of those who urged them "to condemn all aspects of nuclear deterrence." The "political paradox" of deterrence has "strained our moral conception," the bishops admitted, but they could discover no violation of just war criteria in the mere possession of nuclear weapons. In the end, they reaffirmed Pope John Paul II's declaration before the U.N. Conference on Disarmament in June 1981 that nuclear deterrence, at least under present circumstances, remained "morally acceptable."[59]

Indeed, even the bishops' "no" to the use of nuclear weapons seemed more of a "maybe" as the pastoral letter addressed the topic of limited nuclear war. Actually retreating from Archbishop John Cardinal Krol's statement in 1979 that the Church condemned any use of nuclear weapons,[60] the first draft of the pastoral letter suggested that nuclear weapons might be justified in limited retaliation against military targets.[61] Later drafts, including the final draft, expressed more skepticism that the use of nuclear weapons could be kept limited. But proclaiming the policy debate on limited war inconclusive, the bishops declined "trying to adjudicate the technical debate" and begged the question of whether retaliatory use of nuclear weapons could be morally justified if their use could be limited.[62]

The bishops' conclusions about deterrence and limited nuclear war rested upon an explicit rejection of Pax Christi's portrait of a nonthreatening, even victimized Soviet Union. The pastoral letter spoke instead of "a Soviet threat," even a "Soviet imperial drive for hegemony," which "cannot be denied," and it reminded readers of "the significant differences between Christian teaching and Marxism" outlined in the bishops' 1980 pastoral letter. "Many peoples are forcibly kept under communist domination despite their manifest wishes to be free," the bishops observed, and "in some cases" Soviet behavior merited "the adjective reprehensible." At one point, the bishops even seemed to scold Pax Christi for trying to persuade us otherwise:

> The facts simply do not support the invidious comparisons made at times, even in our own society, between our way of life, in which most basic human rights are at least recognized even if they are not always adequately supported, and those totalitarian and tyrannical regimes in which such rights are either denied or systematically suppressed. . . . It is one thing to recognize that the people of the world do not want war. It is quite another thing to attribute the same good motives to regimes or political systems that have consistently demonstrated precisely the opposite in their behavior.[63]

The bishops continued to correct—even scold—Pax Christi as they addressed the obligations of Catholic military personnel and defense industry workers. Again in sharp rebuttal to Pax Christi, the bishops reiterated the conclusion of Vatican II that those "who enter the military service in loyalty to their country should look upon themselves as the custodians of the security and freedom of their fellow-countrymen." The bishops assured Catholic military personnel that it was "surely not our intention in writing this letter to create problems for Catholics in the armed forces," and they expressed their gratitude "for the sacrifice so many in military service must make today and for the service offered in the past by veterans." Similarly, the bishops reassured Catholic defense-industry workers that Church teachings did not condemn their employment or require that they resign. "All Catholics, at every level of defense industries, can and should use the moral principles of this letter to form their consciences," the bishops began. But reiterating the letter's "conditional moral acceptance for deterrence," they argued that those "who remain in these industries or earn a profit from the weapons industry" should find as much support in the Catholic community as those who decided they could "no longer be associated with defense activities."[64]

Media coverage emphasized the pastoral letter's call for "immediate, bilateral, verifiable agreements to halt the testing, production, and deployment of new nuclear weapons systems." Pax Christi lobbied hard for this freeze language, but in the context of the pastoral letter's entire section on policy recommendations their victory proved illusory. Not only did the bishops also endorse the "negotiated bilateral deep cuts in the arsenals of both superpowers" proposed by the Reagan administration, but they even added a footnote insisting that they did not mean the freeze language "to be identified with one specific political initiative."[65] "There is no single freeze resolution, there are several of them," Bernardin explained following approval of the letter, "and we didn't want to be identified with a particular one."[66] With Congress only one day away from a final vote on the freeze issue, the bishops thus declined to choose between the original proposal for an immediate freeze and various modified freezes concocted by some of the most conservative Members of Congress.[67] Specifically, they refused to distinguish between the Kennedy-Hatfield Amendment, which embodied the original language of the Nuclear Weapons Freeze Campaign, and such measures as the Jackson-Warner Amendment, which was endorsed by the administration and proposed a freeze following the Reagan arms build-up.[68]

Whatever one's interpretation of the freeze language, one final point must be stressed: that the pastoral letter drew a clear distinction between *doctores fidei*—those principles of Catholic moral teaching that are binding in conscience—and the bishops' opinions on the various political and technical issues of the nuclear debate. Again at the Vatican's insistence,[69] the pastoral letter strongly emphasized at the outset that "people of good will" could differ with the bishops on specific issues. The "Church expects a certain diversity of views," the bishops wrote, "even though all hold the same universal moral principles." More importantly, the bishops demanded that Catholic political activists also respect the distinction. Quoting the *Pastoral Constitution*, the bishops reminded readers that "no one is allowed . . . to appropriate the Church's authority for his opinion." And toward the end of the letter, they returned to the theme, calling for balanced and objective educational programs based on the letter, and criticizing religious groups who claimed that their opinions were obligatory for Christians or that they were "the only ones that people of good will may hold."[70]

NCCB president John Roach commented during debate over the pastoral letter that "ambiguity has been a legitimate, treasured part of the whole moral tradition of the church."[71] The *Pastoral Letter on War and Peace*, perhaps more than any other Church document in recent memory, reaffirmed that tradition by eschewing specific, doctrinal pronouncements about America's strategic policies. To the extent that the bishops proclaimed America's deterrent policies inadequate "as a long-term basis for peace,"[72] they criticized not just the Reagan administration but all postwar policy makers, and they expressed a universal longing for an alternative to the "balance of terror." With a clear sense of urgency, the bishops encouraged more public debate over nuclear weapons, and they called for a greater emphasis on moral concerns. At the same time, they urged that the debate be conducted with "civility and charity,"[73] and they reminded us that people of good will could arrive at very different conclusions.

## Claiming the Pastoral Letter

Read in isolation or even in the context of secular politics, the *Pastoral Letter on War and Peace* might be interpreted as a radical (if not revolutionary) anti-nuclear statement. But as a rhetorical document, the pastoral letter is best interpreted within its own "particular world,"[74] and that world was generally religious and specifically Catholic. According to J. Bryan Hehir, the bishops' advisor whom many call the real author of the pastoral letter,[75] there were actually two debates over nuclear weapons in the early 1980s, "one religious the other secular," and they seldom intersected.[76] The pastoral letter was unmistakably the product of the religious debate: it evolved out of religious dissent, its revisions were shaped by a religious dialectic, and ultimately it proclaimed the official stance of an ancient religious order. In the religious context, the pastoral letter was not at all a radical statement. On the contrary, it thwarted an attempt to overturn the Church's theological and political tradition.

If Pax Christi had prevailed upon the bishops to condemn the strategic policies of the United States government, it would have signaled a historic change of leadership and philosophy within a traditionally glacial Church. In addition, as Thomas Powers has suggested, it might have provoked "an unpleasant—perhaps an ugly—confrontation between Church and State,"[77] and it conceivably could have resurrected historical animosities toward Catholic citizens.[78] From the point of view of the Church establishment, there probably seemed little to gain and much to lose in a bold departure from traditional Church teachings about war and peace.

Pax Christi continued its crusade for a Catholic peace church following approval of the pastoral letter. According to Matthew F. Murphy, peace activists routinely betrayed the bishops by teaching the pastoral letter as a partisan political document,[79] and some Pax Christi bishops even invoked the pastoral letter to justify direct action against government trains carrying nuclear weapons.[80] Yet more conservative Catholics also embraced the letter,[81] and Catholics in the military and the defense industries found solace in its assurances. For some Catholics, as Susan Chira has written, "the letter represented a striking departure from the traditional posture of the church; for others, it reaffirmed that tradition."[82] As a rhetorical artifact, the *Pastoral Letter on War and Peace* testified to the power of ambiguity in the management of dissent. And much the same might be said about another product of institutional debate: the freeze resolution passed by the House of Representatives in 1983.

## NOTES

1. Catholic Church, National Conference of Catholic Bishops, *The Challenge of Peace—God's Promise and Our Response: A Pastoral Letter on War and Peace* (Washington, D.C.: United States Catholic Conference, 1983), 102. Hereafter cited as *The Challenge of Peace.*
2. Steve Goldzwig and George Cheney, "The U.S. Catholic Bishops on Nuclear Arms: Corporate Advocacy, Role Redefinition, and Rhetorical Adaptation," *Central States Speech Journal* 35 (Spring 1984): 8-23.
3. *The Challenge of Peace*, 60; Forsberg, *Call to Halt the Nuclear Arms Race*, NWFC rev. ed.
4. Edward R. Kantowicz, "Cardinal Mundelein of Chicago and the Shaping of Twentieth-Century American Catholicism," *Journal of American History* 68 (June 1981): 63.
5. Richard N. Ostling, "Bishops and the Bomb," *Time*, 29 November 1982, 68.
6. Eric F. Goldman, *The Crucial Decade—and After: America, 1945-1960*, 2nd ed. (New York: Vintage, 1960), 128, 130.
7. "Peace and Vietnam," in *Pastoral Letters of the American Hierarchy, 1792-1970*, edited by Hugh J. Nolan (Huntington, Indiana: Our Sunday Visitor, 1971), 605. See also James O'Gara, "Peace and the Bishops," *Commonweal*, 23 December 1966, 338.
8. Catholic Church, National Conference of Catholic Bishops, *Resolution on South East Asia* (Washington, D.C.: United States Catholic Conference, 1971).
9. See William A. Au, *The Cross, the Flag, and the Bomb: American Catholics Debate War and Peace, 1960-1983* (Westport: Greenwood Press, 1985), 141-59.
10. See Dougherty, *The Bishops and Nuclear Weapons*, 104-7.
11. "What Theologians Believe: The IEA/Roper Center Theology Faculty Survey," *This World* (Summer 1982): 32, 40-41, 49.

12. See, for example, Thomas C. Fox, "Bishops' Draft Not Encouraging," *National Catholic Reporter*, 30 July 1982, 2; and Michael J. Farrell, "'Prevailing' Despite Court Defeat," *National Catholic Reporter*, 20 March 1981, 3, 18-19, 24.
13. "More on Catholics and Nuclear Arms," *Commonweal*, 12 March 1982, 132.
14. John Garvey, "King of Prussia Eight," *Commonweal*, 30 January 1981, 40.
15. "Archbishop Raymond Hunthausen, Bishop of Seattle, Address at the Pacific Northwest Synod of the Luthern Church in America, July 12, 1981," in *Nuclear Disarmament: Key Statements of Popes, Bishops, Councils and Churches*, edited by Robert Heyer (New York: Paulist Press, 1982), 133, 135-36. See also "Archbishop Raymond Hunthausen, Bishop of Seattle, Interview from *Our Sunday Visitor* by Bruce Smith, August 9, 1981," in *Nuclear Disarmament: Key Statements of Popes, Bishops, Councils and Churches*, edited by Robert Heyer (New York: Paulist Press, 1982), 138-43.
16. See Jim Castelli, *The Bishops and the Bomb: Waging Peace in a Nuclear Age* (Garden City: Image Books, 1983), 53.
17. "Bishop Leroy T. Matthiesen, Bishop of Amarillo, Nuclear Arms Buildup, August 21, 1981," in *Nuclear Disarmament: Key Statements of Popes, Bishops, Councils and Churches*, edited by Robert Heyer (New York: Paulist Press, 1982), 156. Matthiesen's statement led to protests against the United Way's support for the local Catholic Family Services (CFS). Under pressure from Pantex contributors and others concerned that CFS might counsel Pantex workers to leave the plant, the United Way withdrew its support from the agency. See Ronald Kimelman, "Texas Bishop's Stand Against Nuclear Arms Stirs Furor," *Washington Post*, 20 March 1982, B5. For bishop Matthiesen's version of the United Way controversy see Sam Totten and Martha Wescoat Totten, *Facing the Danger: Interviews with 20 Anti-Nuclear Activists* (Trumansburg, New York: The Crossing Press, 1984), 110-11.
18. See, for example, Leroy T. Matthiesen, "Bishop: Don't Help Build Bombs," *National Catholic Reporter*, 11 September 1981, 2; Terri Goodman, "Fatalism, Economic Insecurity Boost Pantex in Texas Panhandle," *National Catholic Reporter*, 2 October 1981, 8; Kenneth A. Briggs, "Religious Leaders Objecting to Nuclear Arms," *New York Times*, 8 September 1981, A1, A20; and Colman McCarthy, "How the 'Peace Bishops' Got That Way," *Washington Post*, 27 December 1981, D5; Colman McCarthy, "Brave Bishops," *Washington Post*, 3 October 1981, A23.
19. See CBS News, "The Bishop and the Bombs," *60 Minutes*, 24 October 1982, microfiche transcript, 13-17; and Totten and Totten, *Facing the Danger*, 109-10.
20. "29 Bishops' Statement That Possession of Nuclear Weapons Is Immoral, October 1981," in *Nuclear Disarmament: Key Statements of Popes, Bishops, Councils and Churches*, edited by Robert Heyer (New York: Paulist Press, 1982), 182-83; Castelli, *The Bishops and the Bomb*, 36. See also "The Bishops as Peacemakers," *Commonweal*, 18 December 1981, 707.
21. Phyllis Zagano, "Media Morality: American Catholic Bishops and Deterrence," *Center Journal* 3 (Winter 1983): 183, 203-04.
22. See Dean C. Curry, "Introduction: The Origins and Relevance of the Bishops' Pastoral Letter," in *Evangelicals and the Bishops' Pastoral Letter*, edited by Dean C. Curry (Grand Rapids: William B. Eerdmans, 1984), 221 n.9; Castelli, *The Bishops and the Bomb*, 47.
23. Garfinkle, *The Politics of the Nuclear Freeze*, 22.
24. Kownacki, ed. *A Race to Nowhere*, iii.

25. Ibid., 58-59, 63. The "just war" theory, developed by St. Augustine and St. Thomas Aquinas, holds that war may be morally justifiable only if it meets certain criteria: the decision for war must be made by a legitimate authority; the war must be fought for a just cause; war must be waged only as a last resort; there must be a reasonable chance of success; the good to be achieved by the war must outweigh the evil that will result from it; and the war must be waged with just means.
26. Kownacki, *A Race to Nowhere*, 63. One is hard pressed to discern which church authorities or documents Pax Christi has in mind in making this statement. *A Race to Nowhere* mentions the examples set by "such leaders as Dorothy Day, Archbishop Romero, Dom Helder Camara, and Daniel Berrigan" (58), but this hardly seems a list of authoritative Church leaders. When the primer does quote from authoritative figures, the statements do not endorse pacifism at all, unless one equates any and all uses of the word nonviolence with an endorsement of pacifist theology. The primer implies that John Paul II endorsed pacifism during a trip to Northern Ireland, for example, because he urged his audience to "turn away from the path of violence" (64). Pax Christi also implies that the bishops of Vatican II endorsed pacifism when they called for an "entirely new attitude" toward war. Arguing from a false dichotomy, Pax Christi concludes that "the old attitude, of course, is the just war theory" (62).
27. Kownacki, *A Race to Nowhere*, 62-64.
28. Ibid., 63.
29. Ibid., 72, 78.
30. Ibid., 17.
31. Ibid., 22.
32. John Corry, Introduction, in *Moscow Meets Main Street: Changing Journalistic Values and the Growing Soviet Presence on American Television*, by Ted J. Smith III (Washington, D.C.: Media Institute, 1988), 5.
33. Kownacki, *A Race to Nowhere*, 25-26.
34. Ibid., 29, 32-35, 44-45.
35. Pax Christi lists *The United States Budget in Brief* for 1981 among its sources on the defense budget. Yet while that document's pie graph shows 24 cents of the budget dollar going to national defense, Pax Christi presents a pie graph showing 46 percent of the budget going to the military. See Kownacki, *A Race to Nowhere*, 29; U.S. President, Executive Office of the President, Office of Management and Budget, *The United States Budget in Brief: Fiscal Year 1981* (Washington, D.C.: Government Printing Office, [1980]), facing 1. See also U.S. Department of Commerce, *Statistical Abstract of the United States, 1987* (Washington, D.C.: Department of Commerce, 1986), 317.
36. Kownacki, *A Race to Nowhere*, 49-51, 66-67.
37. Ibid., 81.
38. Ibid., 81.
39. See Robert Scheer, *With Enough Shovels: Reagan, Bush and Nuclear War* (New York: Vintage Books, 1983).
40. Kenneth A. Briggs, "Bishops Endorse Stand Opposed to Nuclear War," *New York Times*, 4 May 1983, B7.
41. Marjorie Hyer, "How Our War-Blessing Catholic Bishops Got Religion on Nukes," *Washington Post*, 1 May 1983, B1.
42. Goldzwig and Cheney, "The U.S. Catholic Bishops on Nuclear Arms," 10-11.
43. See Castelli, *The Bishops and the Bomb*, 13-15. The letter originated as a varium—a sort of new business item—offered by Bishop P. Francis Murphy, after consultations with fellow Pax Christi bishops. More theologically conservative bishops apparently

went along with Pax Christi because they believed that their "teaching on the sacredness of human life" could not be credible "with liberal and leftist, intellectual, feminist, and youthful Catholics" if they failed to "demonstrate a comparable concern about 'respect for life' in regard to the dangers posed by nuclear weapons" (Dougherty, *The Bishops and Nuclear Weapons*, 8).

44. Pax Christi, "Toward a Christian Response to War and Peace," *Origins*, 17 March 1981, 744.
45. Reflecting the conventional wisdom about the committee's make-up, Patty Edmonds, National Affairs writer for the *National Catholic Reporter*, reported that the committee included "one bishop from the church's right" (Auxiliary Bishop John O'Connor of the Military Ordinariate), "one from the church's left" (Gumbleton), and "two deemed moderates" (Bishops Daniel Reilly of Norwich and Auxiliary Bishop George Fulcher of Columbus). Within just a few months of their appointments, however, both Fulcher and Reilly endorsed a Pax Christi freeze petition and Fulcher formally joined the organization. More importantly, much of the actual writing was done by the committee staff, particularly J. Bryan Hehir, Associate Secretary for International Justice and Peace at the United States Catholic Conference. Hehir had been a champion of liberal foreign policy causes within the Church for a number of years and he became the chief target of conservative critics alleging that the pastoral letter had been written by leftist Church bureaucrats. See Patty Edmonds, "U.S. Bishops Affirm Peace Pastoral," *National Catholic Reporter*, 26 November 1982, 6; Castelli, *The Bishops and the Bomb*, 65-77; Zagano, "Media Morality," 181; Charlotte Hays, "The Voice in the Bishops' Ear," *Washington Post Magazine*, 3 April 1983, 6, 11, 13.
46. For a list of those testifying before the committee see Zagano, "Media Morality," 206-7.
47. This view of the internal workings of the committee is taken from Castelli, *The Bishops and the Bomb*, esp. 65-154. Castelli, a journalist, persuaded NCCB president John Roach and the members of the ad hoc Committee on War and Peace to grant him interviews and access to committee files while the pastoral letter was being written. Castelli's book is thus an authorized, inside account of the pastoral letter, with all the virtues and biases typically associated with such accounts.
48. Pacifist critics seemed to recognize, even at this early stage, that the drafting committee's procedures inevitably would lead to a letter they could not embrace. They proclaimed the first draft unacceptable precisely because it was a compromise—"an accommodation so hideous as to be beyond . . . ordinary human articulation." It read "like a negotiated settlement," complained editor Thomas Fox of the *National Catholic Reporter*. Led by well-known pacifist theologian Gordon Zahn, the pacifists demanded a second draft with "more explicit moral guidance, free from ambiguities, reservations, and exceptions . . . on this most crucial moral issue of our time, perhaps of all remaining time." See Charles E. Kinzie, "First Draft on the Road to the Abyss: Ecclesiastically Endorsed Civil Religion," *National Catholic Reporter*, 24 September 1982, 10-11; Fox, "Bishops' Draft Not Encouraging," 2; Gordon C. Zahn, "Disaster, No; Disappointment, Yes," *Commonweal*, 13 August 1982, 435. For more of the response to the first draft see "War and Peace Draft Hit in Letters . . . and Defended by Gumbleton," *National Catholic Reporter*, 30 July 1982, 18.
49. National Conference of Catholic Bishops, "The Challenge of Peace: God's Promise and Our Response," second draft, *Origins*, 28 October 1982, 305-28.
50. Michael Novak led the conservative Catholic critique, arguing that the letter "recommended a policy whose ultimate logic will demand unilateral nuclear disarmament"

(Michael Novak, "Arms and the Church," *Commentary*, March 1982, 37). See also Michael Novak, "Nuclear Morality," *America*, 3 July 1982, 5-8; and Michael Novak, "Moral Clarity in the Nuclear Age," *National Review*, 1 April 1983, 354-88. For a profile of Novak and his campaign against the pastoral letter, see Colman McCarthy, "The Crossing of the Bishops," *Washington Post*, 11 May 1983, B1, B15.

51. See "A Vatican Synthesis," *Origins*, 7 April 1983, 691-95; "A Positive and Helpful Exchange of Views," *Origins*, 7 April 1983, 695-96; "Vatican Communique: Informal Meeting on U.S. Bishops' Pastoral," *Origins*, 3 February 1983, 545; William P. Clark, "A Letter From the White House," *Origins*, 2 December 1982, 398-401; John P. Lehman Jr. "The U.S. Catholic Bishops and Nuclear Arms," *Wall Street Journal*, 15 November 1982, 28; and "Letter of 24 Congressmen on Bishops' Pastoral," *Origins*, 13 January 1983, 492-96. See also Richard Halloran, "U.S. Tells Bishops Morality is Guide on Nuclear Policy," *New York Times*, 17 November 1982, A1, B4; and Richard Halloran, "Minuet With Catholic Bishops Over Nuclear War," *New York Times*, 16 December 1982, B16.
52. National Conference of Catholic Bishops, "The Challenge of Peace, God's Promise and Our Response," third draft, *Origins*, 14 April 1983, 697-728. For an analysis of the third draft, see Au, *The Cross, the Flag, and the Bomb*, 226-34.
53. See Bernard Gwertzman, "Administration Hails New Draft of Arms Letter," *New York Times*, 7 April 1983, A1. At a news conference, Bernardin downplayed the significance of the revisions, conceding only that certain sections had been "nuanced differently" and that the draft had a "greater degree of flexibility." When media reports continued to suggest that the administration pressured the committee to make the revisions, Bernardin and NCCB President John Roach issued a statement insisting that "the third draft is far more the product of reflection and dialogue within the Catholic community than of dialogue between the drafting committee and the administration." See Michael Getler, "Latest Draft of Bishops More 'Flexible,'" *Washington Post*, 6 April 1983, A5; and "How the Proposed Pastoral Relates to U.S. Policy," *Origins*, 21 April 1983, 738. See also Kenneth A. Briggs, "Bishops Cite Differences," *New York Times*, 10 April 1983, 1, 15.
54. Au, *The Cross, the Flag, and the Bomb*, 235.
55. For the most complete account of the Conference's consideration of amendments see Castelli, *The Bishops and the Bomb*, 155-79.
56. *The Challenge of Peace*, 23-24.
57. At a meeting including Bernardin, a group of European bishops, and Vatican officials in Rome on 18-19 January 1983, the second draft of the Pastoral Letter came under attack for suggesting that there was "a double Catholic tradition" on war and peace. According to a synopsis of the meeting released by the Vatican, "it was clearly affirmed [at the meeting] that there is only one Catholic tradition: the just war theory," and that "the relevant passage in the draft letter would therefore have to be re-elaborated." See "A Vatican Synthesis," 694.
58. *The Challenge of Peace*, 23-24, 72.
59. Ibid., 42-43, 54-55, 60-61.
60. U.S. Congress, Senate, Committee on Foreign Relations, *The SALT II Treaty*, 96th Cong., 1st sess., 1979, part 4, 117.
61. The first draft stated: "If nuclear weapons may be used at all, they may be used only after they have been used against our own country or our allies, and, even then, only in an extremely limited, discriminating manner against military targets" ("The U.S. Bishops on Peace and War," *National Catholic Reporter*, 2 July 1982, 12).

62. *The Challenge of Peace*, 49-50.
63. Ibid., 76-78, 80.
64. Ibid., 93-96.
65. Ibid., 60.
66. Castelli, *The Bishops and the Bomb*, 159.
67. For the most complete account of the congressional debate and the intricacies of the various resolutions and amendments debated, see Waller, *Congress and the Nuclear Freeze.*
68. See U.S. Congress, Senate, S.J. Res 163 [the Kennedy-Hatfield resolution], 97th Cong., 2nd sess., 1982; U.S. Congress, Senate, S.J. Res. 177 [the Jackson-Warner resolution], 97th Cong., 2nd sess., 1982. See also Kennedy and Hatfield, *Freeze*, 125-26, 158.
69. See "A Vatican Synthesis," 693.
70. *The Challenge of Peace*, 4-5, 86-88.
71. See Kenneth A. Briggs, "Bishops Support Letter on Nuclear Arms," *New York Times*, 19 November 1982, D15.
72. *The Challenge of Peace*, 58.
73. Ibid., 5.
74. Edwin Black, *Rhetorical Criticism: A Study in Method*, 2nd ed. (Madison: University of Wisconsin Press, 1978), 39.
75. Hays, "The Voice in the Bishops' Ear," 6.
76. J. Bryan Hehir, "Nuclear Weapons: The Two Debates," *Commonweal*, 13 March 1981, 135.
77. Thomas Powers, "The Moment to Say No," *Commonweal*, 5 November 1982, 583.
78. See James Hennesey, *American Catholics: A History of the Roman Catholic Community in the United States* (New York: Oxford University Press, 1981), esp. 56-58, 116-27, 182-83, 246-47.
79. Matthew F. Murphy, *Betraying the Bishops: How the Pastoral Letter on War and Peace is Being Taught* (Washington, D.C.: Ethics and Public Policy Center, 1987).
80. In a statement explaining their efforts to impede trains carrying warheads to Trident submarine bases, twelve bishops (including Hunthausen and Matthiesen) proclaimed: "Our stand in the pastoral letter is that no further deployment of nuclear weapons can possibly be justified" (Robert Lindsey, "Bishops Protest Train Carrying Atom Weapons," *New York Times*, 24 February 1984, A10).
81. Even Michael Novak concluded that the final draft answered all of the "major objections" conservatives had to earlier drafts and proclaimed it a "valiant text" (Michael Novak, "The Bishops Speak Out," *National Review*, 10 June 1983, 680-81).
82. Susan Chira, "Priests Get Ready for the Questions in Connecticut," *New York Times*, 16 December 1983, B2.

## Chapter Six

# Popular Sovereignty and the House Freeze Debate

No government can continue good but under the control of the people.[1]
Thomas Jefferson

The central paradox of America's constitutional tradition lies in a persistent tension between the moral ideal of popular sovereignty and the practical realities of popular governance. In the *Federalist Papers*, James Madison wrote of a government "which derives all its powers directly . . . from the great body of the people." Yet the *Federalist Papers* also cautioned that the masses might be deluded by "the wiles of parasites and sycophants, by the snares of the ambitious, the avaricious, the desperate."[2] This tension, at bottom, accounts for what has been called the "split personality" of the *Federalist Papers.*[3]

Yet the paradox of popular sovereignty is more than a theoretical tension. It is institutionalized in the government itself, most obviously in the bicameral legislative branch. On the one hand, the Founding Fathers intended the House of Representatives to have a dependence on and a common interest and intimate sympathy with the people.[4] It was to provide a "true picture of the people, possess a knowledge of their circumstances and their wants, sympathize in all their distresses, and [be] disposed to seek their true interest."[5] The Senate, on the other hand, was to be more insulated from the people—"a defense to the people against their own temporary errors and delusions." As Madison explained, there were "particular moments in public affairs" when the people demanded measures which they themselves would "afterwards be the most ready to lament and condemn." At such times, the Senate, a "temperate and respectable body of citizens," was "to suspend the blow mediated by the people against themselves, until reason, justice, and truth" could "regain their authority over the public mind."[6]

Students of American politics rarely dispute the principle that policy making should reflect the will of the people.[7] Yet there has been wide disagreement about the practical influence of public opinion upon policy making, especially in foreign affairs. Traditionally, diplomatic historians simply assumed that public opinion did shape American foreign policy. Writing in 1940, for example, Thomas Bailey asserted that "the American people, exercising their democratic privilege and enjoying freedom of speech and press, have shaped their own foreign policies."[8] Empirical political science fundamentally challenged this assumption in the 1950s and 1960s, creating a portrait of an uninformed and disinterested public[9] and revealing a very tenuous relationship between public opinion and congressional voting behaviors—almost none between public opinion and foreign policy decisions.[10] For a new generation of diplomatic historians, this merely confirmed what they sensed intuitively in the Vietnam era: that American foreign policy in large measure operated independently of public opinion. Gabriel Kolko spoke for many of the New Left revisionists of the 1960s and 1970s when he wrote: "The close and serious student of modern American foreign relations will rarely, if ever, find an instance of an important decision made with any reference to the alleged general public desires or opinions."[11]

In recent years, rhetorical theorists have echoed the skeptical refrains of the revisionist historians. A few still cling to a liberal democratic model of governance, treating the public as a real, concrete entity that authorizes those "deliberating, judging, or acting in its behalf."[12] For the most part, however, we now hear that "the liberal democratic conception of the public" is "only an ideal, a fiction at best."[13] Articulating a common view, Richard Vatz has declared public opinion nothing more than a myth that serves to justify the a priori decisions of policy makers.[14] Similarly, Gerald Hauser and Carole Blair tell us that we now have a "government of, by, and for special interests," while the public has been "reduced to a depoliticized estate" that renders "mass loyalty to a government which does not include them in its decision-making process."[15] Michael C. McGee has theorized the liberal democratic public out of existence altogether, replacing it with a "strictly *linguistic*" phenomenon he labels "the people." The people, McGee declares, are not "objectively real in the sense that they exist as a collective entity in nature." Rather, they are "a fiction dreamed by an advocate and infused with an artificial, rhetorical reality by the agreement of an audience to participate in a collective fantasy."[16]

Theories of the public-as-fiction correctly suggest that the public's role in the policy-making process is a product, not of the actual opinions of the great mass of real people, but of the portraits of the people constructed rhetorically by the policy makers themselves. As political scientist Bernard Cohen has written, we cannot simply assume that public opinion is "absorbed, by osmosis, into the political bloodstream."[17] Rather, we must recognize that public opinion is mediated by policy makers; hence, politically relevant public opinion is discovered, not through survey research, but through examination of rhetorical documents containing history as mediated or filtered by political decision makers.[18]

Yet to say that public opinion is rhetorically mediated is not to say that it is wholesale fiction. Nor is it to say that fictional publics serve only to justify a priori decisions, to thwart the real will of the people, or to maintain only an illusion of popular sovereignty. Instead, it is to say, quite simply, that public opinion is a debatable issue. The question of deference to public opinion, like other political issues, raises an amalgam of philosophical and empirical controversies that are contested rhetorically in political debate.

No generalized theory—whether liberal democratic or neo-Marxist—can account for the public's impact on policy making in each and every case. The public's role in the policy-making process varies situationally, and we have only begun to identify the variables involved. Recalling the Founding Father's ambivalence about deference to the people, we recognize that our political philosophy provides for exceptions to popular rule. Further, we recognize that policy makers are typically confronted with multiple, often competing, portraits of public opinion—portraits constructed rhetorically from ambiguous empirical data. It remains, however, to elaborate precisely the philosophical and empirical *topoi* of debate over public opinion. Why, in some policy debates, does public opinion become a major issue, while in others it plays a minor role? How is the paradox of popular sovereignty in our constitutional tradition manifested in arguments for and against deference to the public? How are vastly differing portraits of public opinion constructed rhetorically in the age of scientific polling? And why do some portraits of public opinion—sometimes even fictional publics—prevail over others?

The fate of the freeze initiative in Congress suggests some intriguing answers to these questions. Throughout the House freeze debate of 1982-1983, public opinion, as mediated by the policy makers themselves, played an important role. Yet that role was far more complicated than either liberal democratic or neo-Marxist theories of the public might suggest. From the outset, supporters and opponents of a freeze resolution disagreed about the public's competence to dictate policy in the realm of strategic nuclear weapons, and they debated at length the breadth and character of public support for a freeze. In 1982, the House narrowly rejected a freeze resolution, only to turn around and overwhelmingly endorse a second freeze resolution in 1983. At first glance, the explanation for this turnabout appears clear: the voters sent a strong pro-freeze message in the elections of November 1982. But upon closer examination, an alternative explanation emerges: the House completely transformed the resolution into a substantively ambiguous endorsement, not of the freeze in particular, but of arms control in general. As a response to general public fears and concerns about nuclear weapons, the House resolution symbolically reaffirmed the sovereignty of the people, acknowledging the public's concern over the arms race. At the same time, however, the resolution reflected skepticism that the freeze campaign had generated informed public support for any particular arms control policy. Like the Catholic bishops' pastoral letter, the House freeze resolution of 1983 ambiguously endorsed all efforts to control nuclear weapons, and it actually helped kill the freeze as a political controversy.

## Public Opinion and the House Freeze Debate

Although the proposal for a mutual freeze on the testing, production and deployment of nuclear weapons originated with disarmament groups on the fringes of American politics, it did not take long for it to reach the floor of the U.S. Congress. With many polls showing strong public support for the initiative and the issue dominating the news, freeze activists introduced resolutions in both houses of Congress in the spring of 1982. Freeze activists pushed first for consideration in the House of Representatives, however, confident that the lower house would be "more susceptible to pressure from hometown freeze groups."[19]

Following a series of arms control hearings beginning in April 1982, the House Foreign Affairs Committee reported out a freeze resolution, designated H.J.Res. 521, by a vote of 28-8. Popularly named for committee chair Clement Zablocki, the Zablocki resolution initially commanded widespread support. But during the day-long floor debate on August 5, supporters of the administration's arms control initiatives introduced a substitute amendment, the so-called Broomfield substitute, calling for "an equitable and verifiable" freeze "at equal and substantially reduced levels." After some ten hours of floor debate, the House, in effect, rejected the freeze by approving this amendment endorsing the Reagan administration's START initiative. The vote, however, was very close: 204 to 202.[20]

Nuclear freeze supporters remained undaunted by their first defeat. In the spring of 1983, Zablocki introduced another resolution calling for a "mutual and verifiable freeze"—this time designated H.J.Res. 13—and again the Foreign Affairs Committee reported it out favorably by a vote of 27 to 9. When the second Zablocki resolution reached the House floor on March 16th, opponents of the freeze again sought to gut the resolution with dozens of amendments, including a "build-down" substitute amendment introduced by Democrat Elliot Levitas of Georgia. This proposed alternative to the freeze went down to defeat, but some thirty other amendments passed, significantly watering down the freeze resolution. After forty-two hours of debate over seven weeks, the House approved this second freeze resolution, 278 to 149.[21]

How does one account for this turnabout on the nuclear freeze issue? What role did the freeze campaign or public opinion generally play in persuading the House to reverse its position? According to observers sympathetic to the freeze, the answer is clear: the freeze campaign, in effect, forced the change-of-heart with a clear demonstration of its political clout in the 1982 elections. As part of the story of how the freeze campaign democratized the nuclear debate, this view of the congressional debate portrays it as a great victory, not only for the freeze campaign but for the people as well. As Rebecca Bjork has put it, the burgeoning public concern inspired by the freeze campaign quickly "permeated all levels of government, eventually including the United States Congress."[22] It was, Bjork and others have suggested, a simple case of democracy at work.

Public concern indeed permeated Congress, but some lawmakers remained skeptical throughout the debate of the public's competence to decide the nation's strategic arms policies. From the beginning of the House freeze debate, opponents of the initiative questioned whether public support for the freeze was more romantic than rational,[23] and they wondered whether the public really understood even the most basic issues involved. Calling the matter "enormously complicated," Republican Henry Hyde of Illinois declared that the issue went beyond the public's "conventional wisdom": "Do you think the average American knows the difference between a Titan II, a Minuteman III, a Pershing, [and] a Poseidon? These are enormously complicated subjects, are they not?"[24] Hyde even suggested that the average citizen might confuse the debate with television advertising: "If you ask the average American what is a Trident, he thinks it is a stick of gum. If you ask the average American what a Minuteman is, he thinks it is an ad for an insurance company."[25]

According to freeze opponents, the public was not only ignorant about nuclear issues but disinterested as well. Republican Edward Derwinski of Illinois insisted that more people were "out watching ball games tonight" than were "worrying about what is said here."[26] Turning the question of deference on its head, Republican William Carney of New York claimed that most Americans preferred to leave such matters to the politicians and the experts: "They want peace, but they believe they should leave that up to their representatives in Congress, and we, in turn, should leave it up to the professional negotiators."[27]

Freeze supporters, of course, painted a much different portrait of the American people. Calling the freeze movement a rational response to the cold war policies of the Reagan administration, Democrat Edward Markey of Massachusetts argued that support for the freeze was not simply a "response to bumper sticker politics, to slogans or easy-to-understand symbols."[28] Pro-freeze representatives insisted that the people were both knowledgeable and concerned about nuclear weapons, and they legitimized the public's views by noting that they were shared by Nobel laureates, former ambassadors, and "dozens of respected leaders in law, medicine, and academics."[29] Throughout America, they argued, the people had "chosen to educate themselves on the issue, to ponder what can be done about it, and to convert their conclusions into political action."[30] Indeed, Markey's portrait of the public, a public suddenly "reawakened to the danger of nuclear war," surpassed even the most idealistic visions of democratic theorists:

> They have begun to study the arcane details of nuclear weaponry. They have begun to analyze the strategic doctrines that will bring us to peace or megadeath. And they have begun to ask questions—questions that have heretofore been the property of that elite group of nuclear theologians who have controlled the fate of this Earth, questions that have left our leaders stammering to explain why they have presided over this insane buildup of nuclear arms, questions that have cut to the very heart of the issue.[31]

Most pro-freeze lawmakers conceded that the average citizen did not possess technical knowledge about nuclear weapons and strategic policies. They admitted that their constituents did not understand "the difference between throw weight and dead weight," and that they were unconcerned with policy details; they just demanded "that the arms race be stopped."[32] The pro-freeze public spoke in "frightened and angry voices,"[33] not with the calm, calculating rationality of the policy expert. Hence, even supporters of the freeze reserved the right to exercise their own best judgment. "Although the urgings of my constituents are of prime importance to me," Democrat Peter Kostmayer of Pennsylvania proclaimed, "I could not and would not support this resolution if I thought it would freeze the United States at an inferior level to the Soviet Union."[34]

Yet unlike the politicians and the experts, the pro-freeze public had the special wisdom of common sense. "What has happened in the past year," Democrat Bob Edgar of Pennsylvania argued, "is that the public has decided that the country's nuclear weapons policy has lost any basis in common sense and that decisions should no longer be left entirely to the experts."[35] For far too long, the American people had been silent while "government leaders and military experts . . . brought us closer to the brink of total destruction."[36] But now the public was "far ahead of the policymakers."[37] Now the public was saying "no" to the "Dr. Strangelove" theorists.[38] As Edward Markey summarized the anti-politician, anti-expert sentiments of the pro-freeze public: "The freeze has caught on simply because it makes good sense. The experts and the administration have been astonished. But as . . . Emerson once said, 'Nothing astonishes men so much as commonsense.'"[39]

With common sense qualifying the public to decide, the pro-freeze case ultimately rested upon a powerful normative appeal: the House's tradition as "a body dedicated to . . . allowing the will of the people to be heard through legislation."[40] "We are the people's House," Republican Jim Leach of Iowa proclaimed. "We have a duty in whatever small way we can to express the concerns of the people of the most awesome democracy ever created on this, the most important issue of our age."[41] Pro-freeze lawmakers insisted that the people had as much "right to be heard in our democracy on foreign and defense policy . . . as on domestic policy."[42] Indeed, they had not only a "right" but a "duty" to "try to improve our policy"; their criticism was "a price we pay for democracy."[43] Thus, pro-freeze lawmakers argued for deference to the people—given that the people had met their obligation to render an informed judgment. "We are not here as leaders," Democrat Norman D'Amours of New Hampshire concluded, "we are here as followers."[44] And with that philosophical principle, none of the lawmakers publicly disagreed.

Still, a crucial question remained to be answered: what, exactly, did the people want? Throughout the House freeze debate, the two sides vigorously disputed the breadth and depth of support for the freeze, and that disagreement spilled over into a number of related questions about public attitudes toward nuclear weapons and strategic policy. These questions, of course, raised primarily empirical rather than normative issues, and they contributed further to the development of two distinctive portraits of public opinion on the nuclear freeze.

## The People Speak

As a "persuasive definition," as rhetorical scholar David Zarefsky has argued, the term "movement" evokes "connotations of motion, determinism, future-orientation, and sympathy for the underdog." For advocates without political power, the term "movement" functions rhetorically "to raise the stakes, enhance the drama of the situation, and impart a sense of destiny" to a political cause. Yet even those in power often claim to speak for movements to "distinguish themselves from their predecessors, to imply that they cannot be co-opted, or to attract attention."[45]

During the House freeze debate, dozens of establishment politicians claimed to speak for a movement—and not just any movement, but a spontaneous and grass-roots movement comparable, in some minds, only to "the revolution which freed us from England."[46] Again and again, freeze advocates emphasized that the resolution before the House was not concocted by politicians or foreign policy experts. Rather, it came "from the bottom up"[47]; the term grass-roots invariably accompanied descriptions of the movement in pro-freeze rhetoric.[48] As portrayed by its supporters, the freeze movement constituted a "profound plea" by millions of "concerned Americans."[49] A "tremendous outpouring of grassroots support" had placed the matter on the national agenda.[50] Thus it was "more than a protest"; it was not just "a fad."[51] Rather, it was a "national grass-roots mandate" that was, according to its supporters, "virtually unparalleled in U.S. history."[52]

Moreover, freeze supporters insisted that the movement was remarkably diverse demographically; it transcended political, economic, and religious distinctions.[53] It was "not a liberal movement, nor a youth movement, nor a partisan undertaking"; it was "quintessentially middle class."[54] It expressed a "growing consensus among Americans from all walks of life, from all political parties," and from all areas of the country—"from Maine to California."[55] It included doctors as well as laborers, civic leaders along with academics and students, admirals and actors, farmers and lawyers, and religious leaders from every denomination.[56] Finally, it was distinguished by its intergenerational makeup. As Mario Biaggi of New York observed, "picture after picture" from freeze demonstrations showed "young and older people marching side by side united in support for an end to the arms race."[57]

Congressman Biaggi was not alone in pointing to demonstrations as proof of the freeze movement's breadth. Demonstrations commonly function as synecdoches for larger political movements,[58] and in the House freeze debate they became symptomatic of—indeed, virtually synonymous with—*vox populi* itself. Thus a single freeze demonstration in Washington, according to freeze advocates, "amply demonstrated the concerns and commitment of the American people." The thousands who participated represented "millions of Americans who have been and are deeply involved and concerned with U.S. nuclear weapons policy."[59] Likewise, the thousands who protested in New York on 12 June 1982 became "the voice of millions and millions of Americans" who did not attend.[60] According to freeze supporters, the crowd in New York ranged from "upward of 500,000," to "more than 700,000," to "almost one million," and it consisted of people "of all ages, races, political persuasions," and "from all parts of the country."[61] Most interestingly, the New York rally not only communicated the public's general fears but also its specific policy preferences. As Democrat Tom Harkin of Iowa argued: "600,000 people marched in New York City the other day in support of the freeze and not START, not the Levitas 2-for-1 build-down proposal, and certainly not the Broomfield amendment."[62]

Public opinion polls provided the final proof of the "genuine outflowing of grassroots sentiment" behind the freeze resolution.[63] Citing numerous polls, House freeze supporters proclaimed "the message from the grassroots . . . clear": the people demanded "an immediate nuclear freeze."[64] Among the polls cited by freeze supporters in 1982 were a *Newsweek* poll showing that "68% of Americans favor a freeze"; a Gallup poll from June 1981 showing 72 percent of Americans favoring a "mutual ban on the production of nuclear weapons"; and a Harris poll indicating that "81 percent of those polled favored a bilateral freeze."[65] In 1983, freeze supporters added still more polls to the list: a Gallup poll from December 1982 showing "71 percent of all American adults" favoring "an immediate nuclear freeze"; a new Harris poll, taken in January 1983, showing "76 percent of the public in favor of a U.S.-U.S.S.R. freeze agreement"; and yet another Harris poll from March 1983 revealing that "79% of the American public" supported "a bilateral freeze."[66] Freeze supporters also claimed that the polls showed growing support for the freeze,[67] and they even cited a poll or two to help account for the phenomenal figures. As Peter Rodino explained:

> The American people are calling for this resolution because they realize, as Einstein predicted, that this is not merely a question of national interest, but of the future of the human race.
>
> According to a Harris poll taken earlier this year, 86 percent of the American people believe that "even a limited nuclear war cannot be won, but will result inevitably in an all-out nuclear war." Also, 70 percent of the American people now believe that "the risks of nuclear war starting by accident are growing because both sides keep adding to the number of weapons." This is the finding of an ABC News-Washington Post poll.[68]

Congressional freeze supporters called upon their colleagues to heed "the voice of the vast majority of the American people who have indicated in polls and demonstrations . . . that they want to see a halt to the arms race."[69] Public opinion polls and marches in the street, they argued, had sent "a message we cannot ignore."[70] Insisting that demonstrations communicated clear policy preferences and that the polls revealed "consistent support for a nuclear freeze," they concluded that the citizens of the United States were "demanding that those of us here in Washington carry out their desires and adopt a plan for a freeze on nuclear weapons."[71]

Conservative lawmakers, of course, were not about to concede such a portrait of American public opinion. Indeed, conservative Democrat Larry McDonald of Georgia denied the very existence of the freeze movement itself: "There is no grassroots movement of support for this resolution." According to McDonald, freeze resolutions by local and state governments had been "orchestrated by small groups of activists," and these were "the same activists who formerly were telling us that the South Vietnamese . . . would be 'better off' under the Communists." Echoing charges by the Reagan administration, McDonald argued that the "so-called peace campaign" was in fact "a Soviet covert action campaign—clandestine political warfare." In McDonald's conspiratorial world view, such pro-freeze organizations as Physicians for Social Responsibility actually promoted the agenda of "Soviet-backed Third World terrorist groups."[72]

Charges that the freeze movement was a communist plot, however, did not carry the day. While pro-freeze lawmakers indignantly dismissed the "allegations and innuendoes" as a "repugnant, inappropriate means of argument,"[73] even some of the staunchest opponents of the freeze downplayed the theme. "I do not think it is fair . . . to say that the Soviet Union is manipulating the freeze movement," conservative leader Henry Hyde conceded during hearings in the Foreign Affairs Committee.[74]

Yet opponents of the freeze remained insistent that the freeze campaign did not speak for the average American. Conservatives generally agreed with McDonald that only the "usual activists" had been involved in the demonstrations, and that the size and significance of the demonstrations had been exaggerated.[75] "We are all aware of [the demonstrations]," Republican Larry Winn of Kansas stated; "It is a form of, obviously, public opinion." Yet disputing pro-freeze claims that the demonstrators represented a cross-section of grass-roots Americans, Winn expressed his feeling that the protestors did not speak for the typical American: "I . . . have a horrible feeling that a great many of the people that are participating in those demonstrations, in those marches, are some of the same people that would not have us spend [a] penny . . . on our own security."[76]

Anti-freeze legislators confirmed Winn's feeling with a very different interpretation of the public opinion polls. While anti-freeze lawmakers had no doubt that the polls showed "the overwhelming majority of Americans" truly wanting "an end to the arms race,"[77] they questioned whether that desire translated specifically into support for the freeze. Exploring the polling data at greater depths than their opponents, anti-freeze lawmakers raised two fundamental challenges to the pro-freeze portrait of public opinion. First, they pointed out that the polls showed the public turning against the freeze if, as a result, "the Soviet Union would gain a military advantage."[78] As freeze opponents pointed out, a "70 percent majority" took this position, rejecting "a nuclear freeze that would leave this country second in defense capabilities to the Russians."[79] Second, anti-freeze lawmakers argued that the polls showed that "the *sine qua non* of any agreement negotiated with the Russians is that it must be verifiable." As Republican Norman Lent of New York observed, 80 percent of Americans opposed a freeze "if either side could cheat."[80] More importantly, freeze opponents cited polls showing that 80 to 90 percent of Americans believed the Soviets would cheat on a freeze agreement.[81] This finding, they concluded, revealed "a strong current of healthy suspicion which flows beneath and erodes away the superficial public support for the freeze movement."[82]

By emphasizing the public's reservations about the freeze, opponents of the measure cast at least some doubt on pro-freeze claims of a clear public mandate. Perhaps some lawmakers also hoped that the administration's vigorous lobbying had blunted the freeze movement's political momentum. Furthermore, some lawmakers may have doubted that the public really cared about the issue. Whatever their thinking, a majority of the lower house thought it safe to oppose the freeze in August of 1982, despite the upcoming November elections.

Yet only six months after the 1982 elections, the big turnabout took place, with the House passing a second freeze resolution by nearly a two-to-one margin. What brought about this dramatic increase in support for the freeze? What role, if any, did debate over public opinion play in the turnabout? For answers to these questions we must examine more closely the 1983 debate. Specifically, we must examine some of the differences between the freeze resolution defeated in 1982 and the version passed in 1983.

## The "Turnabout" on the Freeze

When the House freeze debate resumed in the spring of 1983, a new climate prevailed. As a *New York Times*/CBS News survey revealed, the new members elected in 1982 favored the freeze by 67 to 33 percent, and this alone would have created a 55 percent pro-freeze majority in the new House.[83] The forty-two hours of floor debate between March and May did little to change the figures. When the final vote came, the 81 members of the freshman class voted 53 to 28 in favor of the freeze.

Yet the pro-freeze turnabout went well beyond the freshman class. Analysis of the voting also reveals a strong pro-freeze trend among returning lawmakers. Of the 28 lawmakers who chose not to vote at all on the issue in 1982, all 12 who won reelection voted for the freeze in 1983. Surprisingly, 35 lawmakers who voted against the freeze in 1982 reversed themselves completely, voting for the freeze in 1983.[84]

How does one account for such a remarkable turnabout? The most obvious answer—at least according to freeze advocates in Congress—was that millions of Americans had sent a powerful message in the 1982 elections.[85] In addition to observing that many of their "newer colleagues were . . . aided in their elections by taking a strong stand on this issue,"[86] pro-freeze lawmakers labeled the dozens of freeze referenda approved across the nation a clear "public mandate."[87] As Democrat Lee Hamilton of Indiana summarized the election returns, "one-third of the American electorate had some form of freeze on the ballot," and "a large majority voted in favor."[88] Others reminded their colleagues that, as of election day 1982, 9 states, 340 cities, 63 county councils, 321 city councils, and between 400 and 500 town meetings had passed freeze resolutions, and they calculated that these bodies represented nearly 12 million American voters.[89] Thus freeze supporters did not hesitate to exploit their fellow politicians' most primordial fear: the fear of electoral defeat. As Iowa Republican Jim Leach summarized the message of the 1982 elections, politicians could "ignore the heedings of educated America" only "at political peril for themselves and for their political parties."[90]

Yet a second, more subtle point must be considered when accounting for the turnabout on the freeze. That point, virtually lost in media coverage of the debate, is simply that the House did not approve the same resolution in 1983 that it rejected in 1982. In addition to calling for a "mutual verifiable freeze on the testing, production, and further deployment" of nuclear weapons, the freeze resolution of 1983 carried a host of amendments addressing many of the concerns and reservations raised by opponents of the resolution in 1982. Most notably, the 1983 freeze resolution contained new language insisting upon the maintenance and verification of an equal balance of nuclear forces, and it even endorsed President Reagan's call for reductions in nuclear weapons.[91] As substantive changes, these amendments only obfuscated the resolution, denying what both sides in the debate had long affirmed: that the freeze and Reagan's START initiative were mutually exclusive. As a result, freeze advocates could claim that they won the debate, securing a resolution calling for a "freeze, *then* reductions." But so too could freeze opponents claim victory, arguing that they had "successfully gutted the resolution."[92]

After two years of intense lobbying, prolonged committee hearings, and heated debate on the floor, the House, in effect, declared a draw in the freeze debate. Yet for lawmakers more concerned with public opinion than with the intricacies of strategic arms policy, the ambiguity of the resolution proved its greatest virtue. As Congressman Leon Panetta argued, the resolution could be everything to everybody. "Whether you are a Hawk or a Dove or something in between," he argued, "you can interpret anything you want in this resolution. . . . When you go back home you can say anything you want about this resolution."[93]Furthermore, as

Representative Parren Mitchell pointed out, the resolution "did not mandate anybody to do anything." It was "a powerless piece of legislation"—nothing more than "a vehicle by means of which the people could speak to this Congress and to the President and to the rest of the Nation."[94]

The ambiguity and impotence of the freeze resolution became abundantly clear as the House voted on specific defense policies during the 98th Congress. As Waller has observed, passage of the freeze resolution in 1983 did not "result in a Congress actually ready to halt the arms race." Instead, there was a "return to business as usual," with the House voting on May 24, "just 20 days after passage of the freeze resolution," to fund further production of the MX missile.[95] With the House thus declining to heed its own call to freeze the arms race, the issue all but disappeared from the congressional agenda. Freeze advocates may have claimed victory, but with each new weapon approved their celebration rang hollow.

## A Telepolitical Victory

As a study in the role of public opinion in institutional policy making, the House freeze debate illustrated how the process may be oversimplified by theories declaring that, in each and every case, the public's influence is real or merely a fiction. Policy makers neither simply absorb public opinion and automatically defer to its dictates, nor do they always concoct entirely fictional publics to justify a priori decisions. Rather, they deliberate, in particular cases, their obligation to defer to the people, and they debate how best to interpret ambiguous—often conflicting—empirical data.

The Founders never envisioned a system in which majority opinion invariably prevailed. Designing checks against a tyranny of the majority, they insulated certain policy-making institutions from the will of the people, and they declared the public better equipped to decide some issues than others. In the House freeze debate, both of these variables—the institutional context and the character of the issues—shaped debate over the weight accorded to public opinion. On the one hand, the policy-making context warranted arguments for deference to the people. Voiced in the House of Representatives, appeals to the people drew strength from over two hundred years of constitutional tradition. On the other hand, the complexity of the issues warranted counterbalancing normative arguments. More than most political issues, questions of nuclear weapons and strategic policy reside in the technical rather than the public sphere of argument,[96] and even some freeze supporters expressed reservations about the public's competence to decide the matter. Two powerful impulses thus collided in the House freeze debate, with the result perhaps predictable: a resolution giving voice to the people's general concerns without dictating a specific policy.

Theoretically, one might posit an ideological explanation for the competing philosophies of popular sovereignty manifested in the House freeze debate. In this case, political liberals championed deference to the people, while conservatives were more elitist. In other major congressional debates, however, the roles have been reversed. In the Senate debate over the Panama Canal treaties, for example, conservatives urged deference to the people while liberals doubted the public's competence.[97] It appears, then, that no partisan camp has a monopoly on appeals to the will of the people. Rooted in our common political heritage, the rhetoric of popular sovereignty transcends partisan distinctions.

As a result, the issue of public opinion typically boils down to empirical questions. If public opinion is to influence policy making, it must somehow be communicated to policy makers, and the will of the people on particular issues is rarely beyond dispute. Reducing a diverse multiplicity of voices to a few simple categories, polls inevitably mask important nuances of opinion, and they reveal little about the knowledge or motivations behind public attitudes. Other measures of public opinion—demonstrations and election returns, for example—are even less reliable. On specific matters of public policy, public opinion remains an elusive phenomenon. Faced with voluminous, often conflicting evidence, even policy makers determined to defer to the people typically must decide which public to obey.

In the House freeze debate, proponents defined support for the freeze as a grass-roots movement, and they cited poll after poll indicating overwhelming support for the initiative. Opponents conceded the public's fears and concerns about nuclear weapons, but they disputed that freeze demonstrators spoke for the people. Most importantly, they cited polls revealing important public reservations about the freeze, raising doubts about the character and depth of support for the initiative. As a result, the debate again ended in something of a stalemate. And again the result was perhaps predictable: a watered-down resolution allowing both sides to claim victory.

Polls may never capture fully the reality of public opinion, but some interpretations of the polls are better than others. As is typically the case, the message of the freeze polls proved fuzzy, even contradictory, and the two sides in the House debate interpreted them loosely. Both sides in the debate invoked polls selectively, and neither side attended to nuances of sampling and question-wording that can make enormous differences in the findings.[98] Opponents of the freeze pointed to polls showing public reservations about the freeze, but even they failed to grasp the full significance of those findings. As we shall see, public support for the freeze indeed came heavily qualified—so much so that the polls could have been interpreted, in practical terms, as revealing opposition to the freeze.

Moreover, neither side in the debate paid much attention to polls revealing an almost unbelievable level of public disinterest in the debate. For example, a CBS News/*New York Times* poll in the spring of 1982 revealed that almost 60 percent of Americans considered the freeze issue "too complicated" for the public to decide, while 45 percent admitted they "had not paid attention" to the debate.[99]

As late as April 1982, a *Newsweek* poll revealed that only 43 percent of Americans had even heard of a nuclear freeze movement.[100] In yet another poll taken more than a year later, 45 percent of Americans confessed that they still had not "heard or read anything" at all about a proposed freeze.[101] Nor did surveys support claims that the election returns of November 1982 revealed clear support for the freeze. Post-election polling revealed little correlation between the freeze and candidate preferences in congressional races, and as usual in a midterm election, only a minority of the people voted at all.[102]

All these considerations argue for a rhetorical and situational perspective on the role of public opinion in the policy-making process. Since policy makers themselves debate how to weigh and to read the public's preferences, politically relevant public opinion is discovered, not through survey research, but by examining the will of the people as mediated or filtered by the decision makers themselves. These politically relevant portraits of the people, in turn, can be described precisely only in particular cases. In some situations, policy makers may be persuaded that the public is perfectly qualified to decide an issue, and they may defer to a relatively clear mandate from the people. In other situations, policy makers may conclude that the public is too disinterested or ill-informed to guide a policy decision, or they may defer to a demonstrably fictional portrait of the people.

Freeze activists claimed a great victory in the House of Representatives, and the freeze resolution may indeed have given expression to a new sense of urgency about the arms race—the feeling that something needed to be done. At the same time, however, the debate actually played right into the hands of the Reagan administration, helping to "kill" the freeze issue and to circumscribe the public's role in the nuclear debate. Refusing to endorse the freeze unequivocally in the name of the people, the House nevertheless put the issue to rest. With Reagan's Strategic Defense Initiative capturing more and more attention,[103] the experts again entered the debate. Supplanting the public voice, scientists and policy analysts again posed questions that only they could answer: Was "Star Wars" technologically feasible? Would it be legal under ABM agreements?

Perhaps the House freeze debate should remind us of why the Founding Fathers saw fit to constitute a second legislative body—one with greater powers in foreign affairs—more insulated from the "intemperate passions" and "fluctuations" of the popular will.[104] With one eye on the polls and the other on news coverage of the debate, the House concocted a political illusion: a resolution "headlined" with some of the language of the freeze yet actually supportive of the Reagan administration's policies. Such a maneuver might have reaffirmed the sovereignty of the people symbolically. But as a blueprint for strategic arms policy, the heavily amended freeze resolution achieved little. Even its supporters proclaimed it so ambiguous as to be virtually meaningless as an arms control initiative, and it undoubtedly sent conflicting signals to both U.S. allies and adversaries.

The House freeze debate testified to the difficulty of fashioning policies that are both politically expedient and substantively sound. The public speaks with many voices. In foreign affairs, however, the nation must speak with one. More than that, the House freeze debate testified once again to the impact of journalism on the national political agenda and public dialogue. Why did the House of Representatives suddenly take up the freeze issue in 1982? And why did public opinion become such a central issue in the debate? At least part of the answer undoubtedly lies in the news media's portrait of the freeze campaign—a portrait that characterized the campaign as an unprecedented and politically powerful grass-roots movement.

## Notes

1. Thomas Jefferson, Letter to John Adams, 10 December 1819, in *The Writings of Thomas Jefferson*, edited by Andrew A. Lipscomb (Washington, D.C.: Thomas Jefferson Memorial Association, 1907), 10:153.
2. Alexander Hamilton, James Madison, and John Jay, *The Federalist Papers*, edited by Clinton Rossiter (New York: New American Library, 1961), 241, 432.
3. Ibid., xv.
4. Ibid., 327.
5. Gordon S. Wood, *The Creation of the American Republic* (New York: W.W. Norton, 1969), 515.
6. Hamilton, Madison, and Jay, *The Federalist Papers*, 384.
7. One notable exception is Ernest R. May, who argues that policy making, at least in foreign affairs, should not be influenced by public opinion, but rather "should come to a larger extent from calculation by experts" (May, "An American Tradition in Foreign Policy," in *Theory and Practice in American Politics*, edited by Nelson, 102).
8. Bailey, *A Diplomatic History of the American People*, 756.
9. The classic study is Angus Campbell, et al., *The American Voter* (New York: John Wiley and Sons, 1960).
10. Robert E. Lane and David O. Sears, *Public Opinion* (Englewood Cliffs: Prentice-Hall, 1964), 3.
11. Kolko, *The Roots of American Foreign Policy*, 13.
12. Lloyd F. Bitzer, "Rhetoric and Public Knowledge," in *Rhetoric, Philosophy and Literature: An Exploration*, edited by Don M. Burks (West Lafayette: Purdue University Press, 1978), 75.
13. Gerald Hauser and Carole Blair, "Antecedents to the Public," *Pre-Text* 3 (Summer 1982): 140.
14. Richard Vatz, "Public Opinion and Presidential Ethos," *Western Journal of Speech Communication* 40 (Summer 1976): 201, 204-5.
15. Hauser and Blair, "Antecedents to the Public," 140-41.
16. Michael C. McGee, "In Search of 'the People': A Rhetorical Alternative," *Quarterly Journal of Speech* 61 (October 1975): 239-40.
17. Bernard C. Cohen, *The Public's Impact on Foreign Policy* (Boston: Little, Brown, and Co., 1973), 11.
18. McGee, "In Search of 'the People,'" 249.
19. Waller, *Congress and the Nuclear Freeze*, 102.

20. See U.S. Congress, House, Committee on Foreign Affairs, *Congress and Foreign Policy, 1982*, 98th Cong, 1st sess., 1983, 12-20.
21. See "House OKs, Senate Rejects Nuclear Freeze," *1983 Congressional Quarterly Almanac*, edited by Cohn, 205-11.
22. Bjork, "Reagan and the Nuclear Freeze," 183-85, 192.
23. Henry Hyde in U.S. Congress, House, "Calling for a Mutual and Verifiable Freeze on and Reductions in Nuclear Weapons," 98th Cong., 1st sess., *Congressional Record*, daily ed., vol. 129, no. 52 (21 April 1983), H2279. Hereafter cited as *Congressional Record*, 21 April 1983.
24. U.S. Congress, House, Committee on Foreign Affairs, *Calling for a Mutual and Verifiable Freeze on and Reductions in Nuclear Weapons: Hearings and Markup*, 98th Cong., 1st sess., 2 March 1983, 165.
25. U.S. Congress, House, "Providing for Consideration of House Joint Resolution 138, Calling for a Mutual and Verifiable Freeze on and Reductions in Nuclear Weapons," 98th Cong., 1st. sess., *Congressional Record*, daily ed., vol. 129, no. 33 (16 March 1983), H1216. Hereafter cited as *Congressional Record*, 16 March 1983.
26. U.S. Congress, House, "Calling for a Mutual and Verifiable Freeze on and Reductions in Nuclear Weapons and for Approval of the SALT II Agreement," 97th Cong., 2nd sess., *Congressional Record*, daily ed., vol. 128, no. 106, pt. 2 (5 August 1982), H5348. Hereafter cited as *Congressional Record*, 5 August 1982.
27. U.S. Congress, House, Committee on Foreign Affairs, *Calling for a Mutual and Verifiable Freeze on and Reductions in Nuclear Weapons*, 2 March 1983, 165.
28. *Congressional Record*, 16 March 1983, H1210.
29. Nicholas Mavroules in *Congressional Record*, 5 August 1982, H5291.
30. Olympia Snowe in *Congressional Record*, 5 August 1982, H5288.
31. *Congressional Record*, 16 March 1983, H1210.
32. Tom Harkin in U.S. Congress, House, "Calling for a Mutual and Verifiable Freeze on and Reductions in Nuclear Weapons," 98th Cong., 1st sess., *Congressional Record*, vol. 129, no. 46, daily ed. (13 April 1983), H2063. Hereafter cited as *Congressional Record*, 13 April 1983.
33. George Brown in *Congressional Record*, 5 August 1982, H5314.
34. *Congressional Record*, 16 March 1983, H1256.
35. Ibid., H1285.
36. Louis Stokes in *Congressional Record*, 5 August 1982, H5317.
37. John LaFalce in *Congressional Record*, 16 March 1983, H1293.
38. Pete Stark in *Congressional Record*, 5 August 1982, H5311.
39. *Congressional Record*, 16 March 1983, H1210.
40. Pete Stark in *Congressional Record*, 16 March 1983, H1282.
41. *Congressional Record*, 5 August 1982, H5281.
42. Howard Wolpe in *Congressional Record*, 21 April 1983, H2278.
43. Lee Hamilton in *Congressional Record*, 16 March 1983, H1233.
44. *Congressional Record*, 5 August 1982, H5350.
45. David Zarefsky, "A Skeptical View of Movement Studies," *Central States Speech Journal* 31 (Winter 1980): 248.
46. Mario Biaggi in *Congressional Record*, 5 August 1982, H5312.
47. Jim Leach in *Congressional Record*, 16 March 1983, H1218.
48. See, for example, Leon Panetta in *Congressional Record*, 16 March 1983, H1236; Richard Ottinger in *Congressional Record*, 21 April 1983, H2284; and J.J. Pickle in *Congressional Record*, 5 August 1982, H5290.

49. Jim Leach in *Congressional Record*, 16 March 1983, H1219.
50. James Oberstar in *Congressional Record*, 21 April 1983, H2277.
51. Jim Leach in *Congressional Record*, 16 March 1983, H1219.
52. William Ford in *Congressional Record*, 5 August 1982, H5311; Bruce Vento in *Congressional Record*, 21 April 1983, H2283.
53. Edward Boland in *Congressional Record*, 5 August 1982, H5287.
54. Jim Leach in *Congressional Record*, 5 August 1982, H5281.
55. Stephen Solarz in *Congressional Record*, 16 March 1983, H1237; Jerry Patterson in *Congressional Record*, 5 August 1982, H5307.
56. Silvio Conte and Nicholas Mavroules in *Congressional Record*, 5 August 1982, H5228, H5291; Silvio Conte in *Congressional Record*, 16 March 1983, H1258.
57. *Congressional Record*, 5 August 1982, H5312.
58. As Kenneth Burke writes, the "synecdochic form is present in all theories of political representation," as some "part of the social body" is assumed to be representative of the whole. Todd Gitlin's study of the New Left illustrates specifically how demonstrations can represent a larger movement, particularly in media coverage. According to Gitlin, coverage of New Left demonstrations functioned to trivialize the larger movement, downplay its size, marginalize its participants, disparage its effectiveness, and portray it as violent. See Kenneth Burke, *A Grammar of Motives* (Berkeley: University of California Press, 1969), 508; Todd Gitlin, *The Whole World is Watching: Mass Media in the Making and Unmaking of the New Left* (Berkeley: University of California Press, 1980), esp. 27-28.
59. Bruce Vento in *Congressional Record*, 21 April 1983, H2283.
60. Jonathan Bingham in U.S. Congress, House, Committee on Foreign Affairs, *Strategic Arms Control and U.S. National Security Policy: Hearings and Markup*, 97th Cong., 2nd sess., 11 May 1982, 200.
61. Mario Biaggi, Benjamin Rosenthal, and Bill Green in *Congressional Record*, 5 August 1982, H5312, H5308, H5305; Jonathan Bingham in U.S. Congress, House, Committee on Foreign Affairs, *Strategic Arms Control and U.S. National Security Policy*, 11 May 1982, 200.
62. *Congressional Record*, 13 April 1983, H2063.
63. Letter from Michael Dukakis and other governors in *Congressional Record*, 13 April 1983, H2058.
64. Edward Markey in U.S. Congress, House, Committee on Foreign Affairs, *Strategic Arms Control and U.S. National Security Policy*, 11 May 1982, 52.
65. Jonathan Bingham in U.S. Congress, House, Committee on Foreign Affairs, *Strategic Arms Control and U.S. National Security Policy*, 11 May 1982, 43; Walter Fauntroy in *Congressional Record*, 5 August 1982, H5316; John LaFalce in *Congressional Record*, 5 August 1982, H5299.
66. Lee Hamilton and Edward Feighan in *Congressional Record*, 16 March 1983, H1233, H1234; Letter from Michael Dukakis and other governors in *Congressional Record*, 13 April 1983, H2058.
67. See, for example, Don Edwards in *Congressional Record*, 5 August 1982, H5337.
68. *Congressional Record*, 5 August 1982, H5232.
69. Bingham in U.S. Congress, House, Committee on Foreign Affairs, *Strategic Arms Control and U.S. National Security Policy*, 11 May 1982, 200.
70. Timothy Wirth in *Congressional Record*, 5 August 1982, H5314.
71. John LaFalce and Don Edwards in *Congressional Record*, 5 August 1982, H5299, H5337.

72. *Congressional Record,* 5 August 1982, H5242-43.
73. Bruce Vento in *Congressional Record,* 21 April 1983, H2283.
74. U.S. Congress, House, Committee on Foreign Affairs, *Calling for a Mutual and Verifiable Freeze on and Reductions in Nuclear Weapons,* 8 March 1983, 216. Both sides in the debate acknowledged that the American Communist Party supported the freeze, but so too did the communists support "milk for babies" and "expansion of the national park system." See Henry Hyde and Tom Lantos in U.S. Congress, House, Committee on Foreign Affairs, *Calling for a Mutual and Verifiable Freeze on and Reductions in Nuclear Weapons,* 8 March 1983, 216.
75. McDonald argued that the New York freeze rally attracted only 165,000 actual protestors, with the remainder of the crowd consisting of "young people attracted by the free rock concert." See *Congressional Record,* 5 August 1982, H5242, H5244.
76. U.S. Congress, House, Committee on Foreign Affairs, *Strategic Arms Control and U.S. National Security Policy,* 2 April 1982, 18.
77. Elwood Hillis in *Congressional Record,* 13 April 1983, H2042.
78. Robert Lagomarsino in *Congressional Record,* 5 August 1982, H5354.
79. Larry McDonald in *Congressional Record,* 5 August 1982, H5243. See also Henry Hyde in *Congressional Record,* 16 March 1983, H1216; and Samuel Stratton in U.S. Congress, House, Committee on Foreign Affairs, *Calling for a Mutual and Verifiable Freeze on and Reductions in Nuclear Weapons,* 2 March 1983, 139.
80. *Congressional Record,* 16 March 1983, H1295.
81. Jack Kemp in *Congressional Record,* 5 August 1982, H5259.
82. Herbert Bateman in *Congressional Record,* 13 April 1983, H2028.
83. Hedrick Smith, "New House Seems Less in Tune with Reagan," *New York Times,* 4 November 1982, A18.
84. For comparison of the voting in 1982 and 1983 see *Congressional Record,* 5 August 1982, H5359-60; U.S. Congress, House, "Calling for a Mutual and Verifiable Freeze on and Reductions in Nuclear Weapons," 98th Cong., 1st sess., *Congressional Record,* daily ed., vol. 129, no. 59 (4 May 1983), H2661.
85. Robert Kastenmeier in *Congressional Record,* 16 March 1983, H1274.
86. Mario Biaggi in *Congressional Record,* 16 March 1983, H1275.
87. Jerry Patterson in *Congressional Record,* 16 March 1983, H1289.
88. *Congressional Record,* 16 March 1983, H1233.
89. Clement Zablocki and Edward Feighan in *Congressional Record,* 16 March 1983, H1206, H1234; Donald Albosta in *Congressional Record,* 16 March 1983, H1282; Letter from Michael Dukakis and other governors in *Congressional Record,* 13 April 1983, H2058; Howard Wolpe and Robert Torricelli in U.S. Congress, House, Committee on Foreign Affairs, *Calling for a Mutual and Verifiable Freeze on and Reductions in Nuclear Weapons,* 8 March 1983, 35, 43-44.
90. *Congressional Record,* 16 March 1983, H1218.
91. For the texts of both resolutions, with amendments highlighted, see Appendices E and F in Garfinkle, *The Politics of the Nuclear Freeze,* 232-38.
92. See Waller, *Congress and the Nuclear Freeze,* 286-87.
93. *Congressional Record,* 21 April 1983, H2275.
94. U.S. Congress, House, "Calling for a Mutual and Verifiable Freeze on and Reductions in Nuclear Weapons," 98th Cong., 1st sess., *Congressional Record,* daily ed., vol. 129, no. 56 (28 April 1983), H2462.
95. Waller, *Congress and the Nuclear Freeze,* 290.
96. See Goodnight, "The Personal, Technical, and Public Spheres of Argument," 214-27.

97. J. Michael Hogan, "Public Opinion and American Foreign Policy: The Case of Illusory Support for the Panama Canal Treaties," *Quarterly Journal of Speech* 71 (August 1985): 308-09.
98. On the impact of variations in question-wording, see Ted J. Smith III and J. Michael Hogan, "Public Opinion and the Panama Canal Treaties of 1977," *Public Opinion Quarterly* 51 (Spring 1987): 5-30.
99. Judith Miller, "72% in Poll Back Nuclear Halt If Soviet Union Doesn't Gain," *New York Times*, 30 May 1982, 22.
100. "Newsweek Poll: Nuclear Forebodings," *Newsweek*, 26 April 1982, 24.
101. Peter Begans, "Americans More Worried About Foreign Affairs Than At Any Time in the Reagan Presidency," *ABC News/Washington Post Poll*, press release, 26 September 1983.
102. See Judith Miller, "Nuclear Freeze Debate Important in Few Races," *New York Times*, 19 October 1982, A18.
103. For an analysis of "Star Wars" as a rhetorical strategy designed to undermine support for the freeze, see Bjork, "Reagan and the Nuclear Freeze," 181-92.
104. Alexander Hamilton in *The Debates in the Several State Conventions on the Adoption of the Federal Constitution*, 2nd ed., edited by Jonathan Elliot (Philadelphia: J.B. Lippincott and Co., 1881), 2:301.

# Part III

# Portraits of the Public

Ellen Shub/THE PICTURE CUBE

## Chapter Seven

# The Rhetoric of a Telepolitical "Movement"

> Once in a great while, public opinion seems to rise up with a singular message, as if a great revelation had come to the common imagination. Something on that order may be occurring now . . . as a grass-roots campaign is spreading in support of a bilateral freeze on nuclear weapons.[1]
>
> Bill Moyers, *The CBS Evening News*

Critics on the left have long complained that the news media treat movements unfavorably, ignoring or trivializing their purposes, downplaying their size, marginalizing their participants, disparaging their effectiveness, emphasizing their violence, and privileging their critics.[2] That may have been true in the 1960s, at least before the police riot in Chicago produced a noticeable increase in media sympathy for antiwar demonstrators.[3] But in the 1970s and 1980s, movements generally enjoyed positive, even celebratory coverage by the news media, particularly on television news, and especially in contrast to campaigns and other species of politics-as-usual.

As Austin Ranney has argued, the most striking bias in contemporary television news is not so much an ideological bias as a structural bias against "*all* politicians, and especially against those most identified with electoral politics."[4] While television journalists generally treat movements as spontaneous, grass-roots expressions of the will of the people, they expose campaigns as pseudo-events staged by big-money consultants. While movements have prophecies and visions, campaigns are trivialized—reduced to mere games—by a rhetoric of horserace journalism. While protestors are glamorized as self-sacrificing and idealistic, journalists almost universally view candidates as suspect—"their public images probably false, their public statements disingenuous, their moral pronouncements hypocritical, their motives self-serving, and their promises ephemeral."[5]

No wonder hardly anybody admits to campaigning anymore. From presidential candidates to television evangelists, from environmentalists to advocates on both sides of the abortion controversy, all claim to lead movements against politics-as-usual. Journalists are quick to expose such claims by candidates for elective office, of course. Yet they routinely grant the label movement to a wide variety of special interest causes that are as well-financed, technologically sophisticated, and rhetorically orchestrated as any campaign. As a result, television news has helped transform the American political landscape into a cacophonous jungle of single-issue crusades. Coalition politics—the politics of compromise and concession—is simply too boring for television news.

Coverage of the nuclear freeze campaign provides a case-in-point. Although the freeze initiative arose out of a well-organized coalition of established political groups and eventually attracted support from virtually the entire liberal establishment, television news defined it as a grass-roots movement, celebrating the cause in two major ways. First, television news presented the freeze as the story, not just of any movement, but of an unprecedented and historic movement, international in scope, grass-roots in origins, and enjoying broad-based support from the public at large. On network news, the freeze movement erupted spontaneously and spread like fire, quickly dwarfing even the anti-war and civil rights movements of the 1960s. Magnifying the size and scope of the freeze movement, television news contributed to a widespread illusion that an overwhelming majority of Americans passionately supported the freeze initiative.

Second, television news personalized the freeze movement with sympathetic and ostensibly apolitical characters. On the evening news, the freeze movement's leaders were the intellectual and moral prophets of our age, and they sought only to educate the public. Featuring freeze advocates from the medical and religious communities, the evening news presented positive, even celebratory coverage of the freeze, disguising partisan attacks on the Reagan administration as exercises in public "education." Worse yet, the coverage was not only biased but almost uniformly superficial. Like television coverage of a presidential campaign, it reduced the whole nuclear debate to a contest of personalities, a meaningless political game.

Instead of providing more in-depth reporting about the issues of the freeze debate, documentary and television magazine programs only further dramatized and trivialized the freeze debate. Substituting still more apocalyptic imagery for substantive news, investigative television journalism fleshed out the portrait of a spontaneous grass-roots freeze movement, yet it provided no more politically enabling[6] information about the freeze initiative itself. Reducing the whole nuclear debate to a series of dramatic morality plays, the longer freeze stories only demonstrated once again how dramatic imperatives have led television news to shirk its most fundamental responsibility: "to enable people in a democracy to make decisions based on information."[7]

The rhetorical dynamics of television news may be illustrated by examining closely how one news organization, CBS News, covered the freeze debate. Providing extensive coverage of the freeze on the *CBS Evening News*, as well as in a major documentary and several segments of *60 Minutes*,[8] CBS News celebrated the freeze movement for nearly four years yet reported little about the freeze as an arms control policy. Looking at just one network's coverage, we may miss a nuance or two that distinguished one network from another. But as comparative studies of news content have shown, the differences across networks are largely cosmetic; all appear governed by the same basic values.[9] A close reading of one network's coverage provides a deeper understanding of those "news values" and how they have degraded the public dialogue.[10] Network television news proclaimed the freeze the most important public issue of the early 1980s. But, in the final analysis, it told us little about that issue and created an illusory portrait of an historic grass-roots movement.

## Spreading Like Fire

As Herbert Gans has written, "American news media have always emphasized stories of social disorder,"[11] and television news is particularly attracted to the spectacle of demonstrations in the streets. But demonstrations do more than appeal to the news values of television. They also function as synecdoches for larger political movements,[12] justifying the label movement and supporting claims about their size and significance. Stories about localized demonstrations are invariably framed on television news as symptomatic of larger national movements[13]—the larger and more boisterous the local demonstration, the more significant the movement it represents. At the same time, however, televised demonstrations are largely "decontextualized," or "abstracted from the political situation that provoked them."[14] As a result, demonstrations that may be only tangentially related often come packaged together on television news. In this fashion, television news fostered the signatory image of the 1960s: "that of youthful protestors picketing in massive numbers, singing, chanting, and venting their anger" against the system. Not only did such imagery blend diverse and often warring political factions into a monolithic movement, it also masked the fact that young people generally were far more supportive of the Vietnam war than were older Americans.[15]

Television coverage of the nuclear freeze movement likewise illustrated how demonstrations function as synecdoches—often in misleading fashion. After a decade in which the news media almost totally ignored anti-nuclear protests,[16] CBS News discovered the nuclear freeze movement in the fall of 1981 and instantly proclaimed it historic. As portrayed on the *CBS Evening News*, the freeze movement appeared out of nowhere, "spreading like fire" across both Europe and the United States.[17] Like no movement before, it spread beyond the campuses, beyond youth and political activists, and into the farthest reaches of Middle America. Pointing to the polls, CBS News created the curious spectacle of a protest movement that virtually everybody supported.

The televisual freeze movement began to take shape in coverage of European anti-nuclear demonstrations in the fall of 1981. In October and November alone we witnessed on the *Evening News* "the biggest West German demonstration since the end of World War II," "the largest anti-nuclear rally in Britain in over

20 years," "the largest demonstration in Belgium since World War II," "the biggest peace demonstration ever held in an Eastern bloc country [Romania]," and "by far the biggest demonstration of any kind ever held in the Netherlands."[18] According to CBS News, the anti-nuclear movement had been "gathering strength" rapidly and "spreading across Europe" from "Denmark to Switzerland"; already it represented "a significant portion of European public opinion."[19] Of course, these demonstrations had absolutely nothing to do with the freeze proposed by American peace groups; most arose in response to the planned deployment of American Pershing II and Cruise Missiles on European soil. But determined to find a domestic angle on the story, CBS News quickly made the freeze connection, proclaiming in November 1981 that the European movement had begun to spread to America.

"Not all the strong feelings against nuclear weapons are on the other side of the Atlantic," Bob Schieffer announced on 21 November 1981: "There is also some of that in the United States, but the numbers are different, and so are the tactics." Thus began the top television news story of the early 1980s: the story of a newly emerging nuclear disarmament movement. As the first correspondent to report on this new movement, Chris Kelley began his story of November 21 on a cautious note. To the refrains of protestors singing "Give Peace a Chance," Kelly began: "It is not the same. In this country, the pace has been slow; the voice is reasonable, not shrill; the presence just beginning to be felt." Nevertheless, Kelley insisted that a "new era of activism" was in the making; the new movement already had some support on college campuses, and teach-ins and demonstrations were "attracting thousands across the nation." At this point, Kelley reported, this diverse movement did not criticize or oppose President Reagan. But until "the U.S. and Russia actually begin disarming," he concluded, the "quiet voices" of this new movement were "likely to grow louder."[20]

Grow louder they did, not so much in reality as on the *CBS Evening News.* On 5 December 1981, Bob Schieffer acknowledged that America still had not witnessed anything "on the scale of the mass demonstrations" that had been "going on in Europe."[21] In March of 1982, however, Dan Rather reported that there had been significant growth in the movement over the winter, and a "spring and summer offensive" portended still larger demonstrations to come.[22] Sure enough, the first of several large American demonstrations—demonstrations "modeled after nuclear arms protests that swept across Europe last fall"—erupted in Chicago on 10 April 1982. It was "Chicago's largest ever peace demonstration," CBS reported, and "a prelude to a much bigger demonstration this June in New York."[23] When June rolled around, the prophecy again came true, as a series of demonstrations, both "in this country and throughout the world," marked the occasion of the U.N.'s Special Session on Disarmament in New York.[24] The culmination, of course, came as "the largest anti-nuclear protest in U.S. history engulfed parts of Manhattan" on 12 June 1982. The "peace people" had finally arrived "in very great numbers," Bruce Morton reported, with police estimates of "up to 700,000" inviting comparison to "the largest of the anti-Vietnam rallies of a decade ago."[25]

The televisual freeze movement continued to grow and spread throughout Reagan's first term in office, as virtually any demonstration of anti-nuclear sentiment, no matter how small or unrelated to the freeze initiative itself, suddenly became news. Small, pacifist groups that had been protesting for decades now found themselves performing for the television cameras, as did demonstrators who for years had rallied against specific weapons facilities or military bases in their own backyards.[26] Even demonstrations by groups opposed to the freeze, such as Roger Molander's "Ground Zero" organization, now came packaged as part of the freeze story.[27] In August of 1982, CBS News did a major story on five protestors who stole some scrap metal from a General Electric plant, mistakenly thinking they had swiped a nuclear warhead.[28] In November, just seven protestors at the Trident base in Groton, Connecticut made the *Evening News.*[29] In April 1982, CBS News even reported on a single jogger who "ran for peace at Columbia University."[30] As the protests spread "from Washington state to New York,"[31] no demonstration proved too small or idiosyncratic to warrant national television coverage.

Demonstrations alone, however, did not begin to tell the whole story of this historic new movement. There was something very different—indeed, unprecedented—about this new crusade. It manifested itself not just on campuses and in big-city protest marches, but also in the farthest reaches of Middle America. As Herbert Gans has written, grass-roots is "one of the most complimentary terms in the vocabulary of the news." According to Gans, the "democratic ideal against which [the news media] measures reality is that of the rural town meeting."[32] By that measure, the televisual freeze movement was not just a protest nor even a partisan cause; it became the ultimate exercise in grass-roots democracy.

In Rockwellian images, CBS News reported from "the quiet town of Lyme, Connecticut, population 1800," that residents hoped their new freeze resolution might spur "Connecticut to become the fourth, but not the last state to join the movement."[33] In another major story, Bruce Morton reported from Guilford, Vermont, "no hotbed of radicalism," that a town meeting had just endorsed the freeze. Morton waxed poetic on the larger significance of the small town's decision: "But the movement for a nuclear freeze is wider than just a town meeting in Guilford, Vermont—wider than these New England hills."[34] "Even in rural Southern Indiana," Morton reported in yet another story, the freeze issue was "on people's minds." It was not yet "the main issue," not "the only issue" in the "small farms" and "small towns" around Corydon and New Albany, Indiana. But clearly, Morton concluded, "the nuclear freeze issue is growing here."[35]

By March 1982, five state legislatures and twelve city councils had endorsed the freeze, including even "middle-of-the-road Ft. Wayne, Indiana."[36] According to CBS News, that proved that the freeze attracted a different kind of following, "not predominately radical or college-age,"[37] but consisting of ordinary

Americans from all walks of life. Granted, it was not always easy to get the right spin on the story. There was that man who wanted to complain about taxes, not nuclear weapons, in New Albany, Indiana, and Bruce Morton had to confess that he saw only one "No Nukes" sign at a parade for Congressman Lee Hamilton in neighboring Corydon. Generally, however, the locals were more than happy to oblige the visiting television celebrities by acknowledging that, yes, they too worried about "the possibility of nuclear war."[38]

Public opinion polls provided the ultimate confirmation that the freeze movement had spread to small-town America. The most ubiquitous tool of contemporary "precision" journalism,[39] the polls served to confirm anecdotal reports of a grass-roots uprising; indeed, they legitimized the whole story of the freeze movement as a major news event. Polls, of course, lack the visual appeal and the drama of a demonstration or a spirited town-hall debate. Their primary virtue, as rhetorical critic Roderick Hart has observed, is that they sound "scientific and dispassionate."[40] In coverage of the freeze, however, the polls told a very dramatic story. At least on television news, the polls had begun to write the political obituary of one of the most popular Presidents in U.S. history.

According to CBS News, the polls had "shown repeatedly" throughout Reagan's first term in office that most Americans favored "a mutual, verifiable freeze on nuclear arms production."[41] With Reagan vigorously opposing the freeze, this spelled political trouble, especially since the polls showed such a diverse lot of Americans supporting the initiative. As Linda Douglass reported from California in April of 1982, the freeze movement included "traditional liberal groups, used to marching for causes," and "Hollywood's Democrats" already had "signed up." But the polls showed that, "more than any issue in recent memory, this one cuts across age, income, and political party lines." Citing no particular poll, Douglass asserted that the public supported the freeze "two-to-one," with much of the support coming "from people not previously known for political activism." Without explaining how such information might be gleaned from the polls, Douglass left it to pollster Mervin Field to explain why "the President and politicians in general" would be "watching the California movement closely":

> Mervin Field (pollster): I think what it means for Ronald Reagan and for all politicians who are suddenly . . . alert to this . . . [is that there] appears to be a very strong, unusual, spontaneous grass-roots movement, that they better run fast to get ahead of it.[42]

CBS News reinforced the theme that the polls spelled political doom for President Reagan in a number of other stories. As early as 26 September 1981, CBS News reported that President Reagan's popularity had "taken a substantial drop according to a Gallup Poll released today by *Newsweek* magazine." By way of explanation, CBS noted that the "poll also showed Americans are becoming increasingly worried about nuclear war," finally cementing the connection with talk of the President's upcoming decisions on the B-1 bomber and the "controversial" MX missile.[43] Lesley Stahl predicted trouble for Reagan's 1984 reelection campaign as early as July of that year, reporting from the White House that unnamed administration officials worried "that questions about the President's sincerity on arms control are a political problem." Turning to the "latest CBS News/*New York Times* poll" for confirmation, she noted that 36 percent of the American people thought Reagan insincere in calling for control of the arms race—that he talked about arms control "simply to quiet his critics."[44]

Occasionally, the poll reports on CBS News were obviously, almost unbelievably, flawed. In May of 1984, for example, CBS reported that the polls showed "that 45% of all the Dutch" were in favor of the planned deployment of American missiles in Europe, while "a full majority of 63%" opposed it—for a total of 108 percent of the Dutch expressing an opinion on the matter![45] More often, however, errors of interpretation rather than arithmetic plagued the poll stories. In connecting President Reagan's decline in popularity to questions about nuclear weapons, for example, CBS News neglected to point out that the "decline of nine percentage points" in Reagan's popularity was no more substantial—in fact, was smaller—than the post-election decline seen in the case of every President since Truman.[46] In addition, of course, CBS News had no basis whatsoever for attributing Reagan's decline in popularity to any particular issue, much less to nuclear weapons. The poll itself certainly made no such connection, and academic survey research repeatedly has demonstrated that "a strong concern about nuclear war has seldom been uppermost in the minds of a great majority of Americans."[47]

Only once in four years of coverage did CBS News present detailed information about any of the freeze polls. On 29 May 1982, Bruce Morton reported that the latest CBS News/*New York Times* poll showed support for the freeze to be "very wide, but very shallow." He also explained how "the numbers changed" when qualifications were added: "What if the freeze would give the Russians greater nuclear strength than the U.S.? Our sample was against it. What if the U.S. and the Soviets could cheat on it? The freeze lost again. What if the U.S. had to freeze first? No again." Morton even questioned the public's interest in the issue, observing that "our sample doesn't know a lot about the nuclear freeze issue; only about a third know Ronald Reagan is against it." And in conclusion, Morton contradicted the whole thrust of the network's freeze coverage: "So only about one-fourth of our sample seemed to be hardcore freeze supporters."[48]

Yet CBS News was not about to let even its own poll get in the way of a good story. As the 1984 election approached, the network continued to insist that nuclear war was the number one issue. The Democratic presidential hopefuls were "falling all over each other, trying to court the freeze movement," correspondent Meredith Vieira reported in February 1984, because the polls showed that the fear of nuclear war was "the number one concern on the minds of the voters."[49] As early as December of 1983, freeze activists appeared on the *Evening*

*News* gleefully predicting victory: "We're looking for a million freeze volunteers and contributors to organize millions upon millions of freeze voters in the 1984 election."[50] As election day approached, even Reagan's overwhelming lead in the polls did little to change the story line. As late as September, CBS News insisted that nuclear war remained "high on the list" of voter concerns, with the polls showing that "most Americans want more action" on arms control than they had seen from President Reagan.[51]

The Reagan landslide put an end to such talk, and the freeze movement disappeared from the *CBS Evening News* as suddenly as it had appeared. From a high of twenty-six news stories primarily about the freeze between April and June of 1982, the coverage declined to no major stories about the freeze in the last three months of 1984.[52] Perhaps the American people had indeed supported the metaphor of a freeze on nuclear weapons, but as a grass-roots movement, the freeze was largely a media phenomenon, as fleeting as the sound bites that pass for news in the telepolitical age.

## A "New Breed" of Protestor

Perhaps the most significant biases in news, particularly on television, stem from the imperative to personalize stories.[53] Issues, social problems, causes, trends, ideas, political parties, institutions, and movements cannot be pictured on television news, nor can they utter sound bites for the microphones. People represent political ideas on television news, and the ways journalists personalize the news—the personalities they choose to speak before the cameras, the ways they identify and characterize these sources, the situations in which they present them, and the words they quote from them—can have profound political consequences. As Todd Gitlin has observed, the media selectively elevate political leaders to the status of celebrities, and these media-designated leaders come to define, for good or ill, larger political movements. In the 1960s, according to Gitlin, the media delegitimized the antiwar movement by elevating its most radical and rhetorically strident leaders to the status of celebrities. Thus Mark Rudd became a "household name" in the spring of 1968 and "his rhetoric the standard by which the movement was judged."[54]

CBS News chose a very different sort of personality to speak for the televisual freeze movement. The freeze campaign may have originated with such fringe political groups as the American Friends Service Committee, the Fellowship of Reconciliation, and the Women's International League for Peace and Freedom. On CBS News, however, the movement was led, not by these radicals, but by a "new breed" of protestor, most of whom had "never been involved before" in political protest.[55] According to CBS News, the leaders of the freeze movement had "a different look" and "a different strength";[56] they were more thoughtful and less radical than the protestors of the past. As Chris Kelly explained, their rhetoric was "reasonable, not shrill." Kelley elaborated in the very first story about a freeze movement rally: "The rhetoric was quiet; the purpose, to educate people on the danger of the nuclear buildup."[57]

The educational theme emerged most strongly from the network's heavy reliance upon representatives of Physicians for Social Responsibility (PSR) and the International Physicians for the Prevention of Nuclear War (IPPNW). Introducing the groups as "an extraordinary alliance of doctors" concerned only that "the world's people may be growing oblivious to the horrors of nuclear war," CBS presented the activist doctors not as political animals but simply as thoughtful persons concerned about the "danger of apathy." More importantly, they presented the activist medical professionals as the best available experts on the subject; they were, according to CBS News, "the only people who fully understand what the warnings are about." "We know what probably others do not know," commented a Soviet doctor featured in a major story on the IPPNW. "We know [the] medical consequences of a nuclear war. Catastrophe."[58]

The freeze doctors may have been experts on the medical effects of a nuclear bomb, but they hardly spoke in technical terms. Depicting the gruesome human effects of nuclear bombs, they began, as usual, with recollections from survivors of Hiroshima. "First I remembered seeing . . . a different world . . . sort of a hell," recalled one victim during the first major story about the doctors' crusade, while a second recreated an even more poignant scene:

> Gene Fugita (Hiroshima victim): There was one scene that I—I—I still remember very well, that this little girl just kept on screaming, "Please kill me! Please kill me! I can't stand the pain! And I really did want to go over there and—and—and kill that child.[59]

Building upon these images, the freeze doctors then proceeded to their trademark scenarios of hypothetical nuclear attacks on specific American cities. In one story, Helen Caldicott and Howard Hiatt of PSR explained that a twenty-megaton bomb dropped on Boston would "form a crater half a mile wide and 300 feet deep," turning everything in that volume into radioactive fallout and killing "something of the order of two million people."[60] In another story, PSR doctor Jack Geiger provided an even more graphic description of the medical effects of an attack targeting the SAC base near Omaha:

> Anybody in Omaha that made a reflex glance at the fireball 35 miles away . . . would be blinded by retinal burning. There'd be thousands, tens of thousands, of people on . . . the side of Omaha that's closest to the SAC base with third-degree burns. There would be skull fractures. There would be ruptured lungs. There would be crushing injuries of the thorax. There would be broken backs. There would be deep lacerations and hemorrhage.[61]

Whatever the city, the result was always the same: utter devastation, with no hope of survival. "In practical terms," as Doctor Howard Hiatt explained, "there's nothing that medical science can do if the bombs drop." Portraying a wide range of political and technical issues as medical matters, they characterized their whole political crusade as an exercise in "preventive medicine." As Dr. Bernard Lown of PSR explained: "We have to rise to what physicians have long understood, that if there is an illness for which there is no cure, you must focus on prevention." In the same story, Dr. Caldicott even presented her opposition to Civil Defense policies as a medical judgment: "It's like giving a dying person a placebo sugar tablet. That's medically unethical."[62]

Caldicott herself confessed to practicing "political medicine,"[63] but on CBS News there was nothing at all political about the IPPNW and PSR. According to CBS News, the doctors of the freeze movement did not deliver political speeches or write political manifestoes. Rather, as Lem Tucker reported, they "spread their message through lectures, seminars and, in the most personal terms, talking to their patients."[64] When a PSR doctor released a medical report on nuclear weapons on the same day CBS covered a series of freeze teach-ins, the doctor called the timing sheer coincidence: "The purpose of publishing this report was to educate doctors. It had no political purpose."[65] When a Soviet doctor attacked President Reagan at a meeting of the IPPNW, CBS News again assured viewers that the activist doctors, for the most part, had "managed to walk the thin line between the scientific and political aspects of the nuclear issue."[66] According to CBS News, not even the involvement of Soviet government officials in the IPPNW raised political questions; it merely proved that nuclear war was "not just an American question."[67]

Clearly, CBS News went out of its way to depoliticize the PSR and the IPPNW. In the process, they silenced the numerous critics of such doomsayers as Helen Caldicott, for the medical activists presumably had no political motives; they sought only to educate the public. The IPPNW and PSR spoke not as political combatants but as medical experts engaged only in preventive medicine. At one and the same time, they led an important new movement yet stood above the political fray.

A very different rhetorical dynamic framed coverage of the second major group that CBS News designated as leaders of the new anti-nuclear movement: the bishops of the American Catholic Church. While the bishops in fact addressed nuclear weapons primarily out of theological rather than political concerns, CBS News cast them as the Reagan administration's chief political antagonists, zealously pursuing the dramatic angle of church-state conflict.

As early as November 1981, CBS News reported that the religious community generally had become deeply involved in the movement,[68] and a number of early stories featured Catholic priests and nuns engaged in acts of "political and moral" witness.[69] By April, the bishops stood at the center of the story as leaders of a new "religious movement with political effects"; the bishops, CBS reported, were "on the move."[70]

On April 8, Dan Rather posed the central question that was to frame much of the coverage: "Are [the] bishops of the Roman Catholic Church in this country becoming too political?"[71] Bruce Morton then followed with an in-depth story about "today's prelate"—a bishop who took "a much different view of the world from bishops who went before him." Whereas yesterday's bishop "spoke of duty, honor, and country," today's bishops proclaimed the arms race immoral, called for defense workers to resign from their jobs, and urged Christians to withhold federal taxes destined for the military. The old, hawkish bishops have given way to a new breed, Morton concluded; "the times they are a-changing."

Yet according to Morton, this did *not* mean that the Church had become radicalized. Morton turned to Arthur Jones, Washington bureau chief of the *National Catholic Reporter*, to explain: "You're not looking at political radicals. If they were radicals, they wouldn't be bishops." By definition, then, bishops could not be radicals, but they had begun to move out of the pulpit and into the public arena. And as Morton observed: "Fifty-million Catholics, united, would be a very powerful force. The Church leadership is moving, breaking new ground, raising new issues. The question is, how many of the fifty-million will follow?"[71]

Morton acknowledged that only about one-fifth of the 368 American bishops supported "some sort of a nuclear freeze or a halt in the arms race."[72] Yet on television, as Phyllis Zagano has observed, the personal opinions of this "minority cadre" took on "added moral authority."[73] In effect, this one-fifth became the voice of the entire Church, especially as the bishops began drafting what CBS News called "a strong pastoral letter on nuclear war."[74] Reflecting the spin put on the letter by a handful of pacifist bishops, CBS News framed the story of the pastoral letter as a dramatic tale of church-state conflict, and in the process the network dwelled upon just one word in the 40,000-word document: its call for a "halt" in the "testing, production, and deployment of new nuclear weapons systems."

As told by CBS News, the story of the *Pastoral Letter on War and Peace* pitted a Church courageously determined to endorse the freeze against a reactionary President who often "ripped into the nuclear freeze movement."[75] As the story unfolded, CBS News told of a dramatic back-and-forth struggle, with the President at first getting the upper hand, but with the anti-nuclear bishops ultimately prevailing. Picking up the story near the end of the drafting process, the *CBS Evening News* reported on 5 April 1983, that the third draft of the letter would "please conservative lay Catholics and the Reagan Administration" because it called only for a "curb" rather than a halt in new nuclear weapons systems. "Halt," the report explained, "sounded to many people like an endorsement of the nuclear freeze."[76] Just a few weeks later, however, CBS News reported that the committee drafting the letter had reversed itself again, restoring the word halt and thereby giving the letter "a tougher anti-nuclear stand." An "outright halt" in the arms race, CBS News explained, was "opposed by President Reagan"; it constituted an endorsement of "a freeze on deployment of nuclear weapons."[77] When the entire conference of bishops voted to approve this final draft on 2-3 May 1983, CBS News proclaimed that the bishops had "all but called for a nuclear weapons freeze opposed by President Reagan."[78] The administration could not possibly "be pleased with the final letter," CBS concluded, for the letter had "put church teaching in the vanguard of the nuclear freeze movement."[79]

CBS News dutifully reported that President Reagan claimed to have "no quarrel" with the *Pastoral Letter on War and Peace.* But dismissing the President's response as an attempt to take the high ground in political defeat,[80] CBS News missed the real story: that the bishops had repudiated the Catholic New Left's demands for a letter endorsing pacifism, condemning nuclear deterrence, and criticizing the administration's arms build-up. On the *CBS Evening News*, the whole debate over the pastoral letter was reduced to the spectacle of the bishops quibbling with the President over a single word in the 150-page document. Viewers of the *Evening News* heard nothing about the letter's condemnation of the Soviet Union's "imperial drive for hegemony," nor about the letter's expression of support for Catholic military personnel and defense industry workers. Most importantly, CBS News failed even to mention that the letter coupled its freeze language with an endorsement of Reagan's call for "negotiated bilateral deep cuts in the arsenals of both superpowers."[81] Conservative Catholics may have embraced the final letter as a "valiant text,"[82] and the bishops themselves may have insisted that they did not wish the letter "to be identified with one specific political initiative,"[83] but CBS News would have none of that. Bishops at the "vanguard" of the nuclear freeze movement made for a much more dramatic story.

## Investigative Television Journalism

The documentary, conventional wisdom holds, is a dying art, mortally wounded by the mad competition for ratings, the victim of corporate greed. Once the cornerstone of television's claim to public service, documentaries almost always lost money. Historically, however, the networks have viewed them as worthwhile investments in credibility and prestige. Rocked by the quiz show scandals of the mid-1950s, the networks turned to prime-time documentaries as a demonstration, in David Halberstam's words, of their "good intentions to do more in the public sector."[84] In the 1960s, documentaries still aired regularly, but they became rarer in the 1970s, especially "the kind that arouse controversy and scare away sponsors."[85] By the middle 1980s, they had all but disappeared. In 1986, for example, the three networks aired a total of only 15 prime-time documentaries, down from 79 in 1970.[86] With documentary production units cut back by increasingly cost-conscious networks, talk of the demise of the documentary became common by the late 1970s and early 1980s.[87] By the late 1980s, documentaries had become an "endangered species," clinging to life "at the fringes of the networks' schedules."[88]

Early in the 1980s, however, at least one documentary defied the trend. In June of 1981, CBS News aired a five-part documentary series, *The Defense of the United States*, and part 1 of the series, entitled "Ground Zero," attracted some 40 million viewers—at the time the largest audience for a documentary in the history of television.[89] Bill Leonard, then head of CBS News, had wanted to respond in some "dramatic, all-out way" to the freeze debate, and there was "surprisingly little struggle" over his proposal to "open the eyes of the American people to the nuclear threat." Assigning the project to a young team headed by Howard Stringer (later the producer of the *Evening News* and President of CBS News) Leonard resigned himself to losing "a good deal of money" on the project. But then Stringer came up with the idea that made "Ground Zero" a hit, as Leonard recalled in his memoirs, *In the Storm of the Eye*:

> The team had been working for a couple of months when Stringer walked into my office and gave me his tall, British smile. "Boss, I hope you don't mind, but we're planning to blow up Omaha. He paused for effect.
>
> I did not bite.
>
> "Nuclear, dammit. Nuclear!"
>
> "Sounds like a barrel of laughs," I said finally.
>
> Seriously," said Howard, "we're going to try to show something of what a nuclear bomb would do to a city. Using models, and a lot of effects. And Omaha. It should make the point."[90]

CBS heavily promoted "Ground Zero," not only with "bumpers" but on the *Evening News*. Urging viewers to tune in for a glimpse at this "real-life Armageddon," Dan Rather introduced a preview of the simulated attack as the product of the "best scientific estimates." Rather insisted, "It could happen."[91] Based only upon estimates, of course, "Ground Zero" was no more real-life than ABC's *The Day After*, and the point Stringer hoped to make had important political implications for the freeze debate. Like *The Day After*, "Ground Zero" could best be described as a docudrama, but it made real political arguments: that nuclear war was imminent, that our political and military leaders had betrayed us, and that Civil Defense was a cruel hoax.

Like *The Day After*, "Ground Zero" was set in a typical midwestern town and revolved around the fate of some typical Middle-Americans. We got to know a good, patriotic American family, to witness something of their daily routines, and to peek inside their heads at their innermost fears—before witnessing them "nuked" into oblivion for no apparent reason. In "Ground Zero," of course, Dan Rather and other CBS correspondents addressed some of the issues surrounding nuclear weapons, and we also heard directly from a number of experts. Yet, in the final analysis, dramatic imperatives, not science, dictated the story line, as all the issues, all the experts, served as but preliminaries to the main event: the annihilation of Omaha.

"Omaha, Nebraska," Dan Rather intoned dramatically in introducing the climactic scenario. "Omaha, Nebraska, practically in the center of the country, in the heart of America's farmland. Omaha, on the banks of the Missouri River . . . Omaha, home of the Strategic Air Command." Omaha would be "ground zero" in a Soviet missile attack, Rather explained, before introducing local resident Jerry Allen with a description of his neighbors: "Omaha has about a half a million people—a typical Midwestern town to the degree that people are very hardy, very work-ethic conscious, and very patriotic." After a short trip to Bellevue, "a small community 15 miles from downtown Omaha," we met Jerry's family:

> Jerry Allen represents a national textile concern in the Omaha area. He lives with his wife, Diane, . . . Jerry is 37 years old. He and his wife moved into this house in 1970. They have two children. Michele is eight years old, Julie is twelve.

The kids liked to play soccer, and of course they went to school—only "a couple of miles from home, a couple of miles from the Strategic Air Command." They were, in all respects, the typical American family. Yet for the Allens, there was one big difference: they lived "in the shadow of a nuclear war that just might begin in their back yard."[92]

Naturally, the Allens worried about a nuclear war starting in their own backyard. They tried not to "dwell upon it." But as Jerry Allen admitted, "you always know it's there." As it turns out, they apparently had thought about it quite a bit, at least once they learned they would be featured in a documentary on the subject:

> Jerry Allen: "If you did survive the initial shock and concussion and fireball, you would come out and the radiation levels would be so high that, you know, you're—you would be—have a limited existence. . . . the radiation levels would probably be so high that, you know, you couldn't survive.
>
> Diane Allen: I can imagine that it would be just nothing. There would be nothing. It'd be barren.
>
> Jerry Allen: It would be very terrifying. Very. I don't know if I would walk down to the bomb shelter knowing my family and everybody I know here is probably going to—you know, going to die right then. I don't know if I'd go down to the bomb shelter.
>
> Diane Allen: What is there to do? There's nothing. There's no place to go. I can't run home. There's no place to go. You don't do anything. You say a prayer and that's all.[93]

With the victims properly introduced, CBS then dropped the bomb: a 15-megaton nuclear weapon ground burst in front of the SAC headquarters. As the simulation depicted 53 seconds of general destruction, Rather explained: "The blast from a 15-megaton ground burst would devastate Omaha just that quickly. The fireball would remain on the ground for 20 seconds and open a crater three-quarters of a mile across. It would then rise to a height of 80,000 feet in less than a minute, generating enough heat to cause second- and third-degree burns 16 miles away." Presumably, the Allens would not be among the "simulated burn victims" depicted on the screen. For the Allens, the news would be much worse, as we learned from two of the freeze campaign's experts, Doctors Jack Geiger and Kosta Tsipis:

> Dr. Geiger: Even at 11 or 12 miles, the over-pressures are great enough to take an ordinary window and turn it into a thousand pieces of glass flying at a hundred miles an hour, a lethal weapon for anybody inside that room. And . . . with all of these fires, all of the ignition points . . . a mass conflagration or firestorm would develop and simply burn all of Omaha for the next six or eight hours. The reason that's important is that anybody that was in a shelter would be dry-roasted, as in a crematorium. . . .
> Dr. Tsipis: . . . The weapons now are seventy, a hundred, a thousand times bigger [than the Hiroshima bomb]. . . . There will be many weapons. There would be thousands of weapons . . . . The enemy surely can be killed, but you will also be killed assuredly yourself.[94]

The whole thrust of "Ground Zero" suggested that the threat of nuclear war was not only real but increasing every day. "No general or admiral is ever likely to say enough is enough," Bob Schieffer reported, "so these hydra-headed monsters have continued to multiply and the arms race continues—a race with no finish line." Pressing Secretary of Defense Caspar Weinberger to reveal America's launch doctrine publicly, Dan Rather took the Defense Secretary's refusal to comment as a clear sign that the policy in fact had changed under Reagan—most likely to a hair-trigger doctrine of "launch-upon-warning." The documentary also dwelled upon the possibility "that we could get into war by mistake or by accident," pointing out that there had been 147 false alarms in one 18-month period, triggered by such things as a Soviet training launch, a failed computer chip, and a gas fire in the Siberian pipeline. Finally, the viewer heard from military leaders who barely flinched over the prospect of 10 million Americans dying in a nuclear attack. Ten million dead may sound incredible, Admiral Powell Carter conceded, but "the Soviets lost 20-million Russians in World War II," and they not only "managed to survive as . . . a nation" but went on to achieve "super-power status."[95]

At one point in "Ground Zero," Lieutenant General Kelly Burke declared: "I have always found the—the hypothetical nuclear scenarios inherently implausible. I've never seen one that I thought was really likely to transpire." A bit later, Dr. Geiger conceded that there was "simply nothing in human experience that serves as a precedent" for predicting the impact of even one 15-megaton bomb. After interviewing a number of other experts and military leaders, even Bob

Schieffer confessed that "the more you talk to the people who deal with nuclear weapons the more you realize how little we know about nuclear war." Yet none of these admissions that all such predictions are highly speculative deterred CBS from visually depicting one particular scenario—arguably a worst-case scenario—or from claiming to describe its "exact physical and medical consequences." Nor did they preclude assertions that the United States would be totally incapable of coping medically with such a disaster or even of surviving as a "functioning social unit." "One 15-megaton nuclear weapon exploded near Omaha," Rather predicted, "would result in approximately 132,000 deaths by fire, a million and a half deaths from radiation sickness. Total dead: over 2,000,000 in six weeks' time." For most people, Rather concluded, such was "the stuff of science fiction." But for the Allens, the threat of nuclear holocaust was as real as the missiles in their own backyard.[96]

In Leonard's opinion, all five parts of *The Defense of the United States* were "powerful and informative," but none was quite so explosive as that first segment, "when Omaha disappeared before America's very eyes." Boasting that the series won rave reviews and "nearly every major documentary award for that year," Leonard recalled the project as one of his proudest moments at CBS News: "I felt as if I had done my part to improve the quality of network television." But "Ground Zero" was more than just "quality television," more than an investment in network prestige; it was a big ratings hit. As Leonard pointed out, the normal documentary typically attracted only about 18 percent of the available viewing audience. Yet "nearly twice this many people" tuned in for the first two episodes of *The Defense of the United States*, "or about as many as watch a hit comedy series."[97]

As Thomas Powers has observed, CBS clearly made a political decision to focus "Ground Zero" upon "the consequences of nuclear war, the cost in human terms—not to touch on it in passing but to make it the point."[98] And in doing so, as Meyer has observed, the network "encouraged and legitimized what nuclear freeze activists had been trying to do for more than a year," while reaching "a substantially broader spectrum and greater number of people" than freeze activists could ever have "hoped to reach."[99] But while the political biases of the program may have been obvious, CBS News learned a more important lesson from the program: the bomb sells. Over the next three years, CBS News aired dozens of freeze stories, not only on the *Evening News*, but on all of its news programming. Most notably, similar stories began to air regularly on the network's most popular substitute for full-length documentaries, the highly rated television newsmagazine *60 Minutes*.

As Axel Madsen has written, *60 Minutes* "bumped along in the lower depths of the Nielsen ratings" for a number of years after it debuted in 1968, but it began to climb rapidly in the ratings after 1975. On 26 November 1978, it topped the ratings for the first time—"the only regularly scheduled news and public affairs program to reach this enviable position." By 1981, the program was earning in the neighborhood of $50 million a year for CBS News; one telecommunications economist has "conservatively" estimated the show's annual profits at over $60 million, or some 60 percent of the profits for the entire CBS broadcast group. In 1982, a 30-second spot on *60 Minutes* sold for $175,000—the highest rate in prime-time television. By 1990, *60 Minutes* earned nearly $400,000 for each of its seven minutes of national ad slots. In the headquarters of the program, as Madsen reported, the talk was never about making money; it was about "journalism, of getting 100 stories a year, of continuing the show's reputation for fearless, controversial, provocative journalism." Nevertheless, there clearly was something different about the journalism of *60 Minutes*—something that not only made the show a "TV phenomenon and a national habit" but also inspired a steady stream of libel suits.[100]

The secret of *60 Minutes*' "Nielsen-winning formula," as Jonathan Black has suggested, has never been all that mysterious. Catering to "our crudest entertainment reflexes," *60 Minutes* is "news presented as theater," with its "indefatigable hounds of justice" pursuing the crooks, the swindlers, and the corrupt or incompetent government officials in 13-minute mini-dramas.[101] Following a fairly limited number of set narrative conventions,[102] *60 Minutes* rarely has let the nuances of a complex issue get in the way of a good story line. It is "the hype, the slant, [and] the impulse to dramatize" that makes a *60 Minutes* story.[103] And nowhere was that more evident than in *60 Minutes'* first major response to the freeze debate: a segment aired on 9 May 1982 and entitled, not surprisingly, "The Bomb."

Featuring Ed Bradley, "The Bomb" began with yet another scenario of failed deterrence, yet another glimpse of the impending holocaust: "Imagine that it's 1985. Warsaw Pact forces move into West Berlin. NATO troops offer resistance but are outnumbered and soon overwhelmed. The United States issues an ultimatum to the Soviet Union; withdraw, or face nuclear attack." The Soviets begin a "mass evacuation of their cities." The President considers evacuating our own cites and even the possibility of a pre-emptive first strike. Such a scenario, Bradley declared, was "not all that far-fetched." Echoing Rather's promotion of "Ground Zero," Bradley declared: "It could happen." For the results, of course, we could not look to government officials or to experts in nuclear physics for reliable information. Instead, CBS took us to Grace Cathedral in San Francisco, where an audience listened in "dead silence" to Helen Caldicott's "bombing run" speech:

> [A twenty-megaton bomb] explodes with the heat of the sun. And it would dig a hole three-quarters of a mile wide and 800 feet deep, converting all of [the] human beings and all the buildings, like this cathedral, and all the earth below, to radioactive fallout molecules. . . .
>
> Out to a radius of six miles . . . every building will be flattened, every person killed, many of them actually vaporized. Out to a radius of 20 miles, every person

> will be killed or lethally injured.... There are tremendous over-pressures ... which literally sweep people out of the buildings and convert them into missiles traveling at 100 miles an hour, till they hit the nearest wall, solid object, et cetera.... They rupture the eardrums, producing deafness. If you look at the flash close in, your eyes will disintegrate and melt, as people's eyes did at Hiroshima.[104]

All this had become quite familiar by now. Only Caldicott's arithmetic was new. Instead of the 10 million dead predicted in "Ground Zero," Caldicott (extrapolating to all-out nuclear war) predicted that up to 90 percent of Americans would die within thirty days—a figure well over 200 million.[105] Yet *60 Minutes* rarely dwelled upon statistical nuances. The *60 Minutes* formula dictated conflicts among *people*,[106] and Ed Bradley tracked down the perfect foils for "The Bomb": the bureaucrats of the Federal Emergency Management Agency (FEMA) who labored under the illusion that Caldicott might be wrong—that nuclear war might be, at least in some measure, survivable.

Traveling to Colorado, Bradley began his report with angry citizens denouncing FEMA's "crisis relocation plans" for the city of Boulder. A "smoke screen and an illusion," one citizen called the idea of evacuating the entire city. A "treacherous security blanket," a "mini-air-conditioner for hell," said another. Noting that FEMA's plan called for "the picturesque mountain village of Nederland" to serve as a "host area" for evacuees from Boulder, Bradley naturally drove up Boulder Canyon to take a look. Where would 3,000 people from Boulder stay in Nederland? "Well," Bradley reported, "Nederland has one motel with three rooms, and a school that could be used as an emergency shelter." Unfortunately, Bradley reported, mayor John Workman knew nothing about the plan, nor for that matter did anybody else in Nederland:

> John Workman: Well, the town was not contacted in any way that we were going to be a host area.
> Ed Bradley: How did you find out about it?
> Workman: Well, I read about it in the *Daily Camera* from Boulder....
> Bradley: You mean, no one ever called you?
> Workman: No one called me, or no one called anyone on the board or any of the people in the town hall, or—
> Bradley: When they came up here to—to look around, to see if they could put up people to look at the resources, what did they find? Who'd they talk to?
> Workman: I'm not even sure that they came up here....
> Bradley: Most people have fallout shelters and blast shelters in their homes?
> Workman: No. No. I don't know of one in this town.
> Bradley: Well, what about your public fallout shelter?
> Workman: We don't have one.
> Bradley: Public blast shelter?
> Workman: None.
> Bradley: How do you think they picked you?

Workman (laughing): It would only be a guess on my part. I don't know how they picked Nederland.[107]

Armed with his "scoop," Bradley scurried back down the mountain to confront Frank Mollner, the regional head of FEMA. Confirming that nobody had visited Nederland, Bradley reported that federal officials apparently had just "looked at a map." Edited to follow directly upon the heels of the mayor's prediction that a nuclear blast would block the narrow, winding road up Boulder Canyon, Mollner's response was rendered ridiculous:

Ed Bradley: Have you seen that road up to Nederland?
Frank Mollner: I've driven it several times.
Bradley: Yeah, you know, that's a narrow—
Mollner: Okay, but—but the—
Bradley: Rocks on the side—
Mollner: Yeah, but if you're a native Coloradan, that's kind of fun to drive up that. That—that really isn't bad.[08]

Thus we learned that our government planners thought it might be "fun" to race up Boulder Canyon, with thousands of other panicking drivers, as huge rocks rained down on the cars. We also learned from Dr. Caldicott, in a theme dating back to the Civil Defense debates of the 1950s,[109] that the Russians would become "nervous" at the first sign of such an evacuation and probably "press the button." It would be "medically unwise to frighten the Russians," Caldicott commented, "because they could destroy this nation, and that's not patriotic." Finally, freeze activist Dr. George Kistiakovsky, introduced only as "a key figure in the development of the atomic bomb," declared that, "oh, yes," nuclear war was far more likely today than ever before. And after all this, we returned for one last comment from the head of FEMA, Louis Guiffrida, his assurances rendered absurd, of course, by all that came before it. Yes, Guiffrida insisted, the "country would rebuild itself" following a nuclear attack. The United States would be "different in many significant ways from the way it is now," he conceded, but "a distinctly American nation . . . would come out of this": "We're a nation of survivors, always have been."[110]

All this was vintage *60 Minutes*: the government policy that defied common sense, the innate wisdom of the small-town citizens, the bureaucrats fidgeting in their chairs, and the absurdity, even the black humor, of it all. And "The Bomb," as it turned out, was only the beginning. In October, *60 Minutes* aired another story, introduced as a "real-life morality play," this time featuring Leroy Matthieson, the pacifist Catholic bishop of Amarillo. Matthieson, it seems, had courageously spoken out against the "immorality" of the nearby Pantex nuclear weapons plant. As a result, the local red-necks, led by a local Moral Majoritarian who believed that Jesus Christ would have approved thoroughly of the bomb, had branded Matthieson a traitor and offered him "a one-way ticket to Moscow."[111] In November of 1983, the freeze drama continued on *60 Minutes* with yet another anti-nuclear morality play, this time actually casting a rival network executive as the voice of truth. In a story about the controversy surrounding ABC's airing of *The Day After*, there was ABC's Chief of Motion Pictures, Brandon Stoddard, standing up to the Prince of Darkness himself, Jerry Falwell. Denying that *The Day After* was at all political, Stoddard courageously declared that the movie would air no matter how badly the network might be hurt by Falwell's boycott of sponsors. Would ABC air *The Day After* even if "not a spot sold," even if ABC had to "swallow" the entire $7 million it cost to produce the movie? "Absolutely. Absolutely," Stoddard insisted. "It's going to go on the air."[112]

To the Reagan administration, all of this must have looked like a communist plot. In program after program, all the major themes of the freeze campaign could be heard: the fragility of deterrence, the "human effects" of the bomb, the dangers posed by Reagan's arms build-up, and the absurdity of Civil Defense. Cast as courageous heroes, freeze activists enjoyed virtually free reign to lampoon the Reagan administration, while government officials invariably were cast as evasive, reckless, or ignorant. One can hardly imagine what more CBS News could have done to promote the nuclear freeze.

Yet to interpret such themes as a political bias is to forget the deeper, more insidious biases of contemporary television news: the bias toward overdramatized morality plays, the bias against the information citizens need to deliberate political issues. CBS News portrayed the freeze campaign favorably, but that only reflected how well freeze advocates exploited prevailing, telepolitical conceptions of news. Freeze activists attracted a high level of national coverage, and that coverage was generally positive, even celebratory, in tone. In the long run, however, pandering to television news only contributed to the freeze campaign's demise. While the campaign gained visibility and got its message across, that message provided no foundation for sustained public support.

## Television Journalism's "Crisis of Confidence"

In recent years, more and more media critics have deemed it unproductive to talk of political or ideological bias in the news. Since "allegations of ideological bias" are inevitably "exaggerated by the ideology of the beholder," as W. Lance Bennett has argued,[113] various critics now write not of "liberal" or "conservative" biases but of "structural" and "institutional" biases, "newsworker routines," "mythic structures," "melodramatic imperatives," "fantasy themes," or "rhetorical strictures."[114] Yet try as we may, we seem unable to transcend ideological interpretations of news media bias. Even Bennett's own study of informational biases in the news quickly becomes an angry litany of the media's failure to tell the truth about CIA "subversion," the "U.S. 'Contra' war against Nicaragua," and Reagan's "annual . . . propaganda campaign" to increase the "already sizable" defense budget.[115]

It is only natural that we return to political judgments about the news because the news inevitably has political content and consequences. Notwithstanding efforts by John Fiske and other cultural theorists to obliterate the distinction between news and entertainment programming,[116] the news remains the most obviously political programming on television; it is intentionally, directly, and inextricably bound to the discourse of our civic life. More than other sorts of programming, the news is about—and profoundly impacts—our electoral and policy-making processes. In some ways, the news indeed may be indistinguishable from entertainment programming. But viewers still look to the news for political information, and so it still makes sense to assess the news in ideological terms.

Critics focusing upon news coverage of the nuclear debate continue to sense a conservative, pro-establishment bias. In one recent study, for example, Rubin and Cummings have argued that network television news avoids nuclear issues because they are too politically divisive and too frightening to viewers. In effect, they argue, television has become a "silent, willing partner of government in keeping nuclear issues below the threshold of national consciousness." According to Rubin and Cummings, the television networks have provided only minimal coverage of nuclear issues, and they have refrained from "vigorous adversarial journalism of a type that is lauded in other contexts."[117]

Yet coverage of the freeze campaign could hardly be called minimal. According to one count, the *CBS Evening News* alone ran 28 stories on anti-nuclear protests in just March and April of 1982, compared to only 17 stories spread over the preceding 38 months. This high level of coverage continued until November 1983, when the coverage peaked at 24 stories for the month.[118] Meanwhile, CBS News also produced a major documentary series in response to the freeze debate, as well as at least three segments of *60 Minutes.* And we have not even touched upon the programs with perhaps the most extensive coverage of the freeze campaign: the *CBS Morning News* and *Sunday Morning.*[119]

Nor can it be said that CBS News refrained from "vigorous adversarial journalism" in its coverage of the freeze. Framing the whole story as the tale of a spontaneous grass-roots movement, CBS News, in effect, celebrated a coalition of special interest groups as the voice of the people. Confirming the campaign's small-town, middle-class morality with reports from the heartland and dubious polls, CBS News presented a partisan political campaign as a glorious story of citizen participation in the political process. Personalizing the story with a new breed of protestor, it thoroughly divested the campaign of any traces of radicalism, while it gave freeze activists free reign to prophesize the end of the world. The conclusion is as inescapable as it may be unfashionable: CBS News virtually endorsed the nuclear freeze campaign. Its coverage was not only vigorously adversarial but politically one-sided.

Ideological bias, however, may not be the most insidious bias in television news. In coverage of the freeze campaign, television news may have sided with the Reagan administration's critics, but it provided little substantive information on either side of the freeze debate. Focusing upon the political logistics of the freeze campaign, its supposed political victories, the hoopla of demonstrations, and the findings of the latest polls, the coverage was not, to borrow Bennett's language, "geared for critical debate or citizen action."[120] Reducing the whole freeze debate to "dramatic, digestive, visual moments,"[121] television news sounded the repetitive and shallow notes of a "tin kazoo."[122] And as a result, many Americans became spectators rather than participants in the debate. It hardly seems surprising that Americans who rely mostly upon television for their news tend to be more alienated and less active politically.[123]

Media apologists insist that network news only gives the public what it wants. In recent years, however, there has been growing evidence that people may want more from the news than sound bites and dramatic morality plays. Millions of Americans still watch network television news, but that audience has declined by about a third.[124] Many may have switched to CNN and other news competitors, but so too did many, particularly young adults, apparently quit watching television news altogether.[125] A number of other signs likewise pointed to a growing "crisis of confidence" in television journalism during the 1980s. By an overwhelming margin, the public supported Reagan's exclusion of the press from the Grenada invasion. Major news organizations found themselves fighting an unprecedented number of lawsuits alleging fraud, entrapment, or libel. As early as 1983, it had become major news that the news media itself had lost the public's trust.[126] As Madsen has written, journalists suddenly "discovered that people didn't like them, that they were considered rude and accusatory, more interested in what sells, in scandal, then in reporting the news, and too quick to hide behind the First Amendment." There was even a "popular perception that journalists regarded themselves as detached from, and perhaps even hostile to, the government of their country."[127]

When Jimmy Carter spoke of a "crisis of confidence" in America,[128] he misread a public that lacked confidence in Carter himself. So too do television journalists misread the public's feedback when they attribute journalism's crisis in confidence to a "blame-the-messenger" syndrome or to the public's ignorance about the journalistic profession.[129] As Ted Smith has suggested, many Americans are not so much ignorant as fed up with the rhetoric of crisis and failure on television news. Some even sense that the core values of television's journalistic elite have become a serious threat to American politics and culture.[130] Jamieson may be right that the very nature of the television medium invites visual imagery and sound bites,[131] and time and technological constraints may well account for the superficiality of television news. But the people behind the technology—the journalists themselves—must bear ultimate responsibility for the impoverishment of television journalism. The message, not the medium, has become the problem with television news.

## Notes

1. CBS News, *CBS Evening News*, 22 March 1982, microfiche transcript, 8-9. Hereafter cited as *CBS Evening News*.
2. Gitlin, *The Whole World is Watching*, 27-28.
3. Herbert J. Gans, *Deciding What's News: A Study of CBS Evening News, NBC Nightly News, Newsweek and Time* (New York: Vintage, 1980), 53-55.
4. Austin Ranney, *Channels of Power: The Impact of Television on American Politics* (New York: Basic Books, 1983), 58.
5. Jay Edward Epstein, *News From Nowhere* (New York: Random House, 1973), 228-29.
6. I borrow the term "politically enabling" from David Cratis Williams, "Nuclear Criticism: In Pursuit of a 'Politically Enabling' Deconstructive Voice," *Journal of the American Forensic Association* 24 (Winter 1988): 193-205.
7. John Chancellor quoted in *Believing the News*, edited by Don Fry (St. Petersburg: The Poynter Institute for Media Studies, [1985]), 166.
8. This analysis is based upon more than 400 stories listed under "Nuclear Weapons" in the *CBS News Index*, most from the *Evening News*, but including *CBS Reports*, *60 Minutes*, the *CBS Morning News*, and *Sunday Morning*. All citations to these programs are to the microfiche transcripts. See CBS News, *CBS News Index, 1981-1984*, vols. 7-10 (New York: Microfilming Corporation of America, 1982-1985).
9. In a study of agenda-setting by television news, Behr and Iyengar also focus upon CBS, noting not only that CBS attracted the largest audience at the time, but also that "the network newscasts are so homogenous that bias stemming from the choice of any particular network is minimal" (Roy L. Behr and Shanto Iyengar, "Television News, Real-World Cues, and Changes in the Public Agenda," *Public Opinion Quarterly* 49 [Spring 1985]: 41 n.1). For other studies of content duplication on the three commercial networks' evening news shows, see James B. Lemert, "Content Duplications by the Networks in Competing Evening Newscasts," *Journalism Quarterly* 51 (Summer 1974): 238-44; David L. Altheide, "Three-In-One News: Network Coverage of Iran," *Journalism Quarterly* 59 (Autumn 1982): 482-86; and Joe S. Foote and Michael E. Steel, "Degree of Conformity in Lead Stories in Early Evening Network Television Newscasts," *Journalism Quarterly* 63 (Spring 1986): 19-23.
10. Although this study does not employ the quantitative techniques of "content analysis," its focus on the rhetorical features of newscasts calls to mind Roderick P. Hart, Patrick Jerome, and Karen McComb, "Rhetorical Features of Newscasts About the President," *Critical Studies in Mass Communication* 1 (September 1984): 260-86.
11. Gans, *Deciding What's News*, 53.
12. As Kenneth Burke writes, the "synecdochic form is present in all theories of political representation," as some "part of the social body" is assumed to represent the whole (Burke, *A Grammar of Motives*, 508).
13. See Epstein, *News From Nowhere*, 228-29.
14. Gitlin, *The Whole World is Watching*, 193.

15. William L. Lunch and Peter W. Sperlich, "American Public Opinion and the War in Vietnam," *Western Political Quarterly* 31 (March 1979): 32-33.
16. Gitlin, *The Whole World is Watching*, 287-90.
17. *CBS Evening News*, 19 April 1982, 5.
18. *CBS Evening News*, 10 October 1981, 5; *CBS Evening News*, 24 October 1981, 6; *CBS Evening News*, 25 October 1981, 2; *CBS Evening News*, 14 November 1981, 7; *CBS Evening News*, 21 November 1981, 8.
19. *CBS Evening News*, 20 June 1981, 7; *CBS Evening News*, 21 November 1981, 8; *CBS Evening News*, 5 December 1981, 11; *CBS Evening News*, 21 November 1981, 12.
20. *CBS Evening News*, 21 November 1981, 9-10.
21. *CBS Evening News*, 5 December 1981, 10.
22. *CBS Evening News*, 22 March 1982, 8.
23. *CBS Evening News*, 10 April 1982, 8-9.
24. *CBS Evening News*, 6 June 1982, 4.
25. *CBS Evening News*, 12 June 1982, 6.
26. See, for example, coverage on the *CBS Evening News* of the demonstrations at the Trident submarine base at Groton, Connecticut (11 November 1981, 5; 14 November 1981, 7; 8 January 1983, 9), the Livermore Laboratory in California (1 February 1982, 5; 21 June 1982, 10), the Vandenberg Air Force Base (24 January 1983, 14; 21 March 1983, 10), and the Seneca Army Depot in New York (4 July 1983, 10; 1 August 1983, 9).
27. *CBS Evening News*, 18 April 1982, 3. For Molander's views on the freeze initiative see Garfinkle, *The Politics of the Nuclear Freeze*, 82; and Butterfield, "Anatomy of the Nuclear Protest," 39.
28. *CBS Evening News*, 25 August 1982, 9. As the company pointed out in a statement responding to the incident, "General Electric does not build warheads."
29. *CBS Evening News*, 14 November 1982, 11.
30. *CBS Evening News*, 18 April 1982, 3.
31. *CBS Evening News*, 9 August 1982, 11.
32. Gans, *Deciding What's News*, 44.
33. *CBS Evening News*, 5 December 1981, 10-11.
34. *CBS Evening News*, 3 March 1982, 9-10.
35. *CBS Evening News*, 11 April 1982, 12.
36. *CBS Evening News*, 3 March 1982, 9.
37. *CBS Evening News*, 21 November 1981, 9.
38. *CBS Evening News*, 11 May 1982, 12.
39. See Philip Meyer, *Precision Journalism: A Reporter's Introduction to Social Science Methods* (Bloomington: Indiana University Press, 1973).
40. Roderick P. Hart, *The Sound of Leadership* (Chicago: University of Chicago Press, 1987), 127.
41. *CBS Evening News*, 28 September 1984, 3.
42. *CBS Evening News*, 19 April 1982, 5-6.
43. *CBS Evening News*, 26 September 1981, 3.
44. *CBS Evening News*, 2 July 1984, 1.
45. *CBS Evening News*, 10 May 1984, 12.
46. *CBS Evening News*, 26 September 1981, 3. For discussion of presidential popularity polls and their natural tendency to go down following elections, see Charles W. Roll and Albert H. Cantril, *Polls: Their Use and Misuse in Politics* (Cabin John, Maryland: Seven Locks Press, 1980), 127-29.

47. Howard Schuman, Jacob Ludwig, and Jon A. Krosnick, "The Perceived Threat of Nuclear War, Salience, and Open Questions," *Public Opinion Quarterly* 50 (Winter 1986): 520.
48. *CBS Evening News*, 29 May 1982, 5.
49. *CBS Evening News*, 13 February 1984, 10-11.
50. *CBS Evening News*, 3 December 1983, 5.
51. *CBS Evening News*, 28 September 1984, 3.
52. Ted J. Smith III, "Public Opinion and the Nuclear Freeze Movement of 1980-84," presented to the American Association for Public Opinion Research, St. Petersburg, Florida, 1986, 17.
53. See W. Lance Bennett, *News: The Politics of Illusion*, 2nd ed. (New York: Longman, 1988), 26-35.
54. Gitlin, *The Whole World is Watching*, 146-79.
55. *CBS Evening News*, 21 November 1981, 9.
56. *CBS Evening News*, 3 March 1982, 9-10.
57. *CBS Evening News*, 21 November 1981, 9.
58. *CBS Evening News*, 29 January 1981, 10-11.
59. Ibid., 10-11.
60. Ibid., 11.
61. *CBS Evening News*, 12 June 1981, 13.
62. *CBS Evening News*, 29 January 1981, 10-11.
63. Caldicott, *Nuclear Madness*, 73.
64. *CBS Evening News*, 29 January 1981, 11.
65. *CBS Evening News*, 11 November 1981, 6.
66. *CBS Evening News*, 21 March 1981, 3.
67. *CBS Evening News*, 29 January 1981, 10.
68. *CBS Evening News*, 21 November 1981, 10.
69. See, for example, *CBS Evening News*, 30 May 1982, 3-4 and *CBS Evening News*, 14 June 1982, 14-15.
70. *CBS Evening News*, 8 April 1982, 15.
71. Ibid., 14, 16.
72. Ibid., 14.
73. Zagano, "Media Morality," 183, 203-04.
74. *CBS Evening News*, 15 November 1982, 11.
75. *CBS Evening News*, 31 March 1983, 1.
76. *CBS Evening News*, 5 April 1983, 5.
77. *CBS Evening News*, 29 April 1983, 6 and *CBS Evening News*, 1 May 1983, 15.
78. *CBS Evening News*, 2 May 1983, 1.
79. *CBS Evening News*, 3 May 1983, 3.
80. *CBS Evening News*, 4 May 1983, 4.
81. *The Challenge of Peace*, 60.
82. Novak, "The Bishops Speak Out," 680-81.
83. *The Challenge of Peace*, 60.
84. David Halberstam, *The Powers That Be* (New York: Alfred A. Knopf, 1979), 155.
85. Gans, *Deciding What's News*, 215.
86. Ken Auletta, "Look What They've Done to the News," *TV Guide*, 9-15 November 1991, 6.
87. Gans, *Deciding What's News*, 215.

88. Edwin Diamond, *The Media Show: The Changing Face of the News, 1985-1990* (Cambridge: MIT Press, 1991), 29, 32.
89. *CBS Morning News*, 19 April 1982, 22.
90. Bill Leonard, *In the Storm of the Eye: A Lifetime at CBS* (New York: G.P. Putnam's Sons, 1987), 211-12.
91. *CBS Evening News*, 12 June 1981, 12.
92. CBS News, "The Defense of the United States," part 1: "Ground Zero," *CBS Reports*, 14 June 1981, 14-15.
93. Ibid., 15.
94. Ibid., 15-16, 18.
95. Ibid., 6, 10-11.
96. Ibid., 6, 12, 16-18.
97. Leonard, *In the Storm of the Eye*, 212-13.
98. Thomas Powers, "Sticking to the Grim Point," *The Nation*, 25 July-1 August 1981, 86.
99. Meyer, *A Winter of Discontent*, 122.
100. Axel Madsen, *60 Minutes: The Power and Politics of America's Most Popular TV News Show* (New York: Dodd, Mead and Co., 1984), xiv, 14, 17, 23. The advertising rate for 1990 is from Richard Campbell, *60 Minutes and the News: A Mythology for Middle America* (Urbana: University of Illinois Press, 1991), 60.
101. Jonathan Black, "The Stung," in *Television: The Critical View*, 3rd ed., edited by Horace Newcomb (New York: Oxford University Press, 1982), 248, 256, 259.
102. In a recent study, Richard Campbell identifies four narrative formulas governing stories on *60 Minutes*: news as "mystery," news as "therapy," news as "adventure," and news as "arbitration" (Campbell, *60 Minutes and the News*, 43-136).
103. Black, "The Stung," in *Television*, edited by Newcomb, 256.
104. CBS News, "The Bomb," 2.
105. Ibid., 3.
106. See Madsen, *60 Minutes*, 44-45.
107. CBS News, "The Bomb," 4-6.
108. Ibid., 6.
109. See Mechling and Mechling, "The Campaign for Civil Defense and the Struggle to Naturalize the Bomb," 111.
110. CBS News, "The Bomb," 6-8.
111. CBS News, "The Bishop and the Bombs," 13-17.
112. CBS News, "The Week Before *The Day After*," 7-11.
113. Bennett, *News*, 22.
114. For a summary of these critical alternatives to the ideological perspective, see Hart, Jerome, and McComb, "Rhetorical Features of Newscasts About the President," 261-64.
115. Bennett, *News*, 16, 31, 91.
116. Fiske, *Television Culture*, 281-308.
117. Rubin and Cummings, "Nuclear War and Its Consequences on Television News," 39-40, 45.
118. Meyer, *A Winter of Discontent*, 123-28.
119. With a "soft news" format, morning news shows provided an ideal forum for extended interviews and in-depth stories about the freeze campaign. In April of 1982, the coverage was especially heavy, with *Sunday Morning* airing a special cover story entitled "The Freeze" on April 11, followed by five entire days devoted to Ground Zero Week on the *CBS Morning News*. See CBS News, "The Freeze," *Sunday Morning*, 11 April 1982, 10-15 and CBS News, *CBS Morning News*, 19-23 April 1982.

120. Bennett, *News*, 9.
121. Jamieson, *Eloquence in an Electronic Age*, x.
122. Edwin Diamond, *The Tin Kazoo: Television, Politics, and the News* (Cambridge: MIT Press, 1975).
123. See Norman Ornstein, Andrew Kohut, and Larry McCarthy, *The People, the Press, and Politics: The Times Mirror Study of the American Electorate* (Reading, Massachusetts: Addison-Wesley, 1988), 61-62.
124. Auletta, "Look What They've Done to the News," 5.
125. Although it is impossible to determine whether most former viewers of network evening news switched to other news sources or quit watching television news altogether, data reported by Briller are suggestive. Comparing viewership of all television news in 1990 with viewership in 1965, Briller calls the sharp decline in the number of young adults watching television news "shocking," and he suggests that this decline is related to a decline in "TV news credibility" during the 1980s. See Bert R. Briller, "Zooming in Closer on the News Audience," *Television Quarterly* 25, no. 1 (1990): 107-8.
126. William A. Henry III, "Journalism Under Fire," reprinted from *Time*, 12 December 1983 in *Believing the News*, edited by Don Fry (St. Petersburg, Florida: The Poynter Institute for Media Studies, [1985]), 191-212.
127. Madsen, *60 Minutes*, 174.
128. Jimmy Carter, "Energy Problems: The Erosion of Confidence," *Vital Speeches of the Day*, 15 August 1979, 642-45.
129. See, for example, Briller, "Zooming in Closer on the News Audience," 107-16.
130. Smith, *Moscow Meets Main Street*, 28-29.
131. See my review of Jamieson's *Eloquence in an Electronic Age* in *Quarterly Journal of Speech* 76 (August 1990): 345-47.

## Chapter Eight

# The Rhetoric of Polling

Everybody believes in public opinion polls—everyone from the man on the street all the way up to President Thomas E. Dewey.[1]

Goodman Ace

The "science" of polling has come a long way since the debacle of the *Literary Digest* poll in 1936.[2] The pollsters point to an impressive record in predicting presidential elections, and they imply that they can just as accurately assess public opinion on the issues of the day.[3] With more "scientific" sampling techniques and a variety of other "new technologies available through computers," the pollsters boast that polling has "truly come of age"—a candidate to become the "Fifth Estate" in American politics. Not only can polls now tell us how we will vote, according to the pollsters, but they can also "greatly strengthen the democratic process by providing 'the people' yet another way of making their views known—particularly between elections."[4]

In reality, of course, the pollsters' record in predicting presidential elections has not been all that impressive,[5] and issue polls are significantly less reliable. More scientific methods have done little to reduce the major sources of error in issue polls—problems the pollsters euphemistically call non-sampling error. Specifically, problems with question-wording continue to bedevil the pollsters, as even slight variations in phrasing can produce enormous swings in the findings. In polling on the Panama Canal treaties of 1978, for example, differently worded questions produced results ranging from 78 percent disapproval of the treaties to 65 percent in support.[6] Similarly, the pollsters tell us that while only about 8 percent of Americans support cuts in "aid to the needy," 39 percent favor cutting "public welfare programs."[7] As pollster Burns Roper concedes, results from issue polls are often presented as within three percentage points of what the public actually thinks about a subject, "when, in fact, a differently worded question might—and often does—produce a result that is 25 or 30 points different from the reported result."[8]

The pollsters blame the news media for emphasizing sampling error to the exclusion of question-wording in their poll reports. The emphasis on sampling error, they argue, only conveys a "sense of precision . . . that may be specious."[9]

It is true that the news media, and particularly television, rarely report the wording of poll questions.[10] But that is only part of the problem. The larger problem is that the pollsters themselves ask too many bad questions in the first place. Still concerned more with sample design than with question-wording, the pollsters routinely ask questions that miss the point of political controversies or that bias the results with information about an issue.[11]

Still larger problems arise when the pollsters interpret their data. While they again point fingers at the news media,[12] the pollsters themselves are now more inclined than ever to exaggerate the significance of their findings, to discern lessons from ambiguous data, to predict the future, or to otherwise put dramatic spins on their data. The reason is simple: since the 1970s the polling industry has become virtually a wholly owned subsidiary of the news media. All major polls today are either sponsored directly by a news organization or are syndicated exclusively to media outlets.[13] The pollsters may worry about this conflict of interest, acknowledging that media polls often make news rather than report it, and they criticize news organizations for promoting their own polls to the exclusion of others.[14] But the fact remains that while the pollsters often discover "uncertainty, ambiguity, and low levels of public information and interest on matters of public policy,"[15] their media bosses demand news. And since no election can ever prove an issue poll wrong, as Wheeler has suggested, the pollsters are free to "pontificate about the concerns of the American people without the fear of being caught."[16]

Few issues in American history have inspired more polling—and more pontification about the results—than the nuclear freeze initiative. Asking literally hundreds of questions related to the freeze between 1980 and 1984, the pollsters set out to chart every nuance, every trend, in public attitudes toward the freeze. Driven by journalistic imperatives, they also pontificated at great length about the meaning of the results, telling a dramatic, newsworthy tale of a revolution in public attitudes. In 1982, for example, pollster Patrick Caddell called the freeze movement "the most significant movement since the environmental movement of the late 1960's" and predicted that it would have long-term impacts on the political process.[17] At about the same time, California pollster Mervin Field appeared on the *CBS Evening News* with a warning for presidential candidates: "I think what it means for Ronald Reagan and for all politicians who are suddenly become [sic] alert to this, what I—appears to be a very strong, unusual, spontaneous grass-roots movement, that they better run fast to get ahead of it."[18] Also in 1982, Lou Harris spoke of a new and "urgent hunger for peace" that cut "right across the spectrum of social and political divisions in this country." Calling this change an incredible phenomenon, Harris concluded: "It's an idea that will not go away. It's going to be with us until the final weapons are obliterated."[19] Even as late as 1984, when the freeze had all but disappeared from the news, pollster Daniel Yankelovich reported that "a great change, largely unnoted," had "transformed the outlook of the American electorate toward nuclear arms."[20]

Yankelovich's Public Agenda Foundation even prepared a "briefing book" for the 1984 presidential candidates, suggesting how they might capitalize upon this historic "turnabout" in public opinion.[21]

Candidates who heeded the pollsters did not fare well in 1984,[22] but for several years the myth of a revolution in public attitudes had significant political impacts. With the news media echoing the pollsters' talk of a historic grass-roots movement, peace groups enjoyed unprecedented prosperity, and mainstream political groups by the hundreds jumped upon the freeze bandwagon. The debate left a legacy of nuclear education in our schools, and it nearly splintered the American Catholic Church. In Congress, politicians convinced of the power of the freeze movement twice debated the issue, creating at least the appearance of deference to public opinion. Clearly, the polls proved a potent weapon for nuclear freeze activists. No new arms control policy may have resulted from the whole affair, but the freeze became something of a national political obsession for over three years, and much of the explanation lies in the rhetoric of polling.

Rarely did the pundits or the politicians carefully consider the questions or other methodological characteristics of the polls that inspired the "great debate" over a nuclear freeze. Nor did they consider polls on related issues or polls measuring the public's knowledge and concern about the freeze issue. At best, they developed a superficial understanding of public opinion on the freeze—an understanding based upon only the most general of polls and, in some cases, upon polls flawed by misleading or biased questions.

A closer look at the polling data reveals that public opinion was considerably more complicated, and far less supportive of the freeze, than the pollsters suggested. When one considers the more than 400 freeze-related questions asked by 12 national pollsters between 1980 and 1984,[23] a very different portrait of public opinion emerges. The data, presented in the Appendix,[24] reveal strong support for arms control efforts and for the general concept of a freeze. However, that support came heavily qualified, and some of those qualifications probably should have been interpreted, in practical terms, as opposition to the freeze. Furthermore, the public had serious reservations about the possibility of such an agreement; many simply did not believe the Soviet Union desired an arms control agreement. Most surprisingly, the public simply did not care all that much about the issue. Most Americans paid little attention to the freeze debate, and they were far less enamored of the freeze movement than news reports suggested. In short, grass-roots public support for the nuclear freeze was largely an illusion—the product of a rhetoric of polling driven by journalistic imperatives.

## Support for Arms Control and the Freeze Metaphor

Survey research reveals that "a strong concern about nuclear war has seldom been uppermost in the minds of the great majority of Americans."[25] Over the years, as Tom Smith has observed, "other issues such as the economy, the environment, and the budget deficit have topped the public's list of concerns," with most Americans telling the pollsters "either that they did not think nuclear war would occur or at least that it was not an immediate threat."[26] At the same time, however, Americans historically have expressed concern about nuclear weapons and have supported efforts to negotiate arms control agreements with the Soviet Union. Throughout the nuclear age, as Everett Carll Ladd has observed, survey research consistently has shown the public's "ample appreciation of the bomb's awful destructiveness" and "widespread support for efforts to minimize its destructive potential." According to Ladd, the nuclear freeze campaign did not reflect "some recent change in the public's thinking." Indeed, the most striking finding to emerge from Ladd's review of survey data since World War II was that public opinion on nuclear weapons and war had changed scarcely at all over the nearly four decades of the nuclear age.[27]

As Ladd suggests, Americans historically have supported efforts to negotiate arms control agreements, and they continued to express that support in the early 1980s. Group 1 of the questions in the Appendix includes 23 polls assessing general support for arms control and disarmament. The highest levels of support for arms control were found in polls combining mention of negotiations or agreements with vague references to limitations, reductions, or cutbacks in nuclear weapons. Among the polls included in Group 1, Harris's question about "negotiating an effective nuclear arms agreement that would call for a real cutback" in United States and Soviet arsenals (question 7) produced the highest level of support: 87 percent. Even higher figures (89 to 90 percent) came out of two other polls, not included in the Appendix, mentioning both negotiations and reductions: a June 1984 Harris poll asking whether respondents favored "the U.S. and the Soviet Union sitting down to negotiate an agreement to reduce nuclear weapons on each side," and a November 1984 Gordon Black poll (for *USA Today*) assessing views on the importance of "negotiating nuclear arms limitations or reductions with the Soviet Union."[28] While some polls seemed to indicate an increase in support for arms control negotiations toward the end of the freeze campaign in 1984, the data overall did not support such a conclusion. A series of Roper polls (question 10) revealed a tendency to see negotiations as requiring a greater effort toward the end of the freeze debate, but other series actually revealed some decline in support for arms control between 1981 and 1984 (see questions 1 and 6).

The lowest levels of support for arms control appeared in several polls with problematic questions—questions that illustrated just how dramatically question-wording can affect the findings. For example, a 1982 *Los Angeles Times* poll (question 9) asked: "Do you think the United States should meet with the Soviet Union this year to try to reach agreement on nuclear weapons, or do you think the United States should put off a meeting this year until we are in a better bargaining position—or haven't you heard enough about that yet to say?" This question, which of course implied that the United States would be in a better bargaining position later, resulted in only a bare majority (51 percent) expressing support for negotiations. Three questions posed by Gallup in 1981 also may have been biased against arms control. On two occasions, Gallup asked how respondents would vote in a disarmament referendum sponsored by the United Nations (question 3). The comparatively low support for arms control found in these polls might have resulted from negative opinions about the United Nations or from doubts about the efficacy of such a referendum. The third question (question 2) asked whether respondents would "favor or oppose an agreement between the U.S. and the Soviet Union to destroy all nuclear weapons that have already been built." This question produced the lowest level of support of all the general arms control questions. The explanation may lie in a realization among some respondents that the United States and the Soviet Union were not the only nuclear powers. This suspicion seems confirmed by a series of Harris polls that found much stronger support for an agreement among all nuclear nations to destroy their weapons (question 5).

It is important to note, however, that the polls in Group 1 of the Appendix reveal little about the sort of arms control agreements Americans supported in the early 1980s. Most either made no mention at all of the purpose of negotiating with the Soviet Union, or they suggested only some general objective, ranging from merely limiting nuclear weapons to reducing or even eliminating them altogether. Within Group 1, only two polls aimed to assess public opinion on a specific arms control proposal in the news at the time: the Gallup (question 4) and the Harris (question 8) questions about George Kennan's proposed 50 percent reduction in the arsenals of both superpowers.[29] Although both revealed strong support for the proposal, the questions were flawed in both cases. Gallup's question presented the proposal as if it were President Reagan's initiative,[30] while Harris transformed Kennan's "immediate across-the-boards reduction" into a gradual, five-year reduction. Furthermore, neither pollster assessed whether respondents understood the "50 percent reduction" as a specific alternative to the administration's arms control policies or simply as an arbitrary figure—a figure the pollster just "pulled out of the hat."

By 1982, virtually all major pollsters began asking questions about the freeze. Yet the vast majority of these polls, as revealed by the questions in Group 2 of the Appendix, assessed support only for the general concept of the freeze, perhaps only for the freeze metaphor itself. While it is true that most freeze polls revealed strong, often overwhelming, support for the freeze, those levels of support were comparable to the support typically found in polls assessing general support for arms control and disarmament. Furthermore, they produced no evidence of mushrooming support for the freeze across the period of the freeze debate. Indeed, several series with consistent questions revealed, if anything, a decline in public support for the freeze after 1982 (see, for example, questions 21, 28, and 29).

The pollsters complicated interpretation of support for the freeze by asking a wide variety of questions across the period of the freeze debate. Yet those differences also have some interesting implications about the nature of that support. Questions that included arguments for and against the freeze, for example, actually seemed to decrease support for the concept. The best evidence comes from two ABC polls (question 11) that asked respondents their opinion of a freeze both before and after rating an equal number of pro- and anti-freeze arguments. In both cases, support for a freeze declined, particularly the percentage of those approving strongly of a freeze. In addition, the only question to include both pro- and anti-freeze arguments, the *Los Angeles Times* poll of March 1982 (question 24), found only 52 percent in favor (with an additional 5 percent leaning toward support) of a freeze. Polls revealing higher levels of support sometimes included only pro-freeze arguments (questions 17 and 20), while questions implying that a freeze might be risky (question 12) or mentioning alternatives to the freeze resulted in lower levels of support. For example, some of the lowest pro-freeze figures came in a pair of *Los Angeles Times* polls asking respondents to choose among a freeze, an agreement to reduce both superpower arsenals, an agreement to destroy all nuclear weapons, or no agreement at all (question 23). Similarly, an NBC/Associated Press poll allowing respondents to choose between a freeze and a continuation of the nuclear buildup actually revealed more support for the latter (question 27). One last finding reinforces suspicions that support for the freeze was, at best, fickle. A CBS/*New York Times* poll conducted in May 1982 revealed that 72 percent of the public supported the freeze (question 13)—a finding cited often during the congressional freeze debate. At the same time, however, nearly 40 percent of the same sample called it "more dangerous" for the United States to agree to a freeze than to build "more nuclear weapons" (question 16).

In short, the public strongly, even overwhelmingly, supported the general concept of a nuclear freeze. At the same time, however, there is no evidence that support for the freeze mushroomed throughout the period, or that the public supported anything more specific than the freeze metaphor itself—the imagery of an escalating arms race suddenly frozen in place. The findings suggest that exposure to arguments about the freeze actually reduced public support, and other data help to account for this phenomenon. In April 1983, the Roper poll asked a split sample of 2,000 adults to rate six pro- and six anti-freeze arguments as very convincing, somewhat convincing, not very convincing, or not at all convincing. Respondents rated anti-freeze arguments, on average, "very" or "somewhat convincing" 58 percent of the time, compared to 47 percent for the pro-freeze arguments.

Most importantly, high levels of support for the freeze depended upon several specific conditions. First, the public supported only a bilateral freeze or a freeze among all nuclear nations. Most questions asked only about a bilateral freeze, a freeze between the United States and the Soviet Union, or a freeze among all nations. The absence of any such reference probably explains the unusually low pro-freeze figure in the *LA Times* poll of September 1983 (question 26). Second, very high levels of support for the freeze depended in considerable measure on confidence that such an agreement could be verified. Perhaps the best evidence of this came in the May 1982 CBS/*New York Times* poll (question 13) which revealed that while 72 percent of Americans supported a freeze, 83 percent would support it if assured that each country "could catch the other . . . cheating on the agreement" (question 15). Further evidence came from the *LA Times* series (question 26), in which the addition of a reference to verification in the question in November 1983 resulted in an increase of more than twenty percentage points in "strong" approval of the freeze. Finally, public support for the freeze was conditional upon belief in the equivalency of the two superpowers' arsenals. Again, a follow-up question in the CBS/*New York Times* poll of May 1982 best reveals the effect of this condition. The poll asked those who initially opposed the freeze if they might change their minds if the United States and the Soviet Union were left with "about an equal amount of nuclear weapons." This time the converts combined with those initially supporting the freeze to produce one of the highest pro-freeze figures of all: 87 percent (question 14).

All of these conditions warrant closer examination, for they involve some of the key controversies of the freeze debate. With but a few exceptions, the polls assessed support for a bilateral freeze. Yet freeze opponents denied that such a freeze could be negotiated or verified, and they argued that an immediate freeze would leave the United States at a nuclear disadvantage. In assessing support for the freeze, some pollsters, in effect, resolved these key controversies in favor of the pro-freeze advocates. For example, a number of polls assessed support only for a verifiable freeze, and these polls, not surprisingly, produced some of the highest pro-freeze figures (see questions 18, 19, 22, 24, 25, and 30).[31] The public, however, continued to have its doubts that a freeze could be verified, and it did not wish to see the United States frozen into a nuclear disadvantage. In other words, the public had considerable doubts about the possibility of a bilateral, verifiable, and balanced freeze, as analysis of some additional, more specific polls will demonstrate.

## Reservations About the Freeze

The most important condition underlying public support for the freeze was that it be a bilateral agreement. While support for arms control and the freeze in general remained consistently high throughout the Reagan administration's first term in office, so too did the public consistently reject a unilateral freeze or any sort of moves toward unilateral disarmament. Only about 15 to19 percent of the public supported unilateral disarmament (question 33), while slightly more—approximately 22 to 23 percent—supported a freeze regardless of Soviet compliance (questions 31*, 31**, and 32). It is interesting that approximately a quarter of the population, when given the choice, apparently rejected disarmament under any circumstances (question 35), and at least one poll (question 34) revealed more than twice as many Americans favoring a quest for nuclear superiority as favoring a unilateral freeze. A Public Agenda Foundation poll conducted in May of 1984 (question 36) suggested that a majority of the public might be willing to support a temporary unilateral freeze "to see if the Soviets will follow suit." But with the exception of an anomalous Gallup poll from September 1982 (question 31),[32] the data consistently showed large majorities of the public opposed to any sort of unilateral arms control measures.

The public's rejection of unilateral measures assumes greater significance when one considers attitudes toward verification of arms control agreements with the Soviets. As the questions in Group 4 reveal, overwhelming majorities agreed that verification was essential to any bilateral freeze on nuclear weapons. But the public had considerable doubts about the feasibility of verifying agreements with the Soviets, and hence they may have doubted the possibility of a genuinely bilateral freeze.

Just as the presumption that a freeze could be verified produced overwhelming pro-freeze majorities in Group 2 questions, questions that raised doubts about verification significantly diminished support for a freeze. While one poll found a slight majority proclaiming it an "acceptable risk" to sign an agreement without "foolproof verification" (question 50), another showed the public proclaiming verification more important than halting the growth of the nuclear arsenal by a margin of 67-25 percent (question 42). The most revealing finding, however, came in the only poll that asked specifically about support for the freeze presuming that it could *not* be verified. If either the United States or the Soviet Union "could cheat" on the freeze, according to a CBS/*New York Times* poll in 1982, 71 percent of the public would oppose it (question 41).

Moreover, Americans apparently believed the Soviets (but not the United States) would cheat on a freeze agreement. By clear and often overwhelming majorities, Americans simply did not trust the Soviets to live up to any sort of arms control pact (questions 37, 38, 40, 43, 44, 45, 49, and 51).[33] Furthermore, the public doubted that Soviet cheating could be detected, either because we lacked the means of verification or because the Soviets would not allow such measures as on-site inspection (questions 46, 47, 48, and 52). Taken together, of course, these findings raise fundamental doubts about the public's support for an actual freeze agreement. While the public may have supported the general concept of a freeze, they insisted upon bilateral compliance while expressing strong doubts that such compliance could be verified.

The public's perception of the nuclear balance also had significant effects on support for the freeze, although the findings seem somewhat contradictory. The Penn and Schoen poll of registered voters in April of 1983 revealed that only 36 percent believed that a freeze would be "tilted in favor of the Soviet Union," while 33 percent thought it would be "fair to both countries" (question 63). Similarly, a series of Roper polls not only found less than a majority convinced of Soviet nuclear superiority, but also some decline in that belief between 1980 and 1984 (question 66). These views, of course, conform with pro-freeze arguments about the nuclear balance and the effects of a freeze. Yet at least three other polls suggested that the public agreed with the Reagan administration that an immediate freeze would leave the United States at a nuclear disadvantage. In two ABC/*Washington Post* polls, substantial majorities agreed that a "freeze now" would leave the Soviets with a nuclear advantage (question 54), while 60 percent of the respondents in a Roper poll (question 64) found "very convincing" or "somewhat convincing" the argument that a freeze would leave the Soviets ahead of the United States.

Polls assessing the importance of the nuclear balance likewise seemed somewhat contradictory, although a certain logic could be discerned in the findings. Some polls showed about half of all respondents agreeing that the United States already had more than enough nuclear weapons to deter or destroy the Soviet Union (questions 55, 56, and 60). In two ABC/*Washington Post* polls, for example, nearly 80 percent of the respondents agreed with the statement: "It doesn't matter if the United States or the Soviet Union is ahead in nuclear weapons because both sides have more than enough to destroy each other no matter who attacks first" (question 53). Several other polls, however, produced large majorities agreeing that it was important, necessary, or in the best interests of peace that the United States maintain nuclear equality, even superiority, over the Soviet Union (questions 59, 61, and 65). Even when forced to choose between a "continuation of the nuclear arms build-up" or the United States "falling behind the Soviet Union," more Americans declared the latter a greater threat to peace (question 58). One might speculate that at least some Americans considered nuclear parity important for deterrent purposes or for enticing the Soviets to negotiate—even if it made little difference from a military standpoint. Whatever the explanation, the important point is that the public rejected a freeze that left the Soviets with an advantage. When polls specifically assessed support for a freeze assuming that it would leave the Soviets stronger, support for the idea dropped dramatically to between 30 percent and 36 percent (questions 57 and 62).

## Attitudes Toward the Freeze Debate

In all the media reports of strong public support for a nuclear freeze, one rarely found mention of public attitudes toward the likelihood of the two sides negotiating such an agreement. A number of the poll questions addressed the matter, however, and the results revealed yet another important point about public support for the freeze. In a nutshell, the findings reveal that, while the public may have supported a freeze, many doubted that the two sides would be able to negotiate such an agreement; indeed, large numbers of Americans doubted that any sort of arms control agreement could be negotiated with the Soviets (questions 69, 70, 71, 72, and 73). In general, the public tended to believe that the leaders of the Soviet Union did not share the desire of American leaders to control nuclear arms (questions 74, 75, and 76), and they doubted that Soviet leaders would be as likely as American leaders to agree specifically to a freeze (questions 67 and 68).

Conclusions about public support for the freeze also must be qualified with the observation that the public had mixed feelings about its own role in the nuclear debate. On the one hand, the polls showed large majorities rejecting the notion that the public should be excluded from the decision making—that such matters should be left to political leaders or experts (questions 77, 85, and 86). On the other hand, the CBS/*New York Times* poll of May 1982 revealed that the public had considerable doubts about its own competence to decide such a complicated issue (question 81), and a number of other polls revealed surprisingly little interest in the matter—surprising, at least, in light of all the talk about a grass-roots uprising.

Substantial minorities, ranging from 42 to 45 percent, confessed that they had not paid much attention to the freeze debate or that they had not "heard or read anything" at all about a proposed freeze (questions 78 and 82). During the period of most intensive media coverage—coverage often emphasizing the public's involvement in the debate—basic awareness of the issue never exceeded 57 percent (question 78). To these findings could be added a *Newsweek* poll (conducted by Gallup but missing from the Roper Center data set) which found that only 43 percent of the public had even heard of a nuclear freeze movement. Ironically, *Newsweek* reported this finding as a footnote to a major story on "the ground swell of support for a freeze."[34]

Finally, a number of polls suggested that many Americans had major reservations about the activists behind the freeze campaign. While the public expressed considerable sympathy for the general idea of protesting against the arms race (questions 79 and 83), a large majority said they would refuse an invitation to join a freeze group (question 80). Furthermore, a majority doubted that the freeze campaign constituted a real grass-roots movement. Rejecting media claims that the freeze had attracted a new breed of protestor, less radical and more thoughtful than the protestors of the past,[35] most Americans agreed that the freeze movement consisted of "people who often have been involved in most protest movements in the past" (question 87). Most importantly, few Americans thought the freeze movement helped the cause of arms control. As revealed in the *LA Times* poll of April 1983 (question 84), only 25 percent of Americans thought the freeze movement helped our efforts to negotiate arms reductions with the Soviets, while 31 percent thought it hurt and 28 percent thought it had no effect at all.

All in all, then, we have a surprising portrait of public opinion on the freeze. Clearly, an overwhelming majority of Americans favored arms control and the general concept of freezing the arms race. But there is no evidence of a radical transformation in public attitudes between 1980 and 1984, and the public had serious practical reservations about the freeze proposal itself. Indeed, at least two polls (question 71) showed that 80 percent of Americans doubted that a freeze on nuclear weapons could be negotiated in their lifetime. Moreover, the public simply did not care all that much about the issue. The freeze may have been an appealing metaphor, but most Americans had surprisingly little knowledge about, or interest in, the freeze initiative.

## The Rhetoric of Polling and Democratic Governance

According to the pollsters, polling can "enhance the strength of the democratic process by improving communication between the leader and the led."[36] Yet as Smith and Hogan have pointed out, "complex and important issues of public policy can be illuminated only by polls which are commensurately subtle, specific, and extensive."[37] In polling on the freeze, the pollsters generated extensive data, but much of that data resulted from polls with problematic questions. Moreover, the pollsters based their interpretations largely upon only the most general of questions, going well beyond their own data and ignoring important subtleties of opinion as well as questions of knowledge and salience.

Polling on the freeze issue again called attention to a number of persistent problems of question wording. First, many of the freeze questions were simply too general. Some arguably measured little more than the public's general antipathy towards nuclear weapons and the arms race. As such, they provided little guidance in a policy debate over competing arms control measures, and they glossed over the public's qualified support for the freeze—the fact that the public supported only a bilateral, verifiable, and balanced freeze agreement. Second, the pollsters, as usual, posed widely varying questions and changed questions frequently. As a result, the findings varied dramatically and were difficult to compare. Differences in question-wording might even account for some of the supposed trends in public opinion—the illusion of mushrooming support for the freeze, for example—during this period. Third, the pollsters continued to ignore the hazards of informing respondents about the issues. Some questions examined in this study misrepresented altogether the issue they purported to address (e.g. the questions about Kennan's fifty percent plan). Others risked bias by presenting pro- and anti-freeze arguments; curiously, some questions included only pro-freeze arguments. In any case, the whole business of informing respondents remains hard to justify. The business of polling should be to assess public opinion, not to predict what the public might think if exposed to selected information.

As Michael Wheeler has observed, "for every good poll there are dozens, perhaps hundreds, of bad ones."[38] But even the best poll can be rendered misleading by interpretations that go too far beyond the data—interpretations that speculate about the motivations behind public attitudes or that attempt to predict the future. Dramatic imperatives—the dictates of a good news story—undoubtedly encouraged media reports of a grass-roots movement sweeping the nation, particularly one destined to clash with the Reagan administration. And partisanship no doubt fueled talk in Congress about a public suddenly "reawakened to the danger of nuclear war."[39] In the final analysis, however, the rhetoric of the pollsters themselves created the myth of a revolution in public opinion—the myth of a grass-roots movement that virtually all Americans supported.

## Notes

1. Quoted in Melvin [sic] D. Field, "Opinion Polling in the United States of America," in *The Classics of Polling*, edited by Michael L. Young (Metuchen, New Jersey: Scarecrow Press, 1990), 37.
2. The *Literary Digest* poll, of course, predicted a sweeping victory for Republican presidential candidate Alf Landon over Franklin Delano Roosevelt. Based upon a mail-back sample of over two million, the *Literary Digest* poll is credited, ironically, with enhancing the credibility of polling since George Gallup, with his more "scientific" sampling techniques, predicted that the *Digest* would be wrong. See Michael L. Young, "Editor's Introduction," in *The Classics of Polling*, edited by Michael L. Young (Metuchen, New Jersey: Scarecrow Press, 1990), 2-3.
3. As Richard Vatz and Lee Weinberg have observed, candidate preference polls and polls assessing opinions on issues are often confused, and the pollsters themselves cultivate that confusion. For years, for example, *The Gallup Poll Monthly* (formerly *The Gallup Opinion Index* and *The Gallup Report*) regularly has published a table labeled "Gallup Poll Accuracy Record," showing "the tremendous accuracy of the Gallup survey in predicting the vote in presidential elections." Many—in some cases, all—of the polls inside each issue, however, are opinion polls, not presidential preference polls, which of course are "much more difficult, if not impossible to verify" (Richard E. Vatz and Lee S. Weinberg, "Media and Polling: Measuring and Creating the Salience of George Bush as 'Wimp,'" *Mass Comm Review* 14, no. 3 [1987]: 24).
4. Roll and Cantril, *Polls*, 11-14.
5. As Michael Wheeler pointed out a number of years ago, the pollsters go to extraordinary lengths to assure the accuracy of their election-eve presidential polls, recognizing that "their reputations, and as a consequence their profits, depend on how close they can come to the actual outcome." Yet even though they may double their sample size and "tighten up" their other procedures to avoid being proven wrong, their record since 1948 ("which the pollsters understandably do not like to count") has been, to say the least, undistinguished. As Wheeler pointed out, the pollsters confidently predicted only the obvious landslides between 1952 and 1972, and even then they rarely predicted the vote totals accurately. In more recent elections, their record has not been much better. In 1980, for example, the pollsters completely missed the Reagan landslide, with most major pollsters calling the race a "toss-up" or even predicting that

Carter would win. In 1988, pollsters again "tightened up" their procedures, relying upon more tracking polls to detect last-minute swings. But, again, the results were less than impressive. After reporting wild swings in voter preferences throughout the campaign, the pollsters finally predicted that George Bush would win. Yet only one of the five best-known polls predicted the actual vote for either Bush or Dukakis within three percentage points. In 1992, the pollsters, most notably the Gallup poll, suffered their worst embarrassment since 1936. Choosing to allocate none of the "undecided" voters to third-party candidate Ross Perot, Gallup overestimated Governor Bill Clinton's vote by a whopping 5.8 percentage points. See Michael Wheeler, *Lies, Damn Lies, and Statistics: The Manipulation of Public Opinion in America* (New York: Dell, 1976), 38-43; Mack C. Shelley II and Hwarng-Du Hwang, "The Mass Media and Public Opinion Polls in the 1988 Presidential Election," *American Politics Quarterly* 19 (January 1991): 61, 67-68; and "Gallup Poll Accuracy Record," *The Gallup Poll Monthly*, no. 326 (November 1992).

6. Smith and Hogan, "Public Opinion and the Panama Canal Treaties of 1977," 7.
7. Herbert Asher, *Polling and the Public: What Every Citizen Should Know* (Washington, D.C.: Congressional Quarterly Press, 1988), 42.
8. Burns W. Roper, "The Impact of Journalism on Polling," in *Polling on the Issues: Twenty-One Perspectives on the Role of Opinion Polls in the Making of Public Policy*, edited by Albert H. Cantril (Cabin John, Maryland: Seven Locks Press, 1980), 16.
9. See, for example, Albert H. Cantril, *The Opinion Connection: Polling, Politics, and the Press* (Washington, D.C.: Congressional Quarterly Press, 1991), esp. 119.
10. One of the few empirical studies of poll reporting on network television concluded that only 5 percent of television poll reports included the complete wording of the question, compared to 30 percent of newspaper reports (David Paletz, et al., "Polls in the Media: Content, Credibility, and Consequences," *Public Opinion Quarterly* 44 [Winter 1980]: 505).
11. Pollsters acknowledge that there has not been a great deal of "interest in aspects of opinion research not related to sampling," but they point to a growing body of literature on question-wording since the mid-1970s. However, most pollsters still take a rather technical view of the matter, focusing upon such matters as the number of alternatives offered or the ordering of questions. Rarely do they address whether the substantive content of questions accurately represents real-world political controversies, and they tend to dismiss complaints about informing respondents as themselves coming from biased "issue advocates" (Cantril, *The Opinion Connection*, 125, 211).
12. Pollsters often attribute misleading poll stories to "journalistic criteria of what is newsworthy," and they insist that the problem would be solved if only more polling professionals were involved in the conception, production, and final editing of news stories (Cantril, *The Opinion Connection*, 75-76). See also Roper, "The Impact of Journalism on Polling," in *Polling on the Issues*, edited by Cantril, 16.
13. See Arnold H. Ismach, "Polling as a News-Gathering Tool," in *The Classics of Polling*, edited by Michael L. Young (Metuchen, New Jersey: Scarecrow Press, 1990), 420-37.
14. See Roper, "The Impact of Journalism on Polling," in *Polling on the Issues*, edited by Cantril, 15-19.
15. Asher, *Polling and the Public*, 90.
16. Wheeler, *Lies, Damn Lies, and Statistics*, 43.
17. Butterfield, "Anatomy of the Nuclear Protest," 38.
18. *CBS Evening News*, 19 April 1982, 6.
19. Kalven, "A Talk with Louis Harris," 3, 5.

20. Daniel Yankelovich and John Doble, "The Public Mood: Nuclear Weapons and the U.S.S.R.," *Foreign Affairs* 63 (Fall 1984): 33.
21. Public Agenda Foundation, *Voter Options on Nuclear Arms Policy: A Briefing Book for the 1984 Elections* (New York: Public Agenda Foundation, 1984).
22. See Meyer, *A Winter of Discontent*, 241-51.
23. Most of the poll questions analyzed in this chapter, a total of 361, were obtained from the Roper Center's computerized data base. To these were added approximately 40 other questions identified in a review of published literature. A review of the *American Public Opinion Index* (1981-1984) revealed no additional national polls on the issue, and state polls identified in the *Index* were excluded from the analysis. The search also revealed a detailed opinion study on nuclear arms published by the Public Agenda Foundation (1984); with but a few exceptions, its questions are excluded from the analysis because of the very small sample (N=505).
24. In the Appendix, poll questions are grouped into a rough typology that parallels the discussion. Within each group, questions are ordered alphabetically by pollster. Due to space limitations, not all questions examined in the analysis are discussed or presented in the Appendix. In the case of series, variations in question wording are identified by asterisks. For each question, interview dates, population, and sample size are identified. All figures presented in the Appendix are percentages.
25. Schuman, Ludwig, and Krosnick, "The Perceived Threat of Nuclear War, Salience, and Open Questions," 520.
26. Tom W. Smith, "Nuclear Anxiety," *Public Opinion Quarterly* 52 (Winter 1988): 560.
27. Ladd, "The Freeze Framework," 20, 41.
28. The Harris poll showed 90 percent favoring the two nations "sitting down to negotiate an agreement to reduce nuclear weapons on each side." In the Gordon Black poll, 60 percent listed negotiating an arms control agreement among the "two or three most important" problems facing the government, while an additional 29 percent deemed it an "important" task facing the government. Both polls are available in the Roper Center data base.
29. George F. Kennan, "A Proposal for International Disarmament," the Albert Einstein Peace Prize Acceptance Speech, New York, May 19, 1981, in *The Nuclear Delusion: Soviet-American Relations in the Atomic Age*, 2nd ed., by George F. Kennan (New York: Pantheon, 1983), 175-82.
30. In addition, the Gallup poll presented respondents with a verification plan very different from that proposed by Kennan himself. While Kennan's proposal called for verification by "such national means . . . as now lie at the disposal of the two powers," Gallup asked respondents whether they would favor establishing a "worldwide organization which would make sure, by regular inspection, that neither the United States nor the Soviet Union violates this arms agreement." It is thus misleading for Gallup to report that an "overwhelming majority" favors the "Kennan proposal." See "Kennan Proposal to Break Nuclear Arms Race Supported by Overwhelming Margin; International Inspection Plan Favored," *Gallup Report* 196 (January 1982): 13.
31. The comparatively low levels of support for the freeze in the two *LA Times* polls (questions 24 and 25) may be due to two other factors discussed elsewhere. As noted earlier, the March 1982 *Times* poll may have found less support for the freeze because it included pro- and anti-freeze arguments, while the April 1983 question asked about the freeze movement rather than the concept of a freeze itself. As shown by the questions in Group 7, the polls showed Americans supportive of the idea of a freeze but not very supportive of the activists promoting it.

32. This poll still showed a majority opposed to a unilateral freeze, but the percentage supporting a unilateral freeze was about double that found in other polls. The explanation remains somewhat of a mystery, although it probably involves phrasing the question in terms of a hypothetical national referendum on the freeze issue.
33. A substantial minority (40 percent) also thought that the U.S. would cheat on a freeze agreement (question 39), but that is still far fewer than the number convinced that the Soviets would cheat.
34. Alpern, et al., "A Matter of Life and Death" and "Newsweek Poll: Nuclear Forebodings," 21, 24.
35. *CBS Evening News*, 11 November 1981, 9.
36. Roll and Cantril, *Polls*, 153-54.
37. Smith and Hogan, "Public Opinion and the Panama Canal Treaties of 1977," 28-29.
38. Wheeler, *Lies, Damn Lies, and Statistics*, 301.
39. Edward Markey in *Congressional Record*, 16 March 1983, H1210.

Ellen Shub/THE PICTURE CUBE

# Conclusion

> The perverse and unorthodox argument of this little book is that voters are not fools.[1]
>
> V. O. Key

Ronald Reagan's landslide reelection in 1984 dealt the final blow to the freeze campaign. For more than a year, the campaign had been in decline, with the news media losing interest and freeze activists themselves splintered over questions of strategy. The campaign's partisan opposition to Ronald Reagan sealed its fate. The 1984 election was to be "the final big test for the freeze movement," declared Randall Forsberg, the author of the freeze initiative.[2] Yet despite raising some $3.4 million and fielding about 25,000 volunteer campaign workers, the freeze campaign dramatically failed the test. What was to have been a "watershed year" for the freeze campaign instead "turned into a washout,"[3] and "people in the freeze movement were so disappointed and discouraged," according to Forsberg, that they simply "lost their drive."[4]

Some freeze activists looked to organizational explanations for the campaign's demise. At the fifth national freeze conference in December 1984, a "structure task force" recommended a series of steps designed to allow more people at the local level to participate in the campaign's strategy decisions while streamlining the campaign's national leadership. Yet the conference endorsed only minor structural changes, and the campaign continued to crumble, closing its St. Louis headquarters shortly after the 1984 conference.[5] Two years later, the remnants of the freeze campaign merged with the Committee for a Sane Nuclear Policy (SANE) in a last, desperate attempt to avoid total collapse. Steering the freeze campaign back toward its roots in a broader, more radical agenda, the new SANE/Freeze called for a world without nuclear weapons, ending the Cold War, conversion to a peace economy, and common security among the nations of the world.[6] With the appointment of the Reverend William Sloane Coffin as head of the new group in the spring of 1987,[7] the campaign had come full circle. Peace activists reclaimed the freeze, and mainstream politicians moved on to other issues.

By 1987, however, there was not much of a freeze campaign left to reclaim. Reorganization and new leadership did little to recapture the momentum of what had been considered a historic grass-roots movement. Indeed, the changes did little to address the real reasons behind the campaign's demise: the failure of its rhetorical strategies. By pursuing rhetorical strategies designed, first and foremost, to make news, the freeze campaign won abundant and sympathetic attention from journalists and media commentators. But those same strategies doomed the campaign to failure in institutional political contexts and generated only superficial and transitory public support.

## Telepolitical Eloquence

The freeze campaign marked a milestone in the history of the peace movement. Long relegated to the political fringes by a rhetoric of unilateral disarmament and sympathy for the Soviets, peace activists discovered in the freeze an effective tool of public relations: the simple image of an arms race frozen in place. Promoting the freeze with visual imagery, simple slogans, and bandwagon appeals, they skirted the technical and political controversies of the nuclear debate and disguised their larger, more radical political agenda. For a time, at least, the strategy worked. By the middle of 1982, the freeze dominated the news and Americans appeared to be flocking to the cause by the millions. Yet that very success came back to haunt the peace activists who founded the campaign. Increasingly coopted by mainstream politicians and the news media itself, the telepolitical rhetoric of the freeze campaign took on a life of its own. No longer did it call attention to the peace movement or even the freeze initiative itself. Leaving the peace activists who founded it in the wake of its sudden success, the nuclear freeze became more of a cultural fad than a policy initiative.

The freeze campaign's rhetoric of doom further divorced it from substantive policy concerns, seemingly cultivating fear as an end in itself. Tapping into a long tradition of religious and secular apocalyptic, the rhetoric of doom might have proven effective. But neither the freeze campaign's "bible," Jonathan Schell's *The Fate of the Earth*, nor the most-watched holocaust of the 1980s, ABC's *The Day After*, even mentioned the freeze, much less made an argument in support of the initiative. Indeed, neither offered a real solution of any sort; neither offered much hope. Some may have inferred that the freeze was the answer. Others, however, apparently were unmoved or only grew firmer in their support for a strong nuclear deterrent.

The rhetoric of political medicine, as represented by Helen Caldicott, reflected similarly parochial thinking about rhetorical strategy. Perhaps more than any other political advocate of the 1980s, Caldicott cultivated the eloquence of the electronic age: a talent for visual imagery and sound bites, the ability to telegraph emotions via the news media. Yet Caldicott, like most peace activists, not only failed to channel fear into support for the freeze; she also preached an alien historical faith and insulted those she hoped to persuade. Substituting New

Left historical revisionism for the cultural *mythos* of God's chosen people, Caldicott struck at the very heart of the democratic ethos, railing against a public she considered politically ignorant and culturally depraved.

The same hostility toward mainstream politics and culture manifested itself in the freeze campaign's rhetoric of nuclear education. Convinced of the ignorance and moral bankruptcy of America's adult population, freeze activists went after the children, disguising politically biased, even propagandistic rhetoric as educational curricula. The NEA's *Choices* became the most controversial of these curriculum guides, teaching children that nuclear war was imminent, that the United States was entirely to blame, and that rejecting and rebelling against the corrupt political world of their parents offered the only hope. Meanwhile, freeze activists recruited both parents and their children to the freeze campaign by portraying political activism as effective therapy for virtually all of the ills besetting America's young people. Parading children before the television cameras and dragging them before congressional committees to testify for the freeze, freeze activists created media events with little apparent concern for the children themselves. Of all the rhetorical strategies of the freeze campaign, none raised more troubling questions about public advocacy in the telepolitical age. Even many supporters of the freeze expressed outrage at the rhetoric of nuclear education.

Freeze advocates reveled in the moral righteousness of their cause, claiming that the freeze campaign democratized the nuclear debate and gave voice to the people. But all of the campaign's rhetorical strategies—not only the rhetoric of nuclear education, but the images and slogans, the rhetoric of doom, and the rhetoric of political medicine—raised troubling questions about public discourse in the telepolitical age. There is more to democratic persuasion—or at least there ought to be more—than making the news. Genuinely democratic discourse must not only attract media attention; it must empower citizens to act. It must allow citizens to formulate informed political opinions and to express those opinions in politically meaningful ways.

The rhetoric of the nuclear freeze campaign did not democratize the nuclear debate. To the contrary, it subverted public dialogue and disempowered citizens aspiring to participate in the democratic process. As Kathleen Hall Jamieson has suggested, the "abbreviated forms of communication" that pass for eloquence in today's media climate do not equip citizens to participate meaningfully in the political process. If citizens are to "deliberate fully and judge justly," then "public discourse must be enriched by *logos* as well as *ethos* and *pathos*, statement as well as proof."[8] The nuclear freeze campaign deliberately rejected that premise. Skeptical of the public's intelligence, freeze activists resorted to images and synoptic phrases, fear appeals, and celebrity experts to make their case. In doing so, they may have won over the news media and created the appearance of a grass-roots movement. But, in the final analysis, they underestimated both the demands of institutionalized political debate and the wisdom of the American people.

## INSTITUTIONAL IMPERATIVES

As *Newsweek* reported, the seeds of the nuclear freeze campaign were "carefully sown and cultivated by veteran antiwar activists,"[9] and its tactics included demonstrations and teach-ins reminiscent of the Vietnam era. In many ways, however, freeze advocates conducted more of a conventional political campaign than a protest movement. As Fox Butterfield observed, the leaders of the freeze campaign were "not bearded radicals but middle-aged and middle-class men and women, many accustomed to positions of responsibility and prestige." They included "doctors, lawyers, nurses, scientists, teachers and priests," and their chief battles were fought, "not in street confrontations, but at sermons and lectures, in books and pamphlets."[10] Many of their battles were fought in institutional contexts, as freeze activists lobbied for resolutions from state and local governments, labor unions, business and professional associations, religious organizations, and a diverse array of special interest groups. By 1983, the freeze campaign could boast of literally hundreds of institutional endorsements, ranging from the National Council of Churches and the International Longshoremen's Union to the state legislatures of eleven states.[11]

Freeze activists claimed their greatest institutional victories in the American Catholic Church and the U.S. House of Representatives. Both, it seemed, approved statements endorsing the freeze: the Catholic bishops *Pastoral Letter on War and Peace* and the House freeze resolution of April 1983. Upon closer examination, however, both of these statements actually repudiated key elements of their sponsors' broader political agendas and offered only heavily qualified support for the freeze initiative itself. Reflecting the tendency of institutionalized deliberative bodies toward negotiation and compromise, both the Catholic Church and the House of Representatives symbolically acknowledged the concerns behind the freeze campaign. But both also reaffirmed their long-standing institutional commitments to a strong nuclear deterrent and gave their blessings to the Reagan administration's arms control efforts.

Widely portrayed as a revolution within the Church, the Catholic debate over the *Pastoral Letter on War and Peace* might better be described as a counterrevolution. It served to stifle a radical political challenge to traditional Church teachings. Inaugurated by Pax Christi, the Catholic pacifist group, the debate resulted in a pastoral letter echoing the freeze campaign's call for a halt in the testing, production, and deployment of new nuclear weapons. Yet the bishops also reaffirmed the Church's just war doctrine, and they refused to condemn—indeed, they endorsed—the Reagan administration's efforts to negotiate "deep cuts" in nuclear arsenals. Following an unusually open and democratic procedure, the bishops acknowledged pacifism as one possible option for individual Catholics, but they forcefully rejected pacifism as official Church doctrine. In the end, the *Pastoral Letter on War and Peace* may have echoed some of the freeze campaign's slogans, but it rebuffed virtually all of its substantive political arguments.

Ambiguously affirming a diversity of perspectives, the pastoral letter functioned rhetorically not to foster but to manage anti-nuclear dissent within the Church.

Much the same might be said about the freeze campaign's victory in the House of Representatives. Widely portrayed as an endorsement of the freeze and a major blow to the Reagan administration, the House resolution of 1983 constituted, in reality, a strategically ambiguous affirmation, not of the freeze in particular, but of arms control in general. Debating at length the breadth and depth of public support for the freeze, the House affirmed the sovereignty of the people and acknowledged their fears and concerns about the escalating arms race. But unconvinced of the public's support for any specific initiative, the House endorsed the concept of a freeze while simultaneously encouraging the Reagan administration's nuclear arms build-up. As an arms control measure, the House resolution was contradictory, if not altogether meaningless. Not only did it waffle, but it had no force, no power of law. The freeze campaign claimed victory, and the news media certified that claim. But in the final analysis, the House freeze resolution created only an illusion of victory, while in effect killing the freeze as a policy initiative.

The fate of the freeze in institutional contexts illustrates the dilemma of political activism in the telepolitical era. On the one hand, contemporary news media invite a rhetoric of visual imagery, sound bites, and political confrontation. In today's media climate, the freeze campaign's *dramatis personae* had considerable appeal, and their dramatic scenarios of nuclear armageddon epitomized conceptions of news in the telepolitical age. On the other hand, institutional political debates still demand substantive political argument. They also encourage negotiation and compromise, not dramatic confrontation. When the freeze initiative moved into institutional contexts, its proponents continued to imagine the holocaust and to recite political cliches and slogans. Yet in institutional contexts they faced a different set of rules—rules that mitigated against the success of such strategies.

## Constructing the Public

Historically, survey research has revealed that "a strong concern about nuclear war has seldom been uppermost in the minds of a great majority of Americans."[12] Over the years, as Tom Smith has observed, "other issues such as the economy, the environment, and the budget deficit have topped the public's list of concerns," with most Americans indicating "either that they did not think nuclear war would occur or at least that it was not an immediate threat."[13] A moment or two of heightened public awareness has been evident in the nuclear age: during the Cuban Missile Crisis, for example, and during the campaign for a Nuclear Test Ban Treaty in the early 1960s. For the most part, however, the American public rarely has demonstrated overriding concern about strategic arms policy, apparently content to leave the matter to the politicians and the experts.

In his follow-up to *The Fate of the Earth*, *The Abolition*, Jonathan Schell suggested one possible explanation for public apathy about nuclear weapons. Observing that "the nuclear peril" thus far has left "the world physically untouched," Schell argued that nuclear weapons are simply too "removed . . . from people's direct experience" to inspire public debate and activism. As Schell explained, "most evils arrive in the world a little bit at a time, so that in pushing people into action the bite of painful experience is added to the voice of pure reason." When a factory pollutes the water supply, for example, "the pollution appears gradually, and people are driven to do something before a catastrophe occurs." Since Hiroshima and Nagasaki, however, nuclear weapons have "fortunately stayed unexploded," and people therefore have not been "impelled to think or do very much about them."[14]

But there is another possible explanation for the public's attitudes, one that gives the American people a bit more credit: that they have not been apathetic so much as resigned to the awful necessity of nuclear deterrence. Since the dawn of the nuclear age, as Everett Carll Ladd has observed, survey research has revealed that a significant proportion of Americans has "opposed making, much less using, the bomb," and they have exhibited "an ample appreciation of the bomb's awful destructiveness." At least a plurality of the public has always supported efforts to negotiate arms control with the Soviets. Yet while Americans always have been "appalled" by nuclear weapons, they generally have seen "no realistic alternative to a heavy reliance on such weapons in the country's defense." Considering the Russians "an untrustworthy adversary," Americans may not like the bomb, but they have always considered it "a necessary part of the nation's military deterrence."[15]

Given this history, reports of overwhelming public support for the nuclear freeze campaign came as a considerable surprise. Following Schell's logic, one might have thought that the bomb had gone off, finally forcing people to think. But the history of public attitudes toward nuclear weapons points to a very different conclusion: that the American people never embraced the freeze initiative in the first place. In the news, and especially on television, we witnessed an unprecedented grass-roots movement, but polling data suggest that public attitudes toward nuclear weapons never changed much at all during the freeze debate.

While news media of all sorts portrayed the freeze campaign as a powerful grass-roots movement, television especially reveled in the drama. Attracted by the spectacle of freeze demonstrations, television news presented a spontaneous and nation-wide movement, with anecdotal reports—stories about individual farmers, housewives, and other ordinary citizens who supported the freeze—confirming that the movement had spread throughout America. On television news, the freeze movement did not arise out of the organized structures of the political left, but rather erupted spontaneously in Europe, crossed the Atlantic, and eventually embraced Americans from all walks of life, from all socioeconomic backgrounds, and of all political persuasions. Personalizing the movement with religious leaders, medical doctors, and other "thoughtful people," television news stripped the movement of any taint of political radicalism, even partisanship. Invoking the polls to confirm the visual and anecdotal evidence, the conclusion seemed indisputable: the freeze had spawned an historic political movement that portended serious political trouble for the Reagan administration.

Polling data, however, told a much different story. Clearly, the public feared the bomb, as they have since the dawn of the nuclear age. And they continued to support efforts to negotiate arms control with the Soviets. Yet most Americans supported, at most, the image or the metaphor of a freeze on nuclear weapons. When the pollsters asked specifically about arms control policy, most Americans rejected the freeze as a policy option. They did not believe that a freeze would produce an equal balance of nuclear forces, they doubted its verifiability, and they did not believe that the Soviets would abide by such an agreement. Rejecting the freeze campaign's revisionist portrait of the Soviet Union, Americans believed, as they had since the 1950s, that the Soviets could not be "trusted to uphold the spirit and letter" of any sort of "nuclear arms limitation agreement."[16] Most surprisingly, Americans simply did not pay all that much attention to the freeze debate. Many had not even heard of a nuclear freeze movement, and those who had often viewed it as the same old protestors, people whose activities often hurt rather than helped the cause of arms control.

If anything, confidence in Ronald Reagan actually grew during the freeze debate. A CBS News/*New York Times* poll taken in November of 1984, for example, showed two-thirds of Americans confident that Reagan would "make a real effort to negotiate a good arms control agreement with the Soviet Union." Surprisingly, even 40 percent of Mondale voters had faith that the President would try to negotiate a "good" arms control agreement during his second term.[17] Even the peace movement's own polls showed increased confidence in Reagan. In 1985, a poll commissioned by Women's Action for Nuclear Disarmament (WAND) revealed that, for the first time ever, more Americans thought Reagan's policies made nuclear war less rather than more likely. The same poll also showed that Reagan had "managed to reverse an 11-year trend on the question of which of the two parties was 'best able to keep the U.S. out of World War III.'"[18]

Former freeze activists still refuse to accept such conclusions. Engaged in a sort of psychological denial of their own, some insist that the movement declined only after it had won the debate.[19] Others, like Pam Solo, concede that the campaign failed to "translate its massive public support into real political power," but only because it "strayed from its own original goal of breaking out of arms control 'negotiations as usual' and challenging the new militarism."[20]

But whatever the view of the ultimate outcome, all embrace the great freeze myth: that the campaign, at least for a time, attracted support from an overwhelming majority of Americans from all walks of life—that it inspired a genuine grass-roots movement.

Looking closely at their rhetoric, however, it is easy to see why freeze activists failed to win over most Americans. Freeze activists said little to overcome the historic public distrust of the Soviet Union. Nor did they provide reasons for not believing Ronald Reagan when he spoke of a "window of vulnerability" and promised to negotiate only "balanced" and "verifiable" arms control agreements. Most of all, they never made the case for the freeze as a better alternative, showing why it should be preferred to Reagan's START initiative—or, for that matter, any other approach to arms control. Saying little about competing initiatives, freeze advocates instead wallowed in the horrors of nuclear war. Yet fear of nuclear war, as James Clotfelter has pointed out, does not necessarily translate into support for the peace movement. Often it only encourages "support for leaders who promise security through increased military strength."[21]

In short, the freeze campaign failed to engage the Reagan administration politically. Determined to build broad-based support and appear nonpartisan, freeze activists skirted the key controversies of the nuclear debate. Many freeze activists viewed Ronald Reagan as a dangerous warmonger, but they rarely said so to the American people. Most considered his policies dangerously provocative, but that, too, they kept to themselves. Many advocated unilateral disarmament, and virtually all favored massive cuts in military spending. Yet convinced by decades of political futility that they could not sell such views, they instead hid behind a rhetoric of images and slogans. In doing so, however, they resurrected the dilemma that historically has plagued the peace movement in America: how to sell their ideas without selling out.

## The Strategic Dilemma

For some peace activists, the freeze campaign's demise in 1984 pointed to the futility of working within the system. Frustrated and angry, many returned to direct action against weapons facilities and military bases—to a strategy of confronting the "warmakers." According to a Rand Corporation study of anti-nuclear protests since 1984, both the number of protesters "willing to face arrest, fine, and imprisonment" and the "number of skirmishes between protestors and security personnel" increased significantly in the years following the freeze campaign. In the first eleven months of 1987, for example, 3,000 protestors were arrested for "anti-nuclear civil disobedience," compared to only 1,056 in all of 1984.[22] Some of these activists paid a very high price, receiving prison sentences of 10 years or more for breaking into weapons facilities and damaging government property.[23]

Most peace activists, however, derived a very different lesson from the freeze campaign: that the peace movement needed more televisual strategies, more sophisticated, Madison Avenue appeals. After the demise of the freeze campaign, for example, eight leading peace groups formed the Peace Media Project (PMP), a consulting firm of sorts for peace activists. Convinced that the packaging, not the product, had doomed their earlier efforts, PMP helped peace groups design "costly media campaigns," including mass mailings, television commercials, and "spontaneous" demonstrations timed and promoted for maximum media exposure.[24] Richard Pollack, a spokesman for PMP, described the thinking behind the group's efforts: "It's similar to selling soap, but it's a big departure from that."[25]

Other peace groups arrived at similar conclusions. In 1985, Women's Action for Nuclear Disarmament (WAND) assembled a team of political analysts, pollsters, and media experts to assess the failure of the freeze campaign and to recommend new strategies for "progressive peace groups." Borrowing from the "strategic planning analysis used in most modern presidential campaigns," WAND's nine-month study aimed to develop a "more professional" approach to peace activism, emphasizing survey research, advertising, news management, and fund-raising. Summarizing the results in a slick, 48-page magazine widely distributed within the peace community, WAND argued that too many progressive organizations remained "wedded to old-fashioned notions about citizen participation." For the peace movement to succeed, according to WAND, it needed to emulate the strategies of its "*rival* communicators—television networks, commercial advertisers, [and] political campaigns." WAND even urged peace activists to copy the successful fund-raising methods of the "conservative/Republican coalition," for "the tools of modern communication—television and radio advertising, print advertising, survey research, targeted direct mail, and the associated computer programming—are extremely expensive . . . and, more often than not, they require professional services." WAND concluded that the nature of citizen participation had changed in the 1980s and that, at bottom, political activism now boiled down to "a simple financial transaction": "With less free time, Americans are less able to work on volunteer activities and are more inclined to express their civic, religious, or political activism by simply writing a check."[26]

WAND's recommendations relied heavily upon the results of a *National Survey on Arms Control* commissioned by the group in September of 1985. Summarizing the survey's findings, WAND argued that peace activists needed to "do more to understand the mood of the country," to take account of the "tough-minded realism" of the American public, and to "draw upon enduring American values and concerns." WAND even urged peace activists "to publicly challenge the Soviet government when necessary." According to WAND, this meant only that the movement would have to "change some of its rhetoric"; it did not mean that the movement would have to "change its goals, policies, or objectives with the vicissitudes of public opinion—only that the *way* in which its message is voiced, its arguments for those goals are selected, should be keyed to the public's interest and concerns."[27]

WAND really did not propose anything new. Much the same thinking animated the freeze campaign from the start. In essence, WAND again called upon the peace movement to disguise its real goals, policies, and objectives behind a rhetoric of tough-minded realism—to "draw upon enduring American values and concerns" that they rejected in much of their earlier literature. WAND's survey confirmed what most freeze activists had known all along: that a rhetoric of unilateral disarmament and sympathy for the Soviets could not be sold to the American people. Yet WAND missed the lesson that freeze activists eventually learned: that cosmetic rhetorical changes would not suffice. Not only did most Americans see through the disguise, but the strategy alienated many of the ideological purists at the core of the peace movement.

Moreover, the news media had begun to catch on to the peace movement's public relations gambits. After the Reagan landslide, reporters often called attention to the strategies themselves, exposing how peace demonstrations were being timed for the evening news and "marketed with a promotional flair befitting Madison Avenue."[28] Even when WAND's approach to peace advocacy—the public relations approach—did attract favorable media coverage, that coverage did not necessarily translate into public support. In 1985, for example, a group called People Reaching Out for Peace (PRO-Peace) began planning for what they imagined would be a wildly successful media event: a 255-day, transcontinental anti-nuclear march by 5,000 activists, designed to reach middle America and to get "the movement going again."[29] Headed by a 1960s peace activist turned political consultant, PRO-Peace opened a headquarters on fashionable Beverly Boulevard in West Los Angeles and raised more than $3 million dollars, primarily from such Hollywood stars as Paul Newman, Madonna, Martin Sheen, and Rob Lowe. Heavily promoted with celebrity endorsements on MTV, the plan attracted puff pieces in such popular fare as *People*, *Us*, *Entertainment Tonight*, *Rolling Stone*, and the *Today* program. Yet despite the favorable coverage, the Great Peace March proved a monumental flop, attracting fewer than 900 marchers and staggering to a stop in the California desert after only two weeks. Broke and divided, PRO-Peace folded its tents on March 14, with its leader lamenting that "the support wasn't there." The whole affair only left the peace movement looking even more "flaky in the public eye."[30]

With neither direct confrontation nor the slick, public relations approach to peace advocacy recapturing the momentum of the freeze campaign, some peace activists have invested their hopes for the future in nuclear education. Pam Solo, for example, has urged her fellow activists to organize for the long haul, developing a "comprehensive and coherent political program" and an "on-going political literacy effort" with an emphasis on "nurturing younger activists." Calling for patience, Solo has called upon peace activists to "pace and replace themselves" and to concentrate their efforts on peace education. "Youth programs and outreach to college and high school students will keep the movement alive and growing,"[31] Solo has concluded, and with nuclear education already in place in schools across America her optimism might appear well-founded.

Yet peace education also has proven a double-edged sword, inspiring a whole new debate over propaganda in the schools. As peace educators have expanded their efforts in the post-freeze years, so too have right-wing activists mobilized their forces. And the kids, once again, have been caught in the middle of a political debate—a debate not over how to improve America's schools but over how best to indoctrinate children politically.

## The Legacy of Peace Education

While many freeze groups withered on the vine after 1984, Educators for Social Responsibility (ESR), the chief force behind nuclear education, continued to prosper. ESR remained small in comparison to many special interest groups, claiming only some 15,000 members and an annual budget of about $500,000.[32] But its influence continued to grow after the freeze debate, as it won still more legislative and school board mandates for nuclear education and expanded its network of peace educators not only in the United States but internationally as well.[33]

With nuclear education already widespread, many peace educators developed even greater ambitions in the post-freeze years: to inculcate a global perspective in all areas of study, at all levels of American education. Like nuclear education, of course, global perspective was but a euphemism for the peace movement's political agenda. Yet it better encompassed the broader range of issues that the movement embraced after the freeze: ending apartheid in South Africa, opposing aid to the Contras in Nicaragua, and a variety of other Third World concerns.[34]

Even as ESR and other peace educators expanded their political ambitions, however, they moderated their public face. Stung by criticisms not only of political bias but of elitism, the ESR of the post-freeze era pledged to involve a wider range of parents and teachers in their efforts and to respect opposing viewpoints.[35] As the group's associate director Susan Alexander explained, the group's thinking had been complicated by the realization that all Americans desired peace, even if they did not always agree on the best means to that end.[36] In 1985, ESR pledged a new effort to find the common ground shared by "people with divergent views," to identify "those overlapping interests that the vast majority of Americans share," and to promote "fruitful dialogue" rather than "polarized debates about the crucial issues of our time."[37]

ESR also cultivated a more moderate public face in its curriculum materials and recommended reading lists. In an annotated "Bibliography of Selected Curricula and Teaching Materials" on nuclear war published in 1986, for example, the group not only listed the Harvard Nuclear Study Group's "realist" manifesto, *Living With Nuclear Weapons*, but also two attacks on the freeze published in the *New Republic*. In its section on films, it included the American Security Council's *Countdown for America*, a defense of peace-through-strength, and a film defending the Strategic Defense Initiative, *High Frontier*. Surprisingly, ESR even listed an article published in *Commentary* that disputed the whole premise behind nuclear education: the notion that America's children suffered from nuclear nightmares. And while ESR still recommended the NEA's *Choices* for junior-high-school classes, the group at least acknowledged that some individuals had questioned whether *Choices* presented "sufficiently balanced and diverse viewpoints" and encouraged teachers to supplement the curriculum with materials reflecting "a broad range of points of views."[38]

Still, ESR's reading lists remained dominated by the literature of the peace movement, and the group continued to push, without caveats of any sort, several of its own politically controversial curriculum guides.[39] In addition, ESR continued to annotate moderate and conservative sources with refutations of their major arguments or warnings about their biases. For example, ESR gave its highest recommendation to the Public Agenda Foundation's *The Soviets: What Is the Conflict About?* At the same time, however, the group complained that the source treated better relations with the Soviets as appeasement, and that it assumed that the Soviet Union aimed to "expand its influence and its Marxist ideology." According to ESR, the source also failed, in discussing Nicaragua, to mention "universal literacy, health care, and education" as "the usual byproducts of socialist revolutions."[40] Similarly, ESR warned that such sources as the American Security Council's *Countdown for America* and the Harvard Study Group's *Living With Nuclear Weapons* lacked balance. ESR recommended that both be supplemented with peace movement sources.[41]

Most importantly, the whole business of nuclear education remained, in practice, dominated by teachers passionately involved in the peace movement, teachers who considered themselves "duty-bound" as "socially responsible" educators to promote the cause.[42] As a survey conducted by Robert Erhlich in 1986 revealed, the overwhelming majority of nuclear educators not only held political views far to the left of the political mainstream, but also saw nothing wrong with promoting those views in the classroom.[43] When asked to characterize their own politics, some 75 percent of the nuclear educators placed themselves on the left or liberal end of the political spectrum, as compared to fewer than 20 percent of the general public.[44] On specific issues, nuclear educators were far more likely than most Americans to oppose Reagan's Strategic Defense Initiative and to favor unilateral cuts in America's nuclear arsenal.[45] Most tellingly, nuclear educators expressed far more trust in the Soviet Union than in their own government. When assigning blame for the arms race, for example, only 19 percent of the nuclear educators thought Ronald Reagan sincerely wanted "to reach an arms control agreement with the U.S.S.R.," but only

9 percent doubted Gorbachev's sincerity. Similarly, only a small minority (10 percent) of the nuclear educators considered the Soviet Union primarily responsible for the failure of arms control, while 68 percent blamed the United States.[46]

Teachers have a right to their political opinions, of course, but peace educators still seem to confuse their opinions with the Truth. Generally, the nuclear educators gave the correct response to some of Erhlich's more obviously loaded questions: only about 3 percent agreed that the "position a student takes for or against a controversial nuclear issue" should affect his or her grade, and only about 10 percent disagreed with the notion that "all sides of an issue" should be presented in such a course. Yet a majority of nuclear educators still favored requiring courses in nuclear war, and nearly 40 percent saw nothing wrong with designing such courses "to generate greater public support for specific efforts to stop the arms race, such as the nuclear freeze."[47]

ESR has portrayed all who resist such thinking as part of a growing movement to "empty the classroom of all controversial issues."[48] Yet ESR's critics have never sought to exclude controversial issues from the classroom. To the contrary, most have aimed to introduce the right controversies and the right brand of political indoctrination. In response to the politicized curricula of the left, for example, Phyllis Schlafly and a number of parents' groups launched the so-called "Big 35" campaign, an effort that liberal educators characterized as an attempt to eliminate a list of thirty-five topics such as nuclear war, sex, and religion from the schools. Yet while it is true that Big 35 advocates believed that some issues should not be discussed at all in the schools, their real goal was to have all issues discussed "in the context of traditional, Judeo Christian values." In other words, Big 35 advocates did not want values out of the classroom; they wanted better values in.[49]

Right-wing groups have drawn strength from the excesses of the National Education Association, the ESR, and other advocates of peace education. Blaming the proliferation of non-academic subjects for the 23 million functional illiterates in America, Phyllis Schlafly invoked *A Nation at Risk* as evidence for the effects of the "NEA's radical agenda." Schlafly even managed to couch her crusade in the rhetoric of anti-censorship and civil rights. In one brochure, the Eagle Forum presented teaching about "the proven success of the traditional family, the American Constitution, and the private enterprise system" as a matter of "exposing and ending the radical censorship in school textbooks." Similarly, *The Phyllis Schlafly Report* of November 1985 called liberal educators "the real book banners" for prohibiting the reading of "the great works of literature, biography, and history." The February 1985 issue of *The Phyllis Schlafly Report* even argued that "the NEA and the curriculum writers," instead of "teaching knowledge and training in basic skills," sought "to pry into and manipulate the child's emotions, family problems, sex life, and attitudes toward life and death." This, the *Report* concluded, violated the civil rights of both parents and students: "The protection of the child and his family from the prying eyes and ears of schools which want to engage in psychological manipulation instead of teaching is *the* civil rights issue of the 1980's."[50]

Peace educators have only themselves to blame for the determination of those who campaign for prayer in the schools, creation science, and traditional values in the classroom. By so vigorously pushing their own political agendas, they invited the right-wing backlash and gave credibility to charges of left-wing censorship and political indoctrination. The NEA, ESR, and other peace educators may dismiss Phyllis Schlafly as a kook determined to stifle "critical thinking" and to "turn back the clock."[51] Yet Schlafly's Eagle Forum attracted more than four times as many contributors as ESR in the early 1980s,[52] and it went head-to-head against the NEA to win enforcement of the Hatch Act—the "pupil rights" amendment that gave rise to the Big 35 campaign.[53]

Peace education is but one troubling legacy of the freeze campaign. As American schools have become more of a political battleground, so too has the larger "marketplace of ideas" become impoverished by the proliferation of single-issue crusades employing televisual strategies. Reflecting broader trends toward more strident and uncompromising political activism, the freeze campaign was just one of many telepolitical crusades since the early 1980s. The crusaders have ranged ideologically from neo-Marxists to "born again" Christians, and their causes have included everything from animal rights to stopping abortion.[54] But all are equally convinced of the moral righteousness of their crusade. All consider any and all means justified by their ends, and all pursue those ends with quasi-religious fervor. All view themselves as soldiers in a great war to redefine American culture.

These culture wars, as James Davison Hunter has argued, do not mean that America has become a nation of fanatics. Many of today's "so-called extremists" are actually ordinary people driven to rhetorical extremes by contemporary journalistic dictates—the requirements of making news. Encouraging superficial and sensationalistic rhetoric, even a "grammar of hostility," today's journalistic priorities have led to an "eclipse of the middle," an "impulse toward polarization" in public discussion. As a result, public discourse has become "more polarized than the American public itself," and quiet and reflective voices have become, "for all practical purposes, *silent* in the broader public discussion."[55]

In short, the order of the day has become the politics of unreason. And that bodes ill, not only for the American democracy, but for journalism as well.

## Telepolitical Journalism and Public Disaffection

In a rambling, bitter speech to a women's group in 1986, Dr. Helen Caldicott announced her retirement from the anti-nuclear movement, declaring—startlingly—that "we've achieved nothing." Blaming her own demise, in part, on "a male coup, a palace overthrow" at Physicians for Social Responsibility, she offered an even more intriguing explanation for the failure of the freeze campaign: "It failed because the media killed it."[56] Caldicott returned to her native Australia for a time, but she soon returned to the United States in a new incarnation: as a "lifestyle ecologist." Caldicott remains convinced that the media did her in, however, and she now talks in tones eerily reminiscent of Spiro T. Agnew:

> Let us take a searching look at the media. . . . Too often . . . we get only superficial or sensational news stories. . . . Concentration of press ownership is extremely dangerous for a society. In . . . the United States . . . the press is owned, controlled and manipulated by a small coterie of extremely powerful, wealthy people. . . . The standard of journalism these days is quite low. *USA Today* epitomizes the "sound bite" mentality. . . . Usually, I am given three minutes on the "Today Show" to tell the American people about the medical effects of nuclear war, while some film star is given eight. Important news is trivialized, and the rich, famous, or beautiful people are worshipped. This sort of reporting insults the American public. . . . I think all the major media—TV, newspapers, and radio—should not be privately owned but operated along the lines of . . . the BBC.[57]

Although apparently oblivious to the irony, Caldicott—the media darling of the early 1980s—does have a point. The news indeed has become increasingly superficial and sensational, and a mind-numbing sameness characterizes all of the news, regardless of medium. Increasingly dominated by a tabloid mentality, network evening news programs desperately compete, not so much among themselves, as with *A Current Affair* and *Inside Edition*. Once informative newsweeklies now mimic *People* magazine, reporting the news in gossipy tones and replacing hard news altogether with cynical, pseudo-political features.[58] Even daily newspapers, apparently panicked by competition from *USA Today*, now lay heavy emphasis on "good visuals" and "people-oriented" features. A conspiracy of rich media barons may not explain all this, nor may government ownership be the solution. But Helen Caldicott does have a point: today's journalism indeed insults the American public, and the situation grows worse with each passing day.

Journalists, of course, are quick to blame the politicians or the few "bad apples" among them for the poverty of contemporary political journalism.[59] More commonly, however, they blame the public itself, insisting that they are only giving the public what it wants. Yet since at least the early 1980s, there has been growing evidence that Americans may want more from the news than choreographed images and meaningless sound bites. In droves, Americans have been turning off the news, not so much out of apathy as out of anger.

As early as 1983, signs of public disaffection with the news media had become so clear that even the journalists themselves began to notice. In December of that year, *Time* published a cover story, "Journalism Under Fire," reviewing the evidence of public disenchantment with the news media. Pointing to polling data, libel litigation, and public support for excluding the press from the Grenada invasion, the newsmagazine concluded that the public had become more mistrustful of the press than ever before. Indeed, the evidence pointed not merely to distrust but to a "deep, far-ranging resentment of the press," even a desire to "punish" journalists, for crimes ranging from insensitivity toward grieving victims to hostility toward "the government." *Time* began the story giving voice to the complaints of a growing number of Americans:

> They are rude and accusatory, cynical and almost unpatriotic. They twist facts to suit their not-so-hidden liberal agenda. They meddle in politics, harass business, invade people's privacy, and then walk off without regard to the pain and chaos they leave behind. They are arrogant and self-righteous, brushing aside most criticism as the uninformed carping of cranks and ideologues. To top it off, they claim that their behavior is sanctioned, indeed sanctified, by the U.S. Constitution.[60]

For television journalists, the most painful evidence of public disaffection came in dramatic ratings declines for all three network evening news shows throughout the 1980s. From the "giddy days of yore," when network evening news shows attracted ratings in the low 90 percentiles, the ratings had declined to just above 50 percent by 1990.[61] Worse yet, the greatest decline came in the demographic group that advertisers covet most: young people between the ages of 21 and 34.[62] At the networks, the results were predictable: mass firings in the news divisions, pay cuts for those who remained, closed or downsized news bureaus, and more reliance upon "remotes" and feeds from local affiliates.[63] By the end of the 1980s, as Auletta has observed, network executives began asking serious questions about the future of nightly newscasts:

> Would News have to submit to endless rounds of budget cuts? . . . Would each network have to slash its seventy to ninety highly paid correspondents, replacing them with competent but lower-paid reporter/producers who expected less airtime and fed many of their stories to a dozen or so star correspondents? Would network news lose its coveted half hour each evening?[64]

For viewers of the evening news, all this not only meant more ads for "denture cleaners and backache nostrums,"[65] but also less hard news, more "hype" by reporters desperate to get on the air, more "people-oriented stories," and more "cost effective feature packages" such as ABC's "Person of the Week."[66] The ratings continued to decline, however, and network executives began to ask an even more troubling question: "Would network news have to imitate Fox's lurid *A Current Affair*, Morton Downey Jr., or Geraldo Rivera, in order to attract viewers?"[67] Apparently, the networks never considered the possibility that the public looked to network news for something different than what they found on *Geraldo* or *Oprah*. It never occurred to them that the trend toward "junk news" may have driven away viewers in the first place. And so the trend continues: viewers continue to vote with their remotes,[68] and the evening news continues to lose from 3 to 4 percent of its audience each year.[69]

Journalists have identified a number of scapegoats for the plight of evening news, pointing to "competing demands on viewer time," competition from cable news, and even "the ubiquitous VCR revolution."[70] Most of all, however, they blame the public itself, talking about a blame-the-messenger mentality and insisting that the public lacks a good understanding of the journalistic profession. As Bert Briller, a professional media apologist with the Television Information Office puts it: "The public needs more education on its need for a free press." According to Briller, journalism's problem is merely a problem of public relations and the solution is simple: still more "public service" announcements tooting journalism's own horn.[71]

But could the real problem be that the public understands contemporary journalism all too well? Could it be that they perceptively discern the superficiality, the cynical amorality, and the political nihilism of today's "sophisticated" journalism?

Americans have good reason to resent the arrogance of today's news celebrities and to object to their rude and accusatory behaviors. They are right that too many journalists are "more interested in what sells, in scandal, than in reporting the news," and that they are "too quick to hide behind the First Amendment."[72] They have good reason to suspect that many journalists have lost touch with the public they profess to serve. As Ted J. Smith III has argued, journalism's "crisis of confidence" ultimately boils down to a question of values—to the widespread perception that journalists "have turned some crucial corner," embracing a value system destructive of American culture. According to Smith, this is more than just a matter of blaming the messenger for bad news. Rather, it is a matter of people becoming fed up with the "perfectionistic nihilism" of TV journalism—that rhetoric of crisis and failure that holds that "all events are . . . unfortunate, all institutions flawed, all solutions problematic, and, ultimately, all problems insoluble."[73]

Growing disinterest in the news and in politics generally are troubling trends—trends that bode ill for the future of democratic governance. Yet blaming the public itself may well miss the point. As V. O. Key argued nearly three decades ago, the American public sometimes acts "in odd ways indeed," but in the large the electorate behaves about as rationally and responsibly as we should expect, given the clarity of the alternatives presented to it and the character of the information available to it." Given the character of contemporary news, tuning out might not be so irrational after all. It might be seen as an act of intelligent defiance. Perhaps in rebelling against the journalists, Americans are not withdrawing so much as making a loud political statement. Once again they may be confirming that V. O. Key was right: "voters are not fools."[74]

## Notes

1. Key, *The Responsible Electorate*, 7.
2. Quoted in David Corn, "Election Lessons to Build On," *Nuclear Times*, December 1984, 12.
3. Norman Solomon quoted in Corn, "Election Lessons to Build On," 12.
4. "Setting a New Agenda for Global Arms Control: An Interview with Randall Forsberg," *Technology Review*, November/December 1990, 36-37.
5. See Solo, *From Protest to Policy*, 160, 173.
6. Renata Rizzo-Harvi, "Grass Roots Opt for Unity," *Nuclear Times*, January/February 1987, 29.
7. See Solo, *From Protest to Policy*, 177.
8. Jamieson, *Eloquence in an Electronic Age*, 241.
9. Alpern, et al., "A Matter of Life and Death," 21.
10. Butterfield, "Anatomy of the Nuclear Protest," 14.
11. Nuclear Weapons Freeze Campaign, "Prominent Endorsers List."
12. Schuman, Ludwig, and Krosnick, "The Perceived Threat of Nuclear War, Salience, and Open Questions," 520.
13. Smith, "Nuclear Anxiety," 560.
14. Schell, *The Abolition*, 39-40.
15. Ladd, "The Freeze Framework," 20, 41.
16. Ibid., 41.
17. Adam Clymer, "Americans in Poll View Government More Confidently," *New York Times*, 19 November 1984, B10.
18. Women's Action for Nuclear Disarmament, *Turnabout: The Emerging New Realism in the Nuclear Age* (Boston: WAND Education Fund, 1986), 12.
19. This view rests largely upon the assumption—unproven and unprovable—that the freeze campaign somehow forced Ronald Reagan to moderate his views. As Meyer writes: "The freeze effectively forced an extremely popular president to return to long-established bipartisan policies he had consistently eschewed and had vigorously criticized. The movement vanished then, when it was no longer necessary" (Meyer, *A Winter of Discontent*, 272).
20. Solo, *From Protest to Policy*, xiv, 23.
21. James Clotfelter, "Disarmament Movements in the United States," *Journal of Peace Research* 23 (June 1986): 99.
22. Elizabeth Heneghan Ondaatje, *Trends in Anti-Nuclear Protests in the United States, 1984-1987* (Santa Monica: Rand Corporation, 1989), v.
23. While most anti-nuclear protestors arrested in earlier years served a few days in jail, at most a couple of months, a number of those arrested after 1984 often received surprisingly stiff jail sentences. For example, eight Plowshares activists arrested in April of 1984 for breaking into a Martin Marietta facility to hammer and pour blood on Pershing II missile components served from one to two years in jail, and a Swedish participant was deported after serving one year. In November of 1984, two activists who performed similar rituals in missile silos at Whiteman AFB in Missouri were sentenced to 18 years in prison, another to 10 years, and a fourth to 8 years. In March of 1986, six Plowshares activists once again attempted to deface missile silos at Whiteman and received sentences of 7 to 8 years after refusing to pay fines. Protestor Brian Willson paid the highest price, however. He lost both legs trying to block a weapons train at the Concord Naval Weapons Station in California. See the

"Chronology of Anti-Nuclear and Related Protests: 1984-1987" in Ondaatje, *Trends in Anti-Nuclear Protests in the United States*, 22, 27, 37, 52.

24. Ondaatje, *Trends in Anti-Nuclear Protests in the United States*, 6.
25. Hawkins and Mashek, "Antinuclear Campaign Reawakens," 22.
26. Women's Action for Nuclear Disarmament, *Turnabout*, facing 1, 14, 38-39.
27. Ibid., 8, 46.
28. Robert Lindsey, "438 Protestors Are Arrested at Nevada Nuclear Test Site," *New York Times*, 6 February 1987, A8.
29. "The Long Trek," *U.S. News and World Report*, 27 January 1986, 22.
30. Howard Cushnir, "The Great Peace March That Couldn't," *Mother Jones*, June 1986, 39-43.
31. Solo, *From Protest to Policy*, 180-86.
32. By comparison, the Moral Majority claimed nearly 5 million member/donors and an annual budget of more than $8 million in 1984-85. Even such obscure liberal special interest groups as Citizens in Solidarity with the People of El Salvador and the Infant Formula Action League claimed more members and significantly larger budgets than ESR. See Women's Action for Nuclear Disarmament, *Turnabout*, 42-43.
33. See Dieringer, "The Challenge of Legislation and School Board Resolutions," 1-2, 4; and "New Directions: International Breakthroughs," [Educators for Social Responsibility] *Forum*, Spring 1986, 1, 4.
34. See David Brock, "Selling Globaloney in the Schools," *American Spectator*, December 1988, 22-26.
35. In a keynote address to the ESR's Third Annual Convention in June of 1985, Robert Coles raised the issue of ESR's elitism, apparently causing considerable defensiveness among the peace educators. Observing that ESR drew its support primarily from the "liberal, well-intentioned, middle class," Coles cautioned them against assuming a self-righteous or supercilious attitude toward those concerned more with financial and other day-to-day issues. See Susan Peters Pittman, "Robert Coles Urges a Broader View," [Educators for Social Responsibility] *Forum*, Fall 1985, 9.
36. Quoted in Metta L. Winter, "Nuclear Education Update," *Education Digest*, April 1986, 30.
37. Larry Dieringer, "Days of Dialogue, 1985: Finding Common Ground," [Educators for Social Responsibility] *Forum*, Fall 1985, 1-2.
38. Educators for Social Responsibility, *Knowing the Nuclear World: A Bibliography of Selected Curricula and Teaching Materials* (Boston: ESR, 1986), 2, 7, 14, 19, 25.
39. The three curriculum guides are: *Dialogue: A Teaching Guide to Nuclear Issues*, *Decision Making in a Nuclear Age*, and *Perspectives: A Teaching Guide to Concepts of Peace*. All three, as Andre Ryerson has argued, were even more openly political than *Choices*, and *Dialogue* and *Perspectives* were aimed at even younger children: "Where *Choices* is content to suggest, the guides produced by ESR assert; where the former allows but a glimpse of occasional intimacy with the Left, in the latter this cautionary veil has become completely transparent. . . . While *Choices* is prepared to wait until the young have reached junior high, ESR starts in kindergarten." See Educators for Social Responsibility, *Knowing the Nuclear World*, 3, 5, 10; Andre Ryerson, "The Scandal of 'Peace Education,'" *Commentary*, June 1986, 42.
40. ESR also warned, without explanation, that the cover of the Public Agenda Foundation resource was "belligerent, polarizing, and retrograde" (Educators for Social Responsibility, *Knowing the Nuclear World*, 13).
41. Specifically, the group recommended that the ASC film be shown in tandem with the

anti-nuclear film, *War Without Winners*, and that parts of the Harvard book be read back to back with parts of Schell's *The Fate of the Earth* or Dyson's *Weapons and Hope* (Educators for Social Responsibility, *Knowing the Nuclear World*, 19, 25).

42. Robert Ehrlich, Introduction, in *Perspectives on Nuclear War and Peace Education*, edited by Robert Ehrlich (New York: Greenwood Press, 1987), 3.
43. The survey, conducted at the Conference on Nuclear War Education at George Mason University in 1986, included seventy-one participants in the conference, most of whom had taught a course on nuclear war previously. The survey is of little scientific validity, of course, because of the small and unrepresentative sample. Nevertheless, its findings are suggestive and consistent with other indicators of the political attitudes of "nuclear educators," including statements by such groups as the NEA and ESR and the content of nuclear education courses and curriculum materials. Robert Ehrlich, "Opinions of Nuclear War Educators," in *Perspectives on Nuclear War and Peace Education*, edited by Robert Ehrlich (New York: Greenwood Press, 1987), 219-229.
44. Ehrlich, "Opinions of Nuclear War Educators," in *Perspectives on Nuclear War and Peace Education*, edited by Ehrlich, 225-227.
45. On "Star Wars," 80 percent of the nuclear educators opposed SDI research and 86 percent opposed deployment of SDI, while a Gallup poll from about the same time showed 52 percent of the public in favor of "the development of such a system." The difference on unilateral disarmament is even more striking: while about 72 percent of the nuclear educators favored unilateral cuts in America's nuclear arsenal, surveys of the general public have shown, at most, only about 15 percent of the public favoring such cuts. See Ehrlich, "Opinions of Nuclear War Educators," in *Perspectives on Nuclear War and Peace Education*, edited by Ehrlich, 221; "Star Wars Status," *Public Opinion* (August/September 1985): 33; and the series of NBC/AP polls on unilateral cuts in question 35 of the Appendix.
46. Interestingly, as Erhlich concluded, "reservations about the sincerity and truthfulness" of the American side among nuclear educators were "apparently not limited to Reagan." Only 16 percent of the nuclear educators agreed that U.S. government assessments of Soviet weapons programs were "truthful," and just under half (49 percent) of the nuclear educators considered arms control a mere "fig leaf" used by all Presidents to placate the public. See Erhlich, "Opinions of Nuclear War Educators," in *Perspectives on Nuclear War and Peace Education*, edited by Ehrlich, 221-22.
47. Percentages are calculated from the frequency counts presented in Ehrlich, "Opinions of Nuclear War Educators," in *Perspectives on Nuclear War and Peace Education*, edited by Ehrlich, 220.
48. Susan Peters Pittman, "Politics and the Educator," [Educators for Social Responsibility] *Forum*, Fall 1985, 9.
49. Jacquelyn Mitchard, "A Lesson for Today: Facing the Big 35," [Educators for Social Responsibility] *Forum*, Spring 1986, 3.
50. Eagle Forum, *Eagle Forum: Leading the Pro-Family Movement to Victories Since 1972*, brochure distributed by the Eagle Forum, Alton, Illinios, n.d.; "Hypocrisy About Banned Books," *The Phyllis Schlafly Report*, November 1985, 1-4; "The Radical Agenda of the NEA," *The Phyllis Schlafly Report*, February 1985, 1-3.
51. Mitchard, "A Lesson for Today," 3.
52. Eagle Forum, *Eagle Forum.*
53. As Schlafly recounts the controversy, the Hatch Amendment, passed in 1978, was "never enforced because the Federal bureaucracy refused to issue regulations to provide an opportunity, a procedure, or a place for citizens to file complaints, or a remedy for

violations." After a "crescendo of letters" from Eagle Forum members, however, the Department of Education held hearings over proposed regulations for enforcing the act, but the agency refused to publish the hearings or to act on the matter. After "months of silence" from the DOE, Schlafly herself published a 450-page edited version of the hearings under the title *Child Abuse in the Classroom*, and during this period "Eagle Forum members sent five times as many letters to President Reagan as did NEA members." According to Schlafly, all this forced the DOE finally to issue "the strong Regulations we had been demanding for two years," and President Reagan personally acknowledged the group's support at the Eagle Forum's annual convention in September of 1984. See "The Radical Agenda of the NEA," 2-3.

54. The anti-abortion campaign provides an especially intriguing example. Until about 1984, the pro-life campaign was a mainstream political effort led by "respectable and often well-funded groups with ties to the Catholic Church." The National Right-to-Life Committee (NRLC), the organization spearheading the effort, pursued only legal, institutionalized means of political expression, and its discussions of the moral, legal, and political issues surrounding abortion were carefully reasoned. Yet while the NRLC and similar groups did alter the terms of the abortion debate by focusing attention on the "rights of the fetus," as Marian Faux has observed, they "were never able to stir up much controversy." In other words, they failed to attract much media attention. Then Operation Rescue arrived on the scene, declaring "war" against abortion clinics. Talking of a "holocaust," and displaying giant blow-ups of bloody fetuses, this "small, barely organized group" radically transformed the abortion debate, "stoking the flames of the debate as no one else had managed to do."

The pro-life campaign even discovered its own version of Dr. Helen Caldicott: Dr. Bernard N. Nathanson, host of the controversial anti-abortion documentary, *The Silent Scream*. Like Caldicott, Nathanson appeared, at one and the same time, the medical expert and the impassioned crusader. At times, Nathanson spoke technically of the "science of fetology," but ultimately the point of *The Silent Scream* defied scientific jargon: "And so, for the first time, we're going to watch a child being torn apart, dismembered, disarticulated, crushed, and destroyed by the unfeeling steel instruments of the abortionist."

As if taking another page from the freeze campaign's strategy book, Operation Rescue also cultivated the televisual imagery of a "children's crusade." The group not only exploited children as a media drawing card, but made them central to their strategy of laying siege to abortion clinics. Recruited to travel across the country "rescuing" the unborn, one Georgia-based group called Youth for America trained in civil disobedience, and on cue they performed their ritual: dashing from the ranks of the anti-abortion demonstrators toward the police lines and falling to the ground by the clinic doors. When collared, they went limp and were carried off to jail. But kids served no time and paid no fines, nor did they worry about rough handling by the police. Nine-year-old Joshua Foreman, a veteran of six arrests, explained: "I knew they wouldn't hit us with clubs. . . . I knew they wouldn't shoot us. I knew they'd just drag us away."

All of this made for wonderful television, and the legal and ethical questions raised by such strategies were answered with "higher law." Parading in religious garb and praying on cue for the television cameras, Operation Rescue measured its success by the number of arrests, and the courtroom became just another stage for their dramatic morality plays. Invoking the same necessity defense as many anti-nuclear protesters, the rescuers seldom won their cases—except, of course, in the news media.

See Marian Faux, *Crusaders: Voices From the Abortion Front* (New York: Carol Publishing Group, 1990), 6-7, 155-66; *The Silent Scream*, American Portrait Films, 1984, videocassette; Sandy Banisky, "Children Lead Charge on Abortion Clinics," *Baltimore Sun* 12 July 1992, 1A, 10A; Mark Belz, *Suffer the Little Children: Christians, Abortion, and Civil Disobedience* (Westchester, Illinois: Crossway Books, 1989); and Celeste Michelle Condit, *Decoding Abortion Rhetoric: Communicating Social Change* (Urbana: University of Illinois Press, 1990).

55. Hunter, *Culture Wars*, 135-70.
56. Helen Caldicott, "Nuclear Madness: Helen Caldicott's Farewell Speech," in *Exposing Nuclear Phallacies*, edited by Diana E. H. Russell (New York: Pergamon Press, 1989), 11-12.
57. Helen Caldicott, *If You Love This Planet: A Plan to Heal the Earth* (New York: W.W. Norton, 1992), 179, 189, 191.
58. One example is *Newsweek's* "Conventional Wisdom Watch," a weekly "boxscore" of who's "in" and "out," mostly in Washington politics, but also in sports, entertainment, and other arenas. Rating a number of "players" with up, down, or sideways arrows, the feature offers pithy, satirical assessments of each player's performance in the political "game" that week. The feature could be taken as a parody of the magazine's own "horserace journalism," since it focuses upon many of the same gaffes, sound bites, poll results, and matters of image reported in the magazine's news. In the September 14, 1992 issue, for example, President Bush received a down arrow with the comment: "Porkorama! But hey, Mr. Balanced Budget, you can't buy off the whole country." The sneer referred to Bush's promises that week to victims of Hurricane Andrew, unemployed workers, and farmers—promises all reported in a separate story on the same page. "Conventional Wisdom Watch: Campaign '92 Edition" and "Hey, Big Spender," *Newsweek*, 14 September 1992, 4.
59. At a conference on journalism's credibility problems held at the Poynter Institute in January 1985, John Chancellor led the effort to shift criticisms of television journalism to the politicians, especially the Reagan administration. "We've been beating up on ourselves when we should devote a little bit of time to beating up on the U.S. government," Chancellor argued. "This administration has done more to make us look bad . . . than I have ever seen before in covering news." Throughout the proceedings, examples of irresponsible journalism generally were dismissed as aberrations, with most of the participants insisting, not surprisingly, that the news media generally had become better, more professional, in recent years. As Martin Nolan of the *Boston Globe* summarized the prevailing sentiment: "Despite all our faults, the Janet Cookes and the R. Foster Winans, I do think there's a trend towards improvement." See the proceedings in *Believing the News*, edited by Fry, esp. 36, 65.
60. Henry, "Journalism Under Fire," reprinted from *Time*, 12 December 1983, in *Believing the News*, edited by Fry, 191-212.
61. William Small, "The Changing Face of Network News," *Television Quarterly* 25, no. 1 (1990): 105-6.
62. Briller, "Zooming in Closer on the News Audience," 107-16. As Briller notes, television news viewership among those 21 to 34 years of age declined a "shocking" 21 percent between 1965 and 1990.
63. Edwin Diamond, "Shrinking the News," *New York*, 27 May 1991, 20-21.
64. Ken Auletta, *Three Blind Mice: How the TV Networks Lost Their Way* (New York: Random House, 1991), 530.
65. Briller, "Zooming in Closer on the News Audience," 110.

66. Diamond, "Shrinking the News," 20.
67. Auletta, *Three Blind Mice*, 530.
68. Diamond, "Shrinking the News," 21.
69. Auletta, *Three Blind Mice*, 530.
70. Small, "The Changing Face of Network News," 105.
71. Briller, "Zooming in Closer on the News Audience," 115.
72. Madsen, *60 Minutes*, 174.
73. Smith, *Moscow Meets Main Street*, 28-29.
74. Key, *The Responsible Electorate*, 7.

# Appendix

# Polling on the Freeze

***Group 1: Support for Arms Control Negotiations and General Disarmament***

1. Audits and Surveys: Do you favor or oppose a United States government effort to reach new agreements with the Soviet Union in reducing both nation's nuclear arms?

| | 11/17-22/81<br>Adult<br>*1200* | 9/17-21/83<br>Adult<br>*1205* |
|---|---|---|
| Favor | 77 | 70 |
| Oppose | 10 | 18 |
| No opinion | 13 | 12 |

2. Gallup: Would you favor or oppose an agreement between the U.S. and the Soviet Union to destroy all nuclear weapons that have already been built?

| | 5/8-11/81<br>Adult<br>*1519* |
|---|---|
| Favor | 47 |
| Oppose | 44 |
| No opinion | 9 |

3. Gallup: (Asked after a question about support for a U.N. referendum to be held in every country to vote for disarmament.) If a referendum were held in the U.S., how would you vote—for or against nuclear disarmament?
   *If such a referendum (called for by the United Nations and held in every nation) were held in the U.S. (United States), how would you vote—for or against nuclear disarmament?

| | 5/8-11/81 | *9/18-21/81 |
|---|---|---|
| | Adult | Adult |
| | *1519* | *1540* |
| For | 59 | 52 |
| Against | 30 | 37 |
| No opinion | 12 | 11 |

4. Gallup: Would you approve or disapprove if President Reagan made a proposal to the Soviet Union that both countries reduce their present stock of nuclear weapons by 50%?

| | 11/13-16/81 |
|---|---|
| | Adult |
| | *?* |
| Approve | 76 |
| Disapprove | 19 |
| No opinion | 5 |

5. Harris: Now let me read you some statements about control of nuclear weapons. For each, tell me if you agree or disagree. . . . All countries that have nuclear weapons should agree to destroy them.
*Would you favor or oppose all countries that have nuclear weapons agreeing to destroy them?

| | 3/12-16/82 | *5/25-30/82 | *3/17-20/83 | *4/20-25/83 |
|---|---|---|---|---|
| | Adult | Adult | Adult | Adult |
| | *1249* | *1251* | *1254* | *1253* |
| Agree/Favor | 61 | 74 | 80 | 80 |
| Disagree/Oppose | 37 | 22 | 17 | 16 |
| Not sure | 2 | 4 | 3 | 4 |

6. Harris: Would you favor or oppose every country that has nuclear weapons banning the production, storage and use of those nuclear weapons?

| | 3/5-21/82 | 5/25-30/82 | 3/17-20/83 | 9/9-14/83 | 11/9-14/83 | 3/8-20/84 |
|---|---|---|---|---|---|---|
| | Adult | Adult | Adult | Adult | Adult | Adult |
| | *1599* | *1251* | *1254* | *`1255* | *1252* | *1506* |
| Favor | 73 | 70 | 69 | 68 | 66 | 60 |
| Oppose | 23 | 25 | 25 | 27 | 29 | 34 |
| Not sure | 5 | 5 | 6 | 5 | 5 | 6 |

7. Harris: Do you favor or oppose the U.S. and Russia negotiating an effective nuclear arms agreement that would call for a real cutback in the nuclear weapons each country has?

| | 4/20-25/83 |
|---|---|
| | Adult |
| | *1253* |
| Favor | 87 |
| Oppose | 10 |
| Not sure | 3 |

8. Harris: Now here are some agreements the U.S. (United States) and the Soviet Union might make. Would you favor or oppose each of these agreements? . . . An agreement between the two countries to reduce their total number of nuclear warheads and missiles by 50 percent over a five-year period.

| | 11/26-29/84 |
|---|---|
| | Adult |
| | *1255* |
| Favor | 84 |
| Oppose | 13 |
| Not sure | 3 |

9. *Los Angeles Times*: Do you think the United States should meet with the Soviet Union this year to try to reach agreement on nuclear weapons, or do you think the United States should put off a meeting this year until we are in a better bargaining position—or haven't you heard enough about that yet to say?

| | 3/14-17/82 |
|---|---|
| | Adult |
| | *1503* |
| Meet | 51 |
| Put off | 31 |
| Haven't heard enough | 14 |
| Not sure | 3 |
| Refused | 1 |

10. Roper: There are many problems facing our nation today. But at certain times some things are more important than others, and need more attention from our Federal Government than others. I'd like to know for each of the things on this list whether you think it is something the government should be making a major effort on now, or something the government should be making some effort on now, or something not needing any particular government effort now. . . . Trying to seek agreements with other nations to limit nuclear weapons.

| | 6/5-12/80<br>Adult<br>*2006* | 5/30-6/6/81<br>Adult<br>*2003* | 6/5-12/82<br>Adult<br>*2000* | 5/29-6/3/84<br>Adult<br>*2000* |
|---|---|---|---|---|
| Major effort | 60 | 63 | 70 | 71 |
| Some effort | 29 | 26 | 23 | 21 |
| Need no particular effort | 7 | 7 | 4 | 5 |
| Don't know | 3 | 4 | 3 | 4 |

***Group 2: Support for the Concept of a Nuclear Freeze***

11. ABC/*Washington Post*: Well, would you approve or disapprove of a freeze on nuclear weapons by both the United States and the Soviet Union? . . . Would you say you approve/disapprove strongly or approve/disapprove somewhat? *(Asked after respondents had rated an equal number of arguments for and against the freeze.) We have just gone over some reasons given for and against the proposal for a nuclear freeze by both the U.S. and the Soviet Union. With those reasons in mind, let me ask you once more: would you approve or disapprove of a freeze on nuclear weapons by the United States and the Soviet Union? . . . Would you say you approve/disapprove strongly or approve/disapprove somewhat?

| | 4/21-25/82<br>Adult<br>*1521* | *Repeat | 4/8-12/83<br>Adult<br>*1516* | 9/22-26/83<br>Adult<br>*1506* | *Repeat |
|---|---|---|---|---|---|
| Approve strongly | 61 | 51 | 61 | 63 | 55 |
| Approve somewhat | 15 | 20 | 19 | 17 | 22 |
| Disapprove somewhat | 6 | 9 | 6 | 8 | 8 |
| Disapprove strongly | 14 | 16 | 10 | 9 | 12 |
| Don't know/ refused | 4 | 3 | 3 | 3 | 2 |

12. ABC/*Washington Post*: I'm going to read a few statements that deal with a nuclear freeze. For each, I'd like you to tell me whether you agree with it, or disagree, or if, perhaps, you have no opinion on that statement. . . . Stopping the arms race is so important that we should have a nuclear freeze no matter how risky it seems.

| | 4/21-25/82 |
|---|---|
| | Adult |
| | *1521* |
| Agree | 50 |
| Disagree | 41 |
| Don't know | 9 |

13. CBS/*New York Times*: Do you favor or oppose the United States agreeing to a "nuclear freeze" with the Soviet Union—that is, putting a stop to the testing, production and installation of additional nuclear weapons by both sides? *Do you (favor/oppose) the freeze strongly or only somewhat?

| | 5/19-23/82 | 9/13-18/82 |
|---|---|---|
| | Adult | Reg voters |
| | *1470* | *78%/1664* |
| Favor | 72 | 69 |
| Oppose | 21 | 25 |
| No answer | 7 | 6 |

| | *6/20-26/83 | *9/14/83 |
|---|---|---|
| | Adult | Adult |
| | *1365* | *705* |
| Favor strongly | 50 | 39 |
| Favor somewhat | 19 | 19 |
| Oppose somewhat | 10 | 13 |
| Oppose strongly | 12 | 14 |
| No answer | 9 | 15 |

14. CBS/*New York Times*: What if a nuclear freeze would result in the United States and the Soviet Union having about an equal amount of nuclear strength, would you favor or oppose such a nuclear freeze? (Asked only of Oppose/No answer subsample and computed on the basis of full sample.)

| | 5/19-23/82 |
|---|---|
| | Adult |
| | *1470* |
| Favor | 87 |
| Oppose | 9 |
| No opinion | 4 |

15. CBS/*New York Times*: What if both the United States and the Soviet Union could catch the other country if it were cheating on the agreement—would you favor or oppose such a nuclear freeze? (Asked only of Oppose/No answer subsample and computed on the basis on the full sample).

| | 5/19-23/82 |
|---|---|
| | Adult |
| | *1470* |
| Favor | 83 |
| Oppose | 12 |
| No opinion | 5 |

16. CBS/*New York Times*: Which do you think would be more dangerous for the United States—agreeing to a nuclear weapons freeze, or continuing to build more nuclear weapons?

| | 5/19-23/82 |
|---|---|
| | Adult |
| | *1470* |
| Freeze | 39 |
| Continuing to build | 46 |
| Both/neither (vol.) | 4 |
| No opinion | 11 |

17. Gallup (for *Newsweek*): The advocates of a nuclear freeze say that both the United States and the Soviet Union already have enough nuclear weapons to destroy each other and want both sides to ban all testing, production and deployment of nuclear weapons. What is your view of the nuclear-freeze movement?

| | 3/17-18/82 |
|---|---|
| | Aware Adult |
| | *43% of 757* |
| Strongly favor | 30 |
| Favor | 38 |
| Oppose | 17 |
| Strongly oppose | 8 |
| Don't know | 7 |

18. Gallup: Would you favor or oppose an agreement between the United States and the Soviet Union for an immediate, verifiable freeze on the testing, production, and deployment of nuclear weapons?

| | 11/5-8/82 | 3/11-14/83 | 5/13-16/83 | 6/15-16/83 | 11/18-12/4/83 |
|---|---|---|---|---|---|
| | Adult | Adult | Adult | Adult | Adult |
| | *1540* | *1558* | *1540* | *760* | *1504+514* |
| Favor | 71 | 70 | 75 | 71 | 77 |
| Oppose | 20 | 21 | 16 | 21 | 13 |
| No Opinion | 9 | 9 | 8 | 8 | 10 |

19. Gallup: This card lists various proposals being discussed in this country today. Would you tell me whether you generally favor or generally oppose each of these proposals? . . . An agreement between the United States and the Soviet Union for an immediate, verifiable freeze on testing and production of nuclear weapons.

| | 9/28-10/1/84 |
|---|---|
| | Adult |
| | *1590* |
| Favor | 78 |
| Oppose | 18 |
| No opinion | 4 |

20. Gallup (for *Newsweek*): The advocates of a nuclear freeze say that both the United States and the Soviet Union already have enough nuclear weapons to destroy each other and want both sides to ban all testing, production and deployment of nuclear weapons. What is your view?

| | 1/17-19/83 |
|---|---|
| | Adult |
| | *754* |
| Strongly favor | 30 |
| Favor | 34 |
| Oppose | 19 |
| Strongly oppose | 10 |
| Don't know | 7 |

21. Harris: Would you favor or oppose Congress passing a resolution that would call upon the United States to negotiate a nuclear freeze agreement with the Soviet Union under which both sides would ban the future production, storage, and use of their nuclear weapons?

| | 3/17-20/83<br>Adult<br>*1254* | 4/20-25/83<br>Adult<br>*1253* | 9/9-14/83<br>Adult<br>*1255* | 11/4-7/83<br>Adult<br>*1250* |
|---|---|---|---|---|
| Favor | 79 | 81 | 77 | 75 |
| Oppose | 16 | 15 | 20 | 19 |
| Not sure | 5 | 4 | 3 | 6 |

| | 12/27-30/83<br>Adult<br>*1267* | 7/2-7/84<br>Likely vote<br>*1259* | 7/20-24/84<br>Likely vote<br>*78%/1620* |
|---|---|---|---|
| Favor | 71 | 69 | 68 |
| Oppose | 23 | 24 | 23 |
| Not sure | 6 | 7 | 9 |

22. Harris: Do you favor or oppose . . . the U.S. negotiating with Russia a verifiable freeze on the production, storage and use of nuclear weapons?

| | 6/12-14/84 Adult 1256 | |
|---|---|---|
| | *Ages 20-36* | *Ages 50-64* |
| Favor | 70 | 64 |
| Oppose | 27 | 27 |
| Not sure | 3 | 9 |

23. *LA Times*: At the present time, would you favor or oppose an agreement between the United States and the Soviet Union on nuclear weapons—or haven't you heard enough about that yet to say? (If favor.) What kind of an agreement would you favor most: an agreement not to build any more nuclear weapons in the future . . . or an agreement to reduce the number of nuclear weapons on both sides . . . or would you favor an agreement to destroy all nuclear weapons that have already been built?
*At the present time, would you favor or oppose an agreement between the United States and the Soviet Union on nuclear weapons—or haven't you heard enough about that yet to say? (If favor.) Which kind of agreement

would you favor most: an agreement not to build any more nuclear weapons in the future—in other words, freeze nuclear weapons . . . or an agreement to reduce the number of weapons on both sides . . . or would you favor any agreement to destroy all nuclear weapons that have already been built? (Allows multiple choices).

| | 3/14-17/82<br>Adult<br>*1503* | *7/4-8/82<br>Adult<br>*1102* |
|---|---|---|
| Freeze | 18 | 39 |
| Reduce | 16 | 39 |
| Destroy | 22 | 42 |
| Oppose an agreement | 11 | 18 |
| Haven't heard enough | 28 | 12 |
| Not sure | 4 | 4 |
| Refused | 1 | - |

24. *LA Times*: In some areas of the country, there is an effort to place a petition on the ballot that would urge the United States government to propose to the government of the Soviet Union that both countries agree to immediately halt the testing, production and further deployment of all nuclear weapons, missiles and delivery systems in a way that can be checked and verified by both sides. Supporters of this petition say our government needs to know that Americans do not want the development of more nuclear weapons. Opponents say it would halt production at a time when the United States is behind Russia. If such a nuclear freeze were being voted on today in your area, do you think you would vote for it or vote against it? (If undecided.) Well, as of today, would you lean more in favor of a nuclear weapons freeze or more against it?

| | 3/14-17/82<br>Adult<br>*1503* |
|---|---|
| For | 52 |
| Lean for | 5 |
| Lean against | 5 |
| Against | 33 |
| Not sure | 5 |
| Refused | - |

25. *LA Times*: Do you support or oppose the nuclear freeze movement which calls for the immediate halt to the testing, production and further deployment of all nuclear weapons, missiles and delivery systems in a way that can be checked and verified by both sides?

| | 4/4-10/83<br>Adults<br>*1233* |
|---|---|
| Support | 60 |
| Oppose | 29 |
| Not sure | 9 |
| Refused | 2 |

26. *LA Times*: Generally speaking, do you approve or disapprove of a freeze on nuclear weapons development?
*Generally speaking, do you approve or disapprove of a freeze on all nuclear weapons development in a way that can be verified by both sides?

| | 9/18-22/83<br>Adult<br>*1653* | *11/12-17/83<br>Adult<br>*2004* | *2/4-9/84<br>Adult<br>*1512* | *4/28-5/3/84<br>Reg voters<br>*1898* |
|---|---|---|---|---|
| Approve strongly | 33 | 55 | 55 | 56 |
| Approve somewhat | 16 | 18 | 24 | 21 |
| Disapprove somewhat | 14 | 7 | 7 | 7 |
| Disapprove strongly | 25 | 12 | 7 | 8 |
| Not sure | 11 | 7 | 7 | 8 |
| Refused | 1 | 1 | - | - |

27. NBC/AP: Would you favor a freeze on the production of nuclear weapons in this country, or do you think the United States should continue to produce nuclear weapons?

| | 12/14-15/81<br>Adult<br>*1602* |
|---|---|
| Favor freeze | 34 |
| Favor if other countries do (vol.) | 6 |
| Continue to produce | 49 |
| Not sure | 11 |

28. NBC/AP: Would you favor or oppose a freeze on the production of nuclear weapons in both the United States and the Soviet Union?

| | 3/29-30/82 | 5/10-11/82 | 6/14-15/82 | 10/18-19/82 | 8/9-10/83 |
|---|---|---|---|---|---|
| | Adult | Adult | Adult | Adult | Adult |
| | *1603* | *1599* | *1597* | *1595* | *1594* |
| Favor | 74 | 83 | 78 | 75 | 70 |
| Oppose | 18 | 14 | 16 | 16 | 23 |
| Not sure | 8 | 3 | 6 | 9 | 7 |

29. Penn and Schoen: Do you favor or oppose a freeze on all further development of nuclear weapons by both the United States and the Soviet Union?

| | 6/12-14/82 | 4/23-24/83 |
|---|---|---|
| | Reg voters | Reg voters |
| | *1000* | *1003* |
| Favor | 79 | 70 |
| Oppose | 18 | 23 |
| Don't know | 4 | 7 |

30. Yankelovich: Would you favor or oppose a city or state resolution which would urge the United States government and the government of the Soviet Union to halt the testing, production and deployment of nuclear weapons systems with verification safeguards for both countries?

| | 3/16-18/82 | 10/5-7/82 |
|---|---|---|
| | Reg voters | Reg voters |
| | *1019* | *1010* |
| Favor | 70 | 76 |
| Oppose | 24 | 19 |
| Not sure (vol.) | 6 | 5 |

***Group 3: Support for Unilateral Actions***

31. Gallup: Suppose that on election day, November 2 [1982], you could vote on key issues as well as candidates. Please tell me how you would vote on each of these propositions. . . . A freeze on the production of nuclear weapons whether or not the Soviet Union agrees to do the same.

*Would you favor or oppose a freeze on the testing, production, and deployment of nuclear weapons at this time if the Soviet Union does not agree to a freeze?
**Do you favor or oppose a freeze on the production of nuclear weapons whether or not the Soviet Union agrees to do the same?

| | 9/10-17/82 | *5/13-16/83 | **11/18-12/4/83 |
|---|---|---|---|
| | Adult | Adult | Adult |
| | *1486* | *1540* | *2018* |
| Favor | 45 | 22 | 23 |
| Oppose | 55 | 68 | 68 |
| No opinion | Not asked | 10 | 9 |

32. Harris: Let me ask you about some things that have been suggested to control the nuclear arms race. For each, tell me if you favor or oppose such a step. . . . The U.S. should not produce any new nuclear weapons even if the Russians continue to produce them.

| | 3/12-16/82 |
|---|---|
| | Adult |
| | *1249* |
| Favor | 23 |
| Oppose | 74 |
| Not sure | 3 |

33. Harris: Would you favor or oppose the United States deciding to gradually dismantle our nuclear weapons before getting agreement from other countries to do the same?

| | 3/5-21/82 | 3/17-20/83 | 4/20-25/83 |
|---|---|---|---|
| | Adult | Adult | Adult |
| | *1599* | *1254* | *1253* |
| Favor | 15 | 19 | 17 |
| Oppose | 82 | 78 | 78 |
| Not sure | 3 | 3 | 5 |

34. Harris: In the current debate over east-west nuclear weapons, which of the following best expresses your personal view about what the West should do? . . . Give up all nuclear weapons regardless of whether the Soviet Union does, introduce no more nuclear weapons, not even if the Soviet Union does, introduce just enough nuclear weapons to create a balance between east and

west until an acceptable agreement can be concluded, introduce more nuclear weapons than the Soviet Union has introduced, in order to establish and maintain nuclear superiority.

| | 10/5-11/83<br>Adult<br>*1246* |
|---|---|
| Give up all regardless | 4 |
| Introduce no more | 8 |
| Introduce enough to balance | 63 |
| Introduce more for superiority | 20 |
| No answer | 5 |

35. NBC/AP: Do you think the United States should move toward nuclear disarmament on its own . . . only if the Soviet Union agrees to disarm as well . . . or don't you think the United States should move toward nuclear disarmament at all?

| | 12/14-15/81<br>Adult<br>*1602* | 3/29-30/82<br>Adult<br>*1603* | 5/10-11/82<br>Adult<br>*1599* | 6/14-15/82<br>Adult<br>*1597* |
|---|---|---|---|---|
| On its own | 12 | 14 | 14 | 15 |
| Only if Soviet Union does | 51 | 50 | 50 | 58 |
| Should not disarm | 27 | 26 | 28 | 20 |
| Not sure | 10 | 10 | 8 | 7 |

36. Public Agenda Foundation: It would be an acceptable risk for the U.S. to . . . declare a six month freeze on nuclear weapons development to see if the Soviets will follow suit, even if they might take advantage of it.

| | 5/21-29/84<br>Adult<br>*505* |
|---|---|
| Agree | 61 |
| Disagree | 36 |
| Not sure | 4 |

### *Group 4: Importance of Verification*

37. ABC/*Washington Post*: I'm going to read a few statements that deal with a nuclear freeze. For each, I'd like you to tell me whether you agree with it, or disagree, or if, perhaps, you have no opinion on that statement. . . . The Soviet Union would try to cheat on any nuclear freeze agreement and get an advantage over the U.S.

| | 4/21-25/82<br>Adult<br>*1521* | 9/22-26/83<br>Adult<br>*1506* |
|---|---|---|
| Agree | 80 | 80 |
| Disagree | 13 | 14 |
| Don't know | 7 | 7 |

38. ABC/*Washington Post*: If there were such an agreement to freeze nuclear weapons do you think the Soviet Union would cheat on that agreement or not?

| | 11/3-7/83<br>Adult<br>*1505* |
|---|---|
| USSR would cheat | 79 |
| USSR would not cheat | 14 |
| Don't know | 7 |

39. ABC/*Washington Post*: Do you think the United States would cheat on such a nuclear weapons freeze or not?

| | 11/3-7/83<br>Adult<br>*1505* |
|---|---|
| US would cheat | 40 |
| US would not cheat | 53 |
| Don't know | 7 |

40. Audits and Surveys: If the U.S. and the Soviet Union did come to a new agreement to reduce both nations' nuclear arms, how confident or not are you that the Russians would live up to this agreement?

| | 9/17-21/83<br>Adult<br>*1205* |
|---|---|
| Very confident | 2 |
| Somewhat confident | 13 |
| Not too confident | 36 |
| Not at all confident | 43 |
| No opinion | 6 |

41. CBS/*New York Times*: What if either the United States or the Soviet Union could cheat on the number of its nuclear weapons without being detected by the other side—would you favor or oppose such a nuclear freeze? (Asked only of those supporting a freeze or who had no opinion in a previous question and computed for whole sample.)

| | 5/19-23/82<br>Adult<br>*1470* |
|---|---|
| Favor | 18 |
| Oppose | 71 |
| No opinion | 11 |

42. Gallup (for *Newsweek*): The major problem in arms control is the difficulty in verifying whether the other side is complying with the agreement. Some people feel that verification is essential for such an agreement. Others feel that it is more important for the United States to halt the growth of its nuclear arsenal even if we cannot be sure the other side is doing the same. Which is more important in your view?

| | 3/17-18/82<br>Adult<br>*757* |
|---|---|
| Verification | 67 |
| Halting growth | 25 |
| Don't know | 8 |

43. Gallup: How likely do you think the Soviet Union would be to abide by such an agreement (not to build any more nuclear weapons in the future)—very likely, fairly likely, or not at all likely?

| | 5/8-11/81<br>Adult<br>*1519* |
|---|---|
| Very likely | 6 |
| Fairly likely | 27 |
| Not at all likely | 60 |
| No opinion | 7 |

44. Gallup: How likely do you think the Soviet Union would be to abide by such an agreement (to destroy all nuclear weapons that have already been built)—very likely, fairly likely, or not at all likely?

| | 5/8-11/81<br>Adult<br>*1519* |
|---|---|
| Very likely | 4 |
| Fairly likely | 16 |
| Not at all likely | 73 |
| No opinion | 7 |

45. Gallup: If a nuclear arms treaty were made between the Soviet Union and the United States, do you think the Soviet Union would be likely to live up to this agreement, or not?

| | 7/13-16/84<br>Adult<br>*1532* |
|---|---|
| Yes, would | 17 |
| No, would not | 74 |
| No opinion | 9 |

46. Gallup: Do you think it would or would not be possible to set up a system for verifying or checking whether the Soviet Union is living up to the terms of a nuclear freeze agreement?

| | 11/5-8/82<br>Adult<br>*1540* |
|---|---|
| Yes, would | 39 |
| No, would not | 47 |
| No opinion | 14 |

47. Gallup: Do you think the Soviet Union will or will not agree to on-site inspection of nuclear weapons in their nation?

| | 5/13-16/83<br>Adult<br>*1540* |
|---|---|
| Will agree | 10 |
| Will not agree | 78 |
| No opinion | 12 |

48. Harris: One of the problems in any nuclear arms control agreement between the U.S. (United States) and Russia is the question of verification—how to be sure each side is living up to what has been agreed upon. Do you think it is possible or not to come to a nuclear arms control agreement with the Russians, under which each side would be able to accurately determine if the other is living up to the agreement?

| | 11/26-29/84<br>Adult<br>*1255* |
|---|---|
| Possible | 40 |
| Not possible | 55 |
| Not sure | 5 |

49. *LA Times*: If the United States and the Soviet Union were to reach agreement on nuclear weapons, do you think the Soviet Union could be trusted to keep its part of the bargain, or not—or haven't you heard enough about that yet to say?

| | 3/14-17/82<br>Adult<br>*1503* | 7/4-8/82<br>Adult<br>*1102* |
|---|---|---|
| Could be trusted | 17 | 17 |
| Could not be trusted | 66 | 68 |
| Haven't heard enough | 9 | 8 |
| Not sure | 7 | 7 |
| Refused | 1 | - |

50. Public Agenda Foundation: It would be an acceptable risk for the U.S. to . . . sign an arms control agreement with the Soviets, even if foolproof verification can't be guaranteed.

| | 5/21-29/84<br>Adult<br>*505* |
|---|---|
| Agree | 56 |
| Disagree | 40 |
| Not sure | 5 |

51. Roper: Here are some arguments that have been made against an immediate nuclear freeze. (Card shown respondent.) For an argument to be convincing it has to be both important and true. If it isn't important, or isn't true it isn't convincing. Would you tell me for each of those arguments whether you find it a very convincing argument against an immediate nuclear freeze, or somewhat convincing, not very convincing, or not at all convincing? . . . The Soviet Union cannot be trusted to live up to the terms of a nuclear freeze agreement.

| | 4/23-30/83<br>Adult<br>*1/2 of 2000* |
|---|---|
| Very convincing | 40 |
| Somewhat convincing | 26 |
| Not very convincing | 16 |
| Not at all convincing | 10 |
| Don't know | 7 |

52. Roper: Here are some arguments that have been made against an immediate nuclear freeze. (Card shown respondent.) For an argument to be convincing it has to be both important and true. If it isn't important, or isn't true it isn't convincing. Would you tell me for each of those arguments whether you find it a very convincing argument against an immediate nuclear freeze, or somewhat convincing, not very convincing, or not at all convincing? . . . A freeze would be a real gamble because neither side would know whether the other side was living up to the agreement.

| | 4/23-30/83<br>Adult<br>*1/2 of 2000* |
|---|---|
| Very convincing | 27 |
| Somewhat convincing | 26 |
| Not very convincing | 23 |
| Not at all convincing | 12 |
| Don't know | 13 |

### *Group 5: Importance of the Nuclear Balance*

53. ABC/*Washington Post*: I'm going to read a few statements that deal with a nuclear freeze. For each, I'd like you to tell me whether you agree with it, or disagree, or if, perhaps, you have no opinion on that statement . . . It doesn't matter if the United States or the Soviet Union is ahead in nuclear weapons because both sides have more than enough to destroy each other no matter who attacks first.

| | 4/21-25/82 | 9/22-26/83 |
|---|---|---|
| | Adult | Adult |
| | *1521* | *1506* |
| Agree | 79 | 77 |
| Disagree | 16 | 17 |
| Don't know | 5 | 6 |

54. ABC/*Washington Post*: I'm going to read a few statements that deal with a nuclear freeze. For each, I'd like you to tell me whether you agree with it, or disagree, or if, perhaps, you have no opinion on that statement. . . . The Soviet Union would have an advantage over the United States in nuclear weapons if both countries agreed to a freeze now.

| | 4/21-25/82 | 9/22-26/83 |
|---|---|---|
| | Adult | Adult |
| | *1521* | *1506* |
| Agree | 58 | 55 |
| Disagree | 29 | 32 |
| Don't know | 13 | 13 |

55. ABC/*Washington Post*: I'm going to read a few statements that deal with a nuclear freeze. For each, I'd like you to tell me whether you agree with it, or disagree, or if, perhaps, you have no opinion on that statement. . . . The U.S. should continue developing nuclear weapons because the ones we have now are not enough to make the Russians afraid to attack the U.S. or its allies.

| | 4/21-25/82 |
|---|---|
| | Adult |
| | *1521* |
| Agree | 43 |
| Disagree | 49 |
| Don't know | 8 |

56. ABC/*Washington Post*: I'm going to read a few statements that deal with a nuclear freeze. For each, I'd like you to tell me whether you agree with it, or disagree, or if, perhaps, you have no opinion on that statement. . . . The U.S. already has thousands of nuclear weapons, so new ones would not give us or our allies any more security than we now have against an attack by the Soviet Union.

| | 4/21-25/82<br>Adult<br>*1521* |
|---|---|
| Agree | 50 |
| Disagree | 40 |
| Don't know | 10 |

57. CBS/*New York Times*: What if a nuclear freeze would result in the Soviet Union having somewhat greater nuclear strength than the United States—would you favor or oppose such a freeze? (Asked of those who favored or had no opinion on a freeze in a previous question and computed for whole sample.)

| | 5/19-23/82<br>Adult<br>*1470* |
|---|---|
| Favor | 30 |
| Oppose | 60 |
| No opinion | 10 |

58. Gallup: In your opinion, which of the following increases the chance of nuclear war more—a continuation of the nuclear arms build-up here and in the Soviet Union, or the U.S. falling behind the Soviet Union in nuclear weaponry?

| | 3/11-14/83<br>Adult<br>*1558* | 5/13-16/83<br>Adult<br>*1540* |
|---|---|---|
| Continuation of build-up | 38 | 31 |
| US falling behind | 47 | 51 |
| No opinion | 15 | 17 |

59. Harris: Let me ask you about some things that have been suggested to control the nuclear arms race. For each, tell me if you favor or oppose such a step. . . . If we are stronger than the Russians in nuclear weapons, then the chances of keeping the peace are greater.

| | 3/12-16/82<br>Adult<br>*1249* |
|---|---|
| Favor | 61 |
| Oppose | 35 |
| Not sure | 4 |

60. *LA Times*: Do you think the United States needs more nuclear weapons for its defense, or do you think the United States now possesses enough nuclear weapons to destroy its enemies?

| | 3/14-17/82<br>Adult<br>*1503* |
|---|---|
| More | 31 |
| Enough | 50 |
| Not sure | 18 |
| Refused | 1 |

61. NBC/AP: In thinking about the United States' national defense, how important is it to you that the United States produce as many nuclear weapons as the Soviet Union does?

| | 5/10-11/82<br>Adult<br>*1599* |
|---|---|
| Very important | 42 |
| Somewhat important | 34 |
| Not important | 21 |
| Not sure | 3 |

62. Penn and Schoen: Would you favor or oppose a freeze on all further development of nuclear weapons by both the United States and the Soviet Union, if this proposal put the Soviet Union ahead of the U.S. in terms of the strength of its nuclear arsenal?

| | 6/12-14/82<br>Reg voters<br>*1000* | 4/23-24/83<br>Reg voters<br>*1003* |
|---|---|---|
| Favor | 36 | 35 |
| Oppose | 57 | 50 |
| Don't know | 8 | 15 |

63. Penn and Schoen: Do you think a nuclear weapons freeze at current levels would be fair to both countries, would be tilted in favor of the United States, or would be tilted in favor of the Soviet Union?

| | 4/23-24/83<br>Reg voters<br>*1003* |
|---|---|
| Fair to both | 33 |
| Tilted in favor of US | 10 |
| Tilted in favor of USSR | 36 |
| Don't know/depends | 21 |

64. Roper: Here are some arguments that have been made against an immediate nuclear freeze. (Card shown respondent.) For an argument to be convincing it has to be both important and true. If it isn't important, or isn't true it isn't convincing. Would you tell me for each of those arguments whether you find it a very convincing argument against an immediate nuclear freeze, or somewhat convincing, not very convincing, or not at all convincing? . . . A freeze now would leave the Soviet Union ahead of the U.S. (United States) in nuclear capability.

| | 4/23-30/83<br>Adult<br>*1/2 of 2000* |
|---|---|
| Very convincing | 30 |
| Somewhat convincing | 30 |
| Not very convincing | 19 |
| Not at all convincing | 9 |
| Don't know | 12 |

65. Roper: Do you think it is necessary that the United States be stronger than Russia in nuclear arms capability, or just as strong as Russia, or doesn't the United States need to be as strong as Russia as long as it has enough nuclear arms to knock Russia out?

| | 9/27-10/4/80 | 10/24-31/81 | 12/4-11/82 |
|---|---|---|---|
| | Adult | Adult | Adult |
| | *1/2 of 2005* | *2000* | *2000* |
| Stronger | 58 | 51 | 41 |
| Just as strong | 31 | 36 | 41 |
| Doesn't need to be as strong | 8 | 10 | 15 |
| Don't know | 4 | 3 | 3 |

66. Roper: At the present time do you think the United States is ahead of Russia in terms of nuclear arms capability, about even with them, or behind Russia in nuclear military strength?

| | 9/27-10/4/80 | 10/24-31/81 | 4/24-5/1/82 | 12/4-11/82 | 4/18-28/84 |
|---|---|---|---|---|---|
| | Adult | Adult | Adult | Adult | Adult |
| | *1/2 of 2005* | *2000* | *2000* | *2000* | *2000* |
| Ahead | 15 | 16 | 12 | 14 | 15 |
| About even | 29 | 35 | 32 | 39 | 42 |
| Behind | 43 | 41 | 41 | 39 | 32 |
| Don't know | 13 | 9 | 15 | 9 | 10 |

### *Group 6: Likelihood of Arms Control Agreement*

67. ABC/*Washington Post*: I'm going to read a few statements that deal with a nuclear freeze. For each, I'd like you to tell me whether you agree with it, or disagree, or if, perhaps, you have no opinion on that statement. . . . The U.S. government would never agree to a nuclear arms freeze.

| | 4/21-25/82 | 9/22-26/83 |
|---|---|---|
| | Adult | Adult |
| | *1521* | *1506* |
| Agree | 31 | 28 |
| Disagree | 55 | 61 |
| Don't know | 14 | 11 |

68. ABC/*Washington Post*: I'm going to read a few statements that deal with a nuclear freeze. For each, I'd like you to tell me whether you agree with it, or disagree, or if, perhaps, you have no opinion on that statement. . . . The Soviet Union would never agree to a nuclear arms freeze.

| | 4/21-25/82 |
|---|---|
| | Adult |
| | *1521* |
| Agree | 50 |
| Disagree | 37 |
| Don't know | 13 |

69. Gallup: In your opinion how likely is it that the United States and the Soviet Union will be able to reach an agreement to reduce the size of their nuclear arsenals in the near future?

| | 6/2-3/82 |
|---|---|
| | Adult |
| | *519* |
| Very likely | 7 |
| Fairly likely | 26 |
| Not too likely | 36 |
| Not at all likely | 27 |
| Don't know | 4 |

70. Harris: How likely do you think it is that superpowers such as the United States and Russia will move toward disarmament of their nuclear weapons in the near future?

| | 3/5-21/82 | 4/20-25/83 | 9/9-14/83 |
|---|---|---|---|
| | Adult | Adult | Adult |
| | *1599* | *1253* | *1255* |
| Very likely | 13 | 12 | 11 |
| Somewhat likely | 27 | 35 | 34 |
| Not very likely at all | 57 | 49 | 53 |
| Not sure | 3 | 4 | 2 |

71. Harris: Do you think that (an end to the production, storage, and testing of all nuclear weapons by all countries on earth) will happen in your lifetime or not?

| | 11/23-28/82<br>Adult<br>*1256* | 12/8-12/83<br>Adult<br>*1249* |
|---|---|---|
| Will happen | 15 | 16 |
| Will not happen | 81 | 80 |
| Not sure | 4 | 4 |

72. Harris: How optimistic are you that the U.S. (United States) and Russia will come to an agreement anytime soon to . . . reduce nuclear weapons on each side—very optimistic, somewhat optimistic, not very optimistic, or not optimistic at all?

| | 6/2-7/84<br>Likely voters<br>*1259* |
|---|---|
| Very optimistic | 8 |
| Somewhat optimistic | 24 |
| Not very optimistic | 38 |
| Not optimistic at all | 28 |
| Not sure | 2 |

73. *LA Times*: Do you think that a meeting between the United States and the Soviet Union to try to reach agreement on nuclear weapons would end in success or do you think it would end in failure—or haven't you heard enough about that yet to say?

| | 3/14-17/82<br>Adult<br>*1503* |
|---|---|
| Success | 21 |
| Neither (vol.) | 9 |
| Failure | 45 |
| Haven't heard enough | 15 |
| Not sure | 10 |
| Refused | - |

74. *LA Times*: Do you think the leaders of the Soviet Union really want to reach agreement on nuclear weapons, or not—or haven't you heard enough about that yet to say?

| | 3/14-17/82 |
|---|---|
| | Adult |
| | *1503* |
| Want agreement | 23 |
| Don't want agreement | 48 |
| Haven't heard enough | 15 |
| Not sure | 13 |
| Refused | 1 |

75. *LA Times*: Do you think the leaders of the United States really want to reach agreement on nuclear weapons, or not—or haven't you heard enough about that yet to say?

| | 3/14-17/82 |
|---|---|
| | Adult |
| | *1503* |
| Want agreement | 52 |
| Don't want agreement | 25 |
| Haven't heard enough | 14 |
| Not sure | 8 |
| Refused | 1 |

76. NBC/AP: How likely do you think it is that the Soviets will agree to a bilateral agreement to reduce nuclear weapons?

| | 6/14-15/82 |
|---|---|
| | Adult |
| | *1597* |
| Very likely | 8 |
| Somewhat likely | 31 |
| Not likely at all | 55 |
| Not sure | 6 |

### *Group 7: Public Involvement in the Nuclear Debate*

77. ABC/*Washington Post*: I'm going to read a few statements that deal with a nuclear freeze. For each, I'd like you to tell me whether you agree with it, or disagree, or if, perhaps, you have no opinion on that statement. . . . U.S. government leaders can be trusted to make the right decision about a nuclear freeze without pressure from the public one way or the other.

| | 4/21-25/82<br>Adult<br>*1521* |
|---|---|
| Agree | 36 |
| Disagree | 57 |
| Don't know | 7 |

78. ABC/*Washington Post*: Recently there have been proposals that the United States and the Soviet Union both agree to halt, or "freeze," the testing, production and installation of nuclear weapons. Have you yourself heard or read anything about such a proposed freeze?

| | 4/21-25/82<br>Adult<br>*1521* | 4/8-12/83<br>Adult<br>*1516* | 9/22-26/83<br>Adult<br>*1506* |
|---|---|---|---|
| Yes, have heard | 57 | 56 | 54 |
| No, have not heard | 42 | 44 | 45 |
| Don't know | - | 1 | 1 |

79. ABC/*Washington Post*: Would you say you tend to approve or tend to disapprove of such groups? (that have organized in support of a freeze on nuclear weapons.)

| | 4/21-25/82<br>Adult<br>*1521* |
|---|---|
| Approve | 52 |
| Disapprove | 34 |
| Don't know | 14 |

80. ABC/*Washington Post*: Would you join such a group (that has organized in support of a freeze on nuclear weapons) if invited, or not?

| | 4/21-25/82<br>Adult<br>*1521* |
|---|---|
| Yes, would join | 26 |
| No, would not join | 65 |
| Don't know | 9 |

81. CBS/*New York Times*: Do you think the public can understand the issues involved in a nuclear freeze well enough to vote on it, or is the question of a nuclear freeze too complicated for the public to decide?

| | 5/19-23/82<br>Adult<br>*1470* |
|---|---|
| Public can understand | 35 |
| Too complicated | 59 |
| No opinion | 6 |

82. CBS/*New York Times*: There's been a lot of discussion about a nuclear freeze—a proposed halt to the testing, production and installation of additional nuclear weapons. Have you been paying much attention to the issue of a nuclear freeze, or not?

| | 5/19-23/82<br>Adult<br>*1470* |
|---|---|
| Yes, have been paying attention | 53 |
| No, have not been paying attention | 45 |
| No opinion | 2 |

83. Harris: In many countries of the world, people have been demonstrating against the spread of nuclear weapons. In general, are you in sympathy with the anti-nuclear weapons movement or not?

| | 3/5-21/82<br>Adult<br>*1599* | 4/20-25/83<br>Adult<br>*1253* |
|---|---|---|
| In sympathy | 55 | 45 |
| Not in sympathy | 39 | 48 |
| Not sure | 6 | 7 |

84. *LA Times*: In the talks between the United States and Russia over nuclear weapons reduction, do you think the nuclear freeze movement in America hurts our bargaining position, or doesn't affect the talks one way or the other, or do you think the nuclear freeze movement helps our bargaining position with the Russians?

| | 4/4-10/83 |
|---|---|
| | Adult |
| | *1233* |
| Hurts | 31 |
| Doesn't affect | 28 |
| Helps | 25 |
| Not sure | 14 |
| Refused | 2 |

85. Public Agenda Foundation: The subject of nuclear weapons is too complex for people like me to think about; that should be left to the President and the experts.

| | 5/21-29/84 |
|---|---|
| | Adult |
| | *505* |
| Agree | 21 |
| Disagree | 77 |
| Not sure | 1 |

86. Public Agenda Foundation: The issue of nuclear war is too important to leave only to the President and the experts; citizens must have a say in any decisions that are made.

| | 5/21-29/84 |
|---|---|
| | Adult |
| | *505* |
| Agree | 68 |
| Disagree | 29 |
| Not sure | 3 |

88. Yankelovich: There are many reports of people in the United States today speaking out and protesting against the nuclear arms race. Do you feel that this mostly represents a real grass roots movement, or mostly involves people who often have been involved in most protest movements in the past?

| | 6/8-10/82<br>Reg voters<br>*1010* | 12/8-9/82<br>Reg voters<br>*1019* |
|---|---|---|
| Mostly represents real grass roots movement | 38 | 32 |
| Mostly protesters from the past | 50 | 55 |
| Not sure (vol.) | 12 | 13 |

# Bibliography

## Articles


Adelson, Joseph and Chester E. Finn. "Terrorizing Children." *Commentary*, April 1985, 29-36.

Alpern, David M., et al. "A Matter of Life and Death." *Newsweek*, 26 April 1982, 20-25.

Alsop, Ronald. "'A' is for Atom: Nuclear War Becomes Hot Topic in Schools, Stirs Up Controversy." *Wall Street Journal*, 24 May 1983, 1, 22.

Altheide, David L. "Three-In-One News: Network Coverage of Iran." *Journalism Quarterly* 59 (Autumn 1982): 482-86.

"Americans Assess the Nuclear Option." *Public Opinion* 5 (August/September 1982): 33-40.

Attanasio, Paul. "Big Bang, Little Box." *New Republic*, 5 December 1983, 13-14.

Auletta, Ken. "Look What They've Done to the News." *TV Guide*, 9-15 November 1991.

Banisky, Sandy. "Children Lead Charge on Abortion Clinics." *Baltimore Sun*, 12 July 1992, 1A, 10A.

Behr, Roy L. and Shanto Iyengar. "Television News, Real-World Cues, and Changes in the Public Agenda." *Public Opinion Quarterly* 49 (Spring 1985): 38-57.

Bernstein, Harry. "Teacher Unions Swing Right and Left in Battle." *Los Angeles Times*, 11 July 1983, section 4, pages 1, 5.

"The Bishops as Peacemakers." *Commonweal*, 18 December 1981, 707.

Bjork, Rebecca S. "Reagan and the Nuclear Freeze: 'Star Wars' as a Rhetorical Strategy." *Journal of the American Forensic Association* 24 (Winter 1987): 181-92.

Black, Edwin. "The Second Persona." *Quarterly Journal of Speech* 56 (April 1970): 109-19.

Boyer, Paul. "A Historical View of Scare Tactics." *Bulletin of the Atomic Scientists* 42 (January 1986): 17-19.

Branch, Taylor. Review of *Missile Envy*, by Helen Caldicott. *New York Times Book Review*, 29 July 1984, 13.

Briggs, Kenneth A. "Bishops Cite Differences." *New York Times*, 10 April 1983, 1, 15.

———. "Bishops Endorse Stand Opposed to Nuclear War." *New York Times*, 4 May 1983, A1, B7.

———. "Bishops Support Letter on Nuclear Arms." *New York Times*, 19 November 1982, D15.

———. "Religious Leaders Objecting to Nuclear Arms." *New York Times*, 8 September 1981, A1, A20.

Briller, Bert R. "Zooming in Closer on the News Audience." *Television Quarterly* 25, no. 1 (1990): 107-16.

Brock, David. "Selling Globaloney in the Schools." *American Spectator*, December 1988, 22-26.

Brown, JoAnne. "'A Is For Atom, B Is for Bomb': Civil Defense in American Public Education, 1948-1963." *Journal of American History* 75 (June 1988): 68-90.

Buckley, William F., Jr. "Nuclear Nonthink." *National Review*, 4 February 1983, 140.

Butterfield, Fox. "Anatomy of the Nuclear Protest." *New York Times Magazine*, 11 July 1982, 14-17, 32-39.

Caldicott, Helen. "A Commitment to Life." *The Humanist*, September/October 1982, 5-11.

———. "Growing Up Afraid: The 37th Summer of the Bomb." *Family Weekly*, 8 August 1982, 4-7.

Cantor, Joanne, Barbara J. Wilson, and Cynthia Hoffner. "Emotional Responses to a Televised Nuclear Holocaust Film." *Communication Research* 13 (April 1986): 257-77.

Carter, Jimmy. "Energy Problems: The Erosion of Confidence." *Vital Speeches of the Day*, 15 August 1979, 642-45.

Chapman, Stephen. "Shot From Guns." *New Republic*, 9 June 1979, 14-18.

Chira, Susan. "Priests Get Ready for the Questions in Connecticut." *New York Times*, 16 December 1983, B1-B2.

Clark, William P. "A Letter From the White House." *Origins*, 2 December 1982, 398-401.

Clotfelter, James. "Disarmament Movements in the United States." *Journal of Peace Research* 23 (June 1986): 97-101.

Clymer, Adam. "Americans in Poll View Government More Confidently." *New York Times*, 19 November 1984, A1, B10.

Coalition for a New Foreign and Military Policy. "Join the Coalition Network." *Coalition Close-Up*, Spring/Summer 1982, 1-20.

Cockburn, Alexander and James Ridgeway. "Has the Freeze Failed?" *Village Voice*, 7 June 1983, 22-23.

———. "Will the Freeze Movement Be More Than a Fad?" *Village Voice*, 13 April 1982, 6-7.

Coles, Robert. "Children and the Bomb." *New York Times Magazine*, 8 December 1985, 44-50, 54, 61-62.

———. "The Freeze: Crusade of the Leisure Class." *Harper's*, March 1985, 21-23.

Conventional Wisdom Watch: '92 Edition." *Newsweek*, 14 September 1992, 4.

Corn, David. "Election Lessons to Build On." *Nuclear Times*, December 1984, 12-15.

Cushnir, Howard. "The Great Peace March That Couldn't." *Mother Jones*, June 1986, 39-43.

Diamond, Edwin. "Shrinking the News." *New York*, 27 May 1991, 20-21.

Dieringer, Larry. "The Challenge of Legislation and School Board Resolutions." [Educators for Social Responsibility] *Forum*, Fall 1985, 1-2, 4.

———. "Days of Dialogue, 1985: Finding Common Ground." [Educators for Social Responsibility] *Forum*, Fall 1985, 1-2.

"Disarmament Groups Seek Rallying Point After Faltering on Atom Freeze." *New York Times*, 18 August 1985, 22.

Donner, Frank. "But Will They Come? The Campaign to Smear the Nuclear Freeze Movement." *The Nation*, 6 November 1982, 456-65.

Draper, Theodore. "How Not to Think About Nuclear War." *New York Review of Books*, 15 July 1982, 35-43.

Edmonds, Patty. "U.S. Bishops Affirm Peace Pastoral." *National Catholic Reporter*, 26 November 1982, 1, 6.

Farrell, Michael J. "'Prevailing' Despite Court Defeat." *National Catholic Reporter*, 20 March 1981, 3, 18-19, 24.

Feldman, Stanley and Lee Sigelman. "The Political Impact of Prime-Time Television: 'The Day After,'" *Journal of Politics* 47 (May 1985): 556-78.

Finn, Chester E., Jr. "Teacher Politics." *Commentary*, February 1983, 29-41.

Fisher, Walter, R. "Narration as a Human Communication Paradigm: The Case of Public Moral Argument." *Communication Monographs* 51 (March 1984): 1-22.

Fleisher, Paul. "Teaching Children About Nuclear War." *Phi Delta Kappan* 67 (November 1985): 215-17.

Foote, Joe S. and Michael E. Steel. "Degree of Conformity in Lead Stories in Early Evening Network Television Newscasts." *Journalism Quarterly* 63 (Spring 1986): 19-23.

Foss, Karen A. and Stephen W. Littlejohn. "*The Day After:* Rhetorical Vision in an Ironic Frame." *Critical Studies in Mass Communication* 3 (September 1986): 317-36.

Fox, Thomas C. "Bishops' Draft Not Encouraging." *National Catholic Reporter*, 30 July 1982, 2.

"Freeze March." *Time*, 14 June 1982, 24.

"Gallup Poll Accuracy Record." *The Gallup Poll Monthly*, no. 326 (November 1992).

Garvey, John. "King of Prussia Eight." *Commonweal*, 30 January 1981, 39-40.

Getler, Michael. "Latest Draft of Bishops More 'Flexible.'" *Washington Post*, 6 April 1983, A1, A5.

Gold, Vic. Review of *The Fate of the Earth*, by Jonathan Schell. *American Spectator*, July 1982, 36-37.

Goldwater, Barry. "NEA's Nuclear 'Choices.'" *Washington Post*, 18 June 1983, A20.

Goldzwig, Steve and George Cheney. "The U.S. Catholic Bishops on Nuclear Arms: Corporate Advocacy, Role Redefinition, and Rhetorical Adaptation." *Central States Speech Journal* 35 (Spring 1984): 8-23.

Goodman, Terri. "Fatalism, Economic Insecurity Boost Pantex in Texas Panhandle." *National Catholic Reporter*, 2 October 1981, 8.

Goodnight, G. Thomas. "The Personal, Technical, and Public Spheres of Argument: A Speculative Inquiry into the Art of Public Deliberation." *Journal of the American Forensic Association* 18 (Spring 1982): 214-27.

———. "Public Discourse." *Critical Studies in Mass Communication* 4 (December 1987): 428-32.

———. "Ronald Reagan's Re-formulation of the Rhetoric of War: Analysis of the 'Zero Option,' 'Evil Empire,' and 'Star Wars' Addresses," *Quarterly Journal of Speech* 72 (November 1986): 390-414.

Gottlieb, Jeff. "Prime-Time Patriotism: ABC Atones for *The Day After*." *Mother Jones*, January 1987, 26-44.

Grenier, Richard. "The Politicized Oscar." *Commentary*, June 1983, 68-74.

Gwertzman, Bernard. "Administration Hails New Draft of Arms Letter." *New York Times*, 7 April 1983, A1, B12.

Halloran, Richard. "Minuet With Catholic Bishops Over Nuclear War." *New York Times*, 16 December 1982, B16.

—-. "U.S. Tells Bishops Morality is Guide on Nuclear Policy." *New York Times*, 17 November 1982, A1, B4.

Hart, Roderick P., Patrick Jerome, and Karen McComb. "Rhetorical Features of Newscasts About the President." *Critical Studies in Mass Communication* 1 (September 1984): 260-86.

Hauser, Gerald and Carole Blair. "Antecedents to the Public." *Pre-Text* 3 (Summer 1982): 139-67.

Hawkins, Steve L. and John W. Mashek. "Antinuclear Campaign Reawakens." *U.S. News and World Report*, 27 January 1986, 22.

Hays, Charlotte. "The Voice in the Bishops' Ear." *Washington Post Magazine*, 3 April 1983, 6, 11, 13.

Hehir, J. Bryan. "Nuclear Weapons: The Two Debates." *Commonweal*, 13 March 1981, 135, 159.

"Helen Caldicott on Tactics." *Bulletin of the Atomic Scientists* 42 (May 1986): 45-46.

Hentoff, Nicholas. "Student Letters to Reagan on War Stir Their Own Tempest in Senate." *Wall Street Journal*, 14 September 1983, 30.

Herbers, John. "Widespread Vote Urges Nuclear Freeze." *New York Times*, 4 November 1982, A22.

Herman, Robin. "Rally Speakers Decry Cost of Nuclear Arms Race." *New York Times*, 13 June 1982, 43.

Herndon, Terry. "A Teacher Speaks of Peace." *Phi Delta Kappan* 64 (April 1983): 527-32.

"Hey, Big Spender." *Newsweek*, 14 September 1992, 4.

Hoffman, David. "NEA Criticized for Curriculum on Nuclear War." *Washington Post*, 8 June 1983, A10.

Hogan, J. Michael. "Public Opinion and American Foreign Policy: The Case of Illusory Support for the Panama Canal Treaties." *Quarterly Journal of Speech* 71 (August 1985): 302-17.

———. Review of *Eloquence in an Electronic Age*, by Kathleen Hall Jamieson. *Quarterly Journal of Speech* 76 (August 1990): 345-47.

"How the Proposed Pastoral Relates to U.S. Policy." *Origins*, 21 April 1983, 738-39.

Hyer, Marjorie. "How Our War-Blessing Catholic Bishops Got Religion on Nukes." *Washington Post*, 1 May 1983, B1, B4.

"Hypocrisy About Banned Books." *The Phyllis Schlafly Report*, November 1985, 1-4.

Ivie, Robert L. "Metaphor and the Rhetorical Invention of Cold War 'Idealists.'" *Communication Monographs* 54 (June 1987): 165-82.

Kalven, Jamie. "A Talk with Louis Harris." *Bulletin of the Atomic Scientists* 38 (August/September 1982): 3-5.

Kantowicz, Edward R. "Cardinal Mundelein of Chicago and the Shaping of Twentieth-Century American Catholicism." *Journal of American History* 68 (June 1981): 52-68.

Kehler, Randall. "Message From the National Coordinator." *Freeze Newsletter*, January 1983, 3, 20-21.

Kelly, James. "Fallout From a TV Attack." *Time*, 5 December 1983, 38-41.

———. "Thinking About the Unthinkable." *Time*, 29 March 1982, 10-14.

"Kennan Proposal to Break Nuclear Arms Race Supported by Overwhelming Margin; International Inspection Plan Favored." *Gallup Report* 196 (January 1982): 13-17.

Kerr, Peter. "Physicians Urge End to Arms Race." *New York Times*, 10 June 1984, 17.

Kimelman, Ronald. "Texas Bishop's Stand Against Nuclear Arms Stirs Furor." *Washington Post*, 20 March 1982, B5.

Kinzie, Charles E. "First Draft on the Road to the Abyss: Ecclesiastically Endorsed Civil Religion." *National Catholic Reporter*, 24 September 1982, 10-11.

Krauthammer, Charles. "Kid's Stuff." *New Republic*, 13 February 1984, 10-11.

Ladd, Everett Carll. "The Freeze Framework." *Public Opinion* 5 (August/September 1982): 20, 41.

Lefever, Ernest W. "Teaching History and Politics in the Age of Nuclear Arms." *Phi Delta Kappan* 67 (November 1985): 217-18.

Lefever, Ernest W. and E. Stephen Hunt. "Education, Propaganda, and Nuclear Arms." *Phi Delta Kappan* 64 (June 1983): 727-28.

Lehman, John P., Jr. "The U.S. Catholic Bishops and Nuclear Arms." *Wall Street Journal*, 15 November 1982, 28.

Lemert, James B. "Content Duplications by the Networks in Competing Evening Newscasts." *Journalism Quarterly* 51 (Summer 1974): 238-44.

"Letter of 24 Congressmen on Bishops' Pastoral." *Origins*, 13 January 1983, 492-96.

Levin, Michael. "The Springsteening of Disarmament." *New York Times*, 19 June 1982, 25.

Lewis, Anthony. "The Neglected Question." *New York Times*, 30 July 1981, A19.

Lewis, William F. "Telling America's Story: Narrative Form and the Reagan Presidency," *Quarterly Journal of Speech* 73 (August 1987): 280-302.

Lindorff, Dave. "War in Peace: The Fight for Position in New York's June 12 Disarmament Rally." *Village Voice*, 20 April 1982, 12-14, 25.

Lindsey, Robert. "Bishops Protest Train Carrying Atom Weapons." *New York Times*, 24 February 1984, A10.

———. "438 Protestors Are Arrested at Nevada Nuclear Test Site." *New York Times*, 6 February 1987, A8.

"The Long Trek." *U.S. News and World Report*, 27 January 1986, 22.

Lunch, William L. and Peter W. Sperlich. "American Public Opinion and the War in Vietnam." *Western Political Quarterly* 31 (March 1979): 21-44.

Maddox, John. "What Happened to Nuclear Winter?" *Nature* 333 (19 May 1988): 203.

Maeroff, Gene I. "Curriculum Addresses Fear of Atom War." *New York Times*, 29 March 1983, C1, 4.

Maitland, Leslie. "F.B.I. Rules Out Russian Control of Freeze Drive." *New York Times*, 26 March 1983, 1, 7.

———. "Sources Are Cited for Charge of Soviet Tie to Arms Freeze." *New York Times*, 13 November 1982, 7.

Manoff, Robert Karl. "The Week After." *Nation*, 10 December 1983, 588-89.

Matthiesen, Leroy T. "Bishop: Don't Help Build Bombs." *National Catholic Reporter*, 11 September 1981, 2.

McCarthy, Colman. "Brave Bishops." *Washington Post*, 3 October, 1981, A23.

———. "The Crossing of the Bishops." *Washington Post*, 11 May 1983, B1, B15.

———. "How the 'Peace Bishops' Got That Way." *Washington Post*, 27 December 1981, D5.

McCory, Mary. "Administration Fires Back With Its Own Schoolbook on A-War." *Washington Post*, 9 June 1983, A3.

McDowell, Edwin. "Nuclear Books Proliferating, But Few Sell Well." *New York Times*, 4 November 1982, C25.

McFadden, Robert D. "A Spectrum of Humanity Represented in the Rally." *New York Times*, 13 June 1982, 42.
———. "3 Canadian Films Called 'Propaganda' by U.S." *New York Times*, 25 February 1983, C4.
McGee, Michael C. "In Search of 'the People': A Rhetorical Alternative." *Quarterly Journal of Speech* 61 (October 1975): 235-49.
McGuire, Willard. "Why We Fight." *Today's Education* (1982-83 Annual): 119-20.
Mechling, Elizabeth Walker and Gale Auletta. "Beyond War: A Socio-Rhetorical Analysis of a New Class Social Movement." *Western Journal of Speech Communication* 50 (Fall 1986): 388- 404.
Mechling, Elizabeth Walker and Jay Mechling. "The Campaign for Civil Defense and the Struggle to Naturalize the Bomb." *Western Journal of Speech Communication* 55 (Spring 1991): 105-133.
———. "Hot Pacifism and Cold War: The American Friends Service Committee's Witness for Peace in 1950s America." *Quarterly Journal of Speech* 78 (May 1992): 173-96.
Miller, Judith. "Advocates of Arms Control Ponder Some New Moves." *New York Times*, 5 December 1982, E5.
———. "Nuclear Freeze Debate Important in Few Races." *New York Times*, 19 October 1982, A18.
———. "President Says Freeze Proponents May Unwittingly Aid the Russians." *New York Times*, 11 December 1982, 9.
———. "72% in Poll Back Nuclear Halt If Soviet Union Doesn't Gain." *New York Times*, 30 May 1982, 1, 22.
———. "Soviet Role in Freeze Movement Found Minor." *New York Times*, 10 December 1982, A15.
Mitchard, Jacquelyn. "A Lesson for Today: Facing the Big 35." [Educators for Social Responsibility] *Forum*, Spring 1986, 3.
"More on Catholics and Nuclear Arms." *Commonweal*, 12 March 1982, 131-32.
Morganthau, Tom. "After 'The Day After.'" *Newsweek*, 5 December 1983, 62.
National Conference of Catholic Bishops. "The Challenge of Peace: God's Promise and Our Response." Second Draft. *Origins*, 28 October 1982, 305-28.
National Conference of Catholic Bishops. "The Challenge of Peace: God's Promise and Our Response." Third Draft. *Origins*, 14 April 1983, 697-728.
"New Directions: International Breakthroughs." [Educators for Social Responsibility] *Forum*, Spring 1986, 1, 4.
"Newsweek Poll: Nuclear Forebodings." *Newsweek*, 26 April 1982, 24.
Novak, Michael. "Arms and the Church." *Commentary*, March 1982, 37-41.
———. "The Bishops Speak Out." *National Review*, 10 June 1983, 674-81.
———. "Moral Clarity in the Nuclear Age." *National Review*, 1 April 1983, 354-88.
———. "Nuclear Morality." *America*, 3 July 1982, 5-8.

Nuclear Weapons Freeze Campaign. "The Nuclear Weapons Freeze Campaign." *Freeze Newsletter*, January 1983, 2.

O'Gara, James. "Peace and the Bishops." *Commonweal*, 23 December 1966, 338.

Ostling, Richard N. "Bishops and the Bomb." *Time*, 29 November 1982, 68-77.

Paletz, David, et al. "Polls in the Media: Content, Credibility, and Consequences." *Public Opinion Quarterly* 44 (Winter 1980): 495-513.

Pax Christi. "Toward a Christian Response to War and Peace." *Origins*, 17 March 1981, 744-46.

Pittman, Susan Peters. "Politics and the Educator." [Educators for Social Responsibility] *Forum*, Fall 1985, 9.

———. "Robert Coles Urges a Broader View." [Educators for Social Responsibility] *Forum*, Fall 1985, 9.

"Political Teaching." *Washington Post*, 5 April 1983, A14.

"A Positive and Helpful Exchange of Views." *Origins*, 7 April 1983, 695-96.

Powers, Thomas. "The Moment to Say No." *Commonweal*, 5 November 1982, 583-84.

———. "Sticking to the Grim Point." *The Nation*, 25 July-1 August 1981, 85-87.

"President Says Foes of U.S. Have Duped Arms Freeze Group." *New York Times*, 5 October 1982, A22.

Pringle, Peter. "Putting World War III on Ice." *Inquiry*, July 1982, 13-18.

Quindlen, Anna. "About New York." *New York Times*, 13 June 1982, 43.

"The Radical Agenda of the NEA." *The Phyllis Schlafly Report*, February 1985, 1-3.

Radosh, Ronald. "The 'Peace Council' and Peace." *New Republic*, 31 January 1983, 14-18.

Reagan, Ronald. "United States Foreign Affairs Policy: Arms Reduction." *Vital Speeches of the Day*, 1 December 1981, 98-101.

Reardon, Betty, John Anthony Scott, and Sam Totten. "Nuclear Weapons: Concepts, Issues, and Controversies." *Social Education* 47 (November/December 1983): 473-74.

Ricks, Tom. "Dr. Caldicott Goes to War." *Washington Journalism Review*, October 1982, 36-38.

Rizzo-Harvi, Renata. "Grass Roots Opt for Unity." *Nuclear Times*, January/February 1987, 29-31.

Robinson, Sharon. "Of History, Peace, and Choices." *Social Education* 47 (November/December 1983): 487-88.

Roche, Barbara. "Citizens Lobby for a U.S./Soviet Nuclear Weapons Freeze." *Freeze Newsletter*, January 1983, 4, 21.

Rubin, David M. and Constance Cummings. "Nuclear War and Its Consequences on Television News." *Journal of Communication* 39 (Winter 1989): 39-58.

Rushing, Janice Hocker. "Ronald Reagan's 'Star Wars' Address: Mythic Containment of Technical Reasoning." *Quarterly Journal of Speech* 72 (November 1986): 415-33.

Ryerson, Andre. "The Scandal of 'Peace Education.'" *Commentary*, June 1986, 37-46.

Safire, William. "Bullies in the Pulpit." *New York Times*, 14 March 1983, A15.

Sagan, Carl. "Nuclear War and Climatic Catastrophe: Some Policy Implications." *Foreign Affairs* 62 (Winter 1983/84): 257- 92.

———. "The Nuclear Winter." *Parade*, 30 October 1983, 4-7.

Salholz, Eloise, with Mary Lord and Dianne H. McDonald. "Teaching About Nuclear War." *Newsweek*, 18 July 1983, 78.

Sandman, Peter M. and JoAnn M. Valenti. "Scared Stiff—Or Scared Into Action." *Bulletin of the Atomic Scientists* 42 (January 1986): 12-16.

Schiappa, Edward. "The Rhetoric of Nukespeak." *Communication Monographs* 56 (September 1989): 253-72.

Schlesinger, Arthur M., Jr. Letter to the Editor. *New York Review of Books*, 20 October 1966, 37.

Schuman, Howard, Jacob Ludwig, and Jon A. Krosnick. "The Perceived Threat of Nuclear War, Salience, and Open Questions." *Public Opinion Quarterly* 50 (Winter 1986): 519-36.

"Setting a New Agenda For Arms Control: An Interview With Randall Forsberg." *Technology Review*, November/December 1990, 32-40.

Shelley, Mack C., II and Hwarng-Du Hwang. "The Mass Media and Public Opinion Polls in the 1988 Presidential Election." *American Politics Quarterly* 19 (January 1991): 59-79.

Sheppard, Nathaniel, Jr. "Center for Nuclear Freeze Set Up in St. Louis." *New York Times*, 23 March 1982, A19.

Small, William. "The Changing Face of Network News." *Television Quarterly* 25, no. 1 (1990): 105-6.

Smith, Hedrick. "New House Seems Less in Tune with Reagan." *New York Times*, 4 November 1982, A1, A18.

Smith, Ted J., III and J. Michael Hogan. "Public Opinion and the Panama Canal Treaties of 1977." *Public Opinion Quarterly* 51 (Spring 1987): 5-30.

Smith, Tom W. "Nuclear Anxiety." *Public Opinion Quarterly* 52 (Winter 1988): 557-75.

"Star Wars Status." *Public Opinion*, August/September 1985, 33-35.

Sussman, Barry. "Young People in Area Fear a Nuclear War." *Washington Post*, 19 February 1984, A1, A16-A17.

Talbott, Strobe. "A Grim Manifesto on Nuclear War." *Time*, 19 April 1982, 20-21.

———. "Living with Mega-Death." *Time*, 29 March 1982, 18-26.

Thompson, Starley L. and Stephen H. Schneider, "Nuclear Winter Reappraised." *Foreign Affairs* 64 (Summer 1986): 981-1005.

Totten, Sam. "Orwellian Language in the Nuclear Age." *Curriculum Review* 23 (April 1984): 43-46.

Turco, R. P., et al. "Nuclear Winter: Global Consequences of Multiple Nuclear Explosions." *Science* 222 (23 December 1983): 1283-92.

"26 Groups Join in Campaign for Arms Freeze." *New York Times*, 17 October 1982, 44.

"The U.S. Bishops on Peace and War." *National Catholic Reporter*, 2 July 1982, 11-12, 17-18.

"Vatican Communique: Informal Meeting on U.S. Bishops' Pastoral." *Origins*, 3 February 1983, 545.

"A Vatican Synthesis." *Origins*, 7 April 1983, 691-95.

Vatz, Richard. "Public Opinion and Presidential Ethos." *Western Journal of Speech Communication* 40 (Summer 1976): 196-206.

Vatz, Richard E. and Lee S. Weinberg. "Media and Polling: Measuring and Creating the Salience of George Bush as 'Wimp.'" *Mass Comm Review* 14, no. 3 (1987): 23-29.

Wagner, Tony. "Educating for Responsibility in a Nuclear Age." *Media and Methods* 20 (November 1983): 24-25.

Wallace, James. "Nuclear Freeze Crusade: Gaining or Waning?" *U.S. News and World Report*, 25 April 1983, 18-21.

Walljasper, Jay. "Who's Who in the Nuclear Freeze Campaign." *In These Times*, 21-27 April 1982, 12-13.

"War and Peace Draft Hit in Letters . . . and Defended by Gumbleton." *National Catholic Reporter*, 30 July 1982, 18-19.

"What Theologians Believe: The IEA/Roper Center Theology Faculty Survey." *This World*, Summer 1982, 28-108.

"Who's Who in the Movement." *Newsweek*, 26 April 1982, 22.

Wieseltier, Leon. "Partisan Compassion." *New Republic*, 16 June 1982, 37-39.

Williams, David Cratis. "Nuclear Criticism: In Pursuit of a 'Politically Enabling' Deconstructive Voice." *Journal of the American Forensic Association* 24 (Winter 1988): 193-205.

Winter, Metta L. "Nuclear Education Update." *Education Digest*, April 1986, 30-32.

Yankelovich, Daniel and John Doble. "The Public Mood: Nuclear Weapons and the U.S.S.R." *Foreign Affairs* 63 (Fall 1984): 33-46.

Yudkin, Marcia. "When Kids Think the Unthinkable." *Psychology Today*, April 1984, 18-25.

———. "Young Activists." *Psychology Today*, April 1984, 24-25.

Zagano, Phyllis. "Media Morality: American Catholic Bishops and Deterrence." *Center Journal* 3 (Winter 1983): 177-212.

Zahn, Gordon C. "Disaster, No; Disappointment, Yes." *Commonweal*, 13 August 1982, 435-36.

Zarefsky, David. "A Skeptical View of Movement Studies." *Central States Speech Journal* 31 (Winter 1980): 245-54.

## Books and Pamphlets


Adams, Ruth and Susan Cullen, eds. *The Final Epidemic: Physicians and Scientists on Nuclear War.* Chicago: Educational Foundation for Nuclear Science, 1981.

Alperovitz, Gar. *Atomic Diplomacy: Hiroshima and Potsdam.* New York: Vintage, 1965.

American Friends Service Committee. *A Compassionate Peace: A Future for the Middle East.* New York: Hill and Wang, 1982.

American Friends Service Committee. *Anatomy of Anti-Communism: A Report Prepared for the Peace Education Division of the American Friends Service Committee.* New York: Hill and Wang, 1969.

Asher, Herbert. *Polling and the Public: What Every Citizen Should Know.* Washington, D.C.: Congressional Quarterly Press, 1988.

Au, William A. *The Cross, the Flag, and the Bomb: American Catholics Debate War and Peace, 1960-1983.* Westport: Greenwood Press, 1985.

Auletta, Ken. *Three Blind Mice: How the TV Networks Lost Their Way.* New York: Random House, 1991.

Bailey, Thomas A. *A Diplomatic History of the American People.* New York: F.S. Crofts, 1940.

Belz, Mark. *Suffer the Little Children: Christians, Abortion, and Civil Disobedience.* Westchester, Illinois: Crossway Books, 1989.

Bennett, W. Lance. *News: The Politics of Illusion.* 2nd ed. New York: Longman, 1988.

Bercovitch, Sacvan. *The American Jeremiad.* Madison: University of Wisconsin Press, 1978.

Black, Edwin. *Rhetorical Criticism: A Study in Method.* 2nd ed. Madison: University of Wisconsin Press, 1978.

Boyer, Paul. *By the Bomb's Early Light: American Thought and Culture at the Dawn of the Atomic Age.* New York: Pantheon, 1985.

Brummett, Barry. *Contemporary Apocalyptic Rhetoric.* New York: Praeger, 1991.

Burke, Kenneth. *A Grammar of Motives.* Berkeley: University of California Press, 1969.

Burks, Don M., ed. *Rhetoric, Philosophy and Literature: An Exploration.* West Lafayette: Purdue University Press, 1978.

Caldicott, Helen. *If You Love This Planet: A Plan to Heal the Earth.* New York: W.W. Norton, 1992.

———. *Missile Envy: The Arms Race and Nuclear War.* New York: Bantam, 1985.

———. *Nuclear Madness: What You Can Do!* New York: Bantam, 1980.

Campbell, Angus, et al. *The American Voter.* New York: John Wiley and Sons, 1960.

Campbell, Richard. *60 Minutes and the News: A Mythology for Middle America.* Urbana: University of Illinois Press, 1991.

Cantril, Albert H. *The Opinion Connection: Polling, Politics, and the Press.* Washington, D.C.: Congressional Quarterly Press, 1991.

———., ed. *Polling on the Issues: Twenty-One Perspectives on the Role of Opinion Polls in the Making of Public Policy.* Cabin John, Maryland: Seven Locks Press, 1980.

Carnesale, Albert, et al. *Living With Nuclear Weapons.* New York: Bantam, 1983.

Castelli, Jim. *The Bishops and the Bomb: Waging Peace in a Nuclear Age.* Garden City: Image Books, 1983.

Catholic Church, National Conference of Catholic Bishops. *The Challenge of Peace—God's Promise and Our Response: A Pastoral Letter on War and Peace.* Washington, D.C.: United States Catholic Conference, 1983.

———. *Resolution on South East Asia.* Washington, D.C.: United States Catholic Conference, 1971.

Chivian, Eric, et al., eds. *Last Aid: The Medical Dimensions of Nuclear War.* San Francisco: W.H. Freeman, 1982.

Cmiel, Kenneth. *Democratic Eloquence: The Fight Over Popular Speech in Nineteenth-Century America.* Berkeley: University of California Press, 1990.

Cohen, Bernard C. *The Public's Impact on Foreign Policy.* Boston: Little, Brown, and Co., 1973.

Cohn, Mary, ed. *1983 Congressional Quarterly Almanac.* Washington, D.C.: Congressional Quarterly, 1983.

Condit, Celeste Michelle. *Decoding Abortion Rhetoric: Communicating Social Change.* Urbana: University of Illinois Press, 1990.

Cox, J. Robert, Malcom O. Sillars, and Gregg B. Walker, eds. *Argument and Social Practice: Proceedings of the Fourth SCA/AFA Conference on Argumentation.* Annandale, Virginia: Speech Communication Association, 1985.

Curry, Dean C., ed. *Evangelicals and the Bishops' Pastoral Letter.* Grand Rapids: William B. Eerdmans, 1984.

Daniels, Jonathan. *The Man of Independence.* Philadelphia: J.B. Lippincott Co., 1950.

Dewey, Joseph. *In A Dark Time: The Apocalyptic Temper in the American Novel of the Nuclear Age.* West Lafayette: Purdue University Press, 1990.

Diamond, Edwin. *The Media Show: The Changing Face of the News, 1985-1990.* Cambridge: MIT Press, 1991.

———. *The Tin Kazoo: Television, Politics, and the News.* Cambridge: MIT Press, 1975.

Dougherty, James E. *The Bishops and Nuclear Weapons: The Catholic Pastoral Letter on War and Peace.* Hamden, Connecticut: Archon Books, 1984.

Eagly, Alice H. and Shelly Chaiken. *The Psychology of Attitudes.* Fort Worth: Harcourt Brace Jovanovich, 1993.

Educators for Social Responsibility. *Knowing the Nuclear World: A Bibliography of Selected Curricula and Teaching Materials.* Boston: ESR, 1986.

Ehrlich, Robert, ed. *Perspectives on Nuclear War and Peace Education.* New York: Greenwood Press, 1987.

Elliot, Jonathan, ed. *The Debates in the Several State Conventions on the Adoption of the Federal Constitution.* vol. 2. 2nd ed. Philadelphia: J.B. Lippincott and Co., 1881.

Epstein, Jay Edward. *News From Nowhere.* New York: Random House, 1973.

Faux, Marian. *Crusaders: Voices From the Abortion Front.* New York: Carol Publishing Group, 1990.

Ferry, W. H. *Farewell to Arms: A Case for Unilateral Disarmament.* Nyack, New York: Fellowship Publications, 1978.

Fine, Melinda and Peter M. Steven, eds. *American Peace Directory, 1984.* Cambridge: Ballinger, 1984.

Fiske, John. *Television Culture.* London: Methuen, 1987.

Forsberg, Randall. *Call to Halt the Nuclear Arms Race.* St. Louis: Nuclear Weapons Freeze Campaign, 1980.

———. *Call to Halt the Nuclear Arms Race.* FOR edition. Nyack, New York: Fellowship of Reconciliation, 1981.

———. *Call to Halt the Nuclear Arms Race.* NWFC rev. ed. St. Louis: NWFC National Clearinghouse, 1982.

Fry, Don, ed. *Believing the News.* St. Petersburg: The Poynter Institute for Media Studies, [1985].

Gaddis, John Lewis. *The United States and the Origins of the Cold War, 1941-1947.* New York: Columbia University Press, 1972.

Gans, Herbert J. *Deciding What's News: A Study of CBS Evening News, NBC Nightly News, Newsweek and Time.* New York: Vintage, 1980.

Garfinkle, Adam M. *The Politics of the Nuclear Freeze.* Philadelphia: Foreign Policy Research Institute, 1984.

Gitlin, Todd. *The Whole World is Watching: Mass Media in the Making and Unmaking of the New Left.* Berkeley: University of California Press, 1980.

Goldman, Eric F. *The Crucial Decade—and After: America, 1945-1960.* 2nd ed. New York: Alfred A. Knopf, 1960.

Halberstam, David. *The Powers That Be.* New York: Alfred A. Knopf, 1979.

Hamilton, Alexander, James Madison, and John Jay. *The Federalist Papers.* Edited by Clinton Rossiter. New York: New American Library, 1961.

Hart, Roderick P. *The Sound of Leadership.* Chicago: University of Chicago Press, 1987.

Hennesey, James. *American Catholics: A History of the Roman Catholic Community in the United States.* New York: Oxford University Press, 1981.

Heyer, Robert, ed. *Nuclear Disarmament: Key Statements of Popes, Bishops, Councils and Churches.* New York: Paulist Press, 1982.

Hilgartner, Stephen, Richard C. Bell, and Rory O'Connor. *Nukespeak: Nuclear Language, Visions, and Mindset.* San Francisco: Sierra Club Books, 1982.

Hogan, J. Michael. *The Panama Canal in American Politics: Domestic Advocacy and the Evolution of Policy.* Carbondale: Southern Illinois University Press, 1986.

Horowitz, David. *The Free World Colossus: A Critique of American Foreign Policy in the Cold War.* 2nd ed. New York: Hill and Wang, 1971.

Hunter, James Davison. *Culture Wars: The Struggle to Define America.* New York: Basic Books, 1991.

Jamieson, Kathleen Hall. *Eloquence in an Electronic Age: The Transformation of Political Speechmaking.* New York: Oxford University Press, 1988.

Jefferson, Thomas. *The Writings of Thomas Jefferson.* Vol. 10. Edited by Andrew A. Lipscomb. Washington, D.C.: Thomas Jefferson Memorial Association, 1907.

Jobs with Peace Education Task Force. *Crossroads: Quality of Life in a Nuclear Age.* Boston: Jobs with Peace Education Task Force, 1982.

Kaplan, Lawrence S., ed. *Recent American Foreign Policy: Conflicting Interpretations.* 2nd ed. Homewood, Illinois: Dorsey Press, 1972.

Kennan, George. *The Nuclear Delusion: Soviet-American Relations in the Atomic Age.* 2nd ed. New York: Pantheon, 1983.

Kennedy, Edward M. and Mark O. Hatfield. *Freeze! How You Can Help Prevent Nuclear War.* New York: Bantam Books, 1982.

Key, V. O., Jr. *The Responsible Electorate: Rationality in Presidential Voting, 1936-1960.* New York: Vintage, 1966.

Kolko, Gabriel. *The Politics of War: The World and United States Foreign Policy, 1942-1945.* New York: Random House, 1968.

———. *The Roots of American Foreign Policy: An Analysis of Power and Purpose.* Boston: Beacon Press, 1969.

Kolko, Joyce and Gabriel Kolko. *The Limits of Power: The World and United States Foreign Policy, 1945-1954.* New York: Harper and Row, 1972.

Kownacki, Mary Lou, ed. *A Race to Nowhere: An Arms Race Primer for Catholics.* Chicago: Pax Christi USA, n.d.

Lane, Robert E. and David O. Sears. *Public Opinion.* Englewood Cliffs: Prentice-Hall, 1964.

Lens, Sidney. *The Futile Crusade: Anti-Communism as American Credo.* Chicago: Quadrangle Books, 1964.

Leonard, Bill. *In the Storm of the Eye: A Lifetime at CBS.* New York: G.P. Putnam's Sons, 1987.

Lifton, Robert Jay. *Death in Life: Survivors of Hiroshima.* New York: Random House, 1968.

Lifton, Robert Jay and Richard Falk. *Indefensible Weapons: The Political and Psychological Case Against Nuclearism.* New York: Basic Books, 1982.

Loeb, Paul Rogat. *Hope in Hard Times: America's Peace Movement and the Reagan Era.* Lexington: Lexington Books, 1987.

Maddox, Robert J. *The New Left and the Origins of the Cold War.* Princeton: Princeton University Press, 1973.

Madsen, Axel. *60 Minutes: The Power and Politics of America's Most Popular TV News Show.* New York: Dodd, Mead and Co., 1984.

McBrien, Richard P. *Catholicism.* Minneapolis: Winston Press, 1981.

McCauley, Martin. *The Origins of the Cold War.* New York: Longman, 1983.

McFadden, Thomas M., ed. *Liberation, Revolution, and Freedom: Theological Perspectives.* New York: Seabury Press, 1975.

Meyer, David S. *A Winter of Discontent: The Nuclear Freeze and American Politics.* New York: Praeger, 1990.

Meyer, Philip. *Precision Journalism: A Reporter's Introduction to Social Science Methods.* Bloomington: Indiana University Press, 1973.

Murphy, Matthew F. *Betraying the Bishops: How the Pastoral Letter on War and Peace is Being Taught.* Washington, D.C.: Ethics and Public Policy Center, 1987.

National Education Association. *The NEA Legislative Program for the 99th Congress.* Washington, D.C.: NEA Government Relations, 1985.

Nelson, John S., Allan Megill, and Donald N. McCloskey, eds. *The Rhetoric of the Human Sciences: Language and Argument in Scholarship and Public Affairs.* Madison: University of Wisconsin Press, 1987.

Nelson, William H., ed. *Theory and Practice in American Politics.* Chicago: Phoenix Books, 1967.

Newcomb, Horace, ed. *Television: The Critical View.* 3rd ed. New York: Oxford University Press, 1982.

Nolan, Hugh J., ed. *Pastoral Letters of the American Hierarchy, 1792-1970.* Huntington, Indiana: Our Sunday Visitor, 1971.

Ondaatje, Elizabeth Heneghan. *Trends in Anti-Nuclear Protests in the United States, 1984-1987.* Santa Monica: Rand Corporation, 1989.

Ornstein, Norman, Andrew Kohut, and Larry McCarthy. *The People, the Press, and Politics: The Times Mirror Study of the American Electorate.* Reading, Massachusetts: Addison-Wesley, 1988.

Payne, Keith B. and Colin S. Gray, eds. *The Nuclear Freeze Controversy.* New York: University Press of America, 1984.

Public Agenda Foundation. *Voter Options on Nuclear Arms Policy: A Briefing Book for the 1984 Elections.* New York: Public Agenda Foundation, 1984.

Ranney, Austin. *Channels of Power: The Impact of Television on American Politics.* New York: Basic Books, 1983.

Robinson, Douglas. *American Apocalypses: The Image of the End of the World in American Literature.* Baltimore: Johns Hopkins University Press, 1985.

Roll, Charles W. and Albert H. Cantril. *Polls: Their Use and Misuse in Politics.* Cabin John, Maryland: Seven Locks Press, 1980.

Russell, Diana E. H., ed. *Exposing Nuclear Phallacies.* New York: Pergamon Press, 1989.

Sagan, Carl and Richard Turco. *A Path Where No Man Thought: Nuclear Winter and the End of the Arms Race.* New York: Random House, 1990.

Sayer, Karen and John Dowling, eds. *1984 National Directory of Audiovisual Resources on Nuclear War and the Arms Race.* Ann Arbor: University of Michigan Media Resources Center, 1984.

Scheer, Robert. *With Enough Shovels: Reagan, Bush and Nuclear War.* New York: Vintage Books, 1983.

Schell, Jonathan. *The Abolition.* New York: Avon Books, 1984.

———. *The Fate of the Earth.* New York: Alfred A. Knopf, 1982.

Sibley, Mulford. *Unilateral Initiatives and Disarmament.* Philadelphia: American Friends Service Committee, 1962.

Sloan, Douglas, ed. *Education for Peace and Disarmament: Toward a Living World.* New York: Teachers College Press, 1983.

Smith, Ted J., III. *Moscow Meets Main Street: Changing Journalistic Values and the Growing Soviet Presence on American Television.* Washington, D.C.: Media Institute, 1988.

———., ed. *Propaganda: A Pluralistic Perspective.* New York: Praeger, 1989.

Solo, Pam. *From Protest to Policy: Beyond the Freeze to Common Security.* Cambridge: Ballinger, 1988.

Solow, Barbara. *Mobilizing Media: A National Report on How the Peace Movement Has Used Films and Other Media in Grassroots Organizing and Education.* New York: Media Network, 1983.

Totten, Sam and Martha Wescoat Totten. *Facing the Danger: Interviews with 20 Anti-Nuclear Activists.* Trumansburg, New York: The Crossing Press, 1984.

Union of Concerned Scientists, Massachusetts Teachers Association, and the National Education Association. *Choices: A Unit on Conflict and Nuclear War.* Washington, D.C.: National Education Association, 1983.

Waller, Douglas C. *Congress and the Nuclear Freeze: An Inside Look at the Politics of a Mass Movement.* Amherst: University of Massachusetts Press, 1987.

Wheeler, Michael. *Lies, Damn Lies, and Statistics: The Manipulation of Public Opinion in America.* New York: Dell, 1976.

White, Hayden and Frank E. Manuel. *Theories of History: Papers Read at a Clark Library Seminar, March 6, 1976.* Los Angeles: William Andrews Clark Memorial Library, 1978.

White, Theodore. *America in Search of Itself: The Making of the President, 1956-1980.* New York: Warner Books, 1982.

Williams, Huntington. *Beyond Control: ABC and the Fate of the Networks.* New York: Atheneum, 1989.

Williams, William Appleman. *America Confronts a Revolutionary World, 1776 to 1976.* New York: William Morrow and Co., 1976.

———. *The Tragedy of American Diplomacy.* Rev. ed. New York: Delta Books, 1962.

Women's Action for Nuclear Disarmament. *Turnabout: The Emerging New Realism in the Nuclear Age.* Boston: WAND Education Fund, 1986.

Wood, Gordon S. *The Creation of the American Republic.* New York: W.W. Norton, 1969.

Young, Michael L., ed. *The Classics of Polling.* Metuchan, New Jersey: Scarecrow Press, 1990.

## Government Documents

U.S. Congress. House. "Providing for Consideration of House Joint Resolution 138, Calling for a Mutual and Verifiable Freeze on and Reductions in Nuclear Weapons," 98th Cong., 1st. sess., *Congressional Record,* vol. 129, no. 33, daily ed. (16 March 1983).

———. "Calling for a Mutual and Verifiable Freeze on and Reductions in Nuclear Weapons." 98th Cong., 1st sess. *Congressional Record.* Daily ed. Vol. 129, nos. 46, 52, 56, 59. (13 April, 21 April, 28 April, 4 May 1983).

———. "Calling for a Mutual and Verifiable Freeze on and Reductions in Nuclear Weapons and for Approval of the SALT II Agreement." 97th Cong., 2nd sess. *Congressional Record.* Daily ed. Vol. 128, no. 106. (5 August 1982).

———. Committee on Foreign Affairs. *Calling for a Mutual and Verifiable Freeze on and Reductions in Nuclear Weapons: Hearings and Markup.* 98th Cong., 1st sess., 2 March, 8 March 1983.

———. Committee on Foreign Affairs. *Congress and Foreign Policy, 1982.* 98th Cong., 1st sess., 1983.

———. Committee on Foreign Affairs. *Strategic Arms Control and U.S. National Security Policy: Hearings and Markup.* 97th Cong., 2nd sess., 2 April, 11 May 1982.

———. Select Committee on Children, Youth, and Families. *Children's Fears of Nuclear War.* 98th Cong., 1st sess., 20 September 1984.

U.S. Congress. Senate. Committee on Foreign Relations. *The SALT II Treaty.* 96th Cong., 1st sess., 1979.

———. S.J. Res 163 [the Kennedy-Hatfield Resolution]. 97th Cong., 2nd sess., 1982.

———. S.J. Res 177 [the Jackson-Warner Resolution]. 97th Cong., 2nd sess., 1982.

U.S. Department of Commerce. *Statistical Abstract of the United States, 1986.* Washington, D.C.: Department of Commerce, 1985.

———. *Statistical Abstract of the United States, 1987.* Washington, D.C.: Department of Commerce, 1986.

U.S. President. Executive Office of the President, Office of Management and Budget. *The United States Budget in Brief: Fiscal Year 1981.* Washington, D.C.: Government Printing Office, 1980.

———. *Public Papers of the Presidents of the United States.* Washington, D.C.: Office of the *Federal Register*, National Archives and Records Service, 1953-. Ronald Reagan, 1983.

## Television/Audiovisual Sources

ABC Motion Pictures. *The Day After.* Embassy Home Video, 1983. Videocassette.

ABC News. "'The Day After'—Nuclear Dilemma." *Viewpoint,* 20 November 1983. Microfiche transcript, 1-18.

CBS News. "The Bishop and the Bombs." *60 Minutes,* 24 October 1982. Microfiche transcript, 13-17.

———. "The Bomb." *60 Minutes,* 9 May 1982. Microfiche transcript, 2-8.

———. "The Defense of the United States." Part 1: "Ground Zero." *CBS Reports,* 14 June 1981. Microfiche transcript, 1-18.

———. "The Freeze." *Sunday Morning,* 11 April 1982. Microfiche transcript, 10-15.

———. "The Gospel According to Whom?" *60 Minutes,* 23 January 1983. Network transcript, 1-12.

———. "The Week Before *The Day After.*" *60 Minutes,* 13 November 1983. Microfiche transcript, 7-11.

———. *CBS Evening News,* 1981-1984. Microfiche transcripts.

———. *CBS Morning News,* 1981-1984. Microfiche transcripts.

———. *CBS News Index, 1981-1984.* Vols. 7-10. New York: Microfilming Corporation of America, 1982-1985.

Falwell, Jerry. *Nuclear War and the Second Coming of Jesus Christ.* Lynchburg, Virginia: Old Time Gospel Hour, n.d. Audiocassettes.

*If You Love This Planet.* National Film Board of Canada, 1982. Videocassette.

*The Silent Scream.* American Portrait Films, 1984. Videocassette.

## Unpublished Sources

American Friends Service Committee. *An Introduction to Working With AFSC.* Brochure distributed by the AFSC, Philadelphia, 1984.

———. *Introduction to the American Friends Service Committee.* Brochure distributed by the AFSC, Philadelphia, 1985.

———. *The Choice is Life Itself: AFSC Programs for Disarmament.* Brochure distributed by the AFSC, Philadelphia, 1982, 1984.

———. *The Future Is In Our Hands: Freeze the Arms Race, U.S.-U.S.S.R.* Brochure distributed by the AFSC New Manhattan Project, New York, n.d.

Begans, Peter. "Americans More Worried About Foreign Affairs Than At Any Time in the Reagan Presidency." ABC News/Washington Post Poll. Press release, 26 September 1983.

Eagle Forum. *Eagle Forum: Leading the Pro-Family Movement to Victories Since 1972.* Brochure distributed by the Eagle Forum, Alton, Illinois, n.d.

Keppel, David. "Verification." Connecticut Freeze Campaign Position Paper. Distributed by the NWFC National Clearinghouse, St. Louis, n.d.

McClure, Bob. Telephone interview with David Olsen, 24 April 1986.

National Education Association. *To Speak of Peace.* Brochure distributed by the NEA, Washington, D.C., n.d.

Nuclear Weapons Freeze Campaign. *Freeze: Because Nobody Wants a Nuclear War.* Brochure distributed by the NWFC National Clearinghouse, St. Louis, n.d.

———. "From Popular Mandate to Public Policy: 1983 Strategy Proposal." Presented to the Third National Freeze Conference, St. Louis, January 1983.

———. *Now.* Brochure distributed by the NWFC National Clearinghouse, St. Louis, n.d.

———. "Prominent Endorsers List." Distributed by the NWFC National Clearinghouse, St. Louis, February 1983.

———. *Resources.* Brochure distributed by the NWFC National Clearinghouse, St. Louis, n.d.

———. "State of the Campaign: Proposal for a Mutual U.S.-Soviet Nuclear Weapons Freeze." Distributed by the NWFC National Clearinghouse, St. Louis, 17 February 1983.

———. "The Freeze and Arms Control." *Fact Sheet 5.* Distributed by the NWFC National Clearinghouse, St. Louis, February 1983.

———. "The Freeze and the Military Balance." *Fact Sheet 4.* Distributed by the NWFC National Clearinghouse, St. Louis, February 1983.

———. "The Freeze and the Soviet Union." *Fact Sheet 3.* Distributed by the NWFC National Clearinghouse, St. Louis, January 1983.

———. "The Freeze Campaign: What You Can Do." *Fact Sheet 2.* Distributed by the NWFC National Clearinghouse, St. Louis, January 1983.

———. "The Freeze: Why Now?" *Fact Sheet 1.* Distributed by the NWFC National Clearinghouse, St. Louis, January 1983.

Smith, Ted J., III. "Public Opinion and the Nuclear Freeze Movement of 1980-84." Presented to the American Association for Public Opinion Research. St. Petersburg, Florida, 1986.

Women's International League for Peace and Freedom. *Principles and Policies.* Brochure distributed by the Women's International League for Peace and Freedom, Philadelphia, 1985.

———. *What WILPF Stands For . . . .* Brochure distributed by the Women's International League for Peace and Freedom, Philadelphia, n.d.

# Index


### A

*Abolition, The*, 46, 190
Abzug, Bella, 29
Addams, Jane, 18
Alperovitz, Gar, 67, 70
American Friends Service Committee, the (AFSC), 14, 15, 16-17, 28, 148
*Amerika*, 57n.78
Apocalyptic tradition, American, 38-40

### B

Barnet, Richard, 26, 27
Bauer, Gary L., 89
Becker, Norma, 29
Bernardin, Archbishop Joseph, 107, 116n.53
Biaggi, Mario, 125
"Big 35" campaign, 197, 198
Bilateral freeze, 15, 28, 126, 174, 175-76, 179
Black United Front, the (BUF), 28
Branch, Taylor, 71
Broomfield Substitute, the, 122

### C

Caldicott, Helen: bombing run speech, 62, 64, 69, 73, 157-58, 159; & New Left revisionism, 68-71; & nuclear education, 82-83; & nuclear freeze movement, 61-62, 65-66, 71; & Open Door thesis, 69; & political medicine, 61-66, 73, 74-75, 149, 150, 186-87; public acceptance of, 73-74; retirement of, 198-99; & rhetoric of doom, 54n.3; & Ronald Reagan, 65
Carney, William, 123
Catholic Church: media coverage of, 150-52, 159-60; & nuclear freeze movement, 99, 101-2, 106-11, 114n.43, 150-52, 188-89; & U.S. foreign policy, 100
Catholic New Left, the, 100-101
CBS News, 2, 142-60, 161-62, 163n.8, 166n.119
Chancellor, John, 206n.59
Chazov, Evgueni, 75n.12
Children's Campaign for Nuclear Disarmament, the (CCND), 92
*Choices: A Unit on Conflict and Nuclear War*, 82, 83, 84-91, 93, 94n.10, 187, 196
Church Women United, 33n.19
Citizens Against Nuclear War (CANW), 81
Clergy and Laity Concerned (CLC), 15, 33n.19
Coalition for a New Foreign and Military Policy, the (CNFMP), 16, 26
Coffin, Reverend William Sloane, 185
Coles, Robert, 74, 91, 203n.35
Committee for a Sane Nuclear Policy (SANE), 28, 185
Committee on War and Peace, the, 107, 115nn.45, 47

### D

D'Amours, Norman, 124
Daughtry, Reverend Herbert, 28, 29
*Day After, The*, 47-52, 56n.58, 57nn.73, 76, 77, 79, 58n.82
Defense spending: Russian, 87; U.S., 30, 87, 104-5, 114n.35
Dellinger, David, 29
Derwinski, Edward, 123
Documentaries, television, 152

*E*

Eagle Forum, 197, 198, 204n.53
Edgar, Bob, 124
Educators for Social Responsibility (ESR), 83, 195-97, 203nn.32, 35, 39

*F*

Falwell, Reverend Jerry, 54n.3, 160
*Fate of the Earth, The*, 4, 37, 38, 41-47
Federal Emergency Management Agency, the (FEMA), 57n.79, 158-59
Fellowship of Reconciliation, the (FOR), 14, 17, 28, 148
First National Freeze Conference, the, 16
Fisher, Walter R., 3, 4, 9n.29, 45
Forsberg, Randall: & bandwagon appeals, 26; & decline of nuclear freeze movement, 31, 185; & New York freeze rally, 28-30
Fox, Thomas, 115n.48
Freeze initiatives, state and local, 1, 19, 129, 145
Fulcher, Bishop George, 115n.45

*G*

Gaddis, John, 77n.49
Gallup, George, 180n.2
Geiger, Jack, 149, 155
Goldwater, Barry, 87, 88, 91
Great Peace March, the, 194
Greenpeace, 28
"Ground Zero" (documentary), 153-56
Ground Zero (organization), 53, 145
Guiffrida, Louis, 159
Gumbleton, Bishop Thomas, 102-3, 107, 115n.45

*H*

Hamilton, Lee, 129
Harkin, Tom, 126
Hatch Amendment, the, 198, 204n.53
Hehir, J. Bryan, 111, 115n.45
Herndon, Terry, 81
Hiatt, Howard, 149, 150
House freeze debate, 1, 2, 3, 19-20, 121-32, 189
Hunthausen, Archbishop Raymond, 101
Hyde, Henry, 123, 127

*I*

Ichimaru, Michito, 64
Institute for Defense and Disarmament Studies, the (IDDS), 14, 16
Institute for Policy Studies, the, 26, 27
International Physicians for the Prevention of Nuclear War, the (IPPNW), 62, 75n.12, 149-50

*J*

Jackson-Warner Amendment, the, 110
Jobs with Peace Education Task Force, the, 83
Johnson, Edwin C., 39
June 12 Rally Committee, the, 28
Journalism, television, crisis of confidence in, 160-63, 167n.125, 199-201, 206n.59
Just war doctrine, 103, 108-9, 114n.25, 116n.57, 188

*K*

Kehler, Randall, 20, 27-28, 30
Kennedy-Hatfield Amendment, the, 110
Kissinger, Henry, 51, 56n.71
Kistiakovsky, George, 159
Kolko, Gabriel, 68, 72, 120
Kostmayer, Peter, 124

*L*

LaDuke, Winona, 29
Leach, Jim, 124, 129
Leland, Mickey, 29
Lent, Norman, 128
Leonard, Bill, 153, 156
Levitas, Elliot, 122
Lown, Bernard, 64, 75n.12, 150

*M*

McClure, Bob, 90
McDonald, Larry, 127, 136n.75

McGuire, Willard H., 81, 93n.3
Mack, John E., 85
Maddox, Robert, 77n.49
Markey, Edward, 29, 123, 124
Matthiesen, Bishop Leroy T., 101-2, 113n.17, 159
Melman, Seymour, 29
Mennonite Central Committee, the, 33n.19
Meyer, David S., 6, 31, 156, 202n.19
Mitchell, Parren, 130
Mobilization for Survival (MOBE), 15, 26, 29
Moffett, Toby, 29
Molander, Roger, 53, 145
Mollner, Frank, 159
Moral Majority, the, 203n.32
Murphy, Bishop P. Francis, 114n.43

*N*

Narrative paradigm, theory of, 3, 4, 9n.29, 45
Nathanson, Bernard N., 205n.54
National Conference of Catholic Bishops, the (NCCB), 99-100, 106-11
National Council of Churches, the, 33n.19
National Education Association, the (NEA): & nuclear freeze movement, 81-82, 83, 84-91, 187; political activism of, 81, 93n.3
National Freeze Clearinghouse, the, 20-28, 34n.47
National Right-to-Life Committee, the (NRLC), 205n.54
New Left revisionism, 66-68, 71, 72, 77n.49
New Manhattan Project, the, 15, 25
New York freeze rally, 28-30, 126, 136n.75, 144-45
Novak, Michael, 115n.50, 117n.81
Nuclear education, 82-84, 91-93, 187, 195-97, 204nn.43, 45, 46
Nuclear freeze movement: & bandwagon appeals, 25-28; & bilateral freeze, 15, 28, 126, 174, 175-76, 179; & Catholic Church, 99, 101-2, 106-11, 114n.43, 188-89; & CBS News, 142-60, 161-62, 163n.8, 166n.119; children's participation in, 41, 89, 92-93, 187; & Congress, 1, 2, 3, 19-20, 30, 31, 121, 122-30, 188, 189; & *The Day After*, 47. 51-52, 56nn.58, 59; decline of, 31-32, 185-89, 192; dissention within, 28-30; goals of, 16, 19, 30; media coverage of, 142-52, 156, 157-60, 161-62, 189, 190-91; & nuclear education, 187; & nuclear winter, 52, 58n.86; origins of, 1, 14-16; & peace movement, 1, 5, 13, 14, 15, 16, 18-19, 40, 185-86, 188; & political medicine, 61, 63-65; popular support for, 1-2, 3, 4, 27, 51, 72, 122-28, 129, 131-32, 146, 147, 148, 171-79, 182nn.28, 31, 183nn.32, 33, 188, 190-92, 204n.45, 209-38; & presidential campaigns, 2-3, 29, 30, 31, 51; & protests, 192, 202n.23; & public opinion polls, 2, 126, 128, 131, 146-48, 170-79, 182nn.28, 31, 183nn.32, 33, 191, 209-38; & religious groups, 16, 17-18, 33n.19; rhetoric of, 4, 5, 6-7, 13, 19, 20-28, 32, 187; & rhetoric of doom, 37-38, 40, 41-52, 53-54, 63, 149-50, 186; & Ronald Reagan, 2, 6, 13, , 30-31, 34n.47, 35n.93, 51, 191, 192, 202n.19; & secular groups, 17-18; & *60 Minutes*, 157-60; & telepolitical journalism, 4-5, 7, 37, 47, 186; & unilateral disarmament, 15, 28-29, 65-66, 175-76, 183n.32, 192, 194, 204n.45; & alternative media, 40-41
Nuclear winter, 52, 58nn.86, 87

*O*

O'Connor, Bishop John, 115n.45
Open Door thesis, the, 67-69, 77n.49
Operation Rescue, 205n.54

*P*

Pacifist doctrine, 103-4, 108, 188
Panama Canal, building of, 69, 78n.53
Panetta, Leon, 129
*Pastoral Letter on War and Peace, the*, 99-

100, 106-12, 115nn.48, 50, 116nn.53, 57, 151-52, 188-89
Pax Christi: & New York freeze rally, 28; & nuclear freeze movement, 15, 16, 26, 102-6; & pacifist movement, 17, 103-4; & *Pastoral Letter*, 107-8, 110-12, 188
Peace education, 194-98
Peace film industry, the, 40
Peace Media Project, the (PMP), 193
Peace movement: & nuclear freeze movement, 18-19, 40; & peace education, 194-95; public relations approach of, 193-94
People Reaching Out for Peace (PRO-Peace), 194
Physicians for Social Responsibility (PSR), 62, 149
Political medicine, 61, 63-65, 72, 73, 74-75, 150, 186
Pollack, Richard, 193
Popular sovereignty, 119-21, 130-31
Pro-life campaign, the, 205n.54
Protest movements, media coverage of, 135n.58, 141-42, 143, 148
Public opinion: & House freeze debate, 121, 122-30, 131-32; & U.S. foreign policy, 78n.72, 119-21, 130-31, 132, 133n.7, 178
Public opinion polls: & news media, 170, 181nn.10, 12; & nuclear freeze movement, 2, 126, 128, 131, 146-48, 170-79, 182nn.28, 31, 183nn.32, 33,191, 209-38; & presidential campaigns, 180nn.2, 3, 5; problems with, 131,147,169-70, 172-73,179-80, 180nn.3, 5, 181nn.11, 12

## R

Rabinowitch, Eugene, 53-54
Raskin, Marcus, 27
Reagan, Ronald: & *The Day After*, 51; & Helen Caldicott, 65; & nuclear education, 82; & nuclear freeze movement, 2, 6, 30-31, 34n.47, 35n.93, 191, 202n.19; & Pastoral Letter on War and Peace, 108, 151-52; & public opinion polls, 146-47, 148; & telepolitical journalism, 4, 5
Reilly, Bishop Daniel, 115n.45
Riverside Church Disarmament Program, the, 16, 26, 28
Roach, John, 116n. 53
Robinson, Sharon, 90
Rudd, Mark, 148

## S

Sagan, Carl: & The Day After, 51, 56n.71; & nuclear freeze movement, 52-53, 59n.90; & nuclear winter, 58n.86
Schell, Jonathan, 4, 37, 38, 41-46, 62, 63, 190
Schlafly, Phyllis, 197-98, 204n.53
Schlesinger, Arthur, Jr., 77n.49
Schultz, George, 51, 56n.71
Scientists' movement, 53-54
Second National Freeze Conference, the, 19, 24
Shanker, Albert, 90
Sibley, Mulford, 16
Sidel, Victor, 26
Sisters of Loretto, the, 33n.19
60 Minutes, 156-60, 166n.102
Sojourners, 16, 33n.19
Solo, Pam, 6-7, 31-32, 191, 194-95
START initiative, 34n.47, 129, 132
Stoddard, Brandon, 47-48, 57nn.77, 78, 160
Strategic Defense ("Star Wars") initiative, 13, 53, 132, 137n.103, 196, 204n.45
Stringer, Howard, 153
Sullivan, Bishop Walter, 101

## T

Telepolitical journalism, 4, 7, 9nn.31, 39, 160-63, 189, 199
Third National Freeze Conference, the, 30
Third World and Progressive People's Coalition, the (TWPPC), 28-29
Truman, Harry, 39
Tsipis, Kosta, 155

*U*

Unilateral disarmament, 15, 28-29, 65-66, 109, 175-76, 183n.32, 192, 194, 204n.45
Union of Concerned Scientists, the, 102

*W*

War Resisters' League, the (WRL), 15, 26, 27
Watts, Gary, 90
Wiesel, Elie, 51, 56n.71
Winn, Larry, 127
Williams, William Appleman, 67, 71
Wisconsin school of diplomatic history, the, 67, 77n.49
Women's Action for Nuclear Disarmament (WAND), 193-94
Women's International League for Peace and Freedom, the (WILPF), 14, 15, 16, 18, 26, 148
Women Strike for Peace, 26
World Peacemakers, 16

*Y*

Youth for America, 205n.54
Youth involvement: in anti-abortion campaign, 205n.54; in nuclear freeze movement, 41, 89, 92-93, 187

*Z*

Zablocki, Clement, 122
Zablocki resolutions, the, 122
Zahn, Gordon, 115n.48
Zemora, Rubin, 29